What They Said ...

DROWNED-OUT VOICES

by

Anthony Kerrigan
Sinead Houlihan
Jenifer Kerrigan

GHOST ÉIRE

www.GhostEire.net

First Published in 2021 by The Manuscript Publisher

ISBN - paperback: 978-1-911442-34-9

ISBN - hardback: 978-1-911442-37-0

A CIP Catalogue record for this book is available from the
National Library

Typesetting, page design and layout, cover design by
DocumentsandManuscripts.com

Drowned-Out Voices

Dedication

This is dedicated to those who think it's not what you can do in this life, it's what you can do in the next that matters…

Introduction

"Come away, O human child!
To the waters and the wild
With a Faery, hand in hand,
For the world's more full of weeping
than you can understand."

William Butler Yeats
from *The Collected Poems of W.B. Yeats*

Over the past few years our technique has changed in how we manage a paranormal investigation at GhostÉire. We have become what we consider ourselves today as spiritual counsellors. This incorporates the living on our level and also, those who are currently on another plane.

We, as humans, have a psychological factor so why not, in a supernatural realm, can a Spirit be influenced by their behaviour and mind!

Perhaps we detail too much on our own consciousness and unconsciousness, not giving a care that the Spirit realm could also have an awareness of its surroundings or do stuff or exist without realising. This may open a can of worms to the whole Ouija board and ideomotor phenomenon, the stone tape speculation, exorcisms and our (possibly Spirits too) psychic abilities.

At the moment, our group's intention is not to find if a place is haunted, unfortunately, to those in fear – it already is. So, leaving that aside, we are able to delve deeper, dealing specifically with the history and the occupants who use to frequent (otherwise known as haunt) the location/area that we are investigating. We want to know what they have done, what they are planning to do and so forth.

It means we have to be knowledgeable, knowing what experiments/ sessions/tests to conduct before we even get to the place we are exploring. In doing so, we have to connect with our Spirit guides or angels before, during and after the investigation for direction. We may come across a shady character that has committed an inappropriate act or is still spiteful towards the living on our realm. It is our job to understand the thought process behind its wrongdoing or actions.

In some cases, the events of yesteryear could be misconstrued or entirely false; so we cannot point the finger at someone straight away. Whatever was deemed unpleasant in the past could have been respectable in its day or, would have been the only solution to solve a problem. A belligerent person to some may have been seen as a hero to others. We at GhostÉire have grown and evolved as a group yet, we had to cleanse from within to get where we are today.

To another matter, the common quote made by some paranormal investigation teams is that they are 'non-profit', which is perfect if they are dealing with someone who is concerned about strange occurrences happening in their own house. A great number of times, listening to a person over the phone can sort out a few problems yet, there are times when trying to find an answer to a haunting means a journey has to be made to bring reassurance and a conclusion. At GhostÉire, we request a suggestable fee, taking into account travel expenses. Some might say that we would be taking advantage of a client but where, in any other profession, would you do a job for free!

With the ever-growing popularity of the supernatural on our TV screens, radios, cinemas and in the arts (such as music and literature), some people feel that it is necessary to have their very own private show at home. If it is free, why not? If you take money off a client, you may be regarded as a charlatan but offering services for free could be undermining the whole subject.

Every Halloween, there are widely seen headlines in the media linking paranormal investigators to *Ghostbusters*. It is laughed upon by some and not taken seriously. Bringing in government regulation would stop the charlatans and bring a healthy and respectable operation for those involved in carrying out paranormal studies. Obviously, this is the only way it can progress because as a homeowner, you have to be aware of whom you let in your front door. Nowadays, there is believed to be a tsunami of activity in our homes, happening beyond the scope of normal scientific understanding. So what has become different?

Well, our living and habitat has changed. Electricity is everywhere, fuelling a high electromagnetic field (EMF), especially with the use of plasma televisions, Wi-Fi and other appliances. Such exposure can lead to depression, lack of concentration, insomnia, skin burning or tingling and nausea. We even get freaked out by flickering lights or a kettle suddenly switching on. There could be easy explanations to the strange occurrences but it would alarm many a person who is unaware or has little knowledge of their surroundings. Like fight or flight, there is the other side to an individual; the one that wants to search…

Ghost-hunting apps on mobile or tablet devices are setting a global trend, while most of the equipment that a paranormal investigator would use is now cheaper and widely available to purchase. For businesses around the world, having a haunted story can bring tourists in abundance, creating jobs, revenue and experiences to a wider audience. So, when a client is alleged to be possessed what should you do?

Nine times out of ten, it would not be the dominated soul looking for advice but, more likely, the accompanying elder or friend instead. Making the matters worse, the person who is thought to be controlled by an evil Spirit could be held against their own will.

There is a fine line between possession and channelling. It is how we control it and, how others around react to it that is really important. Channelling or mediumship is the acceptance and ability to serve as a communication tool. Depending on which community you live in and their (religious) beliefs, you could be shortlisted for the Regan MacNeil (the twelve-year-old girl in the film, *The Exorcist*) award if otherwise.

Thankfully, at the present time, better services are being carried out for people suffering from mental illness in some countries but not in others. To bring this full circle, should paranormal investigators be trained in such instances to recognise, care and support clients who symptoms show signs of psychiatric disorder?

Hopefully, the drowned-out voices could be understood, with us and in the Spirit world; that in a time of free speech we are able to speak or give a different slant on things.

To cleanse is to purify and we needed to do this with our team at GhostÉire. It has been a period of peaceful healing and now, we hope to furthermore connect with many otherworldly bodies on our journey in this life. Sometimes it is gracious to concede, be humble and evaluate; then, like in death, we can reach new horizons and the drowned-out voices will be heard.

Map of Locations

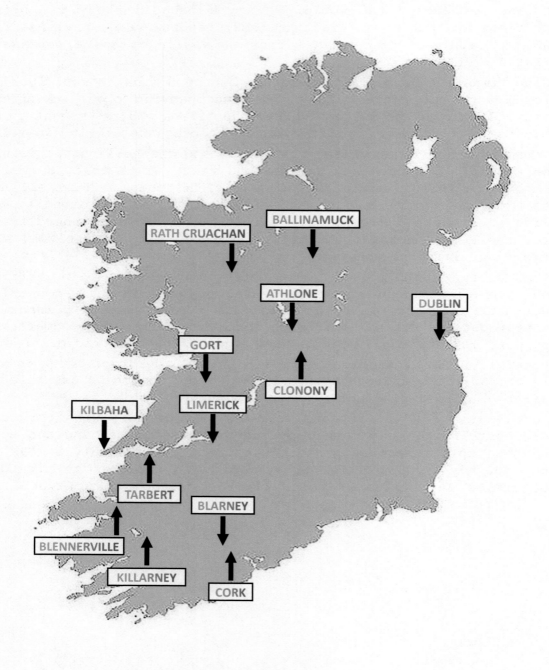

Key to Layout

| FAMINE AREA | Name of room on floor/level |

Windows

Judge's bench

Cut off to another area/room or level

Arched ceiling/opening

Cell bed

Victorian hip bath

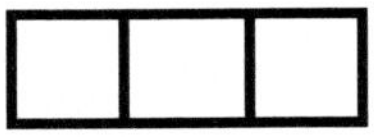

Stairs

Figure sculpture

Sealed doorway

Steam boilers

Gradient rising

Direction to room/area

Road

Mound

Cave

Pillars

Pool table

Curtain

Dumb Waiter

Contents

Equipment

Why do we use such a wide arrange of kit in the paranormal field?

The main emphasis is to enhance the possibility in finding proof and, hopefully, capture unnatural behaviour in our surroundings. Some chose or pretend to be involved in this subject for personal gratification; for close or global recognition and, it might be likely that something regarded as evidence could be plain and simply a hoax or misinterpreted.

Others might be influenced by the television shows, widespread online distributors, paranormal groups and friends, into buying pieces of equipment without understanding its capability or function.

The hard-core investigator will keep an open mind rather than being biased, too quick off the mark or following a trend. In either instance, this implies selecting the right ghost-hunting tools to purchase and, for when you allege to have found something extraordinary or out of this world.

Sometimes it is best not to buy equipment designed for the paranormal market but, to look elsewhere: in science and technology for clarification and in the spiritual practice for evoking.

Using different types of equipment might open more pathways for discovery yet, keep in mind the behaviour of reputed paranormal activity and, how to validate its existence

Video Camera

Catching footage of your investigation has to be centred on video recording equipment. The more cameras you use, the better – if you are to catch anything specific. The prices for video cameras have come down dramatically in the past few years. It is rare to get a video camera with night vision capability. They can be purchased over the World Wide Web and can be bought with an infrared light, to add better picture quality.

Laser Grid

This device, when set up with a video camera, can help create a 3D image of a Spirit, should any obstruction happen with the red laser lines of the grid. Generally, the instrument needs to be positioned behind the camera – for instance, formulating a grid onto the surface of a wall, ceiling, doorway or stairs in front.

Walkie-Talkies

The pressure of setting up experiments and equipment and, finding each other is taken away by using walkie-talkies. They are very handy in big locations. They can become very valuable in times of distress or for calling out what conditions an individual is feeling in a room.

When needing to seek out if an individual is being affected by a Spirit in a dark damp area of a dwelling, you ask for that person to be affected in certain areas of their body or for a change in temperature or, ask for something to happen in their surroundings. If the individual comes back on the walkie-talkie to say they have witnessed a change in that environment, similar to what you asked for, then you may have got a hit.

Always talk with a clear voice over the walkie-talkie. Do not cry wolf and play jokes using them. A good tip is to leave one walkie-talkie in a locked-off room and call out through another walkie-talkie for some activity, from another part of the building or location.

Motion Detectors

Sometimes Spirits can get a bit fidgety or, want to have a wander around, so motion detectors are handy for picking up any movement. Some of these gadgets give out an alarm or chime; others can give an alert through flashing a light. Electronic motion detectors use microwave, optical, acoustic censoring while passive infrared sensors (PIR) take in a source of human heat temperature to a change in room environment, by using infrared wavelengths and black body radiation.

EMF Gauss Master Meter

This instrument uses a needle pointer to record the electromagnetic field, from a scale of 0-10 milliGauss (mG) and an ultra-sensitive setting of 0-1 milliGauss (mG). The meter has an extra feature with an audio buzzer built in. The meter switches itself off after a brief period of time but, is able to give a more precise reading than a K2 meter, making it perfect for baseline tests.

Environmental Multi-Function Meter

This four-in-one digital meter reads sound level (dB), light (lux), humidity (RH) and temperature (Celsius and Fahrenheit). Supplemental to the apparatus is a microphone, temperature probe, humidity sensor and photo detector to give better accurate readings. This instrument is a must for baseline tests. It offers a maximum reading button and data hold button to make recording easier. The only unfortunate problem is that this device is rare and hard to purchase at the present moment.

Full Spectrum Camera

Can capture visible and near infrared (VNIR) and can also detect ultraviolet around 350 nanometres (nm) to 1000 nanometres (nm). Due to modifications on the hot mirror (blocking filter) with an infrared pass or transmitting filter, we are able to see a wider spectrum of colour. The UV light can be essential in finding body fluids, while IR can pick up gun residue and both are useful in archaeological findings. Developed in the 1950s, full spectrum cameras are ideal instruments to have, as they can also block out any orb phenomenon and reflections you might catch on a normal digital camera.

Bells

Commonly used in churches and temples and in our day-to-day life, the use of bells can be traced back to the 3rd century BC. Bells have been rung to signal a death and were used to ward off evil Spirits. They were regularly used in nineteenth century séances, on top of a table, sometimes to detect movement or a Spirit making contact and are still used today in the paranormal community.

Night Vision Camera (tape)

These cameras are ideal for use in low-light conditions. The human eye lacks tapetum lucidum, which many nocturnal animals have for hunting. Near infrared (NIR) or shortwave infrared band (SWIR) are used just below the human eye spectrum in illuminating a particular area. Living sources produce heat, which makes the infrared radiation denser. The difference in temperature to the environment you are in can easily be identified. These cameras were popular in the last decade yet, are very hard to come by now.

K2 Meter

These gadgets use a lighting system to highlight electromagnetic fluctuations. They read a relatively small scale of between 0-20 milliGauss (mG). The meter's shortcoming is that it does not record data but it is an attractive and absorbing instrument in trying to gain a conversation with a Spirit. Newer versions have an audio buzzer, just in case staring at the device becomes a bit too much. Who does not love flashy colourful lights?

Digital Sound Recorder

A huge amount of paranormal phenomenon is found using our sense of hearing. It is much harder to prove however, as many reasonable explanations can discount such good findings. Technology has enhanced the EVP (electronic voice phenomenon) sessions that ghost hunters use today. The digital era has taken a hold on this and improved the way we can listen back to recordings, catch noises that we have not heard earlier and replay them back in much quicker time. Digital recorders, mikes and other audible enhancers can be picked up quite cheaply now. Most electronic recorders are compatible with PCs and other computers. There is certain software you can get as well to enhance and block out any noise disturbances you receive.

Spirit Level

Used in the DIY world, this instrument has an air bubble filled with liquid and is a cheaper form of a seismometer. It shows any imbalance, so it can be essential when used with or as a trigger object. It can aid with identifying movement, vibration or slight inclinations during a séance or table-tilting experiment.

Digital Infrared Thermometer Laser Gun

This handheld instrument uses a laser to pinpoint the surface of certain areas. It can test how hot an object is with a steady hand. Suitable for measuring a flat surface of trigger objects (before and after) in case of movement. Not to be confused with the ambient temperature within a room or area. It can take readings in Celsius and Fahrenheit. Simple, light and easy to use, it is also an affordable piece of kit to buy.

CCTV Surveillance Night Vision Cameras

First used in Nazi Germany in 1942. Otherwise known as close-circuit television; a number of video cameras (some with sound) relay a signal through meshed wire or wireless connections to a motherboard to record. Infrared video cameras that are set up in darkened rooms/areas are recommended and are essential in picking out any disturbance. Some devices have software that let you know if movement has been detected within the cameras scope.

Disposable Camera (Celluloid Film)

Still can bought today at many photography outlets; they are very cheap and reflect the older ways of ghost hunting. Spirit photography became popular in the late nineteenth century with double exposure and falsified film negative.

Oscillating Machine

The base of this mechanism remains stationary as the motor in the main casing enables it to move side to side, in a regular, slow rhythm. By a attaching a video camera to it, you are able to get a wider perspective of a specific room/area. Instead of just focusing on the centre, the video camera can get a good view left and right of the focal point. Keep in mind, although you are surveying a broad space, activity could still occur out of sight.

Mel Meter

The Mel meter was invented by Gary Galka in 2012. It is named in honour of his daughter, Melissa, who died tragically in 2004. In most cases, they help to build a picture of anything electrical inside or outside a location, to provide guidance over high electrical pulses. The Mel meter can take precise readings in varied amounts of Tesla (T) and milliGauss (mG). At the same time, a room/area temperature can be measured (Celsius and Fahrenheit) with an additional probe. It can record on the spot data to the highest and lowest point. The meter comes with glow in the dark display and, in recent years, a P-SB7 integrated Spirit Box. A vibration, touch feature has also been added.

Seismometer

The word derives from the Greek, 'seismos' (shake or quake) and 'metron' (to measure). This device gets triggered by flashing lights when a particular movement or vibration has occurred on a surface it is on. This is ideal if a location has reported pictures falling off walls and creaky uneven floorboards that might be attributed to the structure, causing this phenomenon. Outside influences such as traffic, quarries, roadworks, wind and foundations of the building are just some explanations as to what can cause symptoms such as nausea and restless sleep at a location.

Singing Bowl

First used in China, in 1600 BC and later incorporated into religious rituals and sound therapy. To achieve a musical note, the bowl is struck by a mallet. The sound flowing within the bowl can be enhanced by rotating the mallet around the rim. Quicker revolutions of the mallet result in louder note being played. The singing bowl has been associated with healing powers, relaxation and temporary changes to the mind's state.

Voltmeter

A voltmeter records the difference of electrical capacity between two points in an electric circuit. This analogue voltmeter has three settings – they are off, AC and Circuit DC. There are four slots or terminals at the bottom of the meter for common probe, AC power, DC battery and circuit test functions. One probe, black (negative), goes into the common probe terminal and the other probe, red (positive), goes into the circuit test terminal. The voltmeter is put on a circuit DC setting. One person connects onto the black probe, another person to the red probe then, the two people connect, holding hands with their other spare hand. Ideal for a séance or calling-out vigil, a spike from the pointer of the voltmeter could occur when asking a question or during a certain period of time.

Thermal Imaging Camera

William Herschel made the discovery of infrared in 1800 – a radiation beyond the red light. Previously, he discovered the planet Uranus, in 1791. The thermographic camera produces a heat area picture using infrared radiation, with the wavelengths working as far as 14,000 nanometres (nm). The higher an objects temperature, the greater amount of infrared radiation is discharged. The camera points out these differences in temperature with an image and measurement of heat in Celsius or Fahrenheit, with a few optional contrast viewing modes. It is a perfect piece of equipment to see how people and room/area interact with changes in temperature.

Energy Probes

These are copper, ball-headed, tubed sticks with neon-lighted bulbs that react to high e-fields produced by plasma lamps, ion generators, dangerous high voltage lighting and tesla coils. When set up for a séance or as a trigger object, the e-field waves generate the neon bulbs to light up. When disturbed by a physical force or interrupted in proximity, the bulbs will dim or flash. This can aid your evidence and enhance activity when a Spirit comes forward, as copper is a great conductor. Other potentials for the probes to light up include strange weather conditions, radiation and static charges.

Ultraviolet Torches

Ultraviolet is an electromagnetic radiation, measuring from 400 nanometres to 100 nanometres (nm). It is present in sunlight and can be rarely seen by humans. Ultraviolet LED Torches are limited at around 365 nanometres (nm) to emit light. Ironically, this is the same measurement of ultraviolet that bugs and flies are attracted to. Exposure to UV light can help the nervous system and bone structure however, its sensitivity to skin and the eyes can prove harmful.

Digital Camera

Taking pictures of ghosts (Spirit photography) became popular in the 1860s. William H. Mumler was the first to use the technique but in a fraudulent manner. Interest still grew in capturing ghosts in pictures.

With the birth of digital cameras came orbs, believed to be Spirits (ghost lights) but, in most cases, are a result of the flash from the camera capturing the reflected light from a solid or liquid particle or, dirt within the lens. However, digital cameras are a great option for picking up instant moments of significance. Most are easy to use, compact and display what a location looked and felt like.

Motion Nature Camera

The paranormal community has taken a leaf out of wildlife enthusiasts, hunters and biologists by utilising the trail camera. A sensor is triggered once an animal, person or any other source of movement enters the cameras detection zone. A still frame photo or a short visual recording is stored on its data. Most of them come with infrared capability, able to withstand damage and can be left in a remote spot for a lengthy period of time.

Temperature Gauge

This is a liquid bulb-based thermometer that measures temperature in Celsius ($^{\circ}$C) and Fahrenheit ($^{\circ}$F). The red pointer indicates the highest recorded temperature whilst the blue pointer registers the coldest. The black pointer displays the current temperature in the area/room. The gauge can be reset at any time. The use of this instrument is not to get an instant measurement but, to gather an accurate range or benchmark compared to fluctuations commonly found with electronic thermometers.

PROTECTION PRAYER

You might need this before you read on...

Mother, Father, God.
Life of all creation,
We give you thanks to all that we have
And all that we are.
We evoke the violet flame burning up towards our
bodies, transmuting any energy out of alignment with
our 'I am' presence.

Blessed Be

Baseline Tests

There are a considerable number of factors that can be the cause of alleged paranormal phenomena. It is important to be aware of your surroundings when visiting a site – inside and out. Each location is unique and is different to others. It is important to conduct several baseline tests to distinguish the explainable from the unusual. This helps when reviewing an investigation to see whether the evidence is valid. Depending on how the baseline results read, certain experiments or equipment might be ideal or pointless to use in the study.

If unsure why a 'baseline meter' is giving a peculiar reading, then it is wise to speak to a colleague or ask someone associated with the building/area as to what could be causing it to behave in that way. Nine times out of ten, the meter is doing the right thing. It is also important to gather as much information from owners, staff or witnesses who have experienced paranormal occurrences within or near the property or area. When investigating, you could discover a pattern that might link to individual's testimonies or, to follow-up visits made by you to the location. Some of the statistics vary from the spiritual to the scientific and from progression to evidential.

EMF (Electromagnetic Field)

The EM field is caused by accelerated moving electric charges (electrons). It combines invisible electric and the magnetic fields of force. The Earth has its very own magnetic field. Along with natural sources (thunderstorms), man-made waves originating from house wiring, power lines, mobile phone signals and various other appliances can produce EMF. It is essential to locate and measure EMF, especially if conducting experiments/vigils based around that theme in the investigation. Exposure to EMF is presumed to affect humans, resulting in symptoms such as headaches, tiredness, dysesthesia (itchiness), changes in memory and depression. Most EMF meters operate at a milliGauss (mG) and tesla (T) range.

Internal Temperature

Temperatures inside a building can alter throughout an investigation. Some rooms can be warmer or colder than others for many reasons: such as being largely insulated, have central heating, furnaces and, on the other hand, have open fireplaces, air conditioning, being in a state of neglect or are dilapidated or simply having open windows and doors. The size of the room and where it is situated according to the sun's path can also have an effect.

The amount of people and time going in-and-out of the room has to be taken into consideration too. How you measure the temperature is important. Celsius (°C) and Fahrenheit (°F) are two different measurements of registering heat. Remember Fahrenheit has a larger range on its scale than Celsius. For instance, it has been known that a shift of over 3°C or 6.12°F to a warmer or colder temperature in a very short space of time is a sign of paranormal activity. Taking baseline temperatures prior to the investigation or, at the start of a session, gives reliable feedback on how the building/ rooms cope with temperature changes (or a 'haunting'), should any hot or cold spots be sensed.

External Temperature

It is worth testing the temperature outdoors as well as indoors. A pattern may arise when comparing the two. You might notice how robust or fragile a building is according to the outside conditions. If the type of 'haunting' occurs outdoors, then you may need to do some sessions/vigils around that area. The temperature outside may vary to the inside according to numerous things, including sunlight, shading, wind and shelter (forest), along with man-made influences such as road traffic, street lighting, machinery and even crowds of people. Investigations can be organised around the grounds of a location or places where there are no structures in the locality.

Humidity

The mass of water vapour in the air is known as humidity. Relative humidity (RH, usually given as a percentage) is the amount of water in the air compared to how much the air could hold at that temperature. For instance, if the relative humidity is 75% the air is holding three quarters of the water vapour it can hold. Testing for humidity is useful in predicting weather conditions, including dew, fog and thunderstorms (at a high temperature). High humidity in homes has been known to cause tiredness, fatigue, tighten airways and increase the growth of harmful bacteria, dust mites and moulds (fungus). Sweat can also rest on the skin with the inability to evaporate in high humidity. The 'orb phenomenon' could be explained by high outdoor humidity in the air from water droplets and moisture, with low humidity contributing to floating dust particles and pollen. With low humidity there is a chance of encountering dry skin, lips and hair, bloody noses, cold and flu symptoms and static electricity. It can also make wood crack, making furniture create those 'unsettling creaking noises'.

Lux (Unit of illumination)

The word *lux* means 'more at light' in Latin. It is the unit of illumination (lx) that is used to measure the intensity of light that hits or passes through a surface. Paranormal investigators tend to investigate at night time, so using the available lighting from the building or from your own resources can make a considerable difference and, you might discover a pattern that is interesting. Some sources of light might come from things like suburban street lighting, emergency exit lighting, solar lights, torches, candles, fireplaces and the sun, to name but a few. Documenting how much light is in the location might prove fruitful if, later in the investigation, shadows or flashes of light have been reported; rooms or areas have felt darker or brighter. It is worth keeping in mind reflective objects in the room, such as mirrors, glass, metals and water and not to forget the digital camera flash.

Decibels (Sound)

A major part of a 'haunting' revolves around the subject of sound. Nowadays, paranormal investigators are lucky enough to have sophisticated sensitive recording devices at their disposal, to pick up unaccountable strange noises. This can be a good and a bad thing. Not all noises are done by Spirit although, they find the easiest way to communicate with us on our realm is by creating sounds, so you should not ignore checking how noise affects the location you are investigating. Some areas/rooms might be quieter than others to do vigils or set-up recording equipment. Decibel (dB) is the unit for measuring the intensity of acoustic and electric signal. Basically, the decibel reading will display how noisy it is around you. The 'C weighting level' picks up high frequencies such as engines, machinery and thunder and is used for peak measurements. The 'A weighting level' is the audible frequencies perceived to the human ear, which are commonly low and similar to background noise.

Moon Phase

It is said that paranormal activity and human behaviour changes during specific moon phases. The words lunatic and lunacy come from the Latin meaning for moon, 'Luna'. This is why it is popularly thought within society that an erratic mentality and social tension occur when there is a full moon. There is no proof to suggest this happens yet, studies were carried out on humans and found that we were prone to sleep less when there is a full moon, as the body showed lower levels of the sleep hormone melatonin. The other causes of lack of sleep because of a full moon on a clear night, might be down to environmental factors, such as animals being awake and people out-and-about. There may be a basis around the radiation reflecting on the moon from the sun, causing the different patterns of actions in humans and Spirits. Other theories propose moods change due to the moons gravitational pull (position) around the earth in relation to the sun. The new moon is credited with bringing calmness and good communication. This is when the sun and the moon are in conjunction (aligned) in the same spot of the sky.

Astrological Significance

Similar to the moon phases, the way celestial bodies are positioned in the sky are suspected to play a major role in how we go about our lives; so why not for the Spirits in our realm too, especially if we are all reaching out to one and other? This might affect how an investigation is done. Astrology dates back many centuries. It is the study of movement of celestial bodies through the constellations of the zodiac and where they are situated in relation to others. The sun resembles ego and stamina, whilst Aries (zodiac sign) can represent bravery or selfishness. Put the two together, you would expect a straightforward investigation but with some baffling outcomes. There is no evidence to suggest astrology has any importance on our daily lives yet, it is still ingrained into our culture and was valued and respected, like astronomy, for a science as recently as the start of the 17th century. What science may prove today, in our world, it might not in others.

Forecast

Weather conditions play a part on how investigations are run. Which spots to work in, time spent in that area, which equipment to use and experiments to do, can all depend on how the climate is. Being exposed to heavy rain or a blazing hot sun is not ideal for you, your gadgets or your results. Some 'hauntings' might be attracted to weather patterns, like a hot sunny evening or thunderstorms (like other triggers, for instance, being attached to a piece of music, identical looking people, smells or objects). The weather can be fundamental on how the location/building reacts and, in some cases, was managed. Also, it is worth checking for your own safety what the weather will be like when travelling to and away from the location. So, if you are waiting for continuous number of hot days to do a water experiment (such as a lake or beach) or, visiting a site that is susceptible to floods, always scan the weather forecast.

Most Active Area/Room

There might be a particular area in the place where you are investigating that tends to be more 'lively' than others. This makes it a perfect spot for a study, whether it is from reports of people who had witnessed something abnormal (in that zone), events in its history, first impressions from people within your group (psychics or mediums) or gut instinct. Positioning locked-off equipment or spending an extensive amount of time in the most active area/room could bring its rewards.

Type of Manifestation

There are many categories, according to popular belief, of entities that are presumed to had visited our realm or exist within it. We have listed a few of them that you may encounter on your journeys, attributed to the paranormal activity at the location. Most phenomena collected from accounts made by people are over-exaggerated, based on hearsay or were plainly made-up. Some reports may have been misinterpreted at that moment and are explainable. A rare few may be genuine and a solution behind the phenomena is hard to find so, therefore, is connected to the supernatural.

Here are a few examples of manifestation:

Intelligent

These beings respond to questioning using a method of communication that is mainly oral (for example, speaking or whistling), noises (such as rapping on a table and scratching on walls), influencing objects and the environment around us (for instance, slamming/opening doors or flickering lights) and interacting or affecting us on a mental and physical level (divination, channelling or mediumship, dreams, empathy, touch and so on). Overall, these intelligent Spirits will know of your existence, relate to you and participate by trying to make contact.

Residual

This 'haunting' is connected to an event or incident leftover or being maintained. The hypothesis behind the 'Stone Tape Theory' is that ghosts leave their mark after they had encountered an emotional or distressing situation (like a battle). It may not be all that bad; they could be still 'living in the process of their time'. Two common themes to these Spirits are that they follow a regular routine or pattern and would not notice you around.

There are a few ways of finding out if residual energy is present at a site (such as from reported cases and psychic readings). The main ones are to uncover information or identify an occurrence with the equipment and experiments that had been hidden, forgotten or lost but, is later discovered through questioning and research that links to the residual haunting or history (connecting the residual energy/evidence to the buildings past, in contrast to the location's current state).

Poltergeist

The word poltergeist comes from the German language, meaning 'noisy ghost' or 'noisy Spirit'. This type of 'haunting' is associated with loud noises, objects being moved or destroyed, occasional strange voices and, in rare circumstances, has been known to be bothersome or lethal to people. Activity can last from a few hours to months and even years.

There is a suggestion that psychokinetic energy (PK) – the mental effort by a person to move an object – is the root behind the phenomenon. This ability is triggered through stress, tension and in some instances, puberty and pregnancy. The actual 'haunting' is centred on a particular individual and not the location.

Alternatively, one has to contemplate the mind of an intelligent soul (Spirit guide or wandering ghost) observing changes in its environment or in people they have become accustomed to. With the inability to communicate properly, destructive behaviour is the only method of causing a decisive intervention – and that goes for humans as well as ghosts.

Crisis

A crisis manifestation entails a Spirit that interacts with humans, usually by delivering a message, informing them of a completed (unknowing) event or forthcoming situation that will change their life in the foreseeable future. This omen or task is performed in order to prepare the mental state of the person they had made contact with or, on odd occasions, to drive them into taking immediate action to alter the possible outcome.

Many crisis manifestations happen before/after a loved one's death, some others even warn about the downfall of society but, there are those that foretell of good fortune ahead. They have been known to appear on an anniversary, mainly of their own death, bringing either punishment or reward to anyone whom they come into contact with.

Elemental

These supernatural beings (mainly based on creatures of mythology) are associated with the nature forces (four elements) of our planet: earth, water, air and fire. It is believed that some of these entities can be summoned up using sorcery and can shape-shift, taking on varied appearances and forms (even humans).

Elemental activity might be heavily influenced by anthropomorphism (the human psyche separating and attaching its characteristics, behaviour or traits to a non-human entity, other than its own). This is probably why they've been regarded as having an unpredictable demeanour. So be wary of the ideas and wishes that occur in the mind of the living and other-worldly beings.

Doppelganger

This word means 'double-goer' in German. It refers to an identical looking being of a living person, without any biological connection. Seeing an apparition or double of you (also known as a 'Fetch') is believed to be a warning sign for bad luck or death. The difference with doppelgangers to crisis manifestations is that a description comes from the person who has observed their own lookalike, largely followed by their personal demise.

An explanation for these visions might be down to hallucinations, from disorders like epilepsy and schizophrenia or being in a dream-like state. It is advisable to mention that these 'hauntings' are centred on one person and a singular experience. Other hints include that the individual may had seen a relative in the Spirit world, who looked exactly like them (at that moment 'younger/older looking' to how they imagined to be) or, even a brother or sister they did not know about, who had passed over.

Faerie

Faeries have a tradition of being mischievous, sometimes unruly or helpful, depending on the humans they encounter. In folklore, they are regarded as 'Spirits of nature', too bad for heaven or too good for hell. This is why they are stuck in an in between world. They have been seen to take the guise of mythical and living creatures (horse, goat, rabbit, etc) and also humans. They were believed to have an effect on miscarriages, stillbirths or deformed children and blamed for diseases, people going missing, destruction of property and land and various other things.

Faeries are closely associated with Elementals, the differences being that Faeries were not invited into our world, as they were already here before humans. They tend to move around more freely compared to Elementals, who are genuinely stuck in one place.

There may be a reason for these entities appearing more than Elementals and it is to do with anthropomorphism again and also, with a greater number of people fantasying about the same entity, generating its existence.

Vampire

There are many types of reported stories about Vampires around the world but it was in the early 18th century, in Eastern Europe, that hysteria was at a large scale, with repeated grave diggings and stakes being driven into corpses.

There are many reasons why folklore became a reality in society. Premature burials gave arise to people being 'resurrected from the dead'. Diseases such as tuberculosis, chronic bronchitis, pneumonia (coughing-up blood on lips), rabies (hypersensitivity to light, abnormal sleep pattern and desire to bite), acanthosis nigricans (dark patches around neck); porphyria (skin sensitivity to light and receding gums) and dysfunctional mental attitudes gave grounds to back up vampirism. Drinking the blood of an animal or person (blood ritual) was deemed a way of connecting from the physical to the spiritual. In history, blood was regarded to have good medical properties, even believed to prevent ageing when ingested.

Over the last hundred years, vampirism has been romanticised, mainly due to Bram Stoker's book *Dracula* and recent *Twilight* film sagas. These 'hauntings' cannot be dismissed as only having occurred in the past. Beware of locations where there had been a lust for blood.

Cryptozoology

The subject of Cryptozoology is based on the study of animals whose existence has been noted but yet to be proved – like the Loch Ness Monster, Sasquatch, Mothman and Spring-heeled Jack. They are a cross between myth and geographic disturbances. Hundreds of new species of animals are discovered by biologists each year, whilst animals we thought were extinct can be found alive and well in certain habitats.

A cryptid tends to take a solid form, suddenly appearing then vanishing in the environment that it is in. There are a few reasons for why the cryptid makes itself be known. It could be down to changes in the ecosystem (e.g. territory, dominance and food chain). There are many factors as to why these creatures are evasive. One of them involves crypsis – the capability of an organism to avoid observation or detection. Another factor, a majority of the time, is the inability of the onlooker to properly detail the encounter. These creatures' intentions seem to be unobtrusive, only witnessed by a small few at the most and rarely do they attack the observer.

Demonic

The word *Demon* came from the ancient Greek word, 'Daemon', which means Spirit or divine power. Daemons were treated as deities in classical civilisations but nowadays, mainly thanks to religious and media groups, the term has come to refer to 'fallen angels', dishonourable Spirit or devil.

A Demonic 'haunting' goes hand in hand with possession and, the majority of the time, requires an exorcism, according to religious faiths. Biting, fits, respiratory disorientation, levitation, superhuman strength, talking in peculiar tongue and different languages (at different tones and pitches) are considered to be linked to a demonic presence in a person.

It is important to note that there are only a couple of differences between possession and channelling. Consent or recognition from the person 'possessed' towards the Spirit is withheld or unnoticed, leading towards frustration from the Spirit in being unable to communicate. Channelling works the opposite way.

Predominantly, the weight of the Demonic 'haunting' is observed by an eyewitness or group of bystanders. Their beliefs or attitudes towards the circumstances will concern the consequence of the 'haunting'.

Demons are not just hinged on possession. There have been sightings of human-like beings with hooved feet for centuries. They have been known to be accompanied by bad odours, signs of marks on the body (such as scratches and lesions) and sounds of snorting and growling.

UFO and Extra-terrestrial Encounters

This aspect of the paranormal is mainly separated from ghost hunting section to the study. There is one theory that ley lines can link the two together with the alignment (straight lines) between ancient historical structures, monuments and worship sites.

Unidentified Flying Objects (UFOs) have been seen throughout history but it was around the mid-twentieth century that the term was invented by the United States Air Force (USAF) and the phrase 'flying saucer' was widely used.

In 1947, US aviation pilot Kenneth Arnold witnessed nine objects flying in formation, waving side to side and travelling at an incredible speed over Mount Rainer, USA. Notable cases of UFO sightings include Roswell (1947) and the Phoenix Lights (1997).

The phenomenon is not just restricted to North America. There have been reported worldwide, from all walks of life. Most of these sightings are thought to have logical explanations behind them. Inferior knowledge of the day/night sky, (such as planes and satellites, atmospheric phenomena, present environment and landscape, astronomy etc), hallucinations and poor eyesight are just a few reasons that could mislead people into thinking they have seen a UFO. There are also suggestions they are connected with covert military operations.

Extra-terrestrial encounters are to do with contact with land, objects, animals or people (close encounter) from an alleged alien lifeforce. These includes crop circles, animal mutilations, influencing vehicles or electronic devices, time lapses and abductions.

Magic

Not to be confused with performing tricks, this category is formed around a residual event, either from a single individual or collective group, performing a ceremony, ritual or invocation in an attempt to communicate (invoke) with a deity or Spirit. You may come across a location where spells were cast (witchcraft) or people prayed (worship). Also, a mysterious unexpected event can be put in the same bracket, such as Marian apparitions, ball lightning and the Bermuda Triangle.

False Anomaly Risk

The word anomaly means peculiar, untypical or situations that stray from the usual practices or arrangements. An investigator would regard anomalies as impressions of a supernatural occurrence. The word false means incorrect. The risk of receiving an incorrect odd condition differs at each location you visit.

False anomalies affect our judgement and the only ways it can be identified is through having knowledge of the environment that you are studying in and understanding the equipment that you are using to examine. For an investigator, these anomalies are mainly picked up by three things: peoples experiences, measurements from meters and analysis from recordings. For photography, false anomalies include rain, insects, cast beam of light or shadows, reflection, dust or dirt and so on. People experiencing strange smells or tastes in the air should recognise odours, scents or gases produced from nearby or recently removed sources (which should include humans too).

Here are a few of the guidelines:

Very High: Considerable amount of dust, moisture in the air; nearby airport; road traffic or industrial machines and excessive amount of lighting.

High: High amount of dust; a reasonable amount of moisture in air; suburban town sounds; central heating and sunny or rainy day.

Moderate: Fair quantity of dust; some moisture in air; brief occurrences of noise pollution and standard lighting.

Low: Little dust; small amount of moisture in air; rural or countryside noise and moonlit night.

Very Low: Clean area; dry air; very quiet or isolated sounds; cool environment; pitch black room or cloudy night.

Preface

A definition for the word preface is to 'preliminarily explain'. The journey prior to an investigation can be thrilling yet, met with obstacles on the way. Distance and accessibility are the key. Some places might be easy to get to by vehicle and others, you might have to take an arduous trek on foot. Carrying heavy equipment, going up and down stairs, having to be mindful of your head while walking around (low ceilings and doorways) and footing (uneven ground, loose floorboards and debris) are just some of the ways a location can be hazardous and exhausting to study, though, we all know it is worthwhile. A pre-visit is ideal to get a gist of the time it takes to get to the location and review the surroundings that you will be in before you investigate at a later date.

Here are a few of our guidelines.

Very Good: Easy to find; brilliant access towards location; no problem inside for mobility and high safety.

Good: Reasonably easy to get to; respectable access towards location; good to move around inside and safe.

Moderate: Average.

Poor: Hard to find; problems accessing the location; difficulty inside when moving around and minimal danger.

Very Poor: Trouble finding location; hard to access; hazardous when moving around and dangerous.

Time Duration

Some 'hauntings' can occur at a specific point in the day. This can prove crucial when deciding what time to conduct an investigation. Yet, not all 'hauntings' go by this rule. Some maybe are triggered by certain date, a season in the year, weather condition, lighting and the list goes on.

The length of time the 'haunting' lasts has to be thought out too. There is a chance of recognising a pattern from gathering reports of past activity, maybe from owners, staff or visitors to the location. Day-time investigations can just be as fruitful as night-time investigations, so do not rule them out.

In general, the more time you have to investigate, the better it is. It gives a chance to get your bearings, make less mistakes when setting up, thus affording the spare time to be more relaxed and 'tuned in' to the surroundings and making Spiritual contact. When this cements, the result is a productive investigation, to all intents and purposes.

Chapter 12

Blarney Castle

– *Continued* –

The Investigation

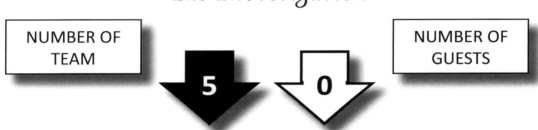

NUMBER OF TEAM	NUMBER OF GUESTS
5	0

Explaining the calibre of this castle is hard to put down to a few words. The height of the castle is immense when first looked upon and compares to the analogue of past, prehistoric structures and other buildings on the grounds for its authenticity.

The weather was perfect for ghost hunting on arrival. Partly cloudy was the forecast. The weather predicted was far tamer but soon, we would be disappointed as the ancient grounds around the premises of Blarney Castle quickly became drenched with pouring rain – just as we were about to start the investigation. This left any opportunity of experiencing anything around the grounds completely worthless.

Before this happened, the team had parked up and met the owner of the castle. The formalities of getting equipment from the cars into the castle were orchestrated; soon, it was time to wander around the ancient grounds and towards Badger Cave.

As various members of the team split up to size up the grounds, thoughts were put into operation as to how we were to set up the experiments, to take photographs, baseline testing, psychic readings and to what structure the investigation should take.

Anthony and a male team member went to conduct the baseline tests. A female team member went on her own to do her psychic readings and Jen, with another female team member, took photographs around the locality.

With the use of walkie-talkies (*See Equipment*) the team met up at numerous points and discussed the criteria of what to do in certain surroundings.

A video camera (*See Equipment*) was set up in the Kennel, Sentry and Dungeons.

A laser grid (*See Equipment*) contraption was placed behind it.

It was only the second time that we had used the laser grid instrument. The video camera might pinpoint any disturbances that could occur within the lines of the red grid. The video camera and the laser grid were both pointed at trigger objects (*See Glossary*), which included a shot glass, drinking-side up and a miniature version of the body mood doll (*See Glossary*).

A motion detector (*See Equipment*) was placed at the entrance to this site.

A full spectrum camera (*See Equipment*) was placed in the Witch's Kitchen. Another motion detector was pointed at a portion of sticks on the ground, to see if the Blarney Witch could contribute a response.

To our dissatisfaction, the heavens started to open as we were in the middle of the protection prayer in the Family Room/Chapel Room on the third floor of the castle. We were just about to start the investigation.

The cameras in the Kennel, Sentry and Dungeons and the Witch's Kitchen had to be activated but because of the distance and harsh weather, it might prove too toilsome to do so. We pondered on this notion and then decided hopefully, midway through the night, that this action could be revised if the weather should change.

In the baseline tests, a reading of up to 8 milliGauss (*See Glossary*) on the EMF gauss master meter (*See Equipment*) was found around Young Ladies Room/Priest Room and a spiral staircase leading up to the Blarney Stone. This was probably due to the floodlights.

A reading of 2-6 milliGauss was found by Badger Cave and Kennel, Sentry and Dungeons, also possibly coming from the outside floodlights.

It was very dark within the castle though: a reading from the environmental multi-function meter (*See Equipment*) gave 002 lux. This would make it impossible to get around within the building. We were prepared with torches however, as we knew upon getting around the castle, we would embark on certain obstacles.

Inside the castle the sound was very mute. We were about a mile away from the town centre of Blarney.

It was thought that the presences of intelligent, residual and magic energies were around us.

The false anomaly risk was high, due to the heavy rain at times, with bugs more easily frequenting the view of the camera lens.

The temperature outside was 22.7°C while inside, it was slightly higher at 22.9°C, making conditions quite warm.

The moon was at first quarter, at 58% of full.

Two hours after we had arrived, we were ready to start proceedings. It was now nine o'clock at night. We were positioned in the Family Room/Chapel Room.

We started with a past enactment experiment (*See Glossary*) to get things going. A recording of battle noises was relayed out. As Blarney was notorious for its many sieges in the past, it was thought that this would be a great idea to assemble the dynamism needed for phenomena to happen.

Two small speakers were placed on a wooden table. The sounds of horses, weapons colliding, shouting and anguish pounded the castle walls as everyone present looked on. A bell (*See Equipment*) was rung to entice some of the 'Spirits' forward.

Anthony, Jen, the two female team members and the male team member all called out their names. Jen was holding the night vision camera (*See Equipment*) scanning around the area; she looked up and down the castle walls, to the centre of the room. She focused the camera onto the table, to where the speakers were positioned.

Anthony called out for the 'Spirits' to come forward.

One of the female team members shouted, "You're under attack, you're under attack!"

A minute later, Jen walked towards a doorway that leads down to the hallway, connecting the Family Room/Chapel Room to the Young Ladies Room/Priest Room. If she wanted to go further, she would have to go down some steps but in front of her was a dark vacuum, in between the bricked walls either side as she peered down the hallway. She turned around and looked through a window slit, towards the battlement grounds of the poison garden.

The male team member and Anthony continued to call out. The male team member was asking for the K2 meter (*See Equipment*), which he was holding to be lit up, to show a 'Spirit' presence.

Twice Jen was enchanted to walk away from the rest of the team, towards the spiral staircase from an off room. She decided not to pursue her intrigue and returned back to the group. Jen viewed with the night vision camera from a window, out onto the oubliette (*See Glossary*) and battlements.

Seconds later, Anthony could smell smoke. As he related this, a drawing in of breath followed by a soft whispering voice that said, 'Horses', could be heard on the night vision camera.

Drowned-Out Voices

Under a minute later, as the male team member called out, another whispering voice could be heard on the night vision camera saying, 'Ah it smells like horses' in a childlike manner.

A croaking grimace could be heard in between these two EVPs (*See Glossary*). It is completely different to the other EVPs caught in this segment, as it is less clear and harder to discern.

Jen viewed with the night vision camera from a window, out onto the oubliette battlements. As she focused away from the window, she turned her attention to another window inlet at the opposite side of the room. A light could be seen shooting up from inside the window inlet as the camera tried to focus.

Two seconds later, the night vision camera focused again, peering straight at the side cavity of the window. The beam of light only lasted for a brief second and was blurry white in its colour. It stuck out a mile due to the pitch darkness we were working in. Torchlight cannot be ruled out but this is disfavoured, with nobody holding a flashlight on the recording at that point of time, also considering the direction that it came in on. Taking this out of the equation, it seemed we may have established a link with smells and children.

Less than ten minutes later, the past enactment experiment had finished. Immediately, the two female team members conversed, sensing energies down by the poison garden battlements. One of them got the sense of footsteps/running around the castle and up the spiral stairs. The past enactment experiment proved quite successful.

Next on the agenda was a Frank's Box (*See Glossary*) séance (*See Glossary*).

The two female team members and Jen were included in on this. They positioned themselves around a table by a window, under a walled ceiling, sheltered from the damp rain pouring down.

A bell, antler, a digital sound recorder (*See Equipment*) and a spirit level (*See Equipment*) were placed alongside the Frank's Box on the table. Anthony held the night vision camera while the male team member continued to hold the K2 meter, monitoring any changes in the electromagnetic field.

A Spanish flag was placed by the disused fireplace.

The Frank's Box was turned on – and so the séance had begun…

Scottish accents were heard coming through the Frank's Box. There could be a connection.

Anthony called out, "Is it to do with helping the Scottish war against the English soldiers from here?"

A reply was picked up by the digital sound recorder. It said something similar to 'compass' followed by 'mustn't' and 'stop'. A

- 24 -

state of confusion was being sensed. Seconds later, a voice said, 'Hello', in Spanish, from the box. Soon after, the word 'Children' is heard twice from the device.

One of the female team members and Anthony sensed they could hear banging noises. The female team member pointed out that it was coming from straight in front of her, towards the opposite end of the Family Room/Chapel Room.

Anthony said it sounded familiar to walking or running.

The Spanish flag took our attention away for a couple of minutes. It was presumed to have moved position from underneath the fireplace.

The female team member described feeling compelled to look to the doorway that led out towards the Young Ladies Room/Priest Room; it is a feeling of being watched. At the same time she expressed a tweak on her shoulder.

The individuals connected at the séance grew into a deeper action of concentration.

The name 'Thomas' was mentioned by one of the female team members. Miraculously, three seconds later, a male voice said, quite clearly on the Frank's Box, 'Thomas'.

Anthony could smell an odour. A female team member started to feel sick. She asked, "Is that you making me feel sick?"

A quick, loud reply from the Frank's Box stated, 'Yeah'.

It was felt that children were coming through: a red-haired, little girl around the age of eight or nine years old along with two boys, who are playing with the flag we had hung up on the window inlets.

One of the female team members said, "I'm really confused" to herself. Meanwhile, Anthony asked, "What do you eat?"

A reply with a strong male Irish accent was heard from the box saying something similar to 'Butter'.

The team laughed in amusement to the answer.

"Who is your queen?"

About ten seconds later, a response was caught on the digital sound recorder coming from the Frank's Box. It said, 'I love babies'. It is not clear if it was in a male or female tone of voice.

Anthony walked over towards the hallway that leads down to the Young Ladies Room/Priest Room. He looked on with the night vision camera in hand for less than a minute, into the vacuum of darkness, calling out questions in Irish.

One of the female team members beckoned him to step away from that area and to come back to the Frank's Box séance. Anthony returned to where the team were. He pointed the night vision camera on the male team member who called out, "Is there somebody here beside us?"

What sounded like a static surge from the Frank's Box followed by a loud hiss that said, 'Yes' could be perceived.

It is not clear if this response came from the Frank's Box, as it is not picked up upon by any individuals around the vigil.

The hallway between the Family Room/Chapel Room and the Young Ladies Room/Priest Room opened our eyes with curiosity.

Jen and Anthony felt distracted by its influence whilst holding the night vision camera. Meanwhile, one of the female team members felt uneasy about the atmosphere within it. It was her and the male team member who were elected to go down to this area and request the 'Spirits' to come forward. The rest of the team took a time out and stayed in the sheltered area of the Frank's Box séance.

The female team member went down the steps to the hallway with the night vision camera. From further on, in the Young Ladies Room/ Priest Room, she could hear footsteps coming towards her. She assumed that they were getting closer.

She called out, with a sense of fear in her voice, "They're coming. I can hear them… coming through that way…is it you I hear walking through the room?"

The calling-out vigil (*See Glossary*) ended, lasting just over a couple of minutes.

The female team member described how she felt the energies called out to her, that they were playing hide-and-seek. She also picked up laughter.

We progressed into the Young Ladies Room. Above us would have been the Priests Room but that floor level did not exist anymore. The area was smaller than the open-top Family Room/Chapel Room that we had been in. We congregated in the Young Ladies Room. A spiral staircase (used by visitors and staff heading up to the Blarney Stone) was situated in one corner of the room.

We would do glass divination (*See Glossary*) using the occupation cards (*See Glossary*) for this experiment. The occupation cards depicted old medieval phrases for types of vocations that a 'Spirit' may have done or, are still doing. The cards also had symbols on them, displaying the type of job they may have been involved in. This was only the second time that we had used these cards. Previously, they proved quite successful on an investigation at the Killegy Cemetery and Chapel of Rest in County Kerry.

The deck of occupation cards was spread out in a circular pattern on the table.

As Jen and a female team member waited at the table, positioned centre of the room, the other female team member rang the bell to start the vigil and to awaken any Spirits.

Anthony held the night vision camera, while the male team member present continued to see if any changes happened on the K2 meter that he was holding.

Bad shivers were felt being around. Members of the team started to lightly clap to release energy – something that is often done at funerals or concerts as recognition.

All three women connected to the upturned glass.

"Can you show us a picture that you like?"

The glass rotated on its rim, then it moved in a fast motion to in between the cards 'Brightsmith', which means 'metal worker' and 'Spittleman', which means 'hospital attendant'.

The glass tilted on its rim and twisted clockwise seven times, before falling on its side, knocking three occupation cards off the table. The glass was put back to the centre of the table. The cards that fell were lined back up on the table.

"I could take the cards off now if you want?" said Anthony.

The glass moved in a fast motion knocking the card 'Brightsmith', meaning 'metal worker', off the table. This card showed a symbol of a sword and the alchemy symbol for metal.

A female team member pondered, "That is really odd movement."

The glass twisted two counter-clockwise circles on its rim before landing on its side.

The occupation cards were replaced with the talking board (*See Glossary*).

It was agreed that a girl with red hair and two boys were strongly present with us.

A female team member and Jen connected to the glass.

"Can you tell us how old you are please?"

The glass moved to 'No'.

The female team member on the glass pointed out, "There are footsteps out there!"

The glass moved from centre of the board to 'No'.

After about five minutes, the glass seemed to unbalance itself around the board, rotating on its rim before repeatedly falling onto its side.

The answers given all seem to be negative.

One of the team members mentioned a priest coming through alongside us.

The glass moved to 'Goodbye' then it tilted on its rim, fell to its side, striking the board hard. Jen and a female team member reacted quickly, stopping the glass from falling off the edge of the table. The glass was placed back at the centre of the board.

"Hello Father. How are you?"

The glass moved in a rapid straight line to 'Goodbye'.

The female team member had to flank one side of the board with her hand, just in case the glass shot off the table with the forcefulness it delivered.

Witticism was used in questions to the 'Spirit'. In reply the glass moved straight to 'Goodbye', in a possible angered act.

This showed the glass could move straight if it wanted to, instead of leading a merry dance on its rim.

The glass was put back on the centre of the board.

"Is that where you are?" Anthony asked.

The glass moved in a straight line to 'Goodbye'.

The glass was put back at the centre of the board. The glass moved a further two times, at a rapid pace, to 'Goodbye' after it had been placed at the centre of the board. This suggested the Spirit was unwilling to make a concession.

"Do you want us to leave?"

The glass moved in a straight line to 'Yes' then reverted diagonally to the opposite side of the board, in a straight line, to 'Goodbye'.

All three women situated around the board attempted to stop the glass from falling off the table by the unforeseen force.

Five minutes later, a cold draft was felt around the board.

"Can you show us the way out?" was asked.

More minutes passed whilst trying to stop the glass from progressing off the table, due to the potency in its adventure.

The male team member asked, "How do you feel that the chapel is gone… that it's just one big room now?"

A screech could be heard on the night vision camera just after this question but no one present at the time picked up on it. It sounded similar to a noise that a crow or a raven would make. These birds were notable Celtic metaphors for war and death.

Latin and Spanish questions were asked but nothing direct, in terms of knowledge, was passed back to us with any plausibility.

A female team member asked, "Okay, I'm going to ask you to step back, going to ask you to step back. You're not protecting anybody, only yourself."

The glass did four to five counter-clockwise circles whilst in motion on its rim.

"You trying to confuse us?"

The glass moved to 'No'.

That was about as clear as it got with the glass's dissentious reputation for direct answers.

We were now nearing the end of the vigil, "Step back, Priest," ordered one of the female team members.

The glass moved to 'No' in its motion, tilting on its rim towards Jen's direction before moving left to right, back towards the centre of the board.

The same female team member expressed that she felt the 'creeps'. She got the feeling of being slightly concerned towards the energy around us.

The vigil only carried on for a few more minutes after this. More notable exchanges were expressed. It was witnessed that the 'Spirit' present was malevolent, possibly into the black arts and reflected on how it could hurt us.

It is presumed that the 'Spirit' was by the spiral stairwell. It was thought to be a very dark energy.

The night vision camera showed signs of low battery power, so it was time to charge it up and to take a break before our last vigil.

This time we ventured down towards the Basement/Banqueting Hall on the ground floor.

A white table was placed at the centre of the room. Four compass points: North, South, East and West were labelled on the table. An orienteering compass was placed centre of this table, in conjunction to the markings on the table. We were about to do some table tilting (*See Glossary*).

On previous investigations, this experiment worked well. The table acted with great vigour in a Fairy Fort in County Cork and in Clonony Castle in County Offaly. It was Blarney, however, where we first used the compass table (*See Glossary*).

During this vigil, we would use red strobe lighting (*See Glossary*) to project an alternative light spectrum to the scene. This was the first time we used this colour in a strobe effect, to see what 'Spirits' would come through.

Anthony and the two female team members connected at the table whilst Jen recorded with the night vision camera. The male team member watched on from the side.

Wooden steps led up to a platform stage in the Basement/Banqueting Hall. To the right of the stage was a wooden staircase, which progressed up to a doorway above on the first floor.

We asked for the table to move in certain directions.

One of the female team members felt a cold breeze on the top of her hands; the table was shaking steadily. She could hear a faint thump coming from above us, from up the stairs. It sounded faint on the night vision camera and it was decided as being out of sync to the tapping noise created by the compass table legs, on the surface of the floor.

Anthony, encouraged by this, exploded into shouting a summoning-in prayer.

"Hear these words! Hear these cries, Spirit from the other side! Come to me I summon thee cross now the great divide!"

The shaking of the table had made the compass dial rotate from 'North 0°' to 'North 20°'. Not a major fluctuation and this could have been a result of the table's gradual altered movement.

Anthony called out, "Come towards us now. Step forward."

A whistle could be heard. It sounded like a puff of breath, obstructed by a solid obstacle.

Anthony turned off the light from his head torch.

There was a decision to bring the energies out from the shadows; to make it easier for them to approach.

As we reset ourselves into position to proceed with the experiment again, one of the female team members shook the table up above her head. She did so in such a reinvigorated state.

The table showed more revitalised movement as soon as she, Anthony and the other female team member reconnected. The table shook vibrantly as we called out several times, in a rhythmic manner, "Light as a feather, stiff as a board."

Anthony shouted, "Rotate this table!"

The compass flew off the middle of the table as it rocked from side to side, heavily tilting in its motion.

We had a pause and quickly reset.

One of the female team members decided to step away from the table.

Anthony shouted out a barrage of encouragement in a deep, croaky voice, "The pain, the sieges, Oliver Cromwell."

The table again tilted heavily, rocking side to side. It broke down to steady shaking as Anthony mentioned, "The four sieges."

Gradually, the table stopped moving after Anthony and the remaining female team member put their hands palm-side up on top of the table. By now, we knew it was just a question of knowing what to say to provoke or evoke.

After a break of just half a minute, Anthony and the two female team members reconnected back at the table.

Anthony whispered out encouragement. One of the female team members let out a bondless tone of garbled words to entice.

Anthony mentioned the Blarney Witch. He then called out, "East, North, South, West."

He bolted back from the table in a surprised demeanour. He thought he had seen an arm appearing to the left of him, invading his focus on the table.

A female team member also bolted back from the table.

They both reprised their positions back at the table quickly.

Anthony demonstrated the action of the arm appearing to the rest of the team. The table reacted to his portrayal, as it bulked up its momentum, which triggered a very heavy rocking state.

The female team member, who earlier had held the table above her head, pushed away her contact from the table. She now stood with her back against a wall, looking deep in contemplation.

The table rotated a third of a circle clockwise. Its movement ceased quickly as Anthony called out, "Use the red light."

Anthony connected back on the table. He was joined by the male team member. The table marginally rocked to the different variation of questions Anthony asked. After a minute or so, the activity stopped.

The other female team member felt she had witnessed something. She claimed to have seen a full-figure apparition of a woman wearing a dress, with her hair tied up, standing by the first-floor doorway.

The female team member, who had her back against the wall, stated that she got pulled off the table, driven right back and that the priest entity came through really clear. She could see his beard and smell his breath.

She explained what the priest said to her, 'So, you think you are safe?'

She explained what she had said in her head in reply, 'Yes… I do not think. I know I am safe.'

She added that the Spirit was right in her face.

She agreed to connect at the table with Anthony.

The table started shaking soon as they were on it.

She started humming. Anthony asked questions in reference to astrology. "Bang the table up in the air?" he asked.

The female team member hummed even louder. The table increasingly shook uncontrollably, until it released a violent rocking motion.

Anthony shouted, "Move the table!"

The table rocked heavily, tilting from side to side.

Anthony started to hum loudly.

The table rotated, counter-clockwise, for half a circle.

Anthony joined in on humming even more loudly.

By now, the female team member only had her left hand on the table. Anthony kept his right hand on top of the table. They both hummed in a high-pitched tone; the table continued to rock, tilting heavily. It twisted a quarter of a clockwise circle then, suddenly came to a halt.

On that note, the end of the night had approached. We did think to have one last go at the castle grounds but fatigue had set in and gathering the equipment was mainly on our minds, after failing to switch the cameras on, due to the rapid flow of the investigation. Blarney Castle has many talkative paths and points.

We packed our cars with all the gear we had brought. We did an end of protection prayer in the Family Room/Chapel Room and left Blarney, knowing what a great experience we had just had. It left us with a great deal to talk about.

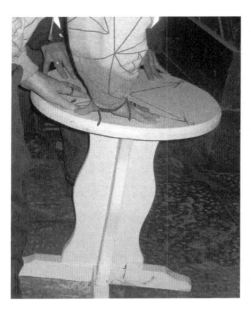

The compass table tilted on its legs

A view from the top of the castle down onto the battlements

Did we catch anything in the Witch's Cave?

Who's on the top of the wooden staircase in the Basement/Banqueting Hall?

A past enactment vigil will get us started

Badger Cave

Outside of the Witch's Cave

There are some wonderful gardens to walk through

Night time at Blarney Castle

An earlier excursion leads to above the Family/Chapel Room

Drowned-Out Voices Investigation footage can be viewed by

Watching the DVD that accompanies this book

Scanning the QR code

Visiting our website

www.GhostÉire.net

Click on the button

Drowned-Out Voices Footage

and enter the password

YourNotAlone

Enter the password

YourNotAlone

Location Background/Biography

The castle, as seen today, is not the actual, original keep. The original castle dates back to before 1200, when a basic wooden structure was believed to have been on the site. This was replaced by a stone fortification by 1210. The castle was destroyed in 1446 but was later rebuilt.

The Blarney Stone (otherwise known as the Stone of Eloquence) is a noted attraction of the castle. It is known to give the 'gift of the gab'. Visitors to the castle can walk the long spiral staircase to the very top of the medieval tower, lie on their back, tilt their head backwards and kiss the stone (almost upside down). All this while twenty-eight metres above the ground.

During the Irish Confederate Wars (*See Glossary*), the castle was besieged and was captured by the parliamentarian forces of Oliver Cromwell's (*See Glossary*) new model army. General Lord Broghill invaded the castle, only for the defending occupying army to escape via the underground caves situated below the battlements, known as Badger Cave.

The castle was restored to Donough MacCarthy (1594-1665) who was later made 1st Earl of Cloncarty. During the Williamite Wars in Ireland, in the 1690's, the 4th Earl of Cloncarty (also named Donough MacCarthy, 1668-1734), a supporter of James II was captured. His lands, including the castle, were seized by the Williamites.

The castle was sold and changed owners a number of times until it was sold to a Sir James St John Jefferyes, Governor of Cork, in 1688. A mansion was built on the grounds by members of the Jefferyes family. This was destroyed as a result of a fire but a replacement, known as Blarney Mansion, was built in 1874 – a type of Scottish Baronial building, which is also open to the public for tours.

Situated around the gardens and pathways of Blarney Castle are numerous rock structures. Dolmans, Druids Circle, Witch's Cave and wishing steps are pleasant acquaintances to the castle.

The Witch Stone is said to have imprisoned the Witch of Blarney. Some say that it was she who told Cormac MacCarthy of the power of the Blarney Stone, after it had already been used in the building of the structure.

The Witch's Kitchen was home to the very first Irish cave dwellers.

A Druidic worship sacrificial altar that dates back to prehistoric times can be found in the gardens too.

Manifestation/Legend

Embers of fire can be seen dying in the early morning dawn. This is lit every night by the Blarney Witch, as she tries to survive the harsh coldness of the night and escape from the Witch Stone.

The wishing steps also hold a solitary legacy. If you walk down and back up on these steps with your eyes closed, without stopping and make a wish, it is believed that the wish will come true within the year.

The Blarney Witch's firewood comes from granting the wishes.

Conclusion

The chance of investigating the castle grounds was thwarted. It was unfortunate, as time and effort had been put in preparing experiments, not only in that area but also in the Kennel, Sentry and Dungeons.

There was a sense that children were around, who needed safeguarding, at the start of the past enactment experiment in the Family Room/ Chapel Room. There had probably been children within the castle keep during various sieges – for instance, before Lord Broghill (Oliver Cromwell's general) succeeded in entering the building, only to find two attendants inside the castle back in 1646. Everyone else had escaped via the underground caves below the castle.

We did capture a child's voice over the night vision camera that we assume said, 'Ah, it smells like horses'.

Anthony could smell smoke just before this too. The children may have had a fundamental interest in horses.

A feeling of sickness had attached to one of the group before she felt a red-haired girl, aged between eight or nine and two boys coming through during the Frank's Box vigil.

It is believed the word 'children' had come over the Frank's Box device twice. It was alleged that these children had joined us in the Young Girls/Priest Room too.

We know that Louisa Jane Jefferyes married Sir George Colthurst in 1846. They had five children. Two of their children (Emily J and Alice Colthurst) possibly died (suspected at a very young age) before Blarney House had been built. Lady Colthurst had demanded the mansion be built. They may have been the last family to occupy the castle. Were the other three siblings – Louisa Mary Julia Bruce, Anne Jane Cape and George St John – the innocent youthful energies that the team member had described?

The team picked up on Scottish accents over the Frank's Box. Ireland and Scotland have mainly had a strong relationship with each other over the centuries or, have shared a common foe in England. Some regard the Blarney Stone as having been given as a gift from Robert the Bruce to Cormac MacCarthy, the King of Munster, after he sent five thousand of his own men to help the Scottish defeat the English at the Battle of Bannockburn in 1314.

The name 'Thomas' was mentioned by a member of the team, ahead of the name plainly transpiring over the Frank's Box. Without more information, we cannot completely identify this person.

Anthony asked, "What do you eat?"

To the team's amazement the answer was, 'Butter' from the Frank's Box radio. The basement served to house cattle and was used as a buttery. The word is separate from butter and lard house (pantry and larder) and correctly means a large cellar used to store liquor. Around the 15th century, butter was eaten fresh, was part of a staple diet for Irish people and is still regarded positively today.

The castle became the property of the Hollow Sword Company (founded in 1691) after estates were forfeited after the Williamite Wars. They produced blades that curved inwards (hollow ground rapiers). The company would cease producing swords by 1702. It was purchased by a group of businessmen, which would later generate the company into a bank. There was an appeal to the Brightsmith occupation card during the investigation that had an image of a sword.

There had been a suggestion that a hostile Spirit was present during the talking-board session, presumably a priest. The inability of the glass's movement was probably not helped by using a half-pint glass, resulting in it being 'top heavy'. Despite that, the glass could move in a straight line with attitude on occasions. In truth, the Priest Room was just above our heads. This being had followed us down to the Basement/Banqueting Hall. He had been described as having a beard.

One matter happening regularly was the sound of footsteps and running heard predominately high up on the third floor of the Family Room/Chapel Room and Young Ladies Room/Priest Room, although there was not a hint of footfalls captured on the recordings.

The vibrancy of the compass table's movement could be exaggerated due to the uneven flooring.

There was no alteration with the trigger objects – body mood doll and shot glass – when collecting the equipment at the end.

Blarney Castle
Co Cork

WEBSITE: blarneycastle.ie
e-MAIL: info@blarneycastle.ie
PHONE: 021 438 5252
TWITTER: @Blarney_Castle

Opened all year round except for Christmas Eve
and Christmas Day

Blarney Castle and Gardens is one of Ireland's top tourist attractions, with numerous events being held throughout the year.

A full day is needed to experience all of the potential of the castle, Blarney House, gardens and lake.

There are numerous plaques that give information around the estate and, if you need to relax, there are plenty of picnic spots and play areas for children.

The Stable Yard Café offers a wide range of fresh cakes, scones and hot beverages.

Layout

Rough Dimensions

COURTROOM, GROUND FLOOR

THOMAS DILLION CELL, GROUND FLOOR

ROOMS/AREAS, FIRST FLOOR

FAMINE AREA

COTTAGE ROOM, GROUND FLOOR

LESLIE CELL

HALLWAY

Chapter 13

Tarbert Bridewell Gaol

Jenifer's Journey

It is January. Everything is quiet in Killarney. Apart from the cold chill in the air, it was not that wintery.

I thought, *let's go for a spontaneous drive.* Anthony agreed with me. We had no other plans, so it seemed a great idea. Just a quick pop into town to do a few jobs and the rest of the day was ours.

After completing what I had to do in town, I made my way back to the car. I spotted Anthony talking to two 'Spinnis' – the radio crew of Spin South West. After a brief chat, they wanted to do a live interview to broadcast on the radio station. It was not every day that you catch a ghost hunter passing by.

Once the interview was over, we quickly checked the road map and recognised that Tarbert, in County Kerry, was worth a gander.

An hour's drive and we were there.

As we drove into the town, I saw a sign for Tarbert Bridewell. We followed it and parked outside the front of the building. My first thought was that it did not resemble what I would expect a gaol to look like.

We entered the reception. This was also part of the cafeteria. We were kindly given tickets by a lady at the counter. A group of women were sitting at a table in blissful conversation.

We came back out from the reception and walked across the front yard, to a door on the opposite side of the building. This was where the tour of the gaol began.

We went around the vast majority of rooms that included wall murals, plaques, props, mannequins – all detailing the lifestyle of those who graced Tarbert Bridewell.

Outside the back of the building was a small exercise yard. If the cells were not cramped enough, then you were not given much space out here too.

After we made our way back in, we noticed a plaque describing what some people were imprisoned or sent abroad for. Some people were sent here for the most surprising things. You would not get a harsher sentence for doing them these days!

Leading off from this room is a cell that details a story about a woman and a baby.

We headed up the stairs to the first floor.

Cordoned off, behind banisters, was a mannequin of a young girl sitting at a wooden table. This area portrayed the basic diet, eaten possibly during the famine times. Laid out on the table were imitations of food, which included apples, baked beans and bread.

One room on this floor had an exhibition dedicated to Tarbert-born art critic, Thomas MacGreevey.

Another cell told the history of the local Leslie family.

We came down the stairs to the Courtroom. A mannequin of a judge sits posing, as though he is about to deliver a sentence.

After finishing the tour, we arrived back at the reception.

Here, we met with one of the patrons of Tarbert Bridewell, Patricia. By chance, we discussed a possible paranormal investigation on the premises. She was very willing and enthusiastic about it. We just had to send on the finer details about what our research entailed.

In the weeks following, the excitement excelled, not just for us but also for the staff and friends of Tarbert Bridewell, when a local newspaper printed an article on the forthcoming investigation that we would d be doing.

On the night, we met up with Sylvie and a female team member outside of the building. Shortly after, we were joined by our three guests, contributors to the Irish pagan magazine, *Brigid's Fire*. They were intrigued about what we might uncover.

As there would be a number of people attending tonight's investigation, Anthony and I promptly got the equipment inside. I got on with setting up the experiments, whilst Anthony did the baseline tests, so as not to keep everyone waiting.

We were getting on with our jobs. Questions were coming from curious participants at every angle. It amazed me how an ex-male team member, who came along with Anthony and I, found the time to sneak over the road to a local pub, for a sly drink! Things took longer than usual for us to get started. Obviously, this was disrespectful and uncalled for, not just to us, the rest of the team but to the onlookers, the Spirits and also to himself.

Anyway, a protection circle was organised for outside of the gaol in the front yard. Some of us were lucky enough to catch the trail of a shooting star across the night sky, when looking upwards for final guidance.

Inside, a coffee table was positioned in the middle of the Courtroom, near the clerk station. Those not participating in the first vigil, table tilting, stood and sat a few metres away at the front of the Courtroom, waiting to see what might unfold.

There we were. We did not know what the verdict could be! What judgement would be passed down and who would plead guilty coming forth?

To deliberate would be the best plan of action.

The Investigation

NUMBER OF TEAM

5

10

NUMBER OF GUESTS

It was early March when the investigation night arrived. We received a very warm welcome from the staff and friends of Tarbert Bridewell. This led to an inspiring few hours.

Outside the main door of the building, during the protection circle, a shooting star with a long yellow tail shone brightly across the sky, for what seemed like an eternity. Thankfully, the weather was clear to see it.

Anthony visited the gaol a few weeks previous to meet with a journalist from the local newspaper. He also examined the EMF whilst he was there.

There was the usual influence from spotlights around the building, from 0-6 milliGauss but interestingly, a reading of up to 10 milliGauss was found in the Cottage Room. This was the first room you would enter when taking the tour. It could relate to the haunting that had occurred at the gaol.

Many staff members have felt unease when locking up the gaol late at night. One worker, who was painting a wall mural late one night, felt on edge and wanted to leave.

A mixture of intelligent and residual essences was felt within the walls. The first floor Leslie Cell, the ground floor Cottage Room and the joining Thomas Dillon Cell were linked to being the most active area/rooms.

Accessibility within and to the gaol was easy. This made the preface (*See Baseline Tests*) very good.

Before the protection circle, Anthony recorded the temperature outside as being 12.1°C but inside, it was colder at 9.9°C. Within the gaol the coldness felt much sharper.

The false anomaly risk was moderate – not to do with the environment but, to the great number of individuals who would be taking part or witnessing the events of the investigation unfold.

An EVP experiment was set up in the Cottage Room, an area of the gaol that showed, upfront, the story of Tarbert Bridewell prisoner, Thomas Dillon.

Mannequins enact the scene of a crime outside a white, thatched replica of a farm cottage.

A digital sound recorder was switched on. In the background, a cassette radio played Latin, Irish, French and German questions, with some Gregorian chant, timed to when the first vigil would start.

Next to this room was the Thomas Dillon Cell. This area would later be used for three separation vigils.

Inside this cell was the mannequin of Thomas Dillon, lying on a mattress of thick coarse material, with a thin, black blanket that barely covered his whole body. Under his bed was a wooden bucket, should one need to relieve oneself.

A high, raised, small window was letting in minimal daylight. This distanced the outside even further, giving a reliable account on how it would have looked like in the past.

We stuck a motion detector in the Hallway of the first floor, in direct line of the Leslie Cell. This was thought to be an active walkway.

Inside the Leslie Cell was a small-sized bed. On the ground, looking towards the right, was a Victorian hip bath. Small candles were lit and placed alongside the bath, close to the trigger objects that we would be using. The trigger objects used were an apple, a fork and a metal bowl, filled with make-believe baked beans. They were gently placed on white baking powder, on top of an A2 white sheet of paper. The candles gave the video camera just the right amount of light it needed to cover the trigger objects, should any disturbance occur.

For now, the Courtroom was where we would focus our main attention. A table-tilting experiment was to be done first.

All the usual aspects of a traditional Courtroom were represented. A royal coat of arms hung on the wall behind the judge's bench. The model of the judge is sitting down, presiding over the court. On his bench are several books on law and a wooden gavel. To the right was another mannequin, this time of a man standing in police uniform, holding his hat under his arm.

In front of the judge's bench is the clerk station. This is where the hearing is documented. The mannequin of the clerk sits, ready to write down in ink, pen to paper on proceedings. The judge, police officer and clerk models are looking over at the defendant on the witness stand.

Other mannequins sit close by, family members of whom, Thomas Dillon had offended. Defendants were brought in the front of the Courtroom through a door, which led to the cells and keeper's quarters.

The Courtroom is half sectioned off by a wooden partition. The other, open half acted as a cut-off point, presumably acting as a bar (an imaginary line), where a bailiff would have stood to keep order in court. On the other side of this would have been where the audience would have gathered in the past, looking in at the trail. This was at the front end of the building.

Apart from a few chairs, this area had more space. So this was perfect for onlookers of the investigation to be as the vigil got started.

It was now half eight in the evening. It was time to get things going. The lights were turned off. The table-tilting experiment was in progress.

Jen and the female team member lightly connected at the table. The female team member called out, "… loads of curious beings; you can probably sense us all here. We're all here for you. We're all here to encourage you, encourage you to show yourselves to us."

The table was already keeping a constant, steady, shaking rhythm. Anthony called out in Latin, "What is your name…? Where are you from…?"

Anthony held an EMF gauss master meter in his hand, pointing it over the table. He was keeping a keen eye should any change occur with the dial. The table gradually built up more of a rocking stance.

A minute later, the female team member called out, "Use the energies to walk this table across the floor."

The table slowly ground to a halt. It paused for a moment, before it continued back to its former rocking state.

Anthony alerted the rest of the onlookers, if they hear or feel anything, to call it out. The female team member declared that she was feeling a cold breeze on her left-hand side.

Harmonia, one of the lady contributors to the *Brigid's Fire* magazine, declared that she was seeing a lot of energy within the room.

Anthony told everybody present that there was Gregorian chant coming through on the cassette radio in the other room (Cottage Room). He made it clear, so that nobody would get freaked out or make false assumptions on what they might hear.

The Gregorian chant could now be heard on the background, louder than before. The table seemed to be inspired by this.

"Now you can hear in the other room. Do you like this energy? You can feed on this energy?"

Anthony walked over to Sylvie, who was behind the night vision camera looking on. He requested her to shine some torch light on the table, in doing so, making it easier for the onlookers witnessing the movement. There was silence but the table was still steadily rocking side to side.

Anthony called out, "Maybe, if you want to, make... change the environment in the room. Make it colder... you can do... or warmer. Whatever you want to do... There's objects across, inside the courthouse. There's an apple and a fork upstairs. If you want to move that, you can do."

The table continued at its pace.

The female team member asked, "Talk to us. Give one of us a tap on the shoulder. Stand by us."

The table gradually built up momentum, rocking faster for about eight seconds before coming to a stop. A tingly sensation was felt by the female team member.

"Were you guilty?"

The table, this time, was rocking to a different beat, slower in its approach.

A male entity was sensed close by.

The table returned to its familiar rocking as the team mentioned the offerings of food and drink left around the gaol. Moments later, Anthony joined the female team member and Jen at the table, as it maintained its rocking action.

Anthony called out, "We want to find answers, to see if there is still life after death. Come towards us."

He let out a summoning-in prayer. The table was rocking quicker. It briefly stopped, interrupted by the red laser light shining on it, from the digital, infrared thermometer laser gun, which Sylvie was holding (*See Equipment*). She quickly directed it away. The table resumed its motion.

Anthony asked, "Were you a... a key holder to this place... were part of the judicial system?"

The table stopped moving, presumably not accepting this as being correct. We might be talking to an inmate of the gaol or someone from another time period.

Talking in Irish was another option we had used. This type of language was seemingly understood.

"What is your name?"

The table initiated the same rocking pattern again, gradually getting more stimulated as we pressed for the Spirit or Spirit's gender. We got the impression that there were men and women around us. We went back to asking questions in English.

Jen and the female team member were feeling the pressure in their bodies from leaning over the table. There was a stoppage to straighten their posture. The table continued its motion as the team reconnected.

"Were you a prisoner?" Anthony asked.

The table carried on moving, signifying a correct answer.

Anthony pushed towards a date. "Was it the nineteen hundreds?"

The table went still and remained so. Anthony asked again, "Was it the eighteen hundreds?"

A few seconds later, Anthony repeated, "Was it…"

The female team member interrupted, "Seventeen hundreds?"

The table rocked. Slower in motion this time, swaying side to side.

Anthony called out, "Are you the energy before this prison was built?"

The table looked balanced as it swayed. We could suggest that Spirits from before the gaol's construction or, from another time-period, were present.

Anthony whispered, "Cold draught on my right hand."

He asked the rest of the people around the room if they were feeling anything. A change in the atmosphere was noticed by some.

Anthony intensified his questioning. "Can you slide the table? Can you come towards us? Come on, come towards us. Come on, step forward. Can you move this table in any direction? Show us what room you…?"

The table, which was steadily shaking, became still just before Anthony could finish the question.

The infrared thermometer laser gun had come up with a reading. The temperature on top of the table was measured a lot higher than what Jen and the female team member were aware of.

Sylvie swapped with Anthony. There were now three women at the table tilting.

Anthony turned on the sound monitor (*See Glossary*). The noise of a heartbeat reverberated around the Courtroom from the device.

A school bell was rung.

On the night vision camera, the legs of the table looked motionless yet, you could see that it was shaking at the top, in a somewhat pulsing manner.

The names Calum and Maureen were mentioned, along with the surname O'Grady.

"Calum is here."

For fifteen seconds, the table increased its motion to a quickening quiver. It then stopped.

Anthony walked over to a doorway, situated to the left of the Courtroom, leading out towards the cells (female quarters) and the cafeteria. He called out aloud, "Am I getting close to where you were?"

The first sound phenomenon of the evening, of countless others, was picked up on the night vision camera. A second or so after Anthony called out, a voice could be heard saying something similar to, 'Table moved'. Listening back at this vocal, it is possible that it could have originated from a lady of senior age. If this came from a Spirit, then we were working with an intelligent entity who knew well of our present surroundings. Could they see us or, could they only see the table moving?

We carried on, oblivious to the voice just recorded. The table started to rock, gradually getting faster as the legs struck the wooden flooring. It was now starting to possess such potential, the Spirit prisoner, who may be holding back a hidden agenda, was finally able to awaken its anger.

Anthony called out, "Pretend that I'm the judge there. Pretend that I'm the judge. Pretend that I'm the judge. Come towards us… come towards us. Pretend that I'm the judge there."

The table, as it rocked, quickly twisted on its spot, counter-clockwise. It slid; the rocking getting faster, locking in on towards the direction where Jen was standing. It moved in a straight line, almost pinning Jen against the seated mannequins by the wooden-partitioned wall. The table slanted on its legs briefly then, as the team members disconnected from the table, its movement stopped. The table was repositioned back into the middle of the open space.

Jen, Sylvie and the female team member connected back at the table. It resumed rocking as soon as they placed their fingers on top. We called out, trying to familiarise ourselves with the circumstances that led to so many at the gaol being convicted.

"We're here to understand what went wrong in this country, with you lot. It's wrong. It was really wrong. Show us how angry this makes you."

Anthony then offered some encouragement.

"Move the table towards me if you can. Move the table towards me if you can. Step forward, step forward. Move towards me if you can…"

The table rocked and moved towards the wooden partition, as though it could be on a mission trying to escape the Courtroom. It remained rocking on its spot, obstructed.

Anthony went over towards the judge's bench and picked up the gavel (the wooden hammer used by the judge to keep order). He asked Patricia if he could use it to knock on the table. Once permission was granted, he walked back over, gavel in hand and lightly struck the head of the gavel six times down on top of the table. The female team member shouted out, "Order in the courtroom!"

Momentarily, the table swayed heavily from its base, almost knocking into Jen as it moved towards her. The motion subsided as the female team member shouted again, "Order in the courtroom!"

Anthony asked Patricia if there were any 'Calums' that might be associated with the gaol. Instead, Patricia said it be more approachable if we mentioned the name Colm.

The table was rocking. Anthony felt a cold draught on his right – the same arm which he was holding the EMF gauss master meter. The conversation continued around the pronunciation of the name.

The female team member called out, directing her questions to the Spirits and to the staff who were present, "And what about O'Grady's, were O'Grady's around then?"

For about seven seconds, the table unleashed a fast, frenzied rocking before stopping. It continued rocking shortly after. We were on the verge of getting more movement from the table.

We were now about twenty minutes into the experiment. Anthony encouraged more action.

"Come on, come towards us. Step forward. Use our energies. Move it in any direction. Tilt the table if you can. Tilt it to one side… tilt it to one side, rotate it clockwise, anti-clockwise, any direction you want to. Come towards us, use our energies. Step forward."

The female team member removed her left hand away from the table. Briefly, the table kept on rocking for a few seconds until ceasing. A well-earned break was needed for the female team member, who was on the table from the start.

Anthony took her place, alongside Jen and Sylvie. This time, all three of them placed their hands palm-side up; the back of their hands were now touching the top of the table. The table slowly swayed a couple of times before all three individuals flipped their hands back over, palms-side down.

For about two minutes, the table was showing the same flow of energy, slowly rocking on its legs side to side, as Anthony called out for the Spirits to cause some drastic action on the table. Moments later, he called out in Latin and then, he followed by talking about the various experiments that would be happening later.

After a change of battery on the night vision camera, the table-tilting experiment was opened up again. This time, Anthony and the male team member connected at the table. Jen was now holding the night vision camera. The sound monitor was still on in the background, playing the same heartbeat pulse. The table very slowly swayed from side to side yet, less potent than before.

"Just heard a knock," said Anthony. He wondered if it was his imagination playing tricks. He called out, "Can you create the heartbeat with taps on the table?"

About eight seconds later, as Anthony was talking, three knocks could be heard on the night vision camera. The first knock was louder than the following two. However, it could have been somebody else, behind the camera: some guest trying to come in through the front door of the Courtroom.

Half a minute later, he called out louder, "Come towards us. Can you make it even colder…?"

Moments later, he felt the sensation of a cold breeze on his right. The table managed to rock slightly more, as various team members shouted out support for more diverse movement.

"A cold blast on my right again… my right hand," said Anthony.

"Where did you stand in the court?"

The table quickened, tapping its legs off the wooden flooring.

"Lift the judge's gavel?"

The movement declined this invitation by stopping.

Anthony asked Patricia if there were any names common with the area that we could use to heighten the activity.

Anthony called out, "Would you have known the Leslies?"

He recognised a change in the environment. He mentioned the table was not moving but something strange was happening. The floor he was standing upon was feeling peculiar and a weird smell had approached. There was a sense that there was something underneath the table as it slowly swayed. Anthony was now feeling heat on his leg and cheek.

"Is there something to do with your cheek, your face?"

Patricia told Anthony some names that might feel familiar with the location: the Blennerhassets, Dennys and Francis Crosbie from Ballylongford.

Anthony called out, "Are you anything to do with the Blennerhassets?"

A very clear young masculine voice came forward on the night vision camera. It said, 'Pierce Crosbie, son of Leslie'.

We had another short break. The night vision camera resumed recording the vigorously rocking table on its legs, with the female team member and Sylvie connected onto it. Anthony turned on the sound monitor; this time it was letting out white noise.

"Was it Mr Leslie who tried you here?"

With more forceful rocking, the table slid. Its legs banged off the floor as it went towards Sylvie, nearly pushing her up against the wall of the Courtroom. The table was put back into position in an open space.

The female team member and Sylvie reconnected. The female team member connected only with her right hand. Her left arm was down by her side. Sylvie was feeling tingling on her hands. Anthony expressed to everyone present that he felt a tingling sensation. The female team member, who had her left hand by her side, returned it to the top of the table. She started to call out in Irish. The table began to pack a punch, rocking faster.

"Were you tried by Mr Leslie… does he make you angry?"

The table started to rotate slowly, counter-clockwise. Anthony shouted for the table to slide across the floor. It was now withdrawing space, restricting Sylvie up against the wall again. Anthony felt a cold draught on his right-hand side as he shouted out, "Slide it, Mr Leslie, come on!"

The night vision camera was focused in at the legs – the base of the table. It had rotated about forty-five degrees counter-clockwise. The table's rocking slowed down as it slid, drawing away from Sylvie, who was up against the wall. We whispered, speaking in a hushed manner, mentioning the judge in charge, "Come on, tell us what you think of him. Go on… go on. Jesus, he was a terrible man…"

The table jumped into life again, rocking a wider bearing than before for a couple of seconds. It moved back opposite yet again, secluding Sylvie's space for the third time. The table shook rapidly, limiting its turbulent motion, until it started rocking from side to side, on opposing legs. Sylvie remained connected whilst taking a step to her right, to avoid the advancing table.

Anthony yelled, "Come on, come towards us. Slide it in any direction. Step forward. Move it to where you are. Move it where you are. Come on! Keep it going! Keep it going! Slide it! Tell everybody where you are!"

The table rotated about forty-five degrees counter-clockwise, moving closer towards the Courtroom wall.

Anthony continued to shout, "Were you part of that area? Were you in one of those cells?"

The top of the table was knocking up against the wall at this stage. An urgent request to alert the Spirit was asked by the female team member. "You're going to chip the paintwork?"

The female team member and Sylvie immediately yielded their contact from the table…

The other side of the Courtroom wall was the cell that belonged to the women and baby mannequins- the women's cells. The Spirit may have chosen the table to move in this direction for a purpose…

The table was pulled away from the wall. The female team member and Sylvie renewed their connection on the table.

The night vision camera recorded again, with the table shaking very fast.

"Was it Cecil Leslie? Was it?" asked the female team member.

The table slanted on its legs from one side to the other, creating loud thuds, as it slammed off the ground. It progressed over towards the same wall again, reducing its motion to a frantic shaking rhythm. It diverted away from the wall, making its way to the open split between the wooden partition and the wall where the bailiff might have stood – the acting bar divide.

The female team member rested her right arm by her side. Her left hand was still connected to the table.

"Maureen O'Grady."

The table slowly lost its power, gradually getting weaker as it shuddered.

We pointed out that we would be doing a séance soon; that the Spirits could come forward if they so wished to. The table shook quickly.

"Now, if you a woman with us right now, can you stop the table, please?"

There was no indication of the table letting up on its mobility.

"If you're a man with us right now…?"

The table immediately stopped. This declared a male presence being with us.

"If you're a man, can you make the table shake…?"

The table started to shake, gradually getting faster.

"If there is more than one Spirit, I want you to not only shake the table, I want you to lift it as well."

The table persistently shook.

"Colm, Colm the angry one… you were a very angry man, are not you, Colm? I'd say you were very angry."

The table vigorously slid on the floor, angling towards an open space. The male team member, sitting on the same seating as the Courtroom mannequins by the wooden partition, was asked to connect on the table.

The night vision camera had stopped recording at this point, due to the battery life being emptied. We had to power the night vision camera whilst recording. The charger lead was attached to the camera and plugged into a power main to be switched back on. Luckily, we did not have to move too far.

Recording started again with the table moving at the same pace – shaking fast. The female team member and Rick – a contributor to the *Brigid's Fire* magazine – were connected on the table; the white noise was still in the background.

After nearly three minutes, Anthony asked, "Should we go into the keeper's quarters to do a séance?"

Seconds later, the table became still. Going by earlier responses, this may have indicated that we were invited to do so yet, we did not pick up on this.

The table re-intervened, by shaking, seconds later. A discussion unfolded about women being held on the upper first floor, although, there was a feeling of a male presence up the stairs. An act of sexual abuse and brutality was sensed to have occurred, with a dominant, malevolent, male entity present in one of the cells above.

The sound of the legs hitting the wooden flooring became louder. "You call that justice? Come on!" said the female team member.

Moments later, "You loved the power; don't you?"

The table slithered against the floor, moving towards the direction of a wooden-seated bench as it rocked aggressively.

The night vision camera was turned off…

We had to be aware of our guard for later tonight. After nearing fifty minutes, it was time to push on to something different.

We stayed in the Courtroom. A long table from the cafeteria was brought in, to be used in a séance. A dining room cloth was draped over it and a Frank's Box, wired up to mini speakers, was placed at the centre of it. It was not turned on yet: we thought it would be best to welcome the energies first, amidst the background of silence.

Sitting with hands flat on the table was the female and the male team member, Harmonia and Rick – contributors to the *Brigid's Fire* magazine – and four of the Bridewell staff. We were now in the front area of the Courtroom, where the audience would have gathered during a hearing.

Looking on, around the sitting was Anthony, who was measuring the EMF levels; Jen, who was holding the night vision camera; Sylvie who was taking photographs; Patricia; Donal, a local historian; another female guest and David, another contributor to the *Brigid's Fire* magazine.

The female team member on the table began the séance.

"You can push a breeze over the top of our hands?"

She began to cough. It became irritating to her. "Stop choking me," she asked calmly. She was finding it hard to talk with uncontrollable fits of coughing. Anthony asked if she was okay if she wanted to sit out from the vigil. She confirmed that she was alright to continue.

A minute later, the same female team member was getting the name, Shaun or Seamus, a particular weighty and rancid energy. Anthony asked the female team member if she had an age for this individual. She replied, "Mid-thirties. He's quite old and he's dark… I'd say, more like a guard or something like that."

Anthony quietly whispered, targeting for a Spirit or Spirits to come closer.

Jen directed the night vision camera away from the séance table and to behind her, towards the judge's bench.

Anthony, a couple of minutes later, was feeling sudden draughts or cold spots. He asked around, "Is anybody else feeling anything?"

Harmonia received a cold sensation on her left. The female team member on the table also felt this on her left leg. Moments later, she informed everyone that there was a freezing draught over her hands.

"I'm getting the name, Fintan in," she added.

It is not clear if this was the name of a place or person.

She carried on, asking, "Come on, build these energies… jump in… you're free Spirits; nobody's hounding you anymore…"

She continued, "I got a right twitch on my right hand then."

Harmonia described that she got something on her right at the same time, on the palm of her hand.

Anthony pressed a button on the EMF gauss master meter, activating it. He started sweeping the space between the female team member on the table and Harmonia, who were sitting next to each other.

Another person on the table started to cough – a lady member of staff. She took a sip from a bottle of water, calming the situation and then placed her hands back on the table, re-establishing the circle of flow.

Donal, the local historian, pointed out that the land on which the Bridewell was built was previously a green field but, an old castle around the back of the gaol once stood, dating back to medieval times.

Jen directed the night vision camera to behind her again. She zoomed in and out at a door beside the judge's bench, which led to the keeper's quarters.

After a few minutes, Anthony went over to the middle of the table and switched on the Frank's Box and mini speakers. This gave time to anyone who wanted to depart from the table to do so. Patricia took this chance and swapped with one of the Bridewell staff. The Frank's Box started scanning…

A very deep croaky vocal could be heard straight away from the Frank's Box.

Jen handed the night vision camera to Anthony.

"Right, you can use these frequencies as well as these energies to talk," said the female team member on the table.

A reply, in a feminine tone that did not seem to come from the Frank's Box said, 'Wow, okay'.

"Talk to us."

A distinct voice came from the Frank's Box. 'Silent' it said, articulated in a posh manner.

"Talk to us… you don't have to be silent in this courtroom. Like I said, we're not here to judge you," said the female team member.

Numerous replies came over the Frank's Box.

The first one was a very deep masculine voice that said something similar to, "I called order."

Next, a women's voice clearly said, 'Seek love' followed, a couple of seconds later, by another clear voice saying, 'Fuck'. This brought a light chuckle to some listening in on the table.

"Use these energies."

Twelve seconds later, the name Susan was thought to have come from the Frank's Box. This was identified as coming clear over the night vision camera recording.

We went on to calling out in German for a brief moment.

"Can you speak German?"

What sounded like 'Buddhist' was heard twice from the Frank's Box. This was only heard by Anthony. After he called out in recognition, the same word appeared again. It came over clearly on the night vision camera he was holding.

Anthony resorted back to English, "Do you have a second name, dear Spirit? Try and use the sound waves on the… on the black box, the middle of the table."

A reply from the box said, 'Bitter' or in German, 'Sorry'.

Anthony resorted to talking in German.

"What is your name?" he asked.

A second later, a women's voice stated, 'Rape' from the Frank's Box.

Patricia was now getting a tingling sensation.

A voice, not apparent from the Frank's Box was heard on the night vision camera.

It said, 'Twenty' in German.

A second later, Anthony asked in German, "What age are you?"

Unknowingly to him, the age was already mentioned but, by whom?

Some of the observers on the table recognised this number (understanding the German language), so it could have been one of them describing what they thought they had just heard from the box.

Another question was asked in German. "How are you?"

What seemed like two replies came from the Frank's Box, both saying, 'Speak up'. The first one was muffled, possibly female. The second one masculine but much clearer. Anthony heard these responses as he panned around the Courtroom with the night vision camera, viewing back to where the judge's bench was.

"Do you speak German?"

A male voice came back from the box, saying, 'What, I…' also in German. Both Anthony and the female team member on the table recalled what they had just heard.

'Yes' came through in German from the Frank's Box. This spoken word was pretty quiet but defined on the night vision camera.

Rick described that he did not feel like crying but he was feeling teardrops running down the cheeks of his face. He also decided to call out in German.

The female team member commented, "My hands are doing very strange things."

Anthony walked over to where she was sitting. He told her, "It could be static."

A clear voice immediately came from the box saying, 'Sensitive'. It was followed by Anthony presuming that the word *talk* had come from the box. The sound that Anthony assumed he had heard was less clear and much louder.

A minute passed, with many individuals at the séance feeling cold breezes. Excitement was flowing.

We went back to asking questions in English.

Anthony called out, "Can you tell us your name, please?"

Three seconds later, a masculine voice returned an answer from the box. 'Peter,' it said, in an Irish accent.

Another response came from the Frank's Box. A female voice in German said, 'Sausage'.

Rick responded to a question that Anthony had asked. Talking in German, he said, "That's heard."

A second later, the word 'heard' came from the Frank's Box, reflecting in the same tone of voice that Rick had just spoken, possibly mimicking what he had just said.

The female team member explained that her right arm was reacting like a pendulum, shaking uncontrollably, whilst Harmonia was also feeling like her right arm was freezing. Supposedly, the energy was circulating, being passed around the séance circle. Anthony pointed the night vision camera towards the female team member's right arm. It looked like her arm was going into spasm.

Anthony asked, "Is anybody else feeling anything on their arms, lads?"

A quick reply, separable to the source of the Frank's Box said, 'Books'. The voice seemed enthusiastic yet, the accent was hard to pin down. It could have been a lady who commented, possibly in regard to what job they held in the Bridewell. Perhaps an employee of the justice system had come forth?

Later, the female team member wanted to find out a couple of things. "Right, I'm going to ask you a couple of questions now…" She added, "If you can make it answer it on the voice box, then we're going to bring the glass in."

She presumed that she had heard the word 'Don't' come from the Frank's Box yet, the reply seemed muffled. A second or two later, something similar to 'No' was heard from the box.

Anthony called out, "Can you respond to that? Do you want us to use the glass, yes or no?"

A female expression that said, 'No' emanated from the Frank's Box.

Many individuals present heard this.

"Is there a reason why you don't want us to use the glass?" asked the female team member.

A couple of suppressed responses were caught on the night vision camera from the box – a plausible 'Yes' and 'Yeah'. Shortly afterwards, a heavy relief of breath was picked up on the night vision camera, not from the Frank's Box but originating from something else in the building.

"Okay, can you tell us your name, please?"

What sounded similar to, 'Colm' was supposed to have come from the box device.

"Can you tell us why you're here?"

Some scattered responses flew from the Frank's Box. A clear spoken female voice from the box said, 'No'. It conveyed a repressed air to it, in such a way that gave the idea of not wanting to reveal.

"Did you commit a crime?"

A reply from the box declared something similar to 'aren't' accompanied, a second later with, 'Done anything'.

Later, a low hushed faint response from the box said, 'Anthony'. This drew the attention of some, presuming it was targeting the team member.

"Did Anthony commit a crime?"

Seven seconds elapsed until a masculine voice clearly said, 'Cause he did' from the Frank's Box.

The name Colm was thought to have come through the scanning device.

Half a minute passed by until another release of a long breath was picked up on the night vision camera. It is not known who is creating this audible…

"Do you like us being here?"

Something similar to the word, 'Go' came from the Frank's Box.

Anthony was now getting a headache at the back of his head.

"Was there rape in this place?"

A couple of replies reverted back to us, furthering to the extreme towards 'Yes'. It may not have been contributed by the Frank's Box; however, it is not a hundred percent clear or certain.

If it was Colm coming through, he must have been a really chatty person, with the direct answers, along with the number of impressions we had received. Or, did the Spirit of Colm only recognise himself, no other, in the Spirit realm?

Seconds later, a female voice said, 'Bad' from the box.

Anthony and Sylvie mentioned that they had heard a bang…

Anthony viewed the table with the night vision camera. He spun around, back behind him and focused on the judge's bench at the foreground of the Courtroom.

He asked, "Can you move one of the dummies?"

A very silent, 'No' came over the Frank's Box.

The female team member asked, "Okay Colm, can I ask you why you're here?"

After eight seconds a man's voice said something similar to, 'torture someone' from the box.

This was recognised by some in on the séance.

Anthony enquired, asking what age Colm was when he died. There seemed to be a distant plea, 'Cold'. This was followed by an array of disconcerted speech from the box mechanism.

The name Francis is believed to have come from the Frank's Box.

Anthony asked how everybody was doing around the room.

"I'm freezing," said Patricia.

The female team member agreed, "Umm, yeah, my tops of my legs are very cold alright."

Patricia added, "All down my left side."

Another member of staff also commented on feeling freezing.

"Can you tell us… is there anybody here that would mean any harm? Is there any Spirit being here that mean any harm to any humans here now?" said the female team member.

Three seconds later, a delicate whistle could be heard on the night vision camera. It did not sound as though it wanted to cause any attraction or was done with any substance.

A few seconds later, 'Go' could be heard from the Frank's Box again.

Some present in the room confirmed that they had heard that answer.

Patricia asked, "Is it Francis? Francis Crosbie?"

A sketchy reply possibly said, 'Yeah' at a high pitch.

It was followed by a male voice, saying something similar to 'cunning' from the box.

The female team member wanted to clarify what Patricia had just asked.

"Did you hear what Patricia said? This Francis, Francis Crosbie?"

A masculine voice said, 'Hello' from the box.

Chatting amongst team members ensued.

Anthony asked, "Which room should we go to Spirit?"

An audible sound, which said 'leave', was reputed to be heard by the male team member at the table from the box. It did sound similar but it was not quite distinct.

"And does this make it unsafe for anybody to be here, if they stay here?" asked the female team member.

A reply from the box, in a Scottish accent said, 'If you like to' followed by, 'No'.

Anthony called out, "Would you like…".

Before Anthony continued the question, a spoken word, 'Water', in hushed desperation was heard. This whisper does not seem to have come from the Frank's Box. The topic of conversation revolved around the subject of drink. Somebody or something chuckled just as Rick said, "Making jokes now, are we?"

'Yes' was heard on the night vision camera, in a whispered tone.

Anthony carried on, "Would you like a drink?"

A man's voice said, 'Yes' followed by a women's voice, which said, 'Orange' came from the box. A pleading, deep voice slowly said, 'Thirsty' shortly after.

It is peculiar how a quick concoction of speech about liquid was filtered into a few brief seconds. Maybe half of these responses were done by people at or around the vigil.

We were coming to the end of the vigil. So much was happening.

"Is that where you used to sell the women? Upstairs, was it?"

Patricia felt the table moving and others felt it too.

Anthony went and grabbed the gavel. He knocked it vigorously five times on the wooden coffee table, used for the table tilting. He shouted, "Order!"

He was asked by a team member to do it again. Just as he made five raps on the table in a quicker succession, a voice said, 'Oh Jesus' from the box.

He shouted louder, "Order in the court!" The female team member also shouted, "Silence!"

A reply from the Frank's Box said something similar to 'again', in a quick, persuasive demeanour.

A new tape had to be put in the night vision camera. Recording began again. This time, the large table from the cafeteria could be seen shaking but this gradually subsided.

"Talk to us through the box as well?" asked the female team member.

It is hard to target what the next response from the Frank's Box meant. It either said, 'I won't' or 'Go home'. Some moments later, another voice said, 'I let you go' in a friendly expression from the Frank's Box.

About a minute of unreliable feedback came back from the instrument.

"Can you tell us your full name, please?"

A soft voice from the box is heard saying, 'Patrick' as the question was being asked. Shortly afterwards, another clear voice said, 'Ready'.

"Can you tell us your second name, please?"

The same style of voice said, 'Dave… is good' or, 'Dave… is Scot' from the box.

Patricia and other people on the séance table agreed that they heard, 'Scot' from the device. Patricia explained where the name Tarbert came from and its link to Scotland.

The name 'Smith' is thought also to have been heard.

The female team member said, "Blacksmith…"

A quick reply said, 'Yeah' from the box.

Patricia made plain that there would have had a good few blacksmiths here down through the years.

Anthony called out, "Can you give us a second name before we do anything else?"

Midway through his question, a man's voice said, 'Yeah' from the scanning radio. Another reply from the box followed yet, harder for an individual to make sense of.

It may have said 'Pat' or 'Mat'.

"Can you say that again, please? We're really stupid," said the female team member.

As Jen turned slowly around with the night vision camera, a lady's voice came from the Frank's Box. It is unclear what was uttered. It possibly said, 'Save you'.

Bordering on a minute later, the female team member on the table asked, "Can you tell me what your trade is?"

A reply said, 'Fish' followed by, 'No' from the box.

Anthony asked, "Where are you from in Scotland, if you are from Scotland?"

A response from the box said, 'Kilmollock' allegedly in an Irish accent.

Patricia felt that it said, 'Kilmarnock' a different interpretation to what was analysed.

The séance session with the Frank's Box had finally ended. There was considerable information being forwarded and quite a bit of physical interaction. We wanted more though; we felt greedy.

The local historian, Donal and four of the staff decided to depart at this stage. We remained in the Courtroom to do a glass divination experiment. Midnight was fast approaching. We did the experiment for about ten minutes yet, there was no movement from the glass. There were, however, some sensations of heat felt on hands but that was all.

In the earlier Frank's Box vigil, we got answers which suggested the use of the glass would not be accepted. We pressed on, however and brought the colour mood frame (*See Glossary*) into play. A total of seven people connected to the glass, which included, Anthony, Jen, Patricia, a staff member with the three contributors to the *Brigid's Fire* magazine: Harmonia, Rick and David. The upturned glass was placed on the centre of the frame.

Around about seven minutes in, Anthony thought that there was something behind the male team member, by the main front door entrance. At this point, the male team member, Sylvie and the female team member were around the vigil, looking in on the experiment.

The female team member replaced Anthony at the glass. She called out, "One push towards me and we'll take this glass off the table."

The glass timidly started to twist on its spot a number of times, rotating slowly before eventually moving thirteen clockwise circles inside the perimeter of the frame.

"Can you tell us who you are, please?"

The glass moved a straight line to 'Orange', meaning 'Unsettled and Mixed Emotions'.

It took a while, at this time, to notice what the glass had gone to. It was pitch dark inside the Courtroom. The glass was placed back in the middle of the frame.

Maybe there was a mixture of good and bad Spirits around? The majority of them might find this place repulsive and disturbing. They might have found us confusing and curious too. With any luck, they could tip over the border, finally being able to reveal the truth. We knew, in our minds, that we might not have been favoured by some Spirits or, one particularly strong soul.

"What mood should we be in?"

The glass went slowly to, 'What you see in the past' (a part designated for the design test, pre-planchette drawing).

"So we're here for historical purposes. Is that what you see? We're here because we want to know who you are. Is that right…?"

Slowly the glass moved, stopping a couple of inches away from 'Yes' and 'Brown', which meant 'Restless' on the frame. We were sure that this indicated 'Yes'.

The Spirit present knew of us being from a different time-period – an understanding that we were from the future on this plain. Moments later, questions were asked about the Irish tricolour flag, which was draped over the judge's bench.

The glass had gone to 'Grey', meaning 'Very Nervous and Anxious'.

"What? We should be very nervous?"

The glass moved to 'Yes' on the frame.

"Is that because you are going to frighten us?"

The glass screeched as it moved off the surface of the table, making its way to between, 'Grey', indicating 'Very Nervous and Anxious' and 'Green', meaning 'Normal and Average'.

Some participants started to giggle. It was possibly a response in relief to not being threatened. This laughter proved infectious, as other individuals laughed at those that were giggling. Maybe this was a way of releasing some tension.

"Are you English?"

The glass divination tool moved at a moderate pace to 'Yes'.

A question was asked if the Spirit was part of the judicial system. The glass did not budge.

Anthony decided to go in a different direction.

"Are you a prisoner?" he asked.

The glass made its journey away from the 'Yes' side of the frame in a straight line, stopping just a few inches away from 'No'.

He asked this question so as to draw the glass away from that area of the frame. The previous question to Anthony's could now be asked again.

"Are you a judge?"

The glass moved to 'Yes'.

So was the judge happy at all with us disturbing the peace? We were given a warning that things could get quite hairy for us. The gavel was used to bring more energy in again. The glass was put back in the middle of the frame.

The name 'Moynihan' was sensed as being close. The glass carried this thought as being correct, moving to 'What you see now' (area used for the design test).

Before long, with obscure glass movement, it was agreed, by some, that the Spirit was moving the glass to show a particular direction.

"Are you pointing at a direction?"

The glass moved up alongside 'Yes' and 'Brown', meaning 'Restless' on the frame.

"Should we go in that direction?"

The glass moved a straight line towards the centre of the frame, briefly stopping then it angled off towards 'Orange', to mean, 'Unsettled and Mixed Emotions'.

The glass then made its way back to the centre of the frame.

"Are you pointing to people around the table?"

The glass went to 'Yes'.

Now it seemed that the Spirit felt unnerved by an individual connected to the glass or, could there still be an ongoing conflict at the Bridewell Gaol?

What came up on the night vision camera was sensational.

A question was asked,

"Are they helping you with their energies?"

A yawn was heard, seemingly coming from Sylvie, who was holding the night vision camera. The glass moved towards the centre of the frame then returned to 'Yes'.

Just before the glass stopped, a very clear female voice, in a Scottish accent was spoken. 'They're saying it's gone,' it said. The recording was incredible. The Spirit identified the energy that the person connected on the glass had in helping them but, was concerned that it might be diminishing at the same time.

Anthony, having just heard something, shushed everybody. He dismissed this sound phenomenon, relating it to the night vision camera but it certainly did not originate from the recording device. It was definitely a Spirit's voice…

The glass continued its motion to 'Grey', to specify 'Very Nervous and Anxious'.

It could be a Spirit of a Scottish lady present with us that was feeling this emotion towards us, possibly towards our safety or, her well-being.

At that moment, a sound was thought to have come from the upper floor.

"Are you there at the balcony looking at us at this minute?" said the female team member.

The glass answered by moving to 'Yes'

The Courtroom is presumed to have had an upper gallery some years ago. This does not exist today but to the Spirit energies up above, it probably still does.

"Do you know there's a ceiling there?"

The glass moved to in between 'Grey', for 'Very Nervous and Anxious' and 'Green', to mean 'Normal and Average'.

"Okay, is there anybody on this table that you want off the table… at this minute?"

The glass moved a direct line to 'Yes'

"Thank you. Can you point to who they are with the glass, please?"

Steadily, the glass went to the direction of the frame to where Jen was sitting.

"You want Jen to get off the table?"

The glass moved to 'Yes'.

The Spirit was pointing the finger at Jen to leave, most probably the person the Spirit was obtaining the energy from.

The Spirit was probably thinking that Jen was best needed somewhere else, to heighten its power, one would figure.

"Is there anybody else you would like to leave the table?"

The glass went to where Jen and Patricia were sitting.

"Patricia?"

The glass went to 'Yes'.

"Anybody else you would like to leave the table?"

Once again, the glass embarked on its journey within the frame to in front of where Jen was sitting.

Patricia said to Jen, "You and me, I'd say."

In a straight line, the glass moved to 'Yes' in agreement.

Anthony asked, "Does that remind you of someone?"

The glass made its way to where Jen was sitting, then travelled back to where 'Yes' was on the frame.

Jen decided to take her finger off the glass.

Soon after, the glass moved to what was recognised as 'Change' on the frame. Whether this was to protect Jen, draw energy from her, resemblance or to single her out, we do not know.

We called out, asking the Spirit if the male team member should join in on the glass experiment.

The answer was 'Green', meaning 'Normal and Average'.

This could have indicated that the Spirit had no intention for this to happen.

A few questions later, Anthony asked, "How should Jen feel now?"

The glass moved to 'White', meaning 'Bored and Frustrated'.

A big bundle of side-splitting laughter intervened. Some found it hilarious that Jen could be like this, after Anthony had asked the question. Putting that aside, the Spirit picked up upon Jen's flow of energy being reduced and that she was better needed in another experiment or area.

"Can you tell us more in what Jen is feeling, please?" asked the female team member.

The glass moved up alongside, 'Brown' meaning 'Restless'.

"How you feeling towards Jen?" asked Anthony.

The glass made its way to 'Pink', which outlined 'Fear and Uncertain'.

The Spirit earlier described how it drained energy from Jen; this might leave it curious to Jen's capability. This would lead to the next interesting question.

"Does Jen frighten you?" said the female team member.

The glass moved to 'Yes' on the frame.

"Should Jen be frightened of you?"

The glass went in a straight line towards the direction of 'No', stopping a few inches away from it. If we're to go by this, Jen had nothing to be scared of. So, we think that if the Spirit present were truthful, it would not be capable of causing any harm.

"Do you mean any harm to Jen and Patricia whatsoever?"

The glass moved to 'Brown', meaning 'Restless' and then to 'Yellow', to mean 'Imaginative'. This combination showed the Spirit wanted to do something inspiring quickly or indeed, reveal itself to them.

The glass later went to 'Symbol' (Design test, pre-planchette drawing/writing section on the frame).

"Is there a symbol of you in this room?"

The glass made its way to 'Yes', then back to the centre of the frame.

Anthony called out, "Move the glass in the direction of where that symbol is."

The glass moved to the side of the frame, in line with the judge's bench, about twenty metres away, up ahead.

Rick asked, "Are you the judge?"

The glass moved to 'Yes'.

We had to rephrase a few questions because we had no responses.

"Can you tell us where you sat with your gavel, please?" asked the female team member.

The glass moved towards the same direction on the frame again, pointing to where the judge's bench was situated in the room. This was correct.

When we discussed where people would have come into the Courtroom, the glass had made its way to 'Grey', which meant 'Very Nervous and Anxious'. It proceeded in the opposite direction to 'Black', meaning 'Stressed, Tense and Nervous'. It then finished by stopping a few inches away from 'No' on the frame. Therefore, the recent colours that the glass went to, were the total opposite of what the Spirit of the judge had described. Possibly, it felt threatened by some of us. This outlined all that it was not: having the ability to be brave and commanding.

The glass carried onto, 'Portrait' on the frame (design test, pre-planchette designated area). Patricia drew our attention to a picture on the Courtroom wall of an illustrated past scene.

Anthony pointed towards the picture and asked, "Is it the Irish Petty sessions, 1855? Are you in the picture here, towards my right that I'm pointing at, dear Spirit?"

The glass moved a few inches away from the side of the frame. It reverted back and knocked against the 'What you see now' section of the colour mood frame. The Spirit might relate well to a particular person depicted in the picture or, it could also be showing what was happening at the court at this precise time.

"Just to clear that up, can you move the glass to Yes?"

The glass screeched off the top of the table and made its journey to 'Yes'.

Harmonia and a female team member headed off to the Thomas Dillon Cell, with a walkie-talkie in hand to do a calling-out vigil. The rest of the team and guests remained in the Courtroom, participating in a talking board (*See Glossary*) vigil. Then, we would use the body-mood-doll experiment with the colour mood frame, to see how the Spirit could affect those who would be in the Thomas Dillon Cell.

No movement of the glass happened in the Courtroom. Nothing in particular happened but for the voice phenomenon during the body-mood-doll experiment.

Anthony called out, "If you're in the other room with the girls, move this glass. Is somebody, other Spirits, that want to communicate with us? Move this glass. Come towards us."

One second later, a faint whisper could be heard. It said, 'I want to'. Some entity was being withheld from doing so, either by another or by lack of potential.

Later, when the female team member and Harmonia returned to the Courtroom, they explained that they were followed into the cell, with a purple aura (*See Glossary*) moving around within: not negative but more on a high-minded spiritual track.

Next, Patricia and Sylvie took their chances in the Thomas Dillon Cell for a second calling-out vigil.

We continued back in the Courtroom, to try out the body-mood-doll experiment for the second time. The body mood doll was placed inside the frame beside the design test, pre-planchette yellow section (halting any advance to that side of the frame). The school bell was rung and the gavel was beaten off the top of the table again, to boost energies.

Four individuals connected on the upturned glass. Jen held the night vision camera. The glass moved slowly in a straight line within the frame, gradually building its strength. It stopped near the centre of the frame.

"Are you the judge that was with us before?" asked the female team member.

The glass moved to 'Yes' on the frame then back to centre.

"Can we ask you to go into the cell with the girls, please?"

The glass began moving; it stopped a few inches away from 'No' on the frame. It then progressed on its way to 'Grey', indicating 'Very Nervous and Anxious' or 'Feet' on the body mood doll. It is hard to determine if this was how the Spirit was feeling. More likely, it was what Sylvie and Patricia should have felt. To correspond with the doll, feet could mean the action of going from the Courtroom to the Thomas Dillon Cell by the Spirit or, in fact, the Spirit would affect their feet.

"Can you make the girls feet hot?"

There was a pause and then the glass moved towards 'Yes' on the frame.

The Spirit made a clear statement of intent by moving back to 'Grey', meaning 'Very Nervous and Anxious', which meant 'Feet' on the body mood doll.

"Are you picking up that the girls are nervous in the cell?"

The glass responded by moving to 'Yes' at a slightly quicker pace.

"Have they any reason to be afraid in the cell?"

The glass moved to, 'Green' to co-inside with 'Normal and Average' or to correspond with 'Head' on the body mood doll. The Spirit was not giving a clear answer. Instead, it probably identified that all will be okay or, that the reason for them being frightened could be all in their heads.

We found out, from the following questions we had asked, that somebody had died in the Thomas Dillon Cell and that they were currently in the cell with Patricia and Sylvie.

Anthony radioed in, via walkie-talkie, to the Thomas Dillon Cell. *Let me know if you're feeling anything there, lads. Over.*

The glass went to 'Green', which linked with the head on the body mood doll. Patricia reported back on the walkie-talkie, stating that Sylvie beside her was complaining of a sore eye. This would tie in with the glass moving to green on the frame. The Spirit confirmed, as a response to affecting Sylvie's eyes, making them go wet with the glass going to 'Yes'.

We queried if Patricia could be affected too.

The glass moved to in between 'Yellow', referring to 'Chest' and 'Grey', meaning 'Feet' on the body mood doll.

"Breathing?"

The glass moved to 'Yes' and then to 'Yellow' again, clarifying 'Chest' on the body mood doll. The glass continued onto 'Change' then to the colour 'Green', to mean 'Head'.

Maybe the Spirit was altering where they were going to affect Patricia next, a change of idea.

"Can you pull their hair?" was asked for a second time.

The glass moved to 'White', meaning 'Hands'. Either the Spirit was going to pull the women's hair using its hands or, focus on affecting their hands. It could relate to making them unconsciously pull their own hair; even possibly tweaking or itching their head of hair. We soon found the answer.

"Can you make them pull their own hair?"

The glass moved to 'Yes'.

We found out, over the walkie-talkie, that Patricia did, in fact, have one hand up around her face but not at her hair!

The glass was at the centre of the frame.

Gunpowder was smelt around the Courtroom.

"Were you shot?"

The glass moved to 'Yes'.

We wanted to find out precisely where on the body this Spirit got shot. The glass moved to 'White' on the frame, to mean 'Hands' on the body mood doll. It might have meant frustration, linking it to an emotion on the colour mood frame.

Soon after, the glass went to 'Change'. The Spirit may have shot his or her self, inflicting their own death.

The glass stayed still: a reluctance to answer any further questions around the subject on how they left this plain. The way the glass had moved considerably to 'Green' could suggest the final act of pointing the gun towards one's head. The Spirit did not identify this as an area of the body in where it was harmed in the process of being deceased yet, its hands were. So could the Spirit have committed suicide? Did it recognise and register those seconds beforehand? That their life was in their own hands?

The glass was at the centre of the frame.

"Were you shot in the head…?" was asked, followed by Anthony mentioning, "Was it the eye?"

The glass moved to 'Yes', then the glass moved to in between 'Green', meaning 'Head' and 'Grey', meaning 'Feet'.

As soon as the glass hit the side of the frame, more sound phenomena occurred, this time, in a form of a very loud bang, otherwise, a mini explosion caught on the night vision camera. One would assume that a pistol had been triggered…

Following this was a looped whistle, ending high in key. All of this was unheard by any individuals on the vigils. Could this be a reoccurrence of what actually happened? Could the glass hitting the side of the frame demonstrate the harsh truth of pulling the trigger? It was expressed, by Anthony, that the glass was closer to 'Green', to mean the 'Head'.

Anthony radioed into the women in the Thomas Dillon Cell. All was fine there.

Two minutes later – "If we put the board out, you move for us?"

The glass moved, answering by going to 'Finish'.

The vigil had ended.

Patricia and Sylvie made their way back to the Courtroom.

Taking their places in the last calling-out vigil in the Thomas Dillon Cell would be the male team member and Rick and David from the *Brigid's Fire* magazine. The rest of us tried the talking board again in the Courtroom.

"We want you to tell us your name," said the female team member.

On the night vision camera was a sound of a door latch opening. It was followed by a faint deep whisper, which said something similar to, 'Ogle' or 'Her goal'. Ogle means to *watch*, *leer* and/or to *eye*.

Various questions were put forward for about five minutes, nothing of which was relevant or significant.

The Spirit answered with the glass, not responding to being a woman so, presumably it was a male Spirit on the board.

"Are you trying to spell the names of those you imprisoned?"

The glass, which was on 'Yes', moved about four inches away in a straight line, then returned to 'Yes'. This could be to do with any Spirit that held authority in the Bridewell or, those who were up against the accused.

After four minutes of very timid movement and nothing making sense, the glass went to, 'Goodbye'.

The next part of the talking-board session proved much more fascinating.

The glass was put back on the centre of the board.

We tried to get some accurate information about the judge.

"Was he ninety when he died?"

With a bit more vigour, the glass moved to, 'H', 'U', 'B', 'U', 'B'.

"We're making too much of a hubbub?"

The glass moved directly to 'Yes'.

"Is this when you get your peace and quiet at night?"

The transparent drinking vessel went to 'No', slightly tilting on its rim on its travel.

"Is this when you're most active? At night?"

The glass moved at a fast pace to, 'Yes'.

"And we're disturbing your activity; is that what's going on?"

The glass moved a couple of inches or so away from 'Yes' on the board and then, returned in a straight line to 'Yes'.

"Don't you like us being here?"

The same pattern of movement occurred, coming back to 'Yes'.

We were not being received with great honour by this particular Spirit. Nothing clearer came of the night. We were found guilty, by the Spirit, in disturbing the peace and, more likely, halting the resident energies of their purpose.

One of the male occupants, in the last separation vigil, picked up a sensation of having a freezing left foot.

It was half past one in the morning and it was time to leave.

No sounds or visuals or any movement from the trigger objects happened in the Leslie Cell above, on the first floor.

The digital sound recorder set up for an EVP experiment in the Cottage Room failed to pick up concrete evidence.

We had a busy week ahead, following up with two more investigations, so rest was much needed. We left Tarbert Bridewell, for now not knowing would there still be or not, order in the court.

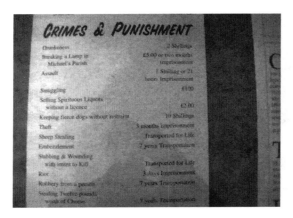

Just some of the sentences handed down for crimes

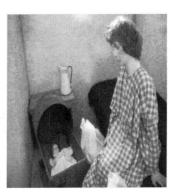

A mother and a baby in the female cell quarters of the Bridewell

The basic diet of a family can be seen in the Famine Area

A motion detector is readied for any movement in the Famine Room

Trigger objects in the Leslie Cell

Thomas Dillon rests in his cell

Proceedings are about to start...

You will be registered as a prisoner in the keeper's quarters

Jen and a mannequin stand in the exercise yard

***Drowned-Out Voices* Investigation footage can be viewed by**

Watching the DVD that accompanies this book

Scanning the QR code

Visiting our website
www.GhostÉire.net

Click on the button
Drowned-Out Voices Footage

and enter the password
YourNotAlone

Enter the password
YourNotAlone

Location Background/Biography

Tarbert Bridewell was built in 1831. The two-storey, detached, limestone building was one of eight bridewells that were in existence in County Kerry. It served as a jail up to 1874 but the courthouse continued its operation until the 1950s.

The Bridewell was used in local court cases. Prisoners who had a sentence longer than three days were held at the Bridewell before being moved to Tralee County Gaol, except if two magistrates verified that they should stay at the Bridewell longer. Many prisoners were tried for petty crimes, with transportation to British penal colonies a customary sentence. Cases were held every thirty days. Those arrested before their trial date would receive a diet of only bread and gruel to eat.

In its early years, Tarbert Bridewell was reported as being in tolerable order. Blankets were scarce. Repairs and painting were needed. One of the four cells was used as a depot for arms, 'placing it in danger'. The yards were not in a particular nice order either.

In 1857, the Bridewell was outlined as being untidy but bedding had been supplied. One of the female cells had been taken over by the keeper's family. The privies were choked with soil and there was no water on the premises. The local inspector visited but did not sign his name and there were cases of illegal imprisonment.

By the 1950s, a local family took up temporary occupancy of the building, shortly after its disuse as a courthouse. The Bridewell was left derelict for about thirty years, until a project group – Tarbert Development Association (TDA) – voted to save the building. By 1993, Tarbert Bridewell was restored and opened as a visitor attraction.

Today, the museum features an insight into the harsh judicial and prison system of the 19th century, including the re-enactment of the trail and judgement of Thomas Dillon. There is a room that documents the poet, art and literacy critic, Thomas MacGreevey. Also, information on the Irish Famine can be found at the Bridewell.

Manifestation/Legend

Workers at the gaol were afraid to be in the building after sunset. Discontent has been felt, especially on the first floor.

During restoration in 1993, a lady who was acrylic writing on the walls late at night, had a sudden urge to leave the building.

Conclusion

There were many outstanding sounds that appeared on the night but there can be uncertainty within credibility, as they may have been generated by the people who attended.

We started off with a lengthy table-tilting experiment. It was claimed that male and female Spirits were present with us. There was considerable unstable movement from the table yet, it was not breath taking and human impact was never far away. Had there been a more open space for the table, fewer obstacles, then we might have had a completely different result.

The multitude of Spirits around may have had something to do with its movement or, it could be down to just one powerful entity, one essence, who was believed to be the judge.

The sense of cruelty was abounding.

An important voice came over the night vision camera. The name Francis Crosbie was mentioned in conversation and, lo and behold, shortly afterwards a man commented, 'Pierce Crosbie, son of Leslie'.

Robert Leslie held the office of Justice of Peace (Judge) for County Kerry. He lived at Tarbert House and married Frances Anne Crosbie in 1790. Pierce Leslie (baptism 1795) is listed as one of their sons. So we have a connection. Pierce Leslie was with us. When his brother's name (Francis Crosbie Leslie) was mentioned later during the Frank's Box session, many individuals felt a cold sensation in the Courtroom.

A substantial number of names were mooted by team members and guests but there were no surnames to back them up or, any history records denoted to those that had, such as Maureen O'Grady.

There was a German sway in the Frank's Box segment of the investigation, followed by Scottish.

During the colour-mood-frame experiment, a woman's voice came across saying, 'They're saying it's gone' in a Scottish intonation, in connection with Jen's energy receding.

Tarbert is a place name in Scotland and Ireland. They are named after a narrow strip of land or isthmus. Travel by water was popular in the 19th century and Tarbert was a key port in the southwest of Ireland. It would have had Scottish people coming into its harbour.

Individuals were experiencing discomfort on their arms. Anthony had asked if this impression was felt around the room. A lady was assumed to have said, 'Books' from the Frank's Box. Maybe this person had been an assistant, carrying out administrative duties or was responsible for the smooth running of the court, possibly an usher, who ensured the security of legal documents. Women may have played a more legal role in trials during the Victorian period, other than being defendants and witnesses.

There was no source of water at the Bridewell back in the day. After Anthony called out, "Would you like..." the word, 'Water' was spoken. There may have been mockery directed at inmates who were dehydrated at the gaol. Water would have had to be brought in from somewhere and it would have needed to be fetched.

The Spirit distinguished Jen and Patricia apart from the rest of persons on the glass, in the colour-mood-frame experiment. It seemed that they possessed capabilities or knowledge threatening to the Spirit at hand.

It liked to control and restrain, putting across that it was not fearful of us. Being so dominant, it could have only been a judge; maybe the other Spirit beings in the background could not get involved.

There was a very nervous and anxious emotion predicted for the Thomas Dillon Cell. After further questioning, we found out that someone may have died in that cell. The head, chest and feet were prominent areas of the body that the Spirit could exploit in the cell. There was a smell of gunpowder and the sound of a gun firing or an explosion caught on the night vision camera. From early records, we find that weaponry was kept in one of the cells at the Bridewell which, in the wrong hands, could prove murderous or lead to a person meeting their fate.

There was an explosion in 2003 from an electricity plant nearby on Tarbert Island, which resulted in two workers being killed. This could have been other-worldly surplus energy left from that circumstance.

The judge was shrewd. He knew which time we were from. Court proceedings were still going on. A picture on the wall signified the judge's intentions, that we were disturbing the peace and have caused a 'hubbub', a noisy situation or chaos. The word 'hubbub' might be of Irish origin from *abú*, used in battle cries.

There was no movement with the trigger objects in the Leslie Cell nor did any EVPs get caught on the digital sound recorder in the Cottage Room though, to this day, the Courtroom was still active.

Tarbert Bridewell Gaol
Co Kerry

WEBSITE: tarbertbridewell.com
e-MAIL: tarbertbridewell@eircom.net
PHONE: 068 36500
FACEBOOK: Tarbert Bridewell

Contact museum for opening hours, admission prices and events

The museum is an ideal place to visit if you are planning a journey by car ferry over the Shannon estuary, to or from Killimer, County Clare.

The Bridewell has a coffee shop, gift shop and toilets.

The gaol hosts many events during the year and has a great community base that welcomes visitors far and wide.

Other local amenities in the area include Tarbert House and the Tarbert Woodland Walk.

OLD FEVER MARKET HOSPITAL

Layout

Rough Dimensions

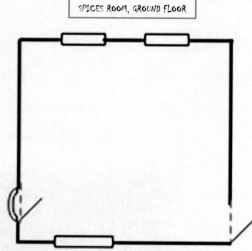

SPICES ROOM, GROUND FLOOR

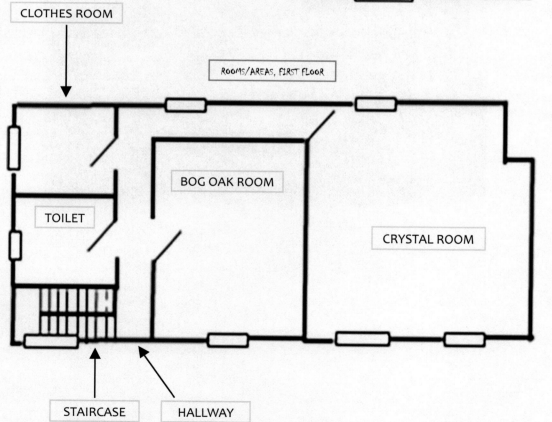

CLOTHES ROOM

ROOMS/AREAS, FIRST FLOOR

BOG OAK ROOM

TOILET

CRYSTAL ROOM

STAIRCASE

HALLWAY

Chapter 14

Old Fever Market Hospital

Jenifer's Journey

After a busy previous week of investigating, we were on to our third location in a matter of seven days. I felt good and my thoughts were optimistic about another great evening.

Anthony got permission to do the Old Fever Market Hospital through a chance phone call. The owners were happy to facilitate us. The impression was that the building was haunted but details were kept silent. That was for us to find out!

Knowing that this used to be a hospital, I was chosen to gather some apparatuses, which would commonly have been used in the occupational fraternity of health and medicine. For example, we would use test tubes for a trigger object experiment.

On the day of the investigation me, Anthony and another male team member took the journey up the N18 motorway from Killarney. It was quite an easy drive.

As it was Tuesday, the roads were quiet and we were in the first week of March. Of course, we took a wrong turn as usual, while driving through Gort but only for a hundred yards. We turned back and saw road signs directing us to the Old Fever Market Hospital.

At first glance, the building looked homely; all the lights were on inside. Who could be haunting this cosy spot?

Sylvie and a female team member had arrived before us. Upon entering the building, we received a warm welcome from the owners. A silver plaque, with a brief description of the history of the location, was embedded onto a wall near the doorway. It triggered a moment for me…

A mouth-watering surprise came to me as I smelt an aroma of hot curry being cooked. This was kindly made for us by the owners but first, I had to help out Anthony with the baseline testing and setting up the equipment. Before doing so, we were shown around the rooms.

There was a crafts workshop on the first floor, which we referred to as the Crystal Room; this was the largest room in the building.

Adjacent to it was the Clothes Room, where we would set up the trigger objects. Two surgical masks, two test tubes and a syringe were placed on a blank piece of A2 paper. I drew around the instruments with a black marker, to see if any altered movement would occur during the investigation. A k2 meter and a walkie-talkie were placed alongside the objects. I also prepared a video camera in a position that was ready to record when switched on.

Downstairs, a delicious concoction of pasta, curries and bread was laid on for us in the cafeteria. A hearty meal before we started was very much appreciated. Over an hour later, we were ready to start.

I felt energies from outside of the building looking in on us. It is a curious impression, not just to us but, perhaps, a common theme to this structure.

The rest of the team and I headed outside the front of the building, to do the protection circle. There would be frost on the cars tonight. After the protection circle, we went back into the building. Anthony and I went up the stairs.

I turned on the video camera in the Clothes Room, to record. Anthony, meanwhile, turned on the digital sound recorder in the Toilet and motion detectors in the Hallway and above the Staircase, on a windowsill on the first floor. We would go down the stairs, leaving the floor above unoccupied.

Everyone had gathered in the Spices Room. We were preparing to do a séance. I was left holding the night vision camera.

The lights were turned off. Just a handful of candles helped illuminate the room.

My thoughts turned to what I first saw upon arriving. Does the former hospital still look cosy from outside in? I could not hold onto that picture now. I had to focus on what was in front of me.

The Investigation

NUMBER OF TEAM **5**   **2** NUMBER OF GUESTS

We carried on to our third investigation in one week. Surprisingly, we were feeling quite fresh and up for the challenge.

Knowing that we were doing our investigation in a former hospital for the sick, we pondered on what would come before us. Nearing the edge of death or the end of mortality could be very bizarre or serene. Diseases that were hard to treat long ago are now, thankfully, more curable.

We arrived at the detached house (yes, house!) standing alone down a cul-de-sac, just off the main town road. We gathered ourselves and entered through a red door. As we wandered in, towards the right, was a stone walling and what seemed to be a semi-circular crown doorway, which opened up to the Spices Room.

The Spices Room had a connecting doorway further on ahead, to the cafeteria. A wooden staircase, with white walling, led to an upper front gable floor towards our left.

We were warmly greeted and, in gentle time, given a viewing of the rooms. We walked up the stairs on the left, then along the timber-surfaced corridor. A room, which held some wooden furnished craftwork, was on the right of the corridor. We called this the Bog Oak Room. It was here that it was thought to be active and, opposite on the left and further along the corridor – the Clothes Room. This was a small compartment with various garments of clothing hung on the door and on a trolley rack. Past this room, further on was a Toilet, where a digital sound recorder would be left recording during the investigation.

We turned a corner on the corridor to the right. Down the adjoining long Hallway was another doorway to the biggest room on the floor: the Crystal Room. Paintings done by artists, candles, t-shirts and many more stock dedicated to homeopathy, spiritual and healthy living were displayed.

It was time to do the baseline tests. Anthony collected the outcomes from the equipment, as Jen organised the trigger objects in the Clothes Room.

The light was fading in the early spring sky although, the forecast was for showers later. The temperature outside was at 15.2°C and the heat inside the building was at 14.8°C. The humidity was at 81.2%. As the evening progressed, it felt much colder outside, when we took our breaks.

The decibel C-low level was at 46.2 while the C-high was at 65.9. This sound level compares to whispering up to normal conversation in volume and also, typical of suburban traffic nearby.

The EMF reading in the whole of the building only peaked at 4 milliGauss, as we were going to work under candlelight. This would reduce any exposure transmitted around by electrical currents or batteries and enhance our serotonin (*See Glossary*).

Pleasant conversation was exchanged and exquisite food was digested. It was now half past nine at night and time to start. Before the team headed into the first vigil, a protection circle was done outside of the building.

As they came back in, Jen and Anthony went up the stairs to the Clothes Room. Jen pressed the record button on the video camera that was set on the trigger objects and turned on the K2 meter. Anthony pressed record on the digital sound recorder in the Toilet and, positioned a motion detector in the Hallway and another on a windowsill above the Staircase. They both came down the stairs and met with the owners and the rest of the team in the Spices Room.

A tricolour Irish flag was draped over a table. Three seats were positioned around the table. They would be occupied by Anthony, a male team member and a female team member.

A séance was about to begin. Jen held the night vision camera while Sylvie stood on the outskirts of the formalities.

The Spices Room was scattered with bottles, such as olive oils and jars of pepper paste, herbs and jams. Newspaper concealed some goods and stock on the cloth-draped display tables. The candles placed in front of the windows offered some more brightness and a mirroring obscurity. Limestone copings stonework helped form the walls, which surrounded and enclosed us.

The three sitting around the table introduced themselves by calling out their names, along with the rest of the team in close attendance. Hands were placed on top of the table. Instantly it shook. Jen primarily focused her attention with the night vision camera to the shaking table.

"Flash," said Sylvie, as she took a photograph with a camera. For a brief second, the room was illuminated.

There was a quirky satisfaction that something or, someone was now with us. We continued cementing our intent by describing the items (trigger objects) above on the first floor. The energy was asked to come forward.

A calming process intervened. As the legs of the table, at either side, tapped a gentle constant rhythm, the tricolour flag could be seen on the night vision camera, mildly rubbing off the stone flooring. Each individual in the séance crossed their ankles underneath the chair they were sitting on, with the end of their toes locking their balance to the surface of the floor. They tried their hardest not to interfere with the flag or the movement of the table.

"Are you a woman?" was asked in Irish.

The table ceased movement to suggest, 'Yes'.

"Are you a man?" was asked in Irish.

For just over a second the table could be seen gently rocking, then ceased to what we presume was 'Yes' also. So, we knew at this stage that there was at least one woman and one man around us.

Jen used the night vision camera to look around the stone framework of the room. The table was now slowly rocking side to side yet, with no sound of tapping in its movement.

"Is there fifteen with us right now?"

The table stopped its motion to mean, 'Yes'.

We carried on asking about the gender of the 'Spirits' that could be around. The table gently rocked; the sound of tapping, again from side to side, was heard.

"You all tired?"

The table ceased moving, to declare an agreement.

The female team member on the table felt her arms ache while Anthony and the male team member stated that their legs were freezing. It seemed we were being listened in on, as the table started gently rocking again.

"… are the patients and doctors here part of the medical crew here?"

The table assumed a stationary position. Nuns and priests were sensed around. The room started to feel somewhat crowded at this stage. Calmness was still apparent.

Anthony asked, "Are you just curious about us?"

The male team member felt tightness around his chest.

Anthony continued, "Are you just curious about us? Is that true?"

The table gently but freely rocked, tapping from opposite leg to leg again, then it halted in agreement to liking the owners of the property, who were present.

Anthony wondered if he had heard a tap on the table; his and the rest of the team's attention turned to this.

Jen panned with the night vision camera to the left of the table, to the front window of the house and then scanned back on the séance.

Sylvie started to feel chest pains. The Spirit may have had a liking to her to discomfort. The table started rocking again.

It halted its movement in regard to a 'Spirit' being around having ginger hair, suggesting 'Yes'

The table mildly rocked; it stopped just as Anthony asked, "Do I look like you?"

Soon after, the table rocked, understanding the process of questioning.

Anthony asked, "Did you use to help the patients here?"

The table looked as though it became still.

Four knocks could be heard. The first knock was loud then gradually they got duller and quicker in succession: almost like a ball being dropped onto the floor.

Doctors were mentioned, which brought the table to a halt.

We talked about an undertaker; Anthony sensed that the table might be sliding.

On further instruction, we asked for the table to tap the floor by rocking how many times dead people were taken out of the hospital. Anthony counted quietly as the table obliged by tapping. The number came to one hundred and forty.

In these couple of minutes of anticipation of the outcome, Jen scanned again with the night vision camera, this time at the original fireplace, to the right. She panned to the left of the séance at the front window and the space in front of it. It was as though there was an interest in that area.

Seconds passed and the female team member on the table asked, "Did you catch the fever yourself…? Did you end up in this hospital yourself?"

The table slowly and gently rocked again, tapping with its legs, only for it to stop a short time later.

We asserted that there was a type of calmness. We moved onto the year the Spirit was from.

"1900s… 1900s, is that true, dear Spirit?" Anthony asked.

Yet again, the table responded by smoothly rocking again and then, fell silent again.

It seemed that we were getting the right answers to what we thought. Possibly we were just being wise to the name and surroundings of the building.

We had to get the Spirit to divulge more.

"Did you die in the 1900s? Move the table if that's correct," said Anthony.

The table returned to a rocking movement.

Jen pointed the night vision camera, viewing at the rear windows of the room as the table took up a more constant rocking, with the team encouraging the energies around to increase. For over a minute the table continued to create this movement.

Cold breezes were felt. Names were starting to come forward in our minds and when we mentioned the name Finbarr, the table came to an abrupt halt.

The subject returned to the bringing of dead bodies, primarily being connected to a mortician (*See Glossary*).

A minute later, Jen switched the night vision camera from infrared to normal light, for a brief second. Total darkness closed in around us.

The conversation now revolved on a judgement as to whether any Spirits here could read and write in English, as later, a talking-board experiment might be used.

"British?" Anthony asked in Irish.

The table resumed a gentle rock.

Two deep breaths could be heard but it was from the male team member on the table, who was starting to feel pressure against his chest. Suddenly the table rocked again, at a slightly faster pace, in acknowledgement of the situation. Anthony, who was concerned at this point, asked the rest of the team and the owners looking on if they felt okay. It was all good for the time being.

Anthony asked the lady owner, Nuala, if there would have been any beds around. This was quite obvious for a hospital but, the number was uncertain.

Nuala explained how air vents ran underneath some of the beds to keep them dry – a natural way of ventilation. As Nuala described this more, unease was felt by the male team member in his chest, as he let out a phlegmy cough.

Despite these physical interactions, Anthony quizzed for more emphasis to become apparent, for the Spirits to use their voice or walk amongst rooms.

Cold blasts of air were felt.

The female team member on the table called out, "I want you to stop the table if you are spitting out blood."

The table obliged by stopping.

This was a symptom of which may have occurred at the hospital. Sensations of blood came through, in taste and smell, to a few of the team.

The male team member soon decided to leave the table. He stood up and let Nuala take his position in the séance. He let out an abundance of coughs.

The table resumed to a gentle rock.

More cold draughts emerged as Anthony encouraged a reaction in a tranquil manner.

Over a minute later, the female team member asked, "… would you like us to leave?"

The table stopped rocking.

Sylvie was now complaining of a headache.

The table resumed rocking.

"Stop the table if there's a priest there who doesn't want us to do any of this?"

The table ceased rocking to confirm this belief.

It is not known whether this would be to do with hidden information or, a warning that what we were doing was sacrilegious. What was known is that we were not appreciated in being around. After further questioning, we were led to believe the priest had stepped back and other Spirits, who were not religious, had stepped forward.

Anthony described an altering motion to the table, a change at the base of it. This was agreed upon by the Nuala and the female team member currently connected on the table.

Anthony ushered Jen to come close with the night vision camera, as he believed he could hear tapping on the table. She scanned the legs of the table, which brought a closer view but nothing had occurred to suggest anything untoward was happening.

Sylvie and the male team member, who were suffering from chest pains and headaches, left the room and went next door to the cafeteria, bringing them out from the inflicted space. It was felt that the energy was becoming draining to some…

As they left the room, Anthony placed an EMF gauss master meter in the centre of the table.

Slight tapping was heard by Anthony and the female team member on the table but, it was very faint and not picked up on the night vision camera.

Anthony asked, "Can you tap twice… underneath the table, on top of the table?"

No sounds were heard but more psychological manipulation came to the fore, as the table was assumed to be slanting to one side. More encouragement was offered; the table, after nearly seven minutes, resumed its natural gentle rocking function.

"Tap on the windows," said Anthony

The table stopped rocking. We could have hit a nerve. There must be an association with windows here! Hands started to feel tingly. The table re-enacted the steady, swaying rock, gradually picking up speed in acknowledgement that we were about to move onto another experiment and that it had the freedom to still roam around in the building. Moments later, the table declared no more movement.

It was very much time to move on. As some of the team took a break and left the room, Anthony, Jen and the gentleman owner – Jack – remained in the vicinity.

Anthony had placed stereo speakers into the Frank's Box on top of the tricolour-draped table. Both the speakers and Frank's Box were switched on. They opted to run straight into the experiment.

Anthony directly asked, "Where you from?"

Some seconds later, a voice returned from the Frank's Box device saying, 'Here'.

"Is there any women here?"

A few unrecognizable responses came back from the box. 'Yeah' was heard in a faint voice and later, 'No' but much clearer.

Could some Spirits not detect other Spirits?

A couple of minutes later, a mature, masculine voice is heard from the Frank's Box saying, 'scum' quite clearly.

Jen, who was recording with the night vision camera, viewed around the area to where she had stood in the previous séance.

Anthony said, "Is there a lady to the left of me, dear Spirit?"

A loud response stated, 'No' followed, in quick succession by fainter replies of 'No'.

There was a type of eagerness for the experiment to take more prominence, so Anthony asked those who were on a break to gather back into the Spices Room.

The female team member and Nuala sat down and connected onto the table, fingers spread palms down. It was mentioned that we did not want any further discomfort happening to anyone present.

Some of the team were taking pictures with their cameras as Anthony held an EMF gauss master meter, pointing the head of the gadget towards the direction of the table.

"The names of you that are around us right now?" asked the female team member.

The name 'Pat' predominately came through.

Anthony asked, "Is Pat your name, dear Spirit?"

What sounded similar to 'No', followed by fainter, masculine voice replied from the Frank's Box saying, 'Alan'. The team struggled to interpret what had just come through.

"Can you say that name again, please?"

Jen backtracked to the door, which led to the entrance of the building and the upper floors. She took in the concentrated look Anthony was possessing. The night vision camera went out of focus. All that could be seen was a clouded screen yet, what sounded like the name 'Bridget' came forth from the box.

The night vision camera retained its scope as Anthony called out, "What age are you?"

There seemed to be a response back, from a frail child saying, 'Nine'. This was confirmed to be heard by Anthony and the female team member on the table.

Fifteen seconds later, the name 'Bridget' popped up again on the Frank's Box.

"Are you a little girl?"

About nine seconds later, a timid, childlike voice said, 'Mummy' from the Frank's Box. A second or two later, followed the same reply, 'Mummy', louder but of similar substance.

The second response may not have come from the Frank's Box. The only other reason for that answer was that a member of the team had mimicked the response they heard previously. It had some of the team puzzled and shocked, as Nuala expressed a sensation that something had channelled through her. It is quite peculiar that the childlike voices were coming through the radio waves late at night and, in a concerning manner.

"Are you looking for Mummy, Bridget?" asked Anthony.

A feeble yet soft clear voice came back from the box saying, 'Yes'.

Knocking could be heard in the background but it was hard to be exact where it came from, as the footage did not show the individuals behind the night vision camera who may have caused it.

"Is Daddy here in the hospital?"

A response, in a male voice, came back from the Frank's Box, similar to 'Yes' or 'Yeah'.

Over the next couple of minutes, we received replies such as, 'Prison', in regard to giving us a message and, when we asked about the workhouse, 'That's what I said' was presumed to have come from the box. So, possibly the Old Fever Market Hospital was a place of last resort and some style of hostile fortress.

The name 'Bridget' was presumed, by many, to materialise regularly on the Frank's Box.

'Hah!' came from the box. It was done in a manner of persuasion – to ask the question again or, of surprise.

The Spirit may not have heard us the first time, could be hard of hearing or, could not understand our language or accents.

Jen viewed away with the night vision camera, gaping at the top corners of the room as we tried to establish a place of origin of the Spirit.

A deep exhale could be heard on the night vision camera, just as Anthony asked, "What did you die of, dear Spirit? I'm sorry to ask you; what did you die from?"

This was followed, ten seconds later, by a reply on the Frank's Box, in a feminine voice, similar to someone saying 'Cholera'. Nuala signified that she heard the word 'consumption', a term related to tuberculosis (*See Glossary*).

"Did you die of consumption?" asked the female team member on the table. A reply came back, in an understanding manner, stating, 'I did' from the Frank's Box.

'Peterswell' was coming up predominantly, as a place of origin for the Spirit.

"Did you have a wife, Pat?" asked Anthony.

A few seconds passed then, what sounded like a child's voice came through again and possibly not via the Frank's Box.

Anthony declared he could hear something upstairs. The female team member and Nuala turned their heads away from the Frank's Box to where Anthony was. The female team member thought she heard the banging too. Nuala broadened this assumption. She described that this was not uncommon and is an occasional occurrence at the building.

It was starting to get more active.

"Do you have a wife, Pat, don't mind me asking?" said Anthony.

Suddenly, Nuala let out a sudden shriek – a moment of channelling one would presume – as she stated out loud, "She died before him."

Jen zoomed in with the night vision camera back at the window to the rear of the room, then zoomed back out. There was an altogether reflective mood at this point. Jen and Anthony discussed hearing bangs from up above as the female team member and Nuala were engaged in conversation.

The table started to rock.

The place, right now, seemed to be alive with paranormal activity, getting busier by the second.

Anthony picked out a digital infrared thermometer laser gun from the equipment bag and repositioned himself around the vigil, pinpointing the red laser dot onto the surface of the tricolour-flag draped table.

More encouragement was asked for the 'Spirit of Bridget' to come forth.

Murmuring came through on the Frank's Box followed, a few seconds later, by a high-pitched soft voice that said, 'I can see you'.

Again, it did not give the impression it came from the Frank's Box device. It seemed to be within the room and on the outskirts of the vigil. It was like what a child would say, amid playing some hide-and-seek or peekaboo game, trying to relate to our presence.

"What's wrong, Bridget?" was asked by the female team member.

An upsetting reply came from the Frank's Box. 'I'm sick' was supposedly said.

"Why are you upset, Bridget?"

A few seconds elapsed and a male voice came from the box.

It said, 'Bridget' but this time, in a sterner voice.

The thought of a child being around made us conscious that it might have died from a disease in the hospital.

"Did you eat any of the food in the garden?"

A clear, masculine voice responded, 'No'.

The table kept rocking; the stereo speakers on the table become unstable. They were eventually placed on an open chair, alongside the table.

Five minutes later, the vigil was ended. It was now necessary to seek what was happening upstairs. The male team member went alone to do some mirror scrying (*See Glossary*) in the Bog Oak Room. Everybody else stayed in the Spices Room.

The female team member, Sylvie and Nuala connected to an upturned glass tumbler placed at the centre of a talking board.

Anthony, with walkie-talkie in hand, kept contact with the male team member who was on the floor above.

Anthony walked around the vigil with an EMF gauss master meter in his other hand.

Over five minutes later and, after plenty of encouragement on the glass, Jen took over from Sylvie on the talking board. Nothing had happened so far; several questions were asked to try to connect with the Spirit. Anthony joined in. He put his index finger on the glass but, still nothing.

Eventually, Anthony left the room with glass in his hand to the cafeteria. He was joined by Nuala and the female team member. It was decided that a wash, to cleanse (*See Glossary*) the glass, might make it more mobile.

Anthony came back into the Spices Room and radioed in to the male team member up in the Bog Oak Room, to see what he was picking up on. He sensed a young woman dressed in black and white and the name, 'Bridget'.

The female team member and Nuala returned with the glass and reconnected on the divination tool with Jen, who had remained seated. As soon as they connected on the glass, to resume the talking-board experiment, the male team member radioed in, clarifying that the entity he saw, through the mirror, had been behind him over the past five minutes...

We had to be more direct on the talking board if we wanted to get more answers. Anthony tried to entice a Spirit to come forward, as he notified those present that he was about to ring the bell. He did so and the glass barely moved a few inches, from the centre of the board to 'Goodbye'.

The male team member radioed in, wanting a member of the team to come up to him to explain what he was getting; for an opinion or to help steady his nerves. Anthony returned to the conversation with the male team member on the walkie-talkie. Just give us five minutes there...

Now the glass showed a determination to respond and moved quite slowly to 'No'.

Whatever was up there in the Bog Oak Room wanted the male team member, either for much longer or less.

Anthony radioed the male team member asking how he was. The male team member replied he was feeling faint and strange.

Urgency took hold of the talking-board vigil. The glass was put back on the centre of the board. The feeling was that the energy was not strong but, it felt close by and we did not know what it would do next!

"You want three of us upstairs?"

The glass finally took a route around the board, positioning itself on 'Yes'.

The Spirit focused on only wanting women on the floor above and for the male team member to come down the stairs straight away. It was time to reorganise. The women would take up position in the Crystal Room while the men would gather in the Spices Room.

During the moment of interchange, Anthony took the motion detector on the windowsill overlooking the Staircase on the first floor and, repositioned it next to the trigger objects in the Clothes Room. The walkie-talkie beside the trigger objects was now turned on. Jen, Sylvie, the female team member and Nuala would do a talking-board session in the Crystal Room. Anthony, the male team member and Jack would do a table-tilting experiment in the Spices Room. We were ready and set to go again.

The Crystal Room was described as being freezing, as the women sorted out their positions for the session. Jen, Nuala and the female team member connected onto an upturned glass placed on the talking board, which was positioned on a small table at the centre of the room. The only option, at the moment, in order to gather around it, was to sit or kneel down on the floor.

The movement of the glass was very casual and, as it did so, a high-pitched, childlike voice was heard on the night vision camera. It could be classified as a giddy expression. It is hard to say what it said: possibly 'Poppy' or 'Puppy'. It did not seem to be coming from the glass or any individual present.

The letters, 'C', 'A', 'F', 'E' were spelled out. The 'Spirit' indicated this was the area of building the women should go down to. Apart from that, what appeared on the talking board was gibberish.

Meanwhile, things were getting animated in the Spices Room below. Anthony could be heard giving a constant barrage of encouragement for any Spirits down there to come forth. He radioed in to the female crew above. He described that the male team member was feeling 'airless'.

It was declared, by Anthony, that the investigation should operate for only another two minutes, as he stated that the table was getting very vigorous. Moments later, 'cold, frantic breezes' were being felt. The glass was now showing more vitality on the board.

"Can you tell us what your name is, please?"

The glass moved to 'M', 'E'.

We took a break, catching up on how each and everybody in the two sessions were coping, to see if it was okay to carry on. It was all good and so, we took up our previous positions.

Ten minutes later, Anthony could be heard roaring this time from the floor below, persuading for more activity to occur on the table, much to the annoyance of the Spirit on the talking board. A few minutes passed and Anthony radioed in. He felt in control yet, he was getting a taste of metal in his mouth.

That was all that the investigation could detail. All that was left was to pack up the equipment, have one last hot beverage in the cafeteria and then head home. It was nearly two o' clock in the morning.

We thought there would be no more freaky incidents as we prepared to set off. We were wrong! As everyone gathered in the cafeteria for the protection circle, the Spirit world wanted to give us one last fright.

As Anthony spoke out, in versed appreciation, for help from Spirit guides/Angels (*See Glossary*), next door, the table that we had been using in the Spices Room was plainly rocking and moving. He was halfway through the prayer; all involved had their eyes shut.

The knocking became louder. There was nobody in that room so, what could be making that noise? Still today, we do not know.

On looking back on the trigger object footage in the Clothes Room, at approximately fifty-two minutes into the investigation, a whine could be heard. Wind or certain draughts within the room cannot be ruled out. All individuals were down on the ground floor at that time.

Trigger objects are set up in the Clothes Room

Another angle of the house

There was another story to these windows...

Who wants soup?

Many gifts could be bought in the Crystal Room

A corridor from the Crystal Room to the Clothes Room and back down the stairs

A plaque describing the fever hospital's history

All hands on deck for the start of the Frank's Box experiment

Spice up your life?

***Drowned-Out Voices* Investigation footage can be viewed by**

Watching the DVD that accompanies this book

Visiting our website
www.GhostÉire.net

Scanning the QR code

Click on the button
Drowned-Out Voices Footage

and enter the password
YourNotAlone

Enter the password
YourNotAlone

Location Background/Biography

The fever hospital was built in 1848. It is located in the heart of Gort town, County Galway. The two-storey limestone building has a keystone with the inscribed '1848' above a Tudor arch door.

A workhouse was built close by in 1831, on seven-and-a-half acres of land and was opened on 11 December 1841. It was constructed to accommodate five hundred people and was the first in County Galway.

The workhouse school was opened on 23 May 1842. Seventy-three boys and fifty-five girls attended.

In December 1843, the workhouse had one hundred and twelve inmates. The Great Famine (*See Glossary*) badly hit numbers attending in the following years. Men were given the job of breaking stones whilst women were made to look after the sick and dying and were, most likely, ill themselves.

Many people died of fever, cholera, flu and other diseases. Life in the workhouse was tough and often, the last resort for many. Food was hardly available; families were separated and orphans were left at the workhouse.

A Doctor Martin Nolan reported on 12 December 1846 about the sick in the workhouse. He said they were, "Scattered through the house, lying in their filth and dirt, without a single person to attend them."

By 1850, there were five hundred and twenty-nine women and children at the workhouse. The Sisters of Mercy came to Gort in 1857. The

Board of Guardians for Gort met. Thomas A Joyce put forward a request for the Sisters of Mercy to visit the workhouse, which was granted but only on Sundays. In 1874, the Sisters of Mercy were asked to take charge of the workhouse.

A Joseph Glynn, a native of Gort, remarked in an article in 1922 about when he was a child, growing up in the 1880s, at the workhouse. He described that the hospital in Gort was like no other. It had 'a woman's touch' to the place. There were flowers in the entrance and a welcome embrace from the nuns. A Christmas party was held each year. The wards were mixed, with a strip of carpet down the centre and a large fire in the winter. Those who were able to get up, sat and read or talked.

In recent years, the fever hospital has been run as a market and a school of homeopathy.

Manifestation/Legend

Many people have seen spectres in and around the former hospital. A man wearing a top hat has been seen moving around in a rushed state.

Footsteps have been heard inside the building, with no explanations.

A woman has also been heard, crying by a window on the first floor.

The sound of children playing outside of the windows of the main building has been reported too.

Conclusion

Nuns did have a major sway on the fever hospital. They were believed to be present in the séance. Priests were also picked up on at the same time. Since many people died in the area, the Last Rites were administered and this is done by a priest.

The table tapped on the floor one hundred and forty times, to the total of dead bodies taken out of the hospital. Over the history of the site being a hospital, the number seems small yet, it may have something to do with an earlier time at the hospital. A Mary Hynes, a contractor or supplied coffins to the workhouse, was owed money in a clerk's report. It becomes comprehensible that the workhouse was unable to keep up with the number of people dying.

Doctors were talked about being present in the same sitting. According to sources, doctors and medical officers did visit, observing the standard of the hospital, detailing names of those who died each week and cause of death. It is self-explanatory that we would reference these types of vocations at or with a hospital.

A Doctor Nolan reported, on the 20 February 1847, the death of a young girl named Bridget Quinn, aged nine years old. What was exceptional is that the name, Bridget came over the Frank's Box when we requested a name and the number nine came through after, when we had asked for an age. The name Bridget came over the Frank's Box again and shortly after, a child's voice said, 'Mummy'.

Our opinion is that the little girl was looking for her mother, who may have died; her father was still around the hospital too. It is claimed that the father's name was Pat, although there is no record of this being correct.

It is unfortunate that Bridget was looking for her mother. She seems to be in an alternative dimension: a segment of time approximately before her own death. It is hard to know whether she chose this existence.

'Bridget' was reckoned to be repeatedly heard transmitted from the radio device later on. Sometimes, voices could be heard but not exactly accepted as coming via the box.

The mother had died before the father, according to Nuala. She also referred to hearing the word 'consumption' (tuberculosis) from the Frank's Box. Otherwise known as TB, this disease can affect the lungs, causing chronic coughing. A couple of team members complained of chest pains, which can also be linked to the sickness. Cold air could be felt when members of the team described their discomfort. This may have been a way the souls wanted to bring their illness to the fore.

Previously, we heard the word 'Cholera' from the device. This is different from TB. It can be contracted by consuming contaminated water or food, causing diarrhoea, dehydration and even death if untreated.

The name 'Peterswell', was believed to be a name of a place where a Spirit had previously lived. Peterswell is situated 5km east of Gort in County Galway.

Earlier, during the séance, the table reacted by becoming still when we asked if the Spirit died in the 1900s, suggesting that it did. This is a completely different time period to when Bridget Quinn died but, possibly, it may have been her father or, another entity that had come in.

Anthony asked, "Tap on the window", which prompted the table to stop rocking.

Many of the unexplainable occurrences at the location have an association of happening next to windows, especially the room that we were in (Spices Room), with sounds often being heard of children playing outside.

Old Fever Market Hospital
Co Galway

The building is now under private ownership.
We thank Nuala and Jack for their time in helping
with our studies.

Ouija Believe It?

This story came from a concerned person...

I was looking for something for my wife and our sixteen-year-old daughter to play over the festive season, around Christmas time. We have shared a keen interest in board games, ever since my daughter was at a young age.

One day, I went into our nearby town to an interesting shop on the high street. I was curious about what to get. I asked the shopkeeper for any recommendations. He showed me a board game that was displayed at the front window.

"You'll love this," he said, holding the board game in front of me.

I felt that my mission had been accomplished, until I went to the shop counter. The shopkeeper briefly peered at another customer at the back of the shop, making sure what he was about to explain would not be eavesdropped. He lowered his glasses down the bridge of his nose, starred into my eyes and whispered, "Be aware though, that when you play it, some will find it hard to cope with the circumstances. The majority of the time, most people... well, really... have a bad experience."

I left the shop with the game, feeling excited yet concerned on what I might unravel or open up.

When Christmas day arrived, the customary turkey, stuffing and roast potatoes were eaten and all was good. It was time to open up the presents...

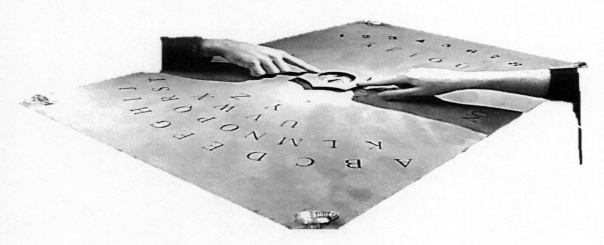

My daughter opened up the present which contained the board game.

"Should we really play this, Dad?" she said. "I have heard so much bad things about it. My friends are afraid to play it."

I replied back, "It is fine. We'll just see how it goes."

My wife was not at all happy or impressed with me. She had an awful experience playing this type of game when she was young.

As we played, words kept appearing on the board, some of which we understood, others seemed rather ridiculous and confusing. It was not long before we all started fighting.

We carried playing on for a matter of hours, until no more words appeared and all fell silent. Maybe it was to do with all the shouting and bickering between us all. All I learned was that I never wanted to play this game again.

Half an hour later, my daughter suggested an idea on what we should do next.

"Let's put the scrabble away and get the Ouija board out."

Away went my anger,

"Yes, we'll do that. It would be much friendlier than that other board game we have just played."

So just remember this Christmas period, when you get your Monopoly, Operation or Mouse Trap out, not all board games are about winning or losing; it is about sharing an experience.

ATHLONE CASTLE

Layout

Rough Dimensions

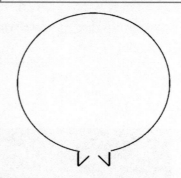

ROOMS/AREAS, FIRST FLOOR

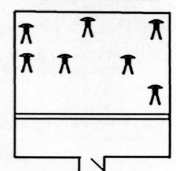

ATHLONE BESIEGED ROOM

SIEGE EXPERIENCE ROOM

ATHLONE CASTLES FIRST 400 YEARS ROOM, GROUND FLOOR

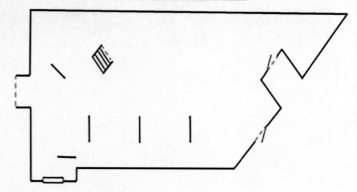

Chapter 15

Athlone Castle

Anthony's Journey

I took a wrong turn one night, driving down the country and ended up going through Athlone town. Signposted was the castle yet, it was not to be seen. What took my eye were the high curtain walls and drum towers. Immense and impressive, I thought – 'wow', there would be bounties of mystery here that I would love to unlock.

Months later, back in 2014, I watched a documentary called, *'Tales of Irish Castles'* presented by Simon Delaney. The series was a joy to watch and Athlone Castle had featured in one of the episodes. It detailed the sieges – my mind fairly digested the knowledge but it was not at the forefront.

Roll onto mid-2015 – I sent an email to the castle, looking to approve a paranormal investigation.

In October of that same year, on a return trip back from county Meath, Jen and I, with time on our hands, had decided to visit the castle, to break up the travelling. We met a lady named Mary at the reception of the visitor centre. We introduced ourselves – she was staggered by our presence of timing. Opened up on her desktop computer was the email I had sent months earlier. After a bustling summer, she was only now getting around to reading it now. Purely coincidence!

We chatted openly and pleasurably about the castle. Afterwards, Jen and I took a walk around the exhibition rooms. The audio-visual show in the Siege Experience Room was simply breath taking. It sent chills down my spine. The People of the Siege room consisted of sculptures of key figures, made out of recycled materials. They looked so lifelike. The visitor centre was so enjoyable that you would hardly notice you were learning at the same time. A dominant facet in the history of the castle are the two sieges, so we would have to plan to include that in our search.

Pleased with the excursion, we headed back down home to Killarney. Mary honourably put forward our proposal to Westmeath County

Council, who thankfully accepted our request. A date was organised for early January.

Ireland suffered severe storms that winter – especially in the month of December – which led to heavy flooding. The water was high on the River Shannon and the national defence forces were called in to help contain it. They were noticeably seen around the banks of the river, a few metres from the castle. Sandbags were aplenty.

Apart from that, we had great optimism during the days going into the investigation. Jen and Sinead would accompany me on the drive up. We arranged to meet another team member – Cameron - in Athlone.

We all arrived in on the town a couple of hours before the investigation, parking up just outside of the castle. We got out of our cars and had a bite to eat at a nearby restaurant. It was a Monday. Christmas had just finished and all was quiet.

With the food finished, we went for a walk. We were surprised to find that many shops in the town were not open – for this day of the week! Even better, as it would make the investigation at the castle even quieter.

The time to enter the fortress was creeping closer, so I rang Mary and she gave approval for us to come into the castle. It was quarter-to-five in the afternoon and the visitor centre would soon be closing its doors. We headed back to the cars to collect equipment.

Cameron, Jen and I would use pedometers (*See Glossary*) (secured to our belongings) to record the amount of distance that we would cover in the castle for the investigation. It might prove fascinating to evaluate at the end of the evening.

Walking from where we had parked to the entrance of the visitor centre, we had racked up a good number of steps. We had almost come full circle around the castle's curtain walls.

We met Mary inside and unloaded ourselves of the cases, bags and equipment we were carrying. We quickly set to work. As usual, I did the base tests, while the rest of the crew got onto the job of getting the CCTV surveillance night vision cameras (*See Equipment*) up and running. This took some time but eventually, they were ready.

Four CCTV cameras were used in total. One in the Athlone Castle's First 400 Years Room and another in the Athlone Besieged Room. Two more were positioned in the Siege Experience Room, in which we would focus our main experiments.

We were later joined by Emmanuel, a friend of Mary's, who had an interest in what the evening's activities were going to tell.

We would begin proceedings in the Siege Experience Room, with the sept/clan cards (*See Glossary*).

Everyone gathered in the same area, except for Jen. I started recording with the video camera. Jen went to check that the CCTV surveillance was working on the plasma television in the People of the Siege room. She also activated the mobile robot (*See Glossary*) and full spectrum camera down below us, in the Self-Sufficient People Room. Cameron and Sinead placed their index fingers on a red heart-shaped planchette (*See Glossary*).

Meanwhile, a couple of minutes in and nothing had happened with the planchette. I was getting frustrated; there were no answers to the questions I was posing. Still, maybe the right one would come up soon. In a way, I did not care if there was no movement; it may have been for a reason…

The Investigation

NUMBER OF TEAM

4

2

NUMBER OF GUESTS

We took a widely variable approach to Athlone Castle.

Surprisingly, there was a fair amount of EMF in the building. The EMF gauss master meter read between 6 and 10 milliGauss throughout the rooms and spaces that we were in. This was mainly from overhead spotlights, emergency exit lighting and interactive computer screens.

The local road traffic noise would have contributed to the 55.7 C low decibel level.

Although it was cold outside, the temperature inside was at 17.3°C. However, this would reduce throughout the night as the heating was turned off.

The lux was 091. There was some illumination coming through from the emergency exit lighting and spotlights in other rooms.

The Siege Experience Room was where we would focus the main operation. We would proceed from there to several other areas. One of these places, the Self-Sufficient People Room, was situated beneath the Siege Experience Room in the same 'donjon' (Castle Keep).

It was a space dedicated to the local people, featuring artefacts used in a variety of trades and lifestyles up to the twentieth century. The objects were displayed behind glass and are easy to skirt around and view.

There was also ample space here to use the mobile robot we had brought. Attached on top of it was the full spectrum camera. We expected to get an extensive view of the room as the mobile robot moved in various directions, hopefully picking up remarkable activity.

The Death and Destruction Room (formerly used to store arms) was another place of interest. In this dimly lit room lay a reminder of what the carnage of war had left behind. For example, on the other side of a large glass panel were sculptures depicting people either sat or curled up in the foetal position. It revealed the harshness of disease and death after the Sieges of Athlone.

A motion pressure board (*See Glossary*) was set-up on the floor beside the glass panel. This included a tyre tractor tube and motion pressure pad sandwiched between two boards. An air pressure gauge was connected to the tyre tubing. It measured 1.2kg/cm^2 at the start of the investigation. We wanted to see if there would be any change in air pressure at the end of the evening.

It was cloudy and the daylight was fading when the team stood outside for the protection prayer. They came back in and went up to the Siege Experience Room, to join the guests and prepare for the sept/clan cards experiment.

The room showcased one of the Sieges of Athlone in a cinematic format. The projector was turned off. Only the bare white circular walls could be seen around us.

The coat of arms shield (*See Glossary*) that Jen had painstakingly made prior to the investigation was placed up against a bench, beside the wall. It displayed the GhostÉire crest, which we hoped might lure some Spirits to come into play.

The sept/clan cards were placed on the back of the talking board and arranged around the edge. A red heart-shaped planchette was placed at the centre. The board rested on a heavy wooden bench with a similar-looking bench next to it. This was where Cameron and Sinead would sit.

A torch shone down on the cards and board. It was clipped into place by a flexible curved gooseneck on a microphone stand.

Emmanuel and Mary looked on. Anthony started filming. Cameron and Sinead connected on the planchette and then, the first question was asked.

"So, the first question is, do you recognise the cards? If you can, tell us which sept/clan you represent?" asked Anthony.

The next six minutes were dull. Several questions were asked but all were void. Not a thing happened.

Showing signs of desperation, Anthony jokingly pleaded for any type of movement from the planchette. He scoured the page of questions he had written in his notebook.

"Umm… which cards, or sept cards, or clan cards represent the leader of this territory… or terrain? Who's the leaders of this territory or terrain – the area we are in…? Come towards us…"

He panned the video camera to behind his left side, to the automatic door and then, back to the cards.

Sinead called out, "If you don't recognise any of these, please move the planchette, if you don't know…"

Finally, the planchette moved in a small, narrow, half, counter-clockwise direction towards Cameron and Sinead but, at a laboured pace. The Spirit present appeared to have no idea what the cards were for. The planchette was repositioned back at the centre of the board.

"We're asking Spirits of Irish decent, maybe a sept or clan to come forward. Step forward," asked Anthony.

Bugger all again… however Sinead graciously intervened.

"Or if you know anybody with these, with these, sur… surnames…?"

The planchette moved in a slow line four inches or so towards Cameron and Sinead's direction, then it moved in a small, narrow, counter-clockwise, circular course as the planchette itself twisted counter-clockwise.

Sinead placed the planchette back at centre.

"If you were killed by a sept/clan… using the cards, represented by the cards, can you tell us which one it is?" said Anthony.

It had been over nine minutes but Jen had eventually managed to enter the room. She may have been the spark that was needed.

Jen and Anthony conversed about the CCTV surveillance cameras. As they did so, the planchette moved in a straight line, six inches or so in a slow manner towards Cameron and Sinead's side of the board.

Inconclusive; the planchette was picked up and placed back at centre.

"They're probably waiting for you to come." Anthony said to Jen, laughing.

"Which sept/clan overall rules this present moment? Who rules this present moment? Which sept/clan rules this present moment? Come towards us."

Although weak, the planchette was beginning to move. As it did, a man's voice came over the walkie-talkie Anthony had in his possession. It was speculated that it came from nearby, notably from the national defence forces, who were communicating with each other. Anthony passed the walkie-talkie to Jen, who gleefully turned the device off.

In the meantime, the planchette had progressed, knocking into the 'Mcloughlin' sept/clan card.

The planchette was placed back at centre.

Anthony wanted more clarification.

"If that's correct, can you move it straight to that card again? More positive, come on, more positive…"

Anthony pressed for a more powerful response.

This time, there was some vigour to the way the planchette moved away from Cameron and Sinead.

It ended up principally knocking into the 'Mcloughlin' sept/clan card again.

The planchette was picked up and placed back at centre.

"Who's the King of Ireland?"

Feebly, the planchette reacted but when Sinead offered encouragement it moved decisively. In the moment of relief and excitement, Anthony failed to accurately record where the planchette had moved to. It was presumed it had gone to the 'O'Neill' sept/clan card.

The planchette was put back to centre.

Anthony went onto the closing question.

"Who is the King of Leinster, represented by the sept/clan cards? Who's the current King of Leinster…?"

Without stopping but at a leisurely pace, it managed to fulfil the answer. It took over thirty seconds for the planchette to travel about fifteen inches, slowly impacting the 'Daly' sept/clan card.

Once more Anthony needed to affirm the response and rightly so but, with a bit more momentum the planchette singled out the 'Daly' sept/clan card.

The next task was to find out what coloured reflection Sinead would look into with the all-seeing-eye pyramid scrying (*See Glossary*) experiment, in the Self-Sufficient People Room. To do so, we would use the colour mood frame. We had twelve coloured, A4-sized pieces of card with us, matching the twelve colours on the frame. One of these pieces of card would slot onto a similar sized picture frame, with a reflective pane of glass inserted onto it. Sinead would direct her gaze to this colour.

The colour mood frame was placed down on the back of the talking board, where the sept/clan cards had previously been. Sinead and Jen sat down on the bench beside it and placed their index fingers on the heart-shaped planchette.

"What colour mirror should I use to see my reflection while scrying downstairs?" asked Sinead.

The planchette moved from the centre of the frame, in a straight line, about twelve inches or so to 'Red'. There seemed to be more strength behind it this time. The Spirit energy was increasing.

Sinead headed down to the Self-Sufficient People Room on her own.

Earlier on, when Jen turned on the mobile robot, she noticed that because of the uneven ground, along with irregular weight distribution of the full spectrum camera, the playback of the footage would be compromised. This meant that the mobile robot had to be turned off after just over a minute; however, the full spectrum camera remained recording. In this time the full spectrum camera had picked up nothing outstanding.

It was Sinead's duty to untie the full spectrum camera from the mobile robot. She placed it about eight feet from her and the all-seeing-eye pyramid scrying board. The scrying board was triangular, gold in colour and had the 'Eye of Horus' symbol within its top angle. It had a square wooden ledge near its base for the picture frame to rest on.

Sinead knelt down in front of the board. She took a deep breath to compose herself then stared into her red reflection through the glass of the picture frame.

In the Siege Experience Room, the rest of the team were preparing an experiment that might reveal the strategic development or consequential positions of some of the armies and figureheads in one of the Sieges of Athlone, from a Spirit's point of view. Before that, we wanted to find out how the Spirit felt.

Anthony asked, "Which mood do you feel?"

Both Anthony and Jen connected on the planchette at the centre of the colour mood frame. Immediately, it went in a straight line to, 'Purple', which described 'Clarity and Sensual'.

Jen placed the planchette back at the middle of the frame.

"What should our mood be in? What? What mood should we be in?"

The planchette did a small, half, narrow, clockwise circle before continuing to move in a relentless clockwise, circular pattern over twenty-one times, finally halting at the 'Blue' segment of the frame, to indicate 'Calm, Relaxed and Loveable'.

The planchette was placed back at the middle.

There was light relief and giggling for a moment, then Anthony pressed on, "What's the general mood in this location…?"

There was a determined type of pressure on the planchette; it moved eight fast clockwise circles, slowing down to target 'Blue', meaning 'Calm, Relaxed and Loveable'.

There seemed to be warmth directed towards us.

The body mood doll was introduced and positioned beside the colour mood frame. Anthony expressed its benefit to the Spirit realm. The coloured parts of the doll were represented on the frame.

"We want know where on the body, if there was going to be, where in the body would you affect Sinead, who is scrying down below?" asked Anthony.

Both Anthony and Jen reconnected on the planchette. Straight away, it had moved, from centre of the frame to a counter-clockwise circle then, it adjusted its direction, making five clockwise circles before pausing at 'Orange', to signify the 'Neck' on the doll.

Next to the frame was an arrangement of cards set in a rectangle formation. There were two types of cards. The nationality cards (*See Glossary*) were positioned at three sides, whilst the Athlone siege figurehead cards (*See Glossary*) were at one side. Anthony placed the planchette at the heart of them and indicated their use.

A sheet of paper with grid reference mapping (*See Glossary*) of the town of Athlone, which included the castle (west side of the River Shannon) and the bridge was employed. It would, optimistically, pinpoint where armies and military leaders were before, during or after one of the sieges.

The map had one to five on the vertical axis and A to D on the horizontal axis. It is important to note that the castle on the map was situated on the right side (east to west). The map was placed on top of a nearby wooden bench.

Anthony specifically asked for Spirits that were involved in a siege of Athlone to come forward.

"… We're going to ask you now… what nationality are you?"

Anthony and Jen connected on the planchette. There was a clear motive in its motion, as it deliberately sought and ended up at the 'Irish' (tricolour) nationality card.

The planchette was placed at the centre of the cards.

Anthony went onto describing the Athlone siege figurehead cards.

There was a need to unravel who the present Irish Spirit had fought under.

"… can you tell us, who did you fight for?"

The planchette appeared to single out the 'Jean De Bonnac, Marquis D'Usson' figurehead card before returning to the centre. Anthony picked up the card and looked at the name that was written on it. Mary commented that this person was French – a Jacobite.

"Can you move it in a circle if that's correct…?"

It seemed to be accurate; the planchette enthusiastically did about five fast, clockwise circles.

Anthony picked up the planchette and placed it at the centre of the colour mood frame. He pointed out where 'Yes' and 'No' were on the frame.

"Did you survive the siege…?" he asked.

The planchette directed us to 'Yes'.

Anthony stood up and retrieved the talking board, placing it on top of the colour mood frame. The planchette was placed at its centre, with Jen and Anthony imminent in reconnecting on it.

Anthony called out, "Okay, so there's A to D; there's one to five. Can you tell us the coordinates of where you were situated, yourself, before the Siege of Athlone? Tell us the letter…?"

The planchette moved onto the letter 'C'.

"… and a number from one to five?"

The planchette swept across the board to number '2'.

Mary picked up the sheet of paper with the map on it.

Astonishingly, this coordinate (square) was relatively part of the room we were currently in. It also included the area just outside of the Castle Keep.

Mary placed the map back on the bench. Anthony put the talking board aside. The planchette was now positioned in the middle of the nationality and Athlone siege figurehead cards. We would try to establish the importance of all the other sections of the grid reference mapping.

"We want you to tell us… A1, who represents A1?"

The 'British' (Union Jack) nationality card was chosen by the planchette.

Then, it was the turn of the colour mood frame.

"Can you tell us, is there any mood or… word of value there…?"

The planchette did one-and-a-half, counter-clockwise circles from centre of the frame, striking up against the side of the frame marked 'No'.

In the moments proceeding this, we alternated between the nationality/Athlone siege figurehead cards and the colour mood frame.

There may have been a voice caught on the video camera, just after the 'Colonel Richard Grace' figurehead card was selected for (B, 4). It came after Anthony placed the planchette divination tool inside the colour mood frame and he said, "Is there any emotion?"

'Yeah' in a whispered yet still deep and masculine voice is believed to have been said.

Cameron, who was holding the camera, could be the only other person identified for this response but it would be out of character for him to comment in that way. There was a strange surge in the amount of circular motion from the planchette in response to the question too; this resulted in it going to 'Grey', to mean 'Very Nervous and Anxious'.

The tension was increasing underneath in the Self-Sufficient People Room…

While Sinead peered into the scrying glass her concentration broke. She looked to her left, towards the full spectrum camera with a sense of trepidation. Something had disturbed her. Over two minutes later, after she relaxed her focus, she talked to the camera, describing that she felt something touch her lower back. She glanced behind her left shoulder, to the empty room for a few seconds before turning back to gaze into the picture frame again. There was plenty of opportunity for something to creep up on her. Shortly afterwards, she described to the camera that she was getting a sensation of anger and frustration and would later attribute this feeling to a young man with a small head and a square jaw.

Back above in the Siege Experience Room, the grid reference mapping experiment was in its concluding stages.

There was an atypical reaction to the (D, 2) grid reference on the map and the 'Scottish' (Royal Standard) nationality card.

Nine times the planchette struck the 'Blue' part of the frame, which signified 'Calm, Relaxed and Loveable'.

There might have been a rationale behind this series of actions.

At the end of the experiment, Mary mentioned to Anthony that many Irish were defending the northern side of the castle, the coordinates matching the ones indicated on the map by the planchette.

With the experiment completed, we moved onto the talking board but, before we could move on, a few queries had to be cleared up to our satisfaction.

Sinead re-joined the rest of the team and guests in the Siege Experience Room. We carried on with the colour mood frame and the nationality/ Athlone siege figurehead cards, in the hope that we would find the answers that we needed.

"Okay dear Spirit, thank you, just clear it up, there's yes and no on this section here. I just want to ask again; was that a Jacobite soldier… that was talking to us before?" asked Anthony.

Sinead and Jen placed their left index fingers on the planchette. It proceeded to 'Yes' from the centre of the frame, then Jen collected the planchette and placed it back to the middle.

"Okay and was that the strategic positions before the siege?"

The response was, 'No' from the planchette.

It was then repositioned back at centre.

"Was that the strategic positions during the siege?"

The planchette moved to the 'Yes' section of the frame.

We were to learn from the Spirit present that there was a fair quantity of different nationalities supposedly with us: Irish, British, French, Scottish and Spanish.

Anthony asked for a soldier from the Williamite army to come forward. The appeal was granted, with the planchette stopping at 'Yes'.

The divination tool was picked up and placed at the central point of the nationality/Athlone siege figurehead cards.

Anthony was still looking to be thorough.

"Who do you fight for…?"

The planchette impacted the Dutch (Batavian Republic) nationality card but it failed to stop moving. It eventually finished its motion at halfway.

Anthony wanted it clear and precise. The planchette was placed at the centre of the colour mood frame.

"Did you die during the siege?"

The planchette went to 'Yes' and was placed back at centre.

Anthony asked if the Spirit was from the Williamite army – there was no budge from the planchette.

In trying to get an answer, Anthony cleverly inquired, "Are you in the Jacobite army?"

In a speedy direct line, the planchette went to 'Yes'. If this was the Jacobite soldier that gave us the grid reference mapping positions before, then it appeared that he had given us a different answer about his outcome after the siege… or did he? Did a Williamite soldier only make a brief impression with us?

The planchette was placed back at centre.

"Did you die during the battle… siege?"

The planchette went to the 'No' side of the frame.

Have we missed something or have we misinterpreted the Jacobite soldier…? An explanation would be found later.

Soon after and still with the colour mood frame, we found out that there were more Spirits with us that had died during the siege and, using the body mood doll, we found that the abdomen was the area of the anatomy inflicted by pain or, had given rise to death to one of them. Nonetheless, there was a response of being unable to talk to us.

For the final time, we hit the nail on the head; the Spirit gave its race as being Irish with the nationality cards.

Next on the agenda was the talking board. Sinead and Jen renewed their touch on the planchette at the centre of the board, whilst Anthony furthermore urged for comprehendible information. He asked, "… first of all, I want to ask you there, are you the same Spirit that was on the board before, talking to us?"

The planchette went towards 'Yes'.

Anthony understood that the Spirit at hand was direct and in control.

Mary asked Anthony for permission to say something. She might have wanted to speak about details relevant to unfolding the puzzle. However, Anthony was lost in his own thoughts.

"… is there a Spirit there that's willing to talk to us from the Williamite army?"

The planchette moved from centre of the board to 'No' and then was placed back at centre.

"Would you not let them talk toward… to us?"

There was a prompt movement to 'No' by the planchette…

"Are you stopping them coming and talking to us?"

The planchette showed some hesitation.

Anthony commented, "Straight answers…?"

There came an anticipated conclusion – the planchette arrived at 'Yes'.

It was inevitable that the same Spirit would stick around for the next phase of the experiment.

Jen had a set of questions, written down on paper, that she wanted to ask.

Anthony and Sinead connected on the planchette at the centre, as Cameron remained filming with the video camera.

"Can you tell us your name?" Jen asked.

After some persuasion by Anthony, the planchette made the word, 'M', 'A', 'R', 'A', 'H'.

Anthony said, "Once you're finished, move it back to centre."

The planchette did a round, counter-clockwise motion, decreasing in size, which then stopped at the centre of the board.

Anthony responded to what had been spelt but he misread the name. This led to the planchette moving to 'No', which left Anthony frankly irritated.

He pleaded for a name.

The letters, 'G', 'A', 'R', 'A', 'I' soon followed but swiftly, so did the word 'No'.

We went onto the next question.

"What age are you?" said Jen.

The numbers '5' and '2' were selected.

"Fifty-two, is that correct?" asked Anthony.

There was no movement.

He picked up the planchette and, in an unsatisfied manner, dropped it at the centre of the board.

He asked again yet, still no response.

It finally moved after Sinead softly said, "Are you fifty-two years old?"

It went to, 'Yes', in agreement.

When asking for a second time, we received the time period that the Spirit was currently present in.

We were presented with the numbers, '1', '6', '9', '0' (zero) for a year.

A couple of minutes later, Jen put forward a distinct type of question, something that we would have never asked before.

"Have you a soul?" she asked.

The planchette moved in a straight line, from centre of the board to 'No' and then, it was placed back at centre.

"Did you see your soul when you… died?"

The planchette went to the opposite side of the board towards 'Yes'.

Anthony repositioned the planchette at the middle of the board.

"Can you feel it?"

The planchette moved by a direct route to 'No'.

Again, Anthony retrieved the planchette and placed it back to centre.

"What does it weigh?"

The number '4' was chosen, followed by the letters, 'T', 'O', 'N'.

Many of the crew were amused by this.

Anthony asked, "Four tons is that correct?"

The planchette moved a large, narrow, half, counter-clockwise circle to 'Yes'.

Roars of laughter ensued.

Jen finished her questioning.

Sinead was curious to know more about the personal experience that she had encountered, in the Self-Sufficient People Room down below.

"… were you injured on your… err… lower back at all?"

The planchette moved from the centre of the board in a half, counter-clockwise circle to 'Yes'.

Anthony put the planchette back to centre and asked, "How many people did you kill during the Siege of Athlone?"

The planchette went to the number '2'.

"Just two is that correct?"

The answer was 'Yes'.

Anthony placed the planchette at centre.

"How many people did you kill… in your lifetime?"

The reaction was similar to the question asked previously: the planchette landed on '2'.

We would soon find a solution to the earlier uncertainty.

Anthony convinced Mary to propose a question to the Spirit.

"Hello Spirit. I'm Mary. I'm wondering, did you come back for the second siege in 1691?"

From the centre of the board, the planchette moved a wide, half, counter-clockwise circle to 'Yes'. The planchette was then placed back at the middle.

"… did you die in the second siege?" asked Anthony.

The planchette went to 'Yes'.

Anthony positioned the planchette back at centre.

"Were you the same Spirit that was talking to us earlier?"

Without doubt, the planchette moved in a straight line, ten inches or so to 'Yes' and was set back at centre.

"… was the coordinates through the second siege?"

The planchette progressed to 'Yes' and was put back to centre.

"And you died during the… and you died during the second siege?"

There was an affirmative response: the planchette moved to 'Yes' again.

"He said he survived… like… don't know," said Anthony in a disheartened manner.

Mary came to the rescue. She stated that there were two sieges. Anthony misconceived the situation, having not clearly specified the second siege to the Spirit earlier.

Showing a change in emotion, feeling merrier, Anthony quickly hopped onto asking for a name.

We obtained a similar word as before. The letters, 'M', 'A', 'H', 'A', 'H' came on the board.

We were lucky enough to get a surname too. 'N', 'E', 'I', 'L', 'L' was spelt on the board.

We had a better grip on what the Irish Jacobite soldier – Mahah O'Neill – was trying to convey.

Lastly, the Spirit confirmed that it would be able to state its name, through the recording equipment, for the last experiment – a séance.

The next examination would involve a couple of members of the team being on their own, to participate in channelling (*See Glossary*).

Cameron and Sinead would be the guinea pigs for this experiment. They both had to select a stance and mentally repeat a sentence, from a choice of envelopes that Anthony had formulated. Inside the envelopes were instructions on how to accomplish this, drawn and written out by Anthony.

Sinead chose an envelope and opened it up. She would have to stand still, with her hands on her ears, whilst saying in her head, "My hands are over my ears; can you make me hear again?"

Cameron then hand-picked his envelope and opened it. He would have to sustain himself in a confrontational approach, during which, he would redo the sentence in his mind, "I'm ready to fight with anger; who are you to stand in front of me?"

As Cameron and Sinead moved to their separate locations, Jen went down to the Death and Destruction Room, to do a calling-out vigil, using the reversion/altered speech device (*See Glossary*). Anthony kept a close eye on Cameron and Sinead by watching CCTV surveillance footage on the plasma television, situated in the People of the Siege room.

Cameron assumed a boxing-style position in the Athlone Castle's First 400 Years Room, on the ground floor. He stood in front of the CCTV surveillance camera. The area was spacious with interactive televisions and artefacts in display cabinets.

Behind Cameron was a door, which could be opened to enter or exit a lift. From this room, up the staircase and on the landing, was the Athlone Besieged Room on the first floor. In here, Sinead stood about two metres in front of the CCTV surveillance camera, with her hands covering her ears. Her hearing would be impaired. This room had inspiring illustrations by creator, Victor Ambrus, on the walls. They portrayed the scenes on the lead up to the Siege of Athlone.

On account of the awkward poses, the channelling experiment would only last for ten minutes. Cameron and Sinead met with Anthony to discuss what they sensed in their respective experiences.

First up was Sinead. She described that she felt really powerful, with a sense of feeling proud but, she did not know what she was proud about.

This was interesting, as the area that she was in contained illustrations of individuals from both sides of the divide: Williamites and Jacobites preparing to go into battle, depicted in a commanding fashion.

Cameron felt like he wanted to move – especially his legs – when he was channelling and happiness was directed into him. This was surprising too, on account of the emotion that he had to sustain during the experiment.

For the final part of the evening, a séance was organised for the Siege Experience Room.

Cameron would take this time to be by himself, in the Death and Destruction Room. He would be in a calling-out vigil, trying to elicit a reaction.

Two hefty wooden benches were placed tightly together for the séance. Mary and Anthony sat on the floor on one side, with Jen and Emmanuel opposite. Sinead was standing a metre or so away, recording with a video camera.

Anthony began to call out, "… dear Spirits I'm asking any Spirits from any era now to come forward; thank you for communicating with us tonight. It's the last chance to give us a name on the recording equipment… umm… maybe if you want to… err… there's a little black/brown box Sinead is holding; you can talk through that… umm… we weren't here to cause you any harm…"

Anthony mentioned that the body mood doll, situated behind him on the wall bench, next to the coat of arms shield, could be touched and that the Spirits could also tap or vibrate the table (benches).

Anthony, Mary, Jen and Emmanuel placed their hands on the benches, palm side down with fingers spread. It was the Spirit world's time to take advantage of the situation. If accepted, there would be more leeway for them to do so.

The big question was: could they do it and, if so, could we detect it?

After about two minutes or so, Anthony fastened a hearing aid (*See Glossary*) instrument onto his right ear. High-pitched whistling feedback came from it, due to sound being forced back on the microphone. He tried tuning it in but, to no avail. There may have been otherworldly, auditory phenomena recorded at his time. What sounded like alternative, lower-pitched whistling or chirping could be heard in the background. This might have been some sort of response from a Spirit. On the other hand, it could just be sound distortion that we were detecting from the hearing aid. Finally, Jen helped Anthony by managing to get it working properly.

As Jen got comfortable again, Anthony resumed calling out, "Okay dear Spirits, can you communicate with us tonight? Thank you… As I was saying there – sorry for the interruption there – you can footsteps around us, make knocks on the table… probably even want to make a whistle, similar to the sound as before. Maybe you want to give us a sing song, a sound with your voice… Maybe you want to give us a date, a year, your name – it would be very much appreciated…"

A couple of minutes later and with nothing happening so far, Anthony instructed Jen to turn on the sound monitor.

The crashing of thunder resonated around the room.

"Maybe this sound may be familiar to you? I don't know what kind of emotion you had through this time… ," said Anthony.

There had been significant damage to the castle and to the town of Athlone from harmful weather in the past.

"… maybe you come through all types of weather, good times and bad… Maybe the sounds are similar to what you heard before; maybe it brings back memories… If you were frightened; were you frightened during this time?"

Anthony adapted his probing, asking for any tribe of the O'Neill's and Mcloughlin's to be present and even asking Mahah O'Neill to draw in.

Later, the volume on the sound monitor was lowered, in favour of the reversion/altered speech device being used.

Anthony continued to call out.

Since the reversion/altered speech device failed to reproduce a decent amount of sound of Anthony's voice, it was put to one side.

Anthony repeated a question that Sinead had asked.

"… what do you think of the British?"

He carried onto to say, "… if you had a chance again, would you… would you liked to have fought harder…?"

The bench on Anthony and Mary's side could now be seen slightly shaking.

"Feel that this table is shaking," remarked Anthony.

He glanced at Mary, who nodded her head slightly in agreement.

He looked at Jen and asked her "Are you feeling anything?"

"No," Jen replied.

Half a minute later, Sinead called out, "Even make a few knocks, if you can?"

Anthony also demanded what Sinead had said.

"Make a few knocks; can you copy me?"

He knocked four times on the bench.

Seconds later he requested, "Three knocks if you like, being in the essence of what you are now?"

Emmanuel looked behind his left shoulder.

Anthony chuckled.

"… thought there was something behind you," said Anthony as he looked over towards Emmanuel.

Anthony closed his eyes again and said, "Four knocks if you don't?"

The bench on which both Anthony and Mary were connected on could be seen shaking persistently again. Unbeknown to everyone, three loud knocks were caught on the video camera recording.

The bench continued to shake, yet there was no more knocking. This meant that the benches hitting into one another could not be to blame for the sound of the knocks.

"Was there something to do with an injury around your waist?"

The bench jiggled from side to side. Knocking sounds could be made out but, less noticeable and pronounced on the video camera than the three knocks heard before.

This new knocking was consistent to the bench moving, making the earlier three knocks stand out as being strange.

"… stop shaking the table if it's the… if there not many of you here left?"

The bench stopped its shaking, appearing to answer yes.

"Shake the table… if there is only yourself there?" said Anthony.

He signalled his regret on what he had just spoken by shaking his head.

"Shake the table if…" said Anthony as he looked up towards the ceiling.

Sinead pooped in to finish the question, "If there's ten or less?"

The bench went active, again waving from side to side, accompanied by knocking sounds.

"Thank you for communicating with us, Mahah. Is it true your fifty-two? Stop the table if that's correct," asked Anthony.

The bench seemed to pick up on its rhythm of movement, to indicate no.

"Is it true? Did you die at that age?"

The bench gradually became still.

On that note, the investigation came to an end but, on a pleasant feeling. Maybe Mahah O'Neill, the lone soldier, managed to get his say – reluctant to give up his post and fought to the bitter end. Hopefully, he found his Elysium.

A team photo was taken outside the castle keep. Goodbyes were said to Mary and Emmanuel, then it was back to the cars to assess the distance Anthony, Jen and Cameron had covered on the investigation. Cameron chalked up the most distance with 3.6km. Jen was second with 3.5km and Anthony last, with 3.1km. Anthony either strolled or was still when doing the baseline check. For the most part, he remained in the Siege Experience Room, controlling operations. Cameron and Jen walked around, setting up equipment and they went down to the ground level areas to conduct vigils.

On the drive back, we were happy and content.

Cameron acknowledged hearing a tap, during the second calling-out vigil, in the Death and Destruction Room. Upon going back over the audio on the digital sound recorder, a tap could be heard but it came five minutes later. What is relevant is that what he perceived and what was recorded are identical. This brought us to the assumption that he was aware at first then, he either had settled into the conditions and did not bother to remark upon the recorded tap or, he was oblivious to it. Tapping might be a common occurrence in this room for a reason.

In closing, did we meet a being in Mahah O'Neill? Well, if that was the case, he was certainly proud and influential.

SIEGE OF ATHLONE 1691

Fig 1: THIS IS AN IRISH JACOBITE SOLDIER 'SPIRIT' WHO FOUGHT FOR JEAN DE BONNAC, MARQUIS D'USSON, WHO DIED DURING THE SIEGE. THIS IS HIS PERSPECTIVE OF THE SIEGE OF ATHLONE. Note: Map is east to west.

BRITISH (UNION JACK)   IRISH (TRICOLOUR)   FRANCE (TRICOLOUR)   SCOTTISH ROYAL STANDARD

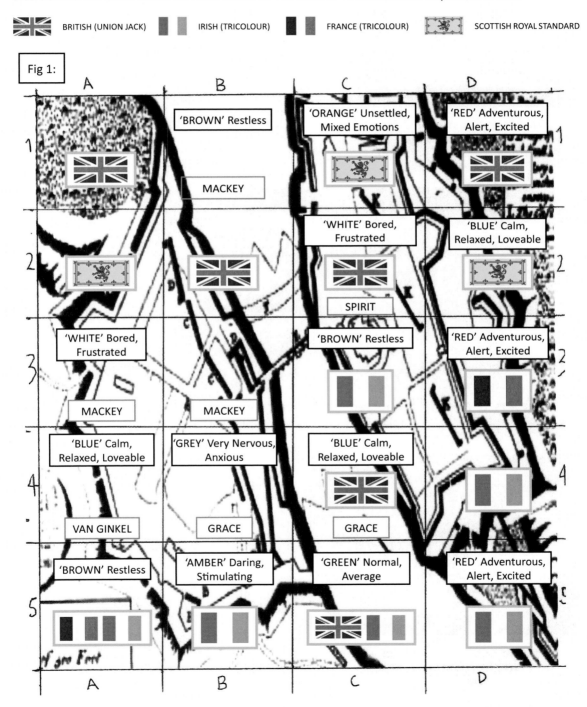

The darkness shrouds the
January night sky

William of Orange, the
leader of the Williamites

The Castle Keep is connected by a corridor leading to the rest of the castle

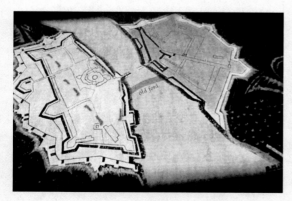

The Siege Experience Room is one of
the many interesting places to see
when visiting

'Custume', one of the
Jacobites' bravest soldiers

The GhostÉire coat of arms, on a shield, designed by Jen

CCTV cameras keep watch

The all-seeing-eye pyramid scrying board

The motion pressure board was put in the Death and Destruction Room

Cameron and Anthony get ready to start a vigil

The sept/clan cards experiment is in full swing

Location Background/Biography

Athlone Castle was originally built in 1129 but the stone structure (Castle Keep) that survives today was built in 1210, for King John, from the orders of John De Gray (Bishop of Norwich).

The castle has a polygonal shape and was constructed on a man-made hill. It was built partly to defend the crossing point of the River Shannon through the town and also, to help Norman expansion into Connaught.

The fortification of the Castle was intensified around 1276, with three round towers (drum towers) and curtain stoned walls, that rise to about twenty-five feet above the present bridge.

The Castle was reconstructed by Sir William Brabazon (Lord Justice of Ireland and elected member of the Privy Council of Ireland) in 1547.

There were two sieges at the Castle, in 1690 and 1691, during the Williamite and Jacobite War. The external walls and towers came under heavy fire in the June siege of 1691. King William III's army, led by Dutch General Godert de Ginkell (Williamite) attacked the bastion on the Leinster side of the town, with minimal resistance from the Jacobite army, who retreated over the bridge and broke its arches to prevent de Ginkell's army from advancing across it.

Over a ten-day period, an estimated 12,000 cannonballs were fired by the Williamite army at the Castle. A pontoon bridge was quickly made by de Ginkell's men, to set up an attack upon the Connaught side of the town. Eventually the Williamite army - consisting of 2,000 elite grenadier force (armed with grenades) progressed up-river, driving the Jacobite army out from the rear. About 500 Jacobites were slaughtered in the final battle. This was in addition to the 1,000 who were killed by the bombardment of the castle beforehand.

In 1697, the castle was hit by lightning, which destroyed even more of the fortification.

During the Napoleonic era, it was modernised, to help store artillery. In later years, the castle became a barracks.

During the 'Big wind' of 1839, the storm, which lasted up to five hours, slowly abated. Athlone suffered severe destruction. It should be noted that a drawbridge existed up until the 1940s.

The castle, by 1966, became a museum, run by the Old Athlone Society and in 1991, a visitor centre was developed by Athlone Urban District Council.

In 2012, it underwent a multi-million-euro renovation, which was hugely transformative. It was turned into a multi-sensory educational experience for visitors. It features eight exhibitions, which include 'Athlone Besieged' and 'The Fabric of Athlone'. A new exhibition opened in 2014, featuring Count John McCormack, Athlone's very own son and world-famous tenor.

Manifestation/Legend

There was no paranormal significance to this location prior to the investigation.

Conclusion

The Castle has a wide variety of corridors and steps - something indicated by the vast amount of distance covered during the investigation.

It was a siege battleground; hence, we went on to base our main experiment (grid reference mapping) for the evening around this.

First up was the Sept Cards in the Siege Experience Room. Little came up in the first few minutes. The Spirit may have felt nothing in connection to what had been asked.

Things got going when the question about who ruled this present moment was put forward. The planchette went to the 'Mcloughlin' card, which symbolised 'Viking'. This was confirmed again seconds later. The Mcloughlin's are derived from the ruling Uí Néill Sept.

The O'Maoilsheachlainns held the Kingdom of Mide (Meath), which included County Meath, Westmeath and parts of County Cavan, Dublin, Kildare, Longford, Offaly and Louth. They were ancestors of the

MacLoughlins. They had a High King, Malachy, from 980-1022 along with several others in earlier years. From O'Mclahlin - it was anglicised to Mcloughlin in 1691. They lost numerous lands and power to the Normans and conceded County Meath, which eventually was absorbed into the separate province of Leinster.

When asked who the High King of Ireland was, the planchette went to, 'O'Neill'. The O'Neills, a Hugh dynasty, ruled from 1185 until 1616 in the lands of Tír Eoghain, now known as County Tyrone. They were heavily involved in the Nine Years War (1594-1603, *See Glossary*), Irish Rebellion (1641, *See Glossary*) and Irish Confederate Wars (1641-1653), so picking this in relation to High Kings (Irish headmen) would be quite accurate.

When asked who the High King of Leinster was, the planchette selected the 'Daly' card, which meant 'Assembles Frequently'. The O'Dalaigh Sept were located in County Westmeath and were distinguished in the field of literature. The 'Daly stone' was moved following the Battle of Aughrim in 1691, after Killimer Castle in Loughrea, County Galway was dismantled. They held various strongholds and seats of power and wealth, which are connected to villages such as Glasson, Kilbeggan and Athlone.

Uí Cheinnselaig were the Kings of Leinster and the earliest descendants of the Daly's to nobility, between the 5th and 8th century.

Red was pinpointed as the colour Sinead would use in the all-seeing-eye pyramid scrying, in the Self-Sufficient People Room. We needed to isolate Sinead, to see if she would come to the same outcome of feelings or sensations to the 'Spirit' or 'Spirits' that were communicating with the rest of the group. She described anger and frustration, that was linked to a young man with a small head and square jaw. Contrary to this, the team came across a Spirit that was genuinely upbeat. The same was also summed-up for other Spirits around.

After Anthony asked what the general mood in the area was, a whisper was caught on the video camera saying, 'Happy', prior to the planchette heading towards 'Blue' on the colour mood frame, to indicate 'Calm, Relaxed and Loveable'.

The neck was the part of the body where the Spirit said it could affect Sinead. It might not have come across to her physical being but instead, in what she saw: the square jaw. She described being touched on her lower back, which is an entirely different section of the body. Still, a Spirit later revealed that it suffered an injury to its lower back.

During the grid reference mapping, we made contact with an apparent Spirit who was an Irish Jacobite soldier, who fought under the command of Jean De Bonnac, Marquis d'Usson at the Siege of Athlone 1691. French Officer, Jean De Bonnac, Marquis d'Usson became garrison commander (Jacobite army), taking over from Colonel Richard Grace. The grid reference of (C,2) was the location of the Jacobite soldier before the siege. This marked the spot in close proximity to where we were undergoing the investigation. This would be the area the Marquis d'Usson had control over.

There are two possible ways in which Colonel Grace died. Colonel Grace may have been killed from bombardment on the western side of the bridge on the same day (20 June 1691) that the Jacobites dismantled it and retreated to the west bank. The grid reference of (C,4) includes part of the western bank (current bridge) and, where the Spirit identified the Colonel Richard Grace figurehead card. The Spirit also detailed Colonel Grace with (B,4) and a very nervous tense emotion. This is where Colonel Grace could have lost his life too. He may have been slain whilst aiding Colonel Fitzgerald (Jacobite).

The influence of Colonel Fitzgerald and his three hundred and fifty men could be linked to (B,5); a daring plot to stop the invasion at the eastern side of the town, to allow Jacobite troops from Limerick to arrive. However, this was thwarted by approaching Williamite army and maybe Godert de Ginkell (Dutch Williamite General), arterially positioned at (A,4). De Ginkell's position at (A,4) holds a safe zone to see what's around. The emotion felt here was most probably calm and relaxed.

The remains of Fitzgerald's army likely met Mackay's (Williamite Lieutenant General, second in command to De Ginkell) army of four thousand men around (A,3) and (B,3). This was where frustration occurred for Mackey. One hundred and fifty members of Fitzgerald's army gallantly fought to their death, trying to rush to the bridge and hold on as fellow soldiers hurried in behind them, to destroy the arches of the bridge.

The grid reference of (D,3) could be the intervention of fifteen hundred horses and foot soldiers sent by St Ruth (French Jacobite Lieutenant General) two miles west of the town. Details of the morning of 29 June revealed that a bridge of boats was placed by Williamite forces, to form an access on the south side of the old bridge. This could be aligned with (B,2) as well.

The restlessness of who appeared to be Mackay on (B,1) could have been attributed to the failed third attempt, along with another one up the river at (C,4).

The grid reference of (C,2) may link with the British finally getting into the defences of Athlone later that day (fourth effort) and drop back of Irish soldiers (a foolish decision to reduce the guard authorised by St Ruth) from that point, leading to an opportunity which the Williamites exploited. Williamite forces crossed and attacked from the rear, which was shown by (C,1) and (D,1). Jacobite soldiers, who were awaiting reinforcements from St Ruth, abandoned the garrison. Only a handful of Jacobite soldiers may have remained at their post.

The square grid (C,5), which includes Irish Tricolour and British Union Jack nationality flags, could be an indication of conflict but it might relate to a contingent of British Jacobite soldiers in support of James II, due to the emotion of normal and average being indicated.

The Royal Scottish standard, in (D,2), could symbolise the calm feeling of Williamite soldiers, with the inevitability of taking the castle after breaching the west bank. What is surprising was the Spirits' general knowledge of the flags. The Irish Tricolour was only first adopted in 1922, the French Tricolour in 1794, the British Union Jack flag in 1801. The oldest flag the Spirit identified with was the Scottish Royal Standard flag of around 1222, used by the sovereign. This flag may have represented Mackay's army, since he was Scottish.

There may have been a brief involvement of a Williamite soldier on the planchette. The Dutch Batavian Republic nationality card was slightly touched upon. This flag was used in the early days of the Kingdom of Holland. It was first introduced in 1796, replacing the Statenvlag (States Flag). The red, white and blue flag – Statenvlag – replaced the older orange, white and blue (Princes flag) in the mid-1600s.

A deep masculine voice said, 'Yeah' on the recording during the grid reference mapping. It came after the Colonel Richard Grace figurehead card was selected and before the planchette went to very nervous and anxious on the colour mood frame for (B,4). The question that got this reaction was, "Is there any emotion?"

This was an important period in the investigation but also, for that area at the Siege of Athlone in 1691. We are unsure who sustained the pain to the abdomen that resulted in death. It could be down to starvation, as Colonel Richard Grace remonstrated to a messenger of Colonel Douglas (General of the Williamite army) in the Siege of Athlone 1690, in which the Jacobites triumphed. He shot with his pistol above the messenger's head and declared, "These are my terms; these only, I will give or receive and when my provisions are consumed, I will defend till I eat my boots."

The Spirit whom we regarded as being Mahah gave the year 1690 on the talking board. There may be a fondness of that particular year of achievement. The name Mahah is of Arabic origin, meaning 'beauty' whilst Marah, in Hebrew means 'bitter' and in Arabic means 'joy'. Mar could also signify impairment of appearance.

We questioned the name of the Spirit again and got another response with the letters, 'G', 'A', 'R', 'A', 'I' before it moved to 'No'. This name has multiple origins.

Jen's questions centred on the soul had us wondering. The Spirit has no soul but saw it when it died. The soul, in the afterlife, could be your actual body or remains, the total opposite (of what we usually think). Four tons was the answer to how much the Spirit's soul weighed. The heavy weight of the soul could be caused by lethargy or - a long shot - by the downward force on the remains of the body in our domain, after being buried.

We trust we got a surname to Mahah. We received Neill as the response. This surname refers to 'Cloud, 'Champion' and 'Passionate', an anglicised version of 'Niall'.

Three noticeable knocks could be heard in the séance. It was a reaction from the Spirit to being happy in the world they were in.

The table ceased movement in agreement that not many Spirits (possibly from the sieges) were currently left in the building.

Jen's vigil in the Death and Destruction Room, with the reversion/ altered speech device brought nothing of importance, nor did anything unexpected happen on the CCTV surveillance night vision cameras and, there was very little change in the air quantity with the motion pressure board.

Athlone Castle
Co Westmeath

WEBSITE: athlonecastle.ie
e-MAIL: info@athlonecastle.ie
PHONE: 090 644 2130
FACEBOOK: AthloneCastle

Open: 10:00am — 5:30pm Tuesday to Saturday and
11:00am — 5:00pm on Sundays. Closed Mondays.

The museum is an enjoyable adventure for all ages, with illustrations, artefacts, 3D maps and hands-on interactive participation.

There is a carpark beside the castle.

Audio-guides are provided in many languages onsite.

A café beside the reception offers inside and outside seating, should you need to refresh.

The castle provides amazing views of the town, River Shannon and the adjacent Church of Saints Peter and Paul.

APPLEROCK STUDIOS

Layout

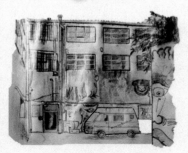

Rough Dimensions

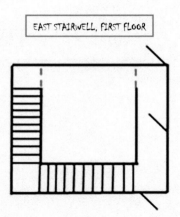

ROOMS/AREAS, GROUND FLOOR

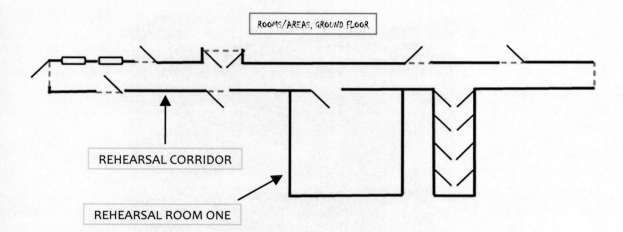

REHEARSAL CORRIDOR

REHEARSAL ROOM ONE

ROOMS/AREAS, SECOND FLOOR

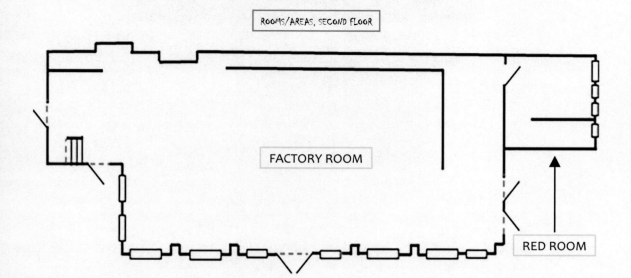

FACTORY ROOM

RED ROOM

Chapter 16
Applerock Studios

Sinead's Journey

When scoping out our next investigation, we decided to venture to Dublin's dark historical times of destitution and disease-induced squalor; a time when surviving each day was the number one priority. Applerock Studios (a multipurpose rehearsal studio and artistic space) would give us just what we were looking for.

Stepping back in time to the 1800s, down the dreary slums of Dublin, the tone of this investigation was going to be quite sombre. What was once a large slum and a notorious red-light district, with over 1,600 prostitutes working in the area at any given time, 'The Monto' (real name Montgomery Street) was once steeped in disease, crime and overcrowding. After the religious order, 'The Legion of Mary', shut down the brothels in the 1920s and put the remaining 'fallen women' into Magdalene laundries, the surrounding area was completely cleaned up and redeveloped.

Apart from apartments and flats, Applerock Studio is one of the last remaining buildings situated in the heart of the area. It is also rumoured to be a 'smothering den' in the past - a place that took those who were suffering out of their misery, in a consensual way. Desperate times in a very bleak world.

I met up with Dermot (the owner of the building) one week before the investigation, to take photos and see what areas were accessible. The place was spacious, with many rooms scattered along the corridors. So many places to hide yet, I doubt that we would be playing a game of 'hide and seek' through our investigation but, you never know - stranger things have happened.

I was extremely impressed with the alternative vibe of the place: unpolished and authentic with back stairwells and high ceilings on the upper floor. A perfect place for any sounds to penetrate through the building.

On the evening of the investigation, Grace and I ventured in together, as we were both situated in Dublin. The rest of the team drove up from Kerry.

On our way in, we discussed how 'The Monto' is slowly being forgotten about, only remembered as part of local history by a tiny section of the older generation. The song, *Monto*, by The Dubliners continues to keep the story alive, etched in the minds of many an Irish person. However, the actual stories are, sadly, beginning to disappear. By investigating this place, we had a chance to restore some of them and, potentially, make some new discoveries. Maybe some of the brothel owners – otherwise known as 'The Madams' – would still be hanging around in Spirit, calling out for customers to come through.

Walking up the silent street towards the building, there was not a soul around. A few people staggered here and there but you would not know that it was a stone's throw away from central Dublin. It was if we were on a secret mission that nobody knew about.

On entering the building, late in the evening, the rest of the team had already arrived. What type of Spirits would be joining us tonight? Could the factory workers, soldiers, nuns, priests, ladies of the night or children still be trapped here?

This used to be a forlorn place of snatched dreams – I had a feeling that the energy here was not going to be too lively.

Jen was already feeling very unwell from the journey down. Could this have foreshadowed what was going to occur later in the night?

Dermot brought us around on a tour of the building, which was full of rehearsal rooms, narrow corridors and artistic graffiti – a true artist's escape.

Weaving our way through the long corridor downstairs, I was instantly drawn to the old creepy looking curtains draped across small cages. Dermot told us they used to be old toilets, which were part of the 'Fiesta Club', where Cilla Black once performed back in the 1970s. It sure felt as though something must be hiding there, cowering away, waiting to make a grand entrance. Also, an ideal place to have somebody separated as well.

Meandering up the East Stairwell, which used to connect two factories together, the excitement was amping up. Already, there was so much exploring to do here, with nooks and crannies scattered all throughout the three floors.

We decided to use the large, wide-open upstairs Factory Room as the main set up, as it was accessible from both sides of the building or alternatively, a perfect place to escape the building, if cornered by something too spooky.

Grace and I thought that we heard a whistle coming from the other part of the room. However, it was not distinctive enough to warrant any rash assumptions.

We followed Dermot all the way to the top of the building, where his office was situated. To make things creepier, he pulled out a child's gas mask from a box, with the date of 21st March 1938 written on it – one year before World War II (*See Glossary*) started.

This building certainly had been through a series of distinct stages. From fear to laughter, creativity to show business, poverty to business, this building had it all. What other surprises lay in store?

Stepping down the opposite stairwell, another team member – Dominic – was hanging from the rafters, wound up in rope, abseiling down the stairs with a high-vis jacket on. The place had now turned in to an acrobatic circus. Could more activity occur if we entertained the Spirits this time around?

This was going to be an interesting night, for sure.

The Investigation

NUMBER OF TEAM		NUMBER OF GUESTS
6	**1**	

The Monto – short for Montgomery Street – was once the name given to the notorious red-light district of Dublin. Between the years 1860 to 1920, thousands of prostitutes worked the streets, within a two-kilometre radius, surviving each day as best they could.

This was until 1925, when 'The Legion of Mary' – a religious order – closed the brothels down and made over 120 arrests. This was practically wiped out of the history books, as if Ireland were ashamed of its 'sinful' past. It was an area that had since gone through renovations and modernisation.

Dominic had a connection with Dermot, the owner of 'Applerock Studio', a building that stood in the heart of 'The Monto' area, now known as Foley Street. He described certain unexplainable noises occurring from within one of the rooms, alongside the feeling of a presence.

During a rehearsal session, an unknown voice had been heard on one of the tapes after a band had been recording. It was enough to spark curiosity about what could be unearthed there. Not only that but, the building had stood the test of time and had been through an array of historical time periods. From being a supposed 'smothering den', a 'factory' alongside a 'theatre'– there was bound to be a mixture of activity awaiting discovery. So, in November 2013, we were more than delighted to investigate this building, situated around such an iconic Dublin location.

On the day of the investigation, Anthony made a four-hour drive from Kerry, accompanied by Jen and a female team member. Sinead and Grace were already situated in Dublin, so they did not have to venture so far.

It was a calm, partly cloudy autumn night. Everyone had arrived by nine o' clock, raring to go apart from Jen, who was feeling extremely ill and wiped out from the car journey. The astrological significance may have played a part in her feelings. With Sun and Mars sextile, there would be notable physical activity. Jen might not be the only one affected or, it might be that circumstances could change around us.

We were provided with a welcoming, informative tour by Dermot. Sinead had visited the building a few weeks prior, to scope out the area, take some photos and see what rooms were accessible. We were over the moon when given leeway to investigate anywhere within the entire building, which was like a maze, with rooms branching out in different directions. There was a glut of information to take in and a lot of area to cover, as the building had a total of two main floors and a smaller room at the very top.

We counted ourselves lucky that it was a weekday night, with limited noise pollution outside the building. This would make distinguishing sounds a lot easier if any strange noises popped up later in the evening.

Downstairs consisted of the rehearsal studios for music, while the upstairs still retained the feeling of an old factory. It was said Princess Diana's clothes were made here at one stage.

This Factory Room was a perfect place to set up for the séance - it was flanked by two stairwells, making it accessible from both sides of the building.

Gravitating towards a small room, just off the Factory Room, known as the Red Room, most of the team felt an unsettling vibe. This was more than likely down to the structure of the room itself, along with the old-fashioned, red, thistle-patterned wallpaper and a secret toilet that accompanied it.

We would set this room up for a scrying experiment, with a video camera facing an oval-shaped mirror. The gazer would also have a view of their back and face from a rectangular mirror, placed opposite. The words 'yes' and 'no' and numbers from 0-9 were marked on the oval mirror. Branded on the wooden edge of the mirror were the alphabet and the Mars and Venus sex symbols (There was a chance that we would use this mirror as a type of talking board, later in the investigation).

The sense of feeling restricted was already quite palpable in this room, giving a good chance that the scrying experience would be enhanced, due to the dense feeling that was already present there.

Wasting no more time, Anthony carried out the baseline tests while setting up the equipment, with Jen, in the chosen rooms.

The Rehearsal Corridor, Red Room and Factory Room had considerable EMF in them. This was partly expected due to compressed spaces, fuse boxes and low-height florescent lighting. We also had to take into consideration everything that accompanied a music recording studio and external factors, such as being situated right in the heart of the city.

The preface was good. It was quite easy to get around, especially to the upper levels with the two stairwells. It was quite mild at the start of the evening. The outside temperature was 9.2°C. The inside temperature was not that much higher, at 11.6°C. We might start to feel the cold in the early hours of the morning.

A digital sound recorder was placed in Rehearsal Room 1, on the ground floor where a distorted croaky voice had been picked up during a music session. The room felt warm because a band had been in earlier, performing some tunes. The walls were insulated with chip wood, to prevent any intrusion of sound. Microphone stands, amplifiers, mixing desks and a drum kit were stored in this room.

Outside of Rehearsal Room 1, another experiment was planned for the dark, long, narrow Rehearsal Corridor. A full spectrum camera was set up, pointing at a trigger object of a baby doll, lying down on a bench with a pillow above its head. Red configurations from a laser beam machine (*See Glossary*) were also aimed at the doll and surrounding walls.

A recording of a baby crying, along with coughing and market noises were prepared to lure any Spirits in. Anthony had pre-recorded a message over the same recording device, in advance of these noises coming on cue. Jen pressed the play button.

You have one minute to leave the building.

Soon, Jen and Anthony declared their leave and departed the Rehearsal Corridor.

With a lot of information taken in and, preparation to do, it was half past one in the morning when we finally managed to get things started. A protection prayer was conducted as we readied ourselves, in the Factory Room, for the séance.

The sides and corners of the room were constructively assorted with, various types of items, from ladders to workbenches and different types of chairs. We did have space to carry out our duties but, mainly in the middle of the room. This was where the séance table would be situated.

Old copper coins were laid across top of the table. As money was scarce in the past, we hoped that this would prove an enticing gesture. A small crucifix was also used – not necessarily as an enticing gesture but, one to resemble the religious order called 'The Legion of Mary', who shut down the brothels. There was a possibility that such a symbol could create friction, resentment or a need for penance or devotion (to faith).

Dermot had placed an old can of Kerry-brand, sweet, condensed milk on the table. He stated that it must have been left behind by plumbers in the attic (above the Factory Room) when they were working up there. Amid the darkness, a pillar (thick) candle was lit. A taper (thin and long) candle was already burning, wedged into an empty spirit bottle at the centre of the table.

Anthony, Jen, Dominic, Dermot and the female team member connected their hands to the table's surface. Sinead and Grace took over the filming while Anthony rang the bell, to summon in the Spirits. A few seconds of silence passed before communication commenced.

A dynamic microphone was suspended over the table and fixed into place by an adaptable gooseneck microphone stand. It was plugged into an amplifier box situated a couple of metres away, on top of a chair. We anticipated noises above the séance table.

"Can you blow the candle? … Can you hear the baby crying? … What do you want to do to that baby? Want to stop it crying? Want to love it?" asked the female team member.

Faint whistling could be heard on the night vision camera but this was barely heard by the team at the time. Given that it was such a calm night, it is doubtful that it was just wind howling through the building.

As Anthony spoke, a couple more whistling sounds occurred. He asked, "Maybe want to talk to through us by willing to … whisper. Maybe you want to whisper to the long sticks that are above us … just there, to amplify, amplify your voice."

About ten seconds later, the table reportedly began to shake.

"Maybe, if you want to open or close a door."

Anthony added that he felt ice cold over his hands.

Two names popped into the mind of the female member of the team – an 'Anne' and a 'Rosie'. The presence of a man was also coming through.

Anthony called out, in Latin, "You are Monk?" Shortly after, he commented, "I feel wavy."

We believed the table to be shaking; although it was also thought that its movement could be happening as a result of an individual's inability to control their pressure on the table. Maybe the Spirits had found a pathway to make themselves be known…

"I feel very sad," said Dermot.

Minutes passed but there was still no concrete sign of communication. Sometimes, during investigations, it takes a while for things to rev up. This was especially true in a location that has not previously been investigated, with Spirits that have been lying dormant for decades.

"Maybe it's been a long time since you communicated; is that true? Come towards us now, step forward, been a long time," Anthony beckoned in a soft tone.

A loud shout, a female voice echoing through the room, a woman howling something, as if in despair. Nobody seemed to notice the scream at the time, remaining stoic and pensive around the table. Nobody questioned it, nor seemed too phased. Everyone around the table remained focused.

"Was there a lot of people that were around here?" asked Anthony.

Dominic muttered some words. A wail was heard but, it was less intense than before. Anthony instantly opened his eyes and turned his head slightly to his left, staring into space in a concerned manner. The female team member remarked, "There are two girls outside of the circle: Sinead and Grace."

A low humming, mumbling voice came across at that point. It is unclear what was said but a definitely female voice was heard. It is possible that the experiment down below, in the Rehearsal Corridor, was contributing to this unfortunate's misery.

Dermot mentioned Montgomery Street. As he was talking, Anthony expressed that he felt a cold breeze on his right hand. The table they were connected on was heavy. Whether it was moving seemed not just surprising but also suspect.

Anthony looked to his left, away from the séance circle. He spoke briefly upon hearing a whistle.

"Did you ever feel loved?" asked the female team member.

Anthony turned his head to his right, drawing his attention back into the séance circle. He whispered, "Cold breeze on my right."

He quickly returned to his natural tone of voice, "Were you in love?" he asked.

A few seconds afterwards, he uttered the same words again, "Cold breeze on my right…"

The activity was increasing, demonstrated also by the fact that everyone could now feel their hands stuck to the table, with a low vibrational buzzing sensation underneath. Dermot expressed that he felt electricity running through him, that he had received a shock!

With his eyes closed and head bowed, Anthony posed a question, "Do you like communicating around here? Do you like showing yourself around here?"

His upper body began to rock back and forth uncontrollably. He spoke out in astonishment as the walkie-talkie moved beside him. The only rational explanation was that it was the table shaking that caused the walkie-talkie (used in communications) to alter its base and settle more comfortably.

The pace was certainly picking up. To elicit a response, the questions were beginning to get serious and exact, cutting to the chase.

"Did you help people to die?" asked the female team member.

Anthony was blunt too, "Was this a smothering den? … Were there people with deformities as well?"

Anthony continued to rock back and forth, as if in a trance-like state. He blew out a puff of air, attempting to remain calm. "Build that energy up. Build that energy up. Come and step forward. Build the energy up."

Anthony's voice, as he spoke, was commanding.

The table began to creak, as if in response to them mentioning smothering dens – places used, consensually but illegally, to put people out of their misery. Anthony's inability to keep still may have caused the noise and shaking on the table, as he exerted a changing pressure on the table's surface with his hands.

The female team member said, "Did you hate being that generation?"

This elicited an emotional response: the table violently shook, with the taper candle rattling in the middle. This startled Anthony and the female team member. Jen also took a moment to lift her head up, to glance across the table, before bowing her head again.

We told the Spirit world that we would hold no judgment over them for their profession, the acts they committed or any deaths they caused during their life in our realm.

"You are not a bad person; feel the love," said the female team member, honest and composed.

"Were you a woman of the cloth?"

"I feel heat there," said Anthony.

He called out, "You can choose to leave at any time; you know that?"

"Yeah, I feel heat as well," said the female team member.

Anthony instantly declared that he sensed the heat and warmth on his back. The female team member recognised what he was saying. She was also feeling the same sensation on her back.

"You didn't do anything wrong; it's just how the times were," she stated – an announcement to erase the sense of guilt or sin for any Spirit trapped in the building.

Anthony's upper body was rapidly seesawing.

"Do any of us resemble you here this evening? … look like you? Is there loads of you around?" asked Anthony.

"Make a sound with your voice; use the energies that are around if you want to move anything in the middle of the table. We're not here to harm you, just to show a presence that you're here … on Montgomery Street."

A second after Anthony finished asking the question, a loud screeching noise pierced through, alongside the sound of furniture being moved. What is interesting is that no similar noises were heard before or after this. It was also bizarre that the noise occurred directly after the question was asked. The street outside was quite silent and there was nobody else in any of the other rooms.

Anthony turned his head, bothered by the noise, looking bewildered as he continued to shake.

The female team member said, "Did you get paid for smothering? … Did you eat well? But it was hard eating?"

Anthony felt a presence in between him and Dominic. Dominic felt someone touching his left shoulder (towards Anthony's right). Whatever Spirit was presenting itself, seemed to be situated around one side of the table. Anthony tried to establish a connection, with whatever was coming through, by asking a question in relation to any children a Spirit being may have had.

"It was hard to make them be educated, was it? Give them a chance; you had to probably offload them there to do your job? Somebody else looked after them, maybe?"

A very faint whistle was caught on the night vision camera then, the taper candle at the middle of the table toppled over, abruptly extinguishing its flame. Laughter ensued and everyone felt livened up.

The Female team member asked the Spirit to show their face in the mirror in the adjoining room, for the scrying session that was about to occur.

With everyone loosening their grip on the table, it started to become clear that some people had already being affected, as the energy coming through was quite sombre and mournful.

Jen's energy was spent. Suffering from exhaustion, she lay down on a couch in the annex room, to get some sleep and refrained from participating in the rest of the investigation.

After a break, Sinead got comfortable in the Red Room for a scrying session, with her walkie-talkie in tow, while the rest of the team set up the occupation card circle in the Factory Room.

As the Red Room was quite tiny, Sinead sat cross-legged in front of the oval mirror, with small candles surrounding her. If any Spirits were hesitant to present themselves during the séance, they would now have the chance to manifest through other means. Pure concentration was needed here, blanking the mind with intense focus straight ahead on the mirror. A video camera was set up behind her, to capture her responses and pick up on anything else that could be occurring.

The occupation cards were set up around the same table used for the séance. They consisted of an amalgamation of different jobs, dating back over the centuries along with some associated with the present day. One circle of cards was arranged on outer edge of the table and another, smaller formation around the centre. An upturned, old-fashioned drinking glass was placed on the table. The female team member and Dermot connected onto it. Anthony filmed with the night vision camera.

A question was asked about the Spirit's occupation. Moving in a jittery, hesitant manner across the edge of the table, the glass arrived at the 'Tapier' occupation card, which signifies 'One who puts the tap on ale cask'.

"Did you sell beer? Did you bring beer here?" asked the female team member.

The glass moved a small, half, counter-clockwise circle but remained conclusively in front of the 'Tapier' card.

"Going to ask any other Spirits, any other energies that are with us right now to come forward and maybe tell us what you do for a living?" asked the female team member.

The glass knocked up and down in the one spot a few times, in another jittery motion.

"What was your trade? How did you make money? How did you eat?"

The glass slowly twisted on the spot clockwise, counter-clockwise then clockwise again, as if having a waltz.

Anthony asked, "Oh just maybe the symbols, pictures on the cards. If you can't read or write… go to the one that is associated with you, that you feel that resembles yourself?"

No movement followed on the glass. However, Sinead radioed in from the Red Room. *I'm getting a lot a sense of anger and my face has grown wider and looks really… I don't know, like just really old.*

"Which picture do you like the best?" said the female team member.

The glass slowly moved a few inches to the 'Drover' card, which means 'One who drives cattle, sheep, etc to market'.

"And which picture don't you like?"

The glass moved in a straight line, towards the middle section of cards more swiftly than before, knocking into the 'Currier' card, to denote 'Cover of hides'.

The glass began to pick up its pace and made its way back to in between the 'Drover' and 'Brewster' card, which means 'Beer manufacturer'.

It managed to swivel on its axis to the next card, 'Mercer', which means 'Cloth merchant'.

"Did you work here in the factory?"

At that exact moment, Sinead radioed in. *Say, like the age, like about fifty or sixty.*

As she was talking, the glass did a small, narrow, counter-clockwise circle, returning to the 'Mercer' card.

As everyone conversed about what the cards could mean or, who the Spirit could be, Sinead radioed in on the walkie-talkie that Anthony was holding. She said that she felt as though she was mourning something.

The glass had stopped moving; the activity had gone quiet in the Factory Room. A static sound came over the walkie-talkie. Anthony radioed into Sinead. "Everything okay, Sinead? Over."

Sinead responded, *Yeah I feel like, I don't know, I feel like…*

She was immediately cut off, so the rest of her sentence did not get through to us. Could the Spirits have been playing havoc with the walkie-talkie?

"They've gone from here into the scrying room," said the female team member.

"You okay, Sinead? Over," said Anthony over the radio. It seemed that his walk-talkie was not sending the transmission through and yet, it was (the video camera in the Red Room deemed that it did).

There was no response.

Anthony spoke slowly and clearly over the walkie-talkie again, "Are you okay, Sinead? Over."

Finally, there was a reply, *Umm, yeah. I just got that, … think it's turning itself…*

Sinead's walkie-talkie was not relaying her entire message.

The female team member called out, "Okay, is that you in there? Can you just hop back here to us for a moment? I want you to move the glass to Dominic for 'Yes' [her left] and to Dermot for 'No' [her right]. Is that you in there with Sinead?"

As the glass moved, Sinead and Anthony conversed over the walkie-talkie. Normal service had resumed over the radio and the glass moved up to the left, towards Dominic's direction, to specify 'Yes'.

There's a really weird… Sinead was cut off once again before she could finish the sentence. On the video camera in the Red Room, she had described a weird vibe and had felt strange.

Back in the Factory Room, the female team member said, "Can you tweak Sinead on the shoulder… maybe knock on the door."

The glass swiftly moved across the table, knocking into a couple of cards, appearing to chiefly touch the 'Mercer' occupation card.

"Okay we're back to the cloth merchant."

"Did you use to work in this area?" enquired Anthony.

Sinead radioed in, sounding quite rattled and uneasy. *I'm literally shaking.*

Anthony offered reassurance back over the walkie-talkie. As he did so, the glass moved a medium, narrow, half, clockwise circle into the middle circle of cards and predominantly to 'Wright', which means 'Workman, especially construction worker'.

"There was roofers here too," explained Dermot.

The building would have had associations with many individuals, with numerous occupations over the years, so it is plausible that whatever was coming through had worked in such a role. The building was also adjacent to the Dublin Docklands, where construction workers used to congregate alongside many people, looking for manual labour on a daily basis.

In the Red Room, Sinead gazed into the mirror. "Come on," she said to herself, as she tried to keep composed. She sighed, expressing how tormented she felt as she bowed and stroked her forehead for comfort. She straightened her back, took a breath in and stared back into the mirror. Whatever she saw there made her sigh heavily again. The screeching whine from the glass's movement off the surface of the table, in the adjoining room, did not help either. It was getting stressful for her.

Returning to the Factory Room, the glass had moved to 'Faulkner', to signify 'Falconer' and again to 'Brewster', for 'Beer manufacturer'.

Sinead described, over the walkie-talkie, that a male presence had been in the room. Dominic notified Anthony about what he was sensing. "Ask her if the male is about fifty, with a black suit and grey hair," he said.

Anthony radioed in, passing on the message to Sinead.

The glass moved directly to the 'Saddler' occupation card, that signifies 'One who makes, repairs and sells saddles'.

Nearly half a minute later, Sinead replied, *Beard for definite here.*

Looking into the mirror she described a man with lots of facial hair and a skinny face.

In the meantime, the glass had taken a shine to the 'Currier' card, which means 'Cover of hides' and the 'Whistler' card, which indicated 'Cloth bleacher'.

A minute passed, with only the odd jolt from the glass as it moved a couple of inches, in a straight line, towards centre of the table.

In the Red Room, Sinead remarked that she was sensing a person who was really old and quite drunk. However, the walkie-talkie did not transmit her announcement.

"Okay Sinead? Over," said Anthony over the walkie-talkie.

Yeah. I'm good… really weird vibe here, like really like, I don't know, lots, lots of anger, answered Sinead.

Every time that Sinead picked up on something, the activity on the glass would cease, as if the Spirit was manoeuvring between the two rooms.

After some light-hearted laughs, Grace swapped seats with the female team member on the table. She connected on the base of the glass with Dermot. A switch of energy might see other Spirits come through, other than the one who had disappeared into the Red Room with Sinead.

My whole body has just started to shake, said Sinead nervously.

Nothing happened for about two minutes, until the glass finally moved, minimally, a couple of inches after the name 'Anne' was mentioned. This name was earlier described as being of importance.

Sinead radioed in again. *A Male, really dark features.*

"Do you know the man that's in the room with Sinead right now?" asked the female team member.

Scruffy, said Sinead on the walkie-talkie.

The names Ellen or Mary Ellen were being picked up by the female team member.

"Are you harlots?… That's a good thing; we have no judgement over you… It's the way to make a living."

It appeared that the Spirits were afraid to show themselves, hiding in the shadows.

Face just changed, said Sinead.

The female team member tried to be persuasive.

"What I'd like to do, just before we go, I'd like to see if we can get the pain reliever back… Hello misses, can we have you back please? Like I said we hold no judgement on you, in any manner whatsoever. Can we have the herbalist back? The woman who helped to euthanise, can you come back?"

There was little movement from the glass yet, very slowly, it did gradually end up at the 'Currier' card once more.

Sinead's walkie-talkie was cutting in and out of transmission. She was getting a person, with a small face, in their late thirties when focusing in on the mirror. Sinead looked tense and her breathing, at times, became shallow. She was also picking up on a factory worker, with a dark face covered in coal and somebody else who worked on the docks.

In the Factory Room, Dominic and the female team member connected back on the glass. The taper candle and pillar candle were removed from the table and placed on the ground.

"Okay, I want you to build up the energies, the fire is on the floor now."

The glass circled the table two-and-a-quarter times clockwise. It screeched around the table as it did so. It jolted and tilted on its rim twice. Dermot mentioned that he could feel considerable heat from it and the female team member could smell cooking.

The energy picked up as the glass shot off again, moving from half a clockwise circle to a wide, counter-clockwise, half circle and eventually moving through and displacing the middle formation of occupation cards. It turned when nearing the edge of the table and reverted, in a straight line, towards the middle again, showing no sign of stopping.

Meanwhile, Sinead's walkie-talkie seemed to have completely cut off. Anthony kept asking if she was alright but something was still stopping her from replying.

The glass continued to move, spiralling slowly in twelve small, counter-clockwise circles, before Dominic relinquished his touch on it. There seemed to be a difference of opinion about the temperature of the glass. The female team member felt a really cold draught on the glass.

"It's like there is a lamp under my hand," said Dermot.

"Well, I'm feeling really cold fucking breathing straight up my arm there," replied the female team member.

The glass responded by moving in a straight line, eight inches or so, stopping at the 'Sheriff' card, which means 'Sheriff'. Was it a warning that the police were coming?

"Are the police coming? Is the Dublin police coming, yeah…?" asked Anthony.

The female team member disconnected from the glass and sauntered off to collect Sinead, who had been scrying for over twenty minutes. The glass moved a slow, small, half, counter-clockwise circle, back to the 'Sheriff' card.

"… is the Dublin police coming? They come to close down all the brothels?"

The glass moved a few inches away, towards the centre of the table.

"… the Dublin police, to do with brothels?" said Anthony.

The glass moved very little: about an inch or so back towards the 'Sheriff' card.

"Did the police use your services?" asked Grace, sounding pleased.

The glass moved in a straight line, steadily pushing the 'Sheriff' card along a couple of inches.

It was Dominic's time to do some scrying in the Red Room, while Sinead joined the rest of the team and Dermot back at the Factory Room, for the next experiment. A planetary board (*See Glossary*) would be used next.

The team began to feel a sense of unease, as if a more restricted presence were around us. Perhaps an entity was preventing some other Spirits from coming through.

The planetary board had symbols of the common heavenly bodies visible from our own skies.

Sinead, Grace and Dermot connected on the upturned glass. Anthony remained filming with the night vision camera.

"Do you like science fiction comics?" asked Grace.

A sudden high pitch screech could be heard. It originated from the dynamic microphone above the table. It only lasted a couple of seconds.

Anthony murmured, "That's interesting, in it?"

The glass moved directly to the symbol for Jupiter, followed by the symbol of the Sun. This movement continued eleven consecutive times, before coming to a halt.

Jupiter indicates growth, expansion and healing, while the Sun signifies the universal father. Anthony alluded to the realisation that the Spirit might be trying to say 'God', the father, leading to the religious association with the street.

"Any high priestesses here?" asked the female team member.

The glass stopped immediately on the 'Sun' symbol, as if either stunned by the question or avoiding it completely – most likely the latter.

"Any nuns?"

The glass moved a couple of inches towards the centre of the board.

We assumed that the Spirit of a priest was present. He was told to step back. As a result, the glass moved in a straight line, stopping at the centre of the board.

Sinead asked, "Don't be afraid to come through. If anybody is in your way, don't let them."

The glass moved to the 'Sun' symbol, then it reversed directly, in the opposite direction, to the 'Saturn' symbol, which means man's material nature.

The priest was thought to be still with us.

The glass finished its action by returning to the 'Sun' symbol.

"What is this place to you?" said the female team member.

The glass moved in a straight line, eight inches or so to in between the 'Mars' and 'Venus' symbols. The Spirit may have been drawing our attention to man and woman.

Like with previous motions, the glass returned to the 'Sun' symbol.

Anthony emphatically called out, "Women, is it the women that you love? I bet its women you love; is that true, yeah?"

The glass responded by moving straight to the 'Venus' symbol, then returned to the 'Sun' symbol.

"Do you come here for sex?"

The glass moved across the board, in a straight line, seven inches or so to the 'Venus' symbol.

Staying within the vicinity of the Factory Room, we took out the direction board. It displays the four cardinal directions – North, South, East and West as well as the four intercardinal directions (Northeast, Southeast, Southwest and Northwest). We placed the board on the table, with all the points lined up like a compass, pointing accurately in each direction.

The purpose of the board, on this occasion, was to provide us with alternative answers to questions in relation to the activity in the building, such as any active areas or places of significance that the Spirits wished to disclose.

Sinead, Grace and Dermot connected with the glass at the centre of the board, while Anthony continued filming.

"What direction are you in at the moment?" asked Sinead.

The glass went in a direct route to the edge of the board, towards 'East – North – East'. It returned to the centre by moving a narrow, half, counter-clockwise circle.

"Northeast. Do you live northeast?" said the female team member.

The glass moved to the edge of the board, towards 'East'.

"Show us where your church is?"

The glass progressed to the opposing side of the board, to 'West' and then made a beeline for the centre.

"Show us where the castle is?"

There was no movement.

"Dublin Castle," said Grace.

The glass went to 'Northeast'.

"And show us where the tunnel is…" asked the female team member.

Before she could finish off the question, the glass retreated a couple of inches in a straight line towards centre.

"… to the castle?"

The glass quickly angled off in response to the 'East – North – East' direction.

Although the question referred to the castle tunnel, the Spirit coming through might have been directing us towards the Monto tunnels, which are now completely covered up.

Dermot began to tell us about the Monto tunnels that soldiers used, when frequenting the brothels from the Custom House (*See Glossary*) Quay. Also used by the upper class of society, the tunnels would provide a layer of secrecy to the whole situation. The shame associated with being caught, at the time, would have been especially costly if you were a notable and respected member of society in those days.

The glass had made its way back to the middle of the board, in advance of Anthony calling out the next question.

"Where? Which direction do you want us to go next… in this building?"

The glass moved back and forth in a line, an inch or so around the centre of the board, before confirming a position with a motion to 'East – South – East'.

This was the direction of the East Stairwell.

After a couple more questions, Anthony asked where the harlots or working girls were. In response to this, the glass ended up at the central point of the board. This pointed to the area that we were currently in, where the recording studios were situated.

The female team member responded, "That's very interesting. Can you tell us where we need to go next?"

The glass moved, at speed, towards the 'East - South - East' direction. No question about it - this intelligent, no-nonsense, matter of fact Spirit wanted us to head to the east side of the building, immediately.

The female team member left the room to check up on Dominic. During his scrying stint, he described being hit by small stones on his left shoulder. He sensed that the room was a prop department of the building and he could see a Spirit of a prop manager in the mirror. He also picked up on a blonde woman, being at the other side of the building (East), who worked in the wardrobe department, bringing people up for fittings.

Grace swapped with Dominic for the final scrying session in the Red Room.

The team started gathering up equipment from other areas of the building, except for the female team member, who went down to the first floor of the East Stairwell, for a solo separation calling-out vigil. As she arrived at the first-floor landing, she mentioned a very cold draught on her left side.

The area was quite lit up, so there was no need for the infrared function on the camera. It was switched to the normal daylight setting. She placed the camera down on the stairs in front of her, facing it towards the landing wall. She squatted with her back against the wall, within the sight of the camera. A beautiful, life-like mural of a large face was painted on the wall behind her. She called out for any energy to step forward, then closed her eyes and remained silent. Over a minute later, she opened her eyes and began to talk.

"There is a sense of being watched… and it doesn't feel horrible, just watched."

She attributed this sensation to the Spirit of Mary Ellen. Later, she expressed that she had a feeling of being tickled and lightly blown on the head. Grace did not seem to detect anything out of the ordinary in her scrying time in the Red Room.

We moved down to the Rehearsal Corridor for the last experiment: table tilting. It was after half past four in the morning. Although weary, we fancied just a bit more interaction with the Spirit world.

The area was now lit up, in stark contrast to the earlier foreboding darkness and noises that had accompanied it. Anthony, Grace and the female team member stood around a small table, each placing their fingertips lightly on top of it. They called out for the table to be moved. Dominic began playing the piano in one of the adjacent rooms, hoping that creating a musical environment could summon in more Spirits.

The continued encouragement had no appeal, yet it looked as if Anthony's arms were shaking, suggesting the table might be moving too. Incantations were used to invite but, there was no movement recognised from the table.

Members of the team felt increasingly impatient, as they knew they were running out of time. Akin to being just short of the finish line during a race, all emotional effort was brought forward, to spur on any activity. Now, everyone meant business. All vocal tones were raised and commanding.

Anthony called out, "The Dublin police are coming in, come on step forward, you got-"

The female team member interjected, "The RIC are here. Quick, quick, quick. Leg it, leg it, leg it. Come on, come on down the tunnel, down the tunnel. You get caught with your pants down, mate, you've had it. Come on, come on, it's a court martial."

"Come on, build the energies up," said Anthony.

The female team member remarked that she felt a really cold breeze on top of her hands. There were a few more interchanges between team members on the table but the energy had completely dissipated. We stepped back from the table and called it a night.

With a long journey back for Anthony, Jen and the female team member, cases and bags of equipment were packed into the car and, after a hot drink to revitalise ourselves, it was time to say our goodbyes.

We kept thinking about what it must have been like for the women back then, focused on survival rather than embracing life. The emphasis on the Catholic Church cleaning the place up and, putting many of them into Magdalene Laundries, would have added another layer to the type of destiny many had.

The investigation at Applerock proved to be calm, if lamenting and opened the doors to energies who seemed to crave a sense of longing. The trepidation of the Spirits coming forward was palpable - with hesitation, they let themselves be known. However, the demanding characters were also present, which created some friction. The theme seemed to revolve around *Religion vs Sin* - or, in this case, objectionable sin.

For the existing Spirits, the ones who perished within the area, we hoped that we provided them a beacon of hope and encouragement, listening to them without judgement, like counsellors.

One thing that will never to be forgotten is the ladies of 'The Monto', who should be remembered for their bravery in the face of all that they endured, each day of their lives. We were delighted to have given them a chance to speak, alongside the others who came through as well. Perhaps they could now move on and forgive themselves, without fearing what would come next.

An overhead view of the Factory Room and a dark, inaccessible doorway opposite – the attic

The séance, about to start, with the microphone set up, ready to enhance any sound phenomenon

A rehearsal room: some strange voices have been picked up in music sessions

Another view of the Factory Room

Looking onto the entrance and some beautiful artwork

The annex room – the safe haven for the night

Anthony is in the background of the Rehearsal Corridor. The trigger object, a baby doll, is set up with a pillow

The Red Room. A scrying experiment is ready to go

***Drowned-Out Voices* Investigation footage can be viewed by**

Watching the DVD that accompanies this book

Scanning the QR code

Visiting our website
www.GhostÉire.net

Click on the button
Drowned-Out Voices Footage

and enter the password
YourNotAlone

Enter the password
YourNotAlone

Location Background/Biography

The Applerock Studios are based at the address of 17/21 Foley Street, formerly named 'Montgomery Street', after Luke Gardiner's wife, Elizabeth Montgomery.

In its heyday, between 1860 and 1920, it is estimated that up to 1600 prostitutes worked in this district, making it the biggest red-light area in Europe at that time. 'Monto', as it was known locally, was contained roughly within the boundaries of Talbot Street, Gardiner Street and Sean McDermott Street (formerly Gloucester Street).

All different manner of customers were catered for.

It was enshrined as 'Nighttown' in the *Circe* chapter of the novel, *Ulysses* by famous Irish writer, James Joyce.

The then Prince of Wales, King Edward VII is said to have frequented the streets of Monto and, allegedly, lost his virginity there.

Its sustainability came from soldiers working in the British Army Barracks.

Monto was very active in IRA pursuit, particularly during the time of Irish War of Independence, 1919-1922 (*See Glossary*) when safe houses (such as former Sinn Féin politician, Phil Shanahan's public house) were used by flying columns (*See Glossary*) to prevent disclosure.

With the growing population, both poverty and disease were rife in the capital. Foley's Street was well known to be the 'smothering den' – a place to help critically ill people, on their deathbed, to receive a quick end with a pillow over the face.

The trade of sexual services was quickly dented by the withdrawal of soldiers subsequent to the Anglo-Irish Treaty of 1921 and the establishment of the Irish Free State in 1922 (*See Glossary*).

From 1923-1925, a Roman Catholic organisation called the Legion of Mary, founded by Frank Duff and a Fr R.S. Devane, worked to close down the brothels. In co-operation with the Dublin Metropolitan Police, in March 1925 they managed to make 120 arrests, after closing down all the brothels.

L.S. Ramsay Ltd, a clothing manufacturer, had operated on the second floor of the site of Applerock Studios. Among their clients were Princess Diana, Queen Elizabeth II and the Queen Mother.

A fiesta ballroom (type of playboy club) operated on the site. It was also used by radio stations, as a broadcasting facility.

Manifestation/Legend

Shadows of people have been seen inside and outside the building.

In Rehearsal Room 1, an unexplainable voice was picked up on recording equipment, as a band was practicing.

A feeling of presences has been picked up by the owner, workers, visitors and musicians at the studio.

Conclusion

There was considerable sensation felt throughout the investigation including, as expected, a large amount during the séance.

As a group, individuals are able relay their emotions and physical feelings out to others. This could either help or hamper a possible outcome. A person might be only willing to comment if they hear that another person has a similar experience beforehand. This can assist in backing up what has been felt.

Yet, in some cases, primary statements might be misleading, (giving a wrong impression) misinterpreted (perceived by others wrongly) and they could be stating the obvious (for instance, feeling a cold draught with windows and doors open in a building, in the middle of winter). We have to look at those supporting comments that stick out.

Anthony expressed twice that he felt a cold draught on his hands, especially on his right hand. As the conversation turned to women of the cloth (perhaps nuns), Anthony was first to feel a warmth on his back. The female team member concurred that she had the same experience.

Shortly afterwards, Anthony could feel a presence between him and Dominic, when a question was asked about payment for smothering. Fascinating was the fact that Dominic felt someone touching his left shoulder (towards Anthony's right). It was not the first time that a strange presence had been sensed.

Did a religious order do the smothering? They may have had no other option than to do so, due to the unyielding, slow and fatal infectious diseases in the area, which needed to be stamped out – Monto being the epicentre.

Smothering (using a pillow or one's own hands to cover mouth and nose) would limit the physical injuries to a victim. Therefore, if they were already ill, it could go unrecognised.

Sexually transmitted diseases, such as herpes and syphilis, can affect the lungs and heart and asphyxia (deficient oxygen supply to the body) could come from respiratory diseases, which might be mistaken for causing death, instead of a premeditated killing. Were babies smothered too and, if so, by whom?

There was obscure whistling on the night vision camera at the start of the séance. The camera might have been picking up on the recording of a baby crying below, in the Rehearsal Corridor.

The harrowing experiment, involving the baby doll, might have given some insight as to why the shouting of a woman could be heard, possibly in grief, as Anthony talked about it being a long time since there had been communication. In such a short space of time, there were the sounds of both wailing and humming. These are very good voice phenomena to have occurred. They came from outside the Factory Room but, in close range – inside the building.

The table violently shook at the mention of hate towards one's age group. There may have been a feeling of remorse.

When talking about offloading children, the taper candle fell to the side of the table. The taper candle could have been already unstable in the spirit bottle and the motion of the table might have picked up, at that stage, as a result of Anthony rocking back and forth. The candle incident came just shortly after the question about payment for smothering and, a presence was felt between Anthony and Dominic.

It is hard to say if we were in close proximity of a parent or a member of a religious order – or both. Overlaying (smothering, in bed, of children who slept with parents) was a frequent form of infanticide (killing of one's own child) in the nineteenth century. Suspicion of murder was low, unless stabbing and beatings occurred.

The names Anne, Rosie and Mary Ellen were mentioned in the investigation. Without surnames, it is hard to be sure that these Spirits were with us.

In the late nineteenth century, an Anne McEachern (Annie Mack) ran top-end brothels (she may have owned eleven houses) in and around Montgomery Street, where beautiful women attracted rich clients, including, potentially, the aforementioned Edward VII.

A Dublin newspaper wrote, in 1879, that Annie Mack was fined after a large supply of liquor was found, on sale, at one of her premises. It was not the last time that she was charged with storing liquor on her property. Madams were often prosecuted for sale of drink after hours and, without a licence.

Annie is believed to be a native of Scotland (born in 1830) and had moved back to her homeland before she died, in 1907.

In the occupation cards the profession of providing beer from a cask was selected. Later, the Brewster card was also chosen - a beer manufacturer. A Brewer is the term used in southern England, while Brewster is chiefly used in midlands, northern England and Scotland. Was this Annie Mack?

Drover (One who moves sheep and cattle from one place to the other) was determined by the Spirit to be the best card and Currier as the worst card. Both of these cards have cattle as their theme.

A Currier would treat skins and hides of animals to produce leather, which was then passed on to the fashion industry. The leather would also be used in saddlery. The Spirit might have displayed a dislike to the process of skinning an animal. Curriers would dye and use certain chemicals to colour the leather.

The Mercer occupation card – cloth merchant (quite significant) – was picked up on three separate occasions, whilst Whistler – cloth bleacher – was selected at one point. It seemed that we were progressing through to the period when the building was used to produce clothing and accessories, though the session ended with the Sheriff card being of value. The brothel raids of Monto come to mind.

During the occupation cards experiment, the glass seemed to remain still when Sinead radioed in, as she described her feelings in the Red Room. The Factory Room showed signs of being void of any Spirit at that time. Nevertheless, the concentration of the participants, who were connected on the glass, might have been diverted to Sinead's situation, so its stillness was expected.

Dominic got the sense, as he was scrying, that there was a blonde woman, who did wardrobe fittings on the east side of the building.

He also sensed a prop manager coming through, which could be assigned to the assumed past of the building as a theatre.

Sinead had picked up on a factory worker with a dark face (covered in dirt) and a person that worked on the docks. Twice, she mentioned seeing an old person (in their fifties or sixties) who was hostile. There was nothing to distinguish between the entity being male or female and when it was present, Sinead's body shook. Again, we are left clueless without any names for these Spirits.

It was thought that a Priest was coming through on the planetary board, considering the symbols that the planchette had gone to. Father Richard Devane played a pivotal part in helping women escape prostitution. Before the raids were carried out in 1925, priests had visited Monto, to give the impression they were taking notes of any men who were attending the brothels. Behind the women, who were well dressed and tidy, there was another class left suffering. Many of them were alcoholics, who had been on the game for years and needed help.

The high-pitched squeal from the dynamic microphone might be because of the night vision camera that Anthony was holding. He was standing over the planetary board, close to the dynamic microphone at the time, which probably caused the distortion.

With the direction board, the Spirit was presumed to be in the same course as a tunnel at East — North — East. There are tunnels underneath Dublin, with one that reportedly runs from Monto to the Custom House. These tunnels were mainly used for the brothels, so that well-known clients could go on impulse or, make a quick escape. However, Custom House is south of Foley Street. There may have been a tunnel (East — North — East) underneath, which extended from the boundary of the former red-light district to where Amiens Street is today.

The glass went to Northeast, for Dublin Castle. This is wrong. The castle is situated southwest from Foley Street.

The Spirit did identify that prostitutes were situated exactly where we were in the studio: the glass moved to the centre of the direction board.

There was nothing to note from the full spectrum camera recording in the Rehearsal Corridor or, from the digital sound recorder in Rehearsal Room 1.

Changes in the table tilting were negligible and are not worth considering, as the team's attention dwindled.

Applerock Studios
Co Dublin

The building is now under private ownership.
We thank Dermot for his time in helping in our
studies.

OLD CORK WATERWORKS

Layout

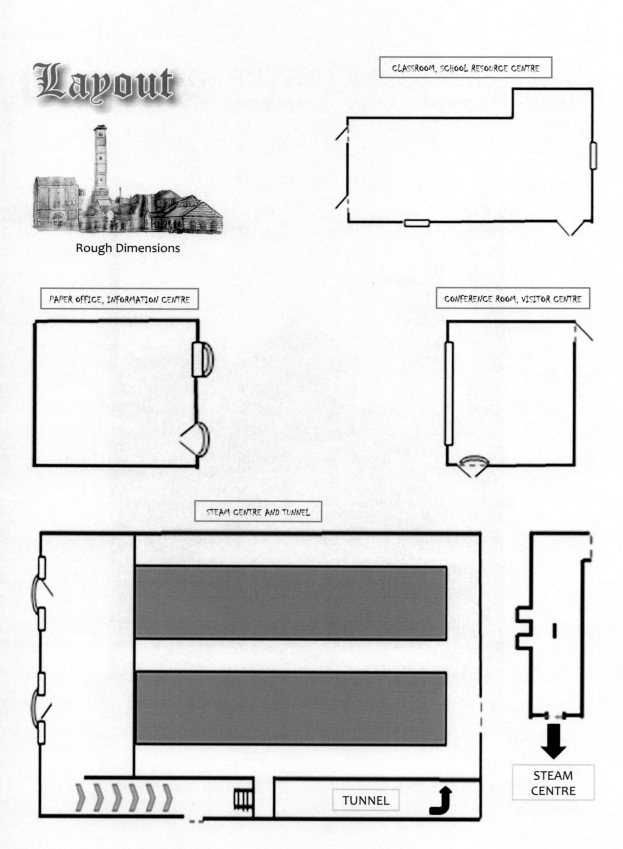

Rough Dimensions

CLASSROOM, SCHOOL RESOURCE CENTRE

PAPER OFFICE, INFORMATION CENTRE

CONFERENCE ROOM, VISITOR CENTRE

STEAM CENTRE AND TUNNEL

TUNNEL

STEAM CENTRE

Chapter 17

Old Cork Waterworks

Anthony's Journey

As you come along the Carrigrohane Road, heading into Cork City, there on the left, above the River Lee, are some of the finest examples of red-bricked Victorian structures. On the northern bank of the Lee Road stands the Old Cork Waterworks. Above that is Saint Kevin's Hospital, which was built in 1893 and operated as a mental asylum.

It was not Saint Kevin's that fascinated me; it was the building below it. A tall chimney had me captivated. We had done an interview on a local Cork community radio station. The radio presenter, curious as to our plans for the future, asked us about places we intended or would like to explore. The Old Cork Waterworks was mentioned.

We left details on how the public could contact us, if they had any locations that we should follow up around the Cork City area. To my astonishment, I got a message from Mervyn Horgan, manager of the Old Cork Waterworks and Lifetime Lab, which welcomed us to come visit and carry out a paranormal investigation.

It took nearly eighteen months to actually commence the investigation, due to family commitments and holidays. A female team member and I managed to pay a visit on an afternoon in May. After parking the car up across the way, beside the River Lee, we crossed the road and walked up a series of steps (you can also take a lift).

We met Mervyn in the Visitor Centre, where we would be given a guided tour of the buildings. There is a Conference Room to the left as you walk in, toilets to the far left and a cafeteria and reception desk straight ahead. To the right is the interactive, multimedia area. Here, children and adults can be educated in the field of sustainability and recycling, in the former Engine Rooms of the Waterworks plant.

When we retreated back out of the Visitor Centre, we saw a marquee to our right as we stepped on cobblestones. Twenty metres ahead, to our left, was the Steam Centre with the hundred-foot chimney beside it. I was busy taking pictures with my disposable (celluloid film) camera (*See Equipment*). I had to tilt my head back to get the height of the chimney into the view of my lens.

We walked towards the Steam Centre, opening large glass doors to where the boilers are. The opened cast-iron doors give one an example of how high the coal had to be lifted over, waist height, into the stove of the boilers. The two boilers are about ten foot in height. Beside them, on the right, is a ramp that leads up to a viewing station. It overlooks three triple extension engines, which are situated opposite on a lower steel platform.

Moving from the Steam Centre, out the glass doors to our right, is the School Resources Centre (formerly a weigh house). To the left is a lane, closed off by an iron gate. This was the entry-point, where coal used to be brought in by horse and cart and weighed. A couple of metres outside of the School Resources Centre were the old scales. A ramp led up towards the door.

Upon entering the building, to our right there was a Classroom. Desks and chairs filled the room, situated in view of a whiteboard. Posters on the wall gave an insight into the local wildlife.

We left the School Resources Centre and headed back into the Visitor Centre. We sat down in the cafeteria and chatted with Mervyn about what we do and to set a date to return. We settled for a date within the upcoming weeks. I left with a happy smile, feeling delighted at the prospect of touching another part of history, intent and industry.

Jen, who would not be attending the investigation due to work commitments, had a dream a few days before our return to the Waterworks. She had a vision of a blonde girl, aged around six or seven. There were children playing on a red-cobbled street, with other people around. The dream continued onto the inside of the building, with the blonde girl, coated in black soot, inside a tunnel or archway. She wanted some paper and colours to draw with. It made me think of including an experiment featuring automatic drawing/writing (*See Glossary*) in the investigation.

The day came for our return. There would be only four of us in the team heading up to Cork. Two volunteers would meet us later that evening, to open the building and to lend any support or help if needed.

I remember parking the car up in a private carpark allocated for the museum. Shane sat in the passenger seat beside me. We talked about the weather conditions. It was late June but it had been raining all day and it was muggy. I heard a loud noise overhead. I looked up and saw a plane flying at a low altitude. Visibility might have been hard coming into land or, the pilots were trying to avoid the moisture-laden clouds.

I took pictures of the outside of the Waterworks with a full spectrum camera. Not many pictures however, as it was starting to rain again.

The female team member had arrived and she parked up in the same carpark as we did. We unloaded the cars and brought the equipment up the steps, into the Visitor Centre.

The semi-final of the Euros (football) was on - Spain against Portugal. This absorbed the interest of the male volunteer, who was content to watch the match on his laptop behind the reception desk.

I received a phone call. Sinead had arrived in Cork City by bus from Dublin. She was finding it hard to get directions to the Waterworks. The female team member went out in her car to collect her.

I walked around the buildings, accompanied by Shane, to conduct baseline tests. We would focus on the Conference Room in the Visitor Centre, the Steam Centre and the Classroom in the School Resource Centre. We also added the Paper Office in the Information Centre (not mentioned before), situated across from the Steam Centre.

After this, I had trouble in finding an extra extension lead to help plug in an oscillating machine (*See Equipment*), with the intent of this helping guide a video camera to scan a larger area of the Classroom in the School Resource Centre. I could not find one, so this did not happen.

I received another phone call. The female team member and Sinead were finding it hard to locate each other. Sinead was now told to stay put and not wander around, so the female team member could pick her up more easily.

We had now been at the Waterworks for an hour and a half. The rain was now coming down in buckets - so heavy that it made difficult to get around to each building.

I had setup a chair and a table in the Steam Centre, upon which I placed the Frank's Box with attaching speakers. A lamp mechanism for a strobe lighting experiment was positioned alongside the oscillating machine and video camera. They were laid out in view of the chair and table. This would be hub for the separation (*See Glossary*) vigils later.

We were ready to start. We had to wait a little longer for Sinead and the female team member to arrive. Shane and I had to play the waiting game.

The rain was pouring down. I took more pictures with the full spectrum camera from inside the School Resource Centre, looking opposite out towards the Steam Centre and the River Lee below it. We seemed trapped by the elements but, I did not envisage what was going to happen later that night.

The Investigation

NUMBER OF TEAM **4**

2 NUMBER OF GUESTS

We had set our sights on the Old Cork Waterworks and had finally reached our destination. Our clothes were soaked through from the heavy downpours but, even this could not sour our excitement.

Almost two hours after we initially arrived, the female team member and Sinead finally showed up and joined Anthony and the Shane in the School Resource Centre. It was approaching half nine in the evening. The forecast for the night was for sprinkles but this severely underestimated the weather that was to come.

The humidity was high, at 86.6% and the temperature inside and outside was measured at 21.1°C. There was a high concentration of moisture in the air due to the heavy rains, which increased the false anomaly risk. It would affect our recording equipment.

There was not much EMF in the four buildings. Only the compression box in the Steam Centre recorded 0.1 milliGauss. There were only 2 milliGauss recorded where the old coal shoot used to be, on the north-western outside wall of the Conference Room.

As some of the team took a breather, the rest of us set upon starting the first experiment. This would be away from the School Resource Centre, which unfortunately, looking back, appeared to be the most active area/room.

Sinead, Anthony and Shane gathered at the Conference Room in the Visitor Centre. This room had originally been used to store coal. Rows of singular seats faced a white science lab workstation, with a white board to the left of it. Underfoot was a blueish/greyish carpet. The walls were decorated with black-and-white pictures.

We would be doing some automatic drawing/writing. We might be able to shine a light upon Jen's dream of the young girl who wanted to draw.

Sinead and Shane sat in front of a workstation, facing each other. Both sat upright. Placed on top of each of their laps were cardboard folders acting as easels, to support the A4, white, blank piece of paper that they would be drawing or writing on.

Anthony blindfolded them. He wrapped fabric bandages around their heads to cover their eyes. For the duration of this three-part vigil, they would both have to forgo their sense of sight.

Anthony placed a K2 meter alongside a modern, gothic hourglass on the floor, in between where Sinead and Shane were sitting. Using just their sense of touch, Sinead and Shane randomly selected a coloured marker pen from a cardboard casing, which Anthony was holding in front of them. Sinead picked a grey marker pen to use, whilst Shane picked a yellow marker pen.

Anthony started recording with the night vision camera. The camera was left on a normal daylight setting, as the room was well lit up. No need to go into night mode just yet. He turned the hourglass over. Grains of orange sand trickled down to the bottom compartment.

Anthony explained to both team members that they would hear certain noises. These would be coming from the sound monitor.

"Sorry, I just want you to relax, blank your mind out."

He pressed a button on the sound monitor. The sound of running stream water was heard.

Anthony continued, "I'm going to be silent for about five minutes there so, block, blank your mind, whatever comes in, let it come in."

Both Sinead and Shane gently gripped the coloured marker pen that they had chosen. The tips of the pens were lightly touching the sheets of paper.

Anthony explained, "If you're feeling anything emotional, just speak up and say it if you can and the camera will pick it up."

Sinead started to scribble. She was drawing lines a couple of inches in size with synchronised strokes on the top left of the paper.

With the night vision camera, Anthony zoomed out and zoomed back in on the hourglass. He took a few steps forward then concentrated the camera on the K2 meter, which was on a constant green light (giving a reading of below 1.5 milliGauss). No shift in the circumstances. He slowly zoomed out.

He moved the camera to Sinead on his right. She was starting to draw wavy lines around the centre of the sheet of paper. Shane seemed content but drew little, without the same sense of intention and purposefulness as Sinead.

Anthony panned the camera to his right, to scan the pictures on the wall. One picture included the boilers in the Steam Centre being loaded with coal, shovelled in by a labourer. He then spanned the night vision camera back left, a full 360° and did the same again, this time turning right, trying to get good scope of the room. He set his camera back on the K2 meter.

Sinead was now drawing around the top-right corner of the sheet of paper. The drawing appeared to be divided into three sections. After four minutes had passed, Anthony called out, "You got one minute left."

He looked in on the hourglass and saw the bottom half was full: time had run out. Anthony turned off the night vision camera.

Sinead's drawing was separated into three parts of wriggly vertical lines. The centre section seemed to depict a style of dress worn by Victorian or Edwardian women. It seemed to show a large round hat, head, torso with cleavage and flowing wriggly lines at the lower area, where legs should be. The right section looked like a series of boxes or squares.

Sinead and Shane received another blank sheet of A4, white paper from Anthony, for the second session of automatic drawing/writing. They both switched to different coloured marker pens. Shane picked a brown marker pen while Sinead picked out a blue marker pen. Anthony coordinated the next stage. He switched on the night vision camera to record and prepared to press a button on the sound monitor.

"Okay now, folks, umm, the sound you're going to be hearing now is … thunder."

He pushed the button on the sound monitor. The crackling of thunder that it played added more hype to the occasion. Sinead stroked the paper with the top of the marker pen. Her right arm was fully rested in front of her, as she lightly gripped the pen with her thumb and index finger.

Anthony took a few steps forward, then knelt on one leg and turned the hourglass upside down, to time the session. He repositioned the K2 meter, placing it in front of the hourglass.

Sinead started to quicken her touch on the sheet of paper.

Anthony stood upright, to relieve the stress on his legs from kneeling. He pointed the night vision camera towards the door behind him, then he swung back left, to bring Sinead and Shane, the K2 meter and the hourglass into sight. He zoomed back in to what Sinead was drawing. For the next three minutes, her drawing became more erratic, with various concentrations of detail across numerous areas of the sheet.

The top half of the hourglass was empty, indicating that five minutes had passed. Anthony ended the recording and brought the second session to an end. Shane, as in the first session, added minimal detail to his drawing. Sinead, however, scribbled on the sheet of paper what looked like the letter 'T' or a cross. At the centre, above the centre and at the top right corner of the sheet, she drew a series of looped circles and wriggly lines. It was spread out at the top, giving it the likeness of smoke engulfing the ceiling of a room. At the bottom right corner of the sheet, she had written what seemed to be the number '8', followed by something resembling the number '9' or the letter 'g'. Below these markings there was something that resembled a thickly drawn signature.

It was now coming up to eleven o'clock. For the final automatic drawing/writing session, Shane picked out a black marker pen, whilst Sinead picked out a light green marker pen. Anthony began recording once more with the night vision camera, having flipped back over the hourglass. He pressed another button on the sound monitor.

"White noise."

What came from the sound monitor sounded like a constant flow of static.

After a couple of minutes, Anthony directed the camera to observe upon Sinead's drawing. She was drawing shapes and symbols this time, on different areas of the paper.

Time passed and then Anthony gave a one-minute warning. The final grains of sand fell onto the bottom of the hourglass and the session came to a close shortly after.

Sinead had drawn what looked like a triangular tree trunk. Straight above, it was a both pointy and curved shape, which resembled the leafy crown of the tree. At the centre of the page, there seemed to be an arrow pointing to wavy horizontal lines and straighter vertical lines, along with several looped shapes underneath. These configurations looked like ankle-high boots or some other certain footwear. She drew what looked like an 'S' at the top left of the sheet. Alongside this there is what could be either a triangle or else an arrow, which pointed to the 'S'.

Anthony, Sinead and Shane vacated the Conference Room in the Visitor Centre. Sinead went to join the female team member in the Paper Office at the Information Centre. Anthony and Shane went over to the Steam Centre. As they walked in, a dim motion light was activated. It was still dark enough to proceed with the next experiment. This was where Shane would remain for the next half an hour, alone with the Frank's Box on in the background, in a separation calling-out vigil.

Shane sat on the chair that Anthony had readied earlier. He would be blindfolded for the whole vigil. The green strobe lamp was switched on and the light flickered across Shane. Being much darker meant it was more effective. Shane clutched the Frank's Box in his left hand. It was already scanning the airwaves. On the table beside Shane was a small black speaker, connected by a lead to the Frank's Box and the digital sound recorder, which Anthony had gotten prepared and started recording. Two doorway motion detectors were positioned, facing each other, on the ramp that led up to the viewing station. An infrared beam was discharged about three feet across to the other, a few inches off the ground. They were set-up a couple of metres behind Shane's left shoulder.

Anthony picked up the walkie-talkie and tested it to see if it was working, communicating with the female team member in the Information Centre. All was loud and clear. Anthony put the walkie-talkie on the table. He placed a K2 meter, face-up, in Shane's right hand. This would help pick out any changes in the EMF through the flickering of lights. The walkie-talkie would not be touched unless necessary, like if the individuals alone in that room felt compromised.

Anthony left the Steam Centre and walked to the Information Centre, the smallest building at the Waterworks. Inside were Sinead and the female team member, sat around a desk opposite each other. An empty chair was on the smaller width of the desk beside them.

A talking board was placed at centre of the desk with an upturned glass situated at its centre. To the left of the talking board was the hourglass, a torch, the body mood doll and a brass school bell. Anthony held the night vision camera. This time, in the darker room, it needed to go into infrared mode.

Anthony turned the hourglass over and radioed into Shane, "… you can ask away questions now; we are starting the experiment."

Over at the Steam Centre Shane had started to call out.

"Hi, anybody would like to talk to us lads… I'm just here to say hi, say hello?"

Coming from the Frank's Box, two replies came about a second apart, both saying, 'Yes' very clearly. Half a minute later, he asked, "Are you from Cork?"

Another two replies could be heard from the Frank's Box saying, 'Yes'. The first reply sounded masculine, the second feminine.

He asked the same question again, "Are you from Cork?" A quick reply from the Frank's Box seemed to state the word, 'City'.

He moved on to asking, "Were you working here long… five years maybe?"

An interesting sound came back. It seemed to be the sound of a door slamming shut. Five seconds later, a masculine voice said,

'Six', quickly followed by a voice saying, 'Seven' and moments after that, another voice that said, 'Eight'.

A few minutes after this, another reply was heard from the Frank's Box saying, 'Tyler', in reference to asking for a name. Sobbing, crying and high-pitched wailing could also be heard.

Back at the Paper Office in the Information Centre, the female team member and Sinead connected with their index fingers on the base of a glass. We all introduced ourselves, calling out our names. We figured out what was likely around us. Names were coming through, which we assumed were associated with the location: 'Mac', 'Collette', 'McCarthy' and 'O'Sullivan'. However, there was no movement on the glass.

Anthony turned his attention to what was around the room. The room consisted of filing cabinets. We were in a compact space. Anthony called out a summoning-in prayer but the glass remained still. Anthony turned off the torch that had been placed on the desk. Although we were only four minutes into the vigil, with the lack of activity, it felt as though time was passing by far too slowly.

Anthony and Sinead called out in Irish.

Anthony suddenly got distracted, "Wow! White light, flash outside the window there."

He walked a few steps over to a small window on the right. He directed the night vision camera to the buildings opposite: the Visitors Centre and the Steam Centre. Anthony was astonished, unable to believe his eyes. "That was a massive flash."

He turned the night vision camera back and walked a few steps to where had previously been watching the talking board.

"It could be lightning; I don't know where it's coming from."

The team returned their concentration to the glass. Excited, they began to ask questions in rhyme.

Sinead asked, "Do you like it here?"

A second or two later Anthony heard something.

"Oh… thunder."

There were smiles all round as the team experienced the clap of thunder and flash of lightning. They felt safe and charged in energy but the realisation that a storm was brewing above our heads also gave rise to a pinch of uncertainty. Would this bring the night's investigation to a whole new level?

Anthony talked about the sound monitor in the previous experiment. "That's interesting; we had the thunderstorm here in the automatic writing."

The female team member stated that she could feel the glass was rocking on its spot.

Anthony walked back to the window on his right. He directed the night vision camera towards the Steam Centre, where Shane remained by himself. An outside spotlight only offered a small degree of glare on the glass doors of the Steam centre. Inside, the motion sensor light was still on but Anthony saw that it was still very shaded and dark within. Anthony returned to the desk and sat on the seat that he sat on previously, to get comfortable.

The glass was visibly shaking. It got increasingly pronounced, starting to tap the surface of the board. Anthony called out, "There no need to be scared either. We're not here to harm you."

The glass moved a couple of inches then slanted in the direction of the female team member.

Sinead asked, "Are you a man?"

The glass returned, with all its rim touching the board, immediately moving in half of a clockwise circle to '1'.

The glass tilted several times in different directions, gradually making its way back to centre of the board.

Sinead asked, "Did you work here?"

The glass started to shudder on the spot again.

"Kevin's; do you know Kevin's hospital?"

The glass rattled off the surface of the board, making three rapid thuds on the board before moving in a straight line to in between '1' and '2'.

We directed our questions to Saint Kevin's Hospital, situated on the bank above us.

Anthony radioed in on the walkie-talkie, asking Shane to stop asking questions and remain silent for now. Shane yielded to what was going to be asked from the Paper Office. Anthony followed up by talking through the walkie-talkie. "Are you from Saint Kevin's Hospital? Over."

All was still with the glass in the Paper Office.

Anthony radioed in again. "Are you O'Sullivan?"

The questions could be heard in the Steam Centre. About seven seconds later, the video camera in the Steam Centre picked up a voice from the Frank's Box, which was high pitched and seemingly in distress, that said, 'Take me too'.

Back in the Paper Office, the glass started to rock on its spot again. The team were discussing certain countries of origin. Anthony radioed in again, this time speaking in Irish. "Are you English?"

Five seconds later, to the same question in the Steam Centre, a feminine voice from the Frank's Box clearly said, 'Who did?'

Meanwhile, the glass in the Paper Office moved to in between '2' and '3'. Sinead was starting to feel shivers. Anthony got on the walkie-talkie again. "Are you twenty-three years old?"

At the Steam Centre, six seconds after the question was asked, a muffled reply could be heard on the Frank's Box saying, 'Thirty'.

The glass remained still after several more questions were asked. It was placed back to the centre of the board.

We turned our attention to religion. We asked the Spirit if it had a connection to being Catholic. The glass tilted and swung on its rim for a couple of seconds. Anthony radioed in. "Are you Catholic?"

A mixed arrangement of vocals came back, from the Frank's Box, in response to this question. Some replies seemed to indicate agreement whereas, others were groans or grunts. Half a minute later, Anthony told Shane that he could resume calling out.

Returning to the Paper Office, the glass was steadily shaking at the centre of the board. It was steadily shaking. During this time, Anthony wandered back to the window and gazed out towards the Steam Centre.

The team discussed some ideas about what they thought happened around the Waterworks. Sinead mentioned fire. Anthony went back on the walkie-talkie again, to tell Shane to be silent. He followed up by radioing in. "Was there a fire around here?"

The female team member concluded that present there was a little girl, around the age of seven or eight, who had died in a fire.

Anthony recalled what Jen had witnessed in her dream, "This is interesting. I remember Jen saying to this, we should use pictures and drawing, young kid, young child, wants to draw."

Sinead and the female team member stared back over at Anthony. The glass could be heard gently clattering on the board. Realising that Shane's half of the vigil had finished, Sinead began to feel spooked. She was to take over from Shane, to be on her own in the Steam Centre.

Anthony headed over towards the Steam Centre. Thankfully, all was fine with Shane. He seemed undeterred by what was going on. On the video camera, when Shane asked, "Can you come and touch me? Can you touch my arm?", a reply could be heard from the Frank's Box saying, 'Yes'.

Later, when the team were picking up the young girl in the Paper Office, Anthony had radioed in to ask, *Do you like to draw pictures?*

A couple of seconds later, a voice could be heard softly saying, 'Yeah' followed by a much swifter masculine voice saying, 'Yes'.

After a short conversation Shane and Anthony departed from the Steam Centre. Anthony then returned with Sinead, to do the second separation, calling-out vigil of the night.

The two entered the room through the glass door. The video camera was still recording on the oscillating machine, with the green strobe lighting ongoing. Sinead sat down on the chair in front of the video camera. Anthony told Sinead to hold the Frank's Box and to press a button on it, should it stop scanning. He also handed her the K2 meter. Sinead grasped it in her right hand. Anthony proceeded to blindfold Sinead.

Sinead and Anthony discussed the requirements for the experiment. As they did, a deep voice came up on the recording. It sounded like it was saying, 'She looks pretty'.

No one heard it.

Sinead let out a tense shudder. "Oh God!"

She was preparing herself to be alone. Anthony turned the digital sound recorder back on and took some pictures with the full spectrum camera. Sinead let out a nervous cough, "I feel a bit spooked."

Anthony reassured her, "Don't worry, just stay with it."

He then exited the room, back through the glass doors. Over thirty seconds later, as Sinead awaited instruction through the walkie-talkie, a voice could be heard from the Frank's Box saying, 'Hello'.

Anthony made his way back to the Paper Office. He sat down where Sinead had been sitting previously. The upturned glass was placed on the desk, an equal distance between Anthony and the female team member. We would be doing glass divination.

The talking board had been repositioned on the desk, in front of the vacant empty chair to Anthony's right and the female team member's left. The bottom right corner of the board was marked 'No', to Anthony's near right whilst the bottom left corner of the board, which was marked 'Yes', was to the female team member's near left.

Anthony talked into the walkie-talkie. "Okay Sinead, you can ask questions. Fire away. Over."

He reached out to the hourglass on the far side of the desk and turned it upside down. The vigil had started. He placed his right index finger on the glass and the female team member connected with hers as well. Shane was now holding the night vision camera. It was approaching a quarter to midnight.

"Are you a little girl? Is that correct?" asked Anthony.

The glass moved a straight line in Shane's direction, where he was standing close to the desk. The glass moved again, reversing, ending up by the bottom-left corner of the board, signifying 'Yes'.

The impact of hail stones could be heard pattering on the window and it got heavier and heavier.

The glass was put back to its starting position, midway between Anthony and the female team member. Anthony declared that a strange scent was coming forth. The glass was removed and replaced by the brass school bell, minus the tongue. Anthony and the female team member attempted to use the bell as a divination tool. Since the glass was faltering, it might work - why not? Both placed an index finger on the upper crown of the bell, below the handle.

"Get underneath the bell and make a noise," asked the female team member.

The bell slid across, in a straight line, to Anthony's left, towards the edge of the desk, making the female team member stretch, at arm's length, to try to keep contact. In accordance with this, the bell was repositioned to midpoint, to make things easier.

Anthony and the female team member pushed for answers. Anthony looked behind his left shoulder, staring towards the door, licking his bottom lip. He pondered the notion of 'fire'. His elbow rested on the armrest of the chair and he tapped his mouth, in a position of thought. A burned odour was coming in strong.

"Did you fall in a fire?"

The bell moved in a straight line, about twelve inches or so before stopping at the left side of Anthony. We were hitting the mark. It would not be long till we asked some questions over the walkie-talkie, aimed at the Steam Centre.

Anthony radioed in. "Okay, you got two more minutes, Sinead: two more minutes of asking questions. Over."

We wondered if the Spirit died at the Waterworks. Anthony asked, "Was it close by?"

The bell moved in a straight line to the bottom left corner of the board. This meant 'Yes'.

On further movement of the bell, it was claimed that the Spirit was from a house nearby. However, the Spirit did not connect with having lived in the house. Nor did the Spirit connect the house with the place in which it had fallen in the fire. So, it is possible that the Spirit died at the Waterworks. We had been connecting with an orphan child, considering its lack of affiliation to any one place. A sense of being lost was felt.

Back at the Steam Centre, Sinead asked, "What is your name?"

A reply from the Frank's Box said, in a nervous manner, 'Damien'.

Sinead clarified this by saying, "Did I hear, 'Damien'?"

Sinead continued, asking questions about hobbies and occupations. She then questioned the number of Spirits that were around. "Umm, how many of you are here?"

A couple of seconds later, a mellow voice came back from the Frank's Box, 'Seven'.

Sinead called out to what she thought had heard, "Did I hear, 'seven'?"

A quick, clear response came back from the Frank's Box – a masculine voice saying, 'Yes'. It seemed that there was a conversation brewing.

Sinead asked, "Umm, who is your king… or your queen?"

A stern voice came back saying, from the box, 'Women'.

Sinead continued, "Who is your Taoiseach?"

Seconds passed, with some mumbled words coming back from the box. "You didn't have one," replied Sinead.

A voice came back from the Frank's Box saying, 'We did'.

A couple of minutes later, Sinead asked, "Do you like to dance? Do you like music?"

A masculine voice, saying something that sounded like, 'Yes' came from the box.

Sinead started calling out in Irish.

"Music and dance."

A voice said, 'I do', followed by a lady's voice, in a Dublin accent, saying something that sounded like 'Greatly'.

Things were starting to develop in the Paper Office. It was about to get even more gripping, for all. It was now time for Anthony to call out questions. Sinead had to remain silent.

"Okay, stop asking questions, Sinead. We'll ask the questions from now on. Over."

Shortly afterwards, he asked through the walkie-talkie, "What is the name of the city you lived in?"

Over at the Steam Centre, a whimper could be heard from the Frank's Box, followed by a woman's voice saying, 'Tralee'.

Back in the Paper Office, Shane decided to sit down on a chair beside the desk, to get comfortable.

The female team member asked, "Is there anybody around here, right now, that works here?"

The bell moved five inches or so, stopping directly in front of Anthony. This made Anthony think more.

"There bodies here? Is there bodies buried here?"

The bell moved another three inches or so towards Anthony, stopping just at the edge of the desk. It seemed, to us, that the Spirit present might be offering a place of significance. The bell had moved to the direction of the opposite building, the Steam Centre.

"Did you go down the tunnels?"

The bell seemed to heavily slide off the surface of the desk this time. It promptly moved in a straight line, screeching as it travelled, stopping at the bottom left corner of the talking board. This meant 'Yes'.

The female team member gasped in astonishment. She asked Anthony, "Did you hear the bell whistle then?"

Anthony was also surprised by what happened.

"Shit."

He fed the same question through the walkie-talkie. "Are you, are you underneath in the tunnels?"

The bell moved, in a straight line, to halfway between Anthony and the female team member then returned, in a straight line, screeching off the face of the desk, ending up at the bottom left corner of the talking board, at 'Yes'.

The female team member wiped the front of her face. She was getting goose pimples.

The bell moved again, fifteen inches in a straight line, stopping midway between Anthony and the female team member.

Unsuspectingly, things got scarier in the Steam Centre. Murmuring could be heard and then, a voice responding, 'Yeah' to Anthony's previous question about the tunnels. However, things got even more unnerving as Anthony enquired, over the walkie-talkie, *Are you from the catacombs underneath? Are you buried there?*

A clear, tense voice said, 'Yes'.

Nineteen seconds later, the room was plunged into darkness. The inside motion sensor light had, surprisingly, turned off. The illumination of the flashing green strobe lighting became more apparent, offering a small reward of intermittent viewing for the video camera.

Sinead, unaware, was now shrouded in darkness all around her. Anthony radioed in. *Did you get caught in the tunnel?*

Not much came back in response to this.

Anthony continued, ... *second name?*

More whimpering could be heard, which sounded like a child in distress.

At the Paper Office, the female team member asked, "Were you in the hospital?"

The bell howled in its movement, going in a direct line from midpoint and stopping alongside the bottom left corner of the board, to possibly mean 'Yes'. At this moment, Anthony had his head turned away. He was looking behind his left shoulder at the door. It was as if he was trying to figure out what was happening over at the Steam Centre.

We found out that the Spirit present could read but not write.

The wooden handle was unscrewed off the bell.

Anthony radioed into Sinead. "Okay, Sinead, ask questions now just for two more minutes. Over."

We asked a question in reference to stealing food because of hunger. The bell reacted by moving a straight line, twenty inches or so, towards Anthony's direction, stopping in front of him.

Anthony asked, "... are you hiding?"

The bell moved a couple of inches towards the edge of the desk in front of Anthony. The direction that the bell was pointing to appeared to be the Steam Centre.

The bell was placed back between Anthony and the female team member on the desk. Anthony told Sinead to stop asking questions. He radioed in. "Do you smuggle stuff?"

This time, the bell slowly and quietly moved and finished up alongside the bottom right of the talking board, presumably to mean 'No'. A few seconds passed with silence and then, the bell curled slowly a small, quarter, counter-clockwise circle before stopping near the edge of the desk in front of Anthony.

"Do you want us to go in the... umm... engine room?"

By this, Anthony meant the Steam Centre.

The bell moved eighteen inches or so, stopping alongside the bottom centre of the talking board, closest to the numbers '5' or '6'.

Anthony spoke into the walkie-talkie. "Do you want us to go into the engine room?" (Steam Centre).

The bell moved hesitantly a couple of inches in the female team member's direction, pausing somewhat, then reverted in a straight line back next to the bottom right corner of the board, presumably to indicate 'No'.

In a daring wicked way, Anthony directed the Spirit's intentions over at the Steam Centre, he radioed in. "Do you like Sinead?"

He opened his mouth wide open, dropping his jaw in an expression of humoured disbelief about what he had just said. The bell reacted by moving forcefully in a straight line, stopping at the edge of the desk in front of Anthony. Anthony let out a short whistle of surprise and looked back at the door, as to reflect on what could be unfolding in the Steam Centre. He wondered if Sinead could be affected. "Can you, can you touch Sinead? Touch Sinead on the right shoulder?"

The bell slowly moved off towards the far side of the desk. It crept up to the body mood doll, slightly knocking into it, causing it to wobble and twirl to its left.

The female team member pointed to the right shoulder on the body mood doll. She asked, "Can you touch Sinead there? Sinead is the girl in the engine room (Steam Centre) in the big boiler room?"

Over the walkie-talkie, Anthony told Sinead to ask more questions and that the vigil would end in one minute. As he finished the question, the bell moved a few inches away from the body mood doll and then slammed back into it. This sent the body mood doll toppling over, striking the surface of the desk with force. Anthony whistled again in disbelief and commented, "I hope she hasn't collapsed in there now."

He made his final comment over the walkie-talkie. "Okay Sinead. I'm coming over to get you. Over."

He then stuttered and laughed as he tried to explain that she could now take the blindfold off. When Anthony arrived at the Steam Centre, the motion sensor light came on as he opened the glass door. Thankfully, Sinead did not come to any harm. She explained to Anthony that when he had said, "Do you like Sinead?" a clear voice came through to her and said, 'Who is she?'

Anthony headed towards the video camera to stop the recording and to turn off the oscillating machine, lamp, digital sound recorder, Frank's Box and speaker. By this point it had been persistently raining heavily for half an hour.

The team all gathered at the Steam Centre. The oscillating machine was turned on again, with the video camera set to record. The team concluded that a calling-out vigil would be adequate for the next experiment.

The team walked up the ramp, hopping over the motion detectors. They bypassed the viewing station on their right and went up a three-foot ladder on the left, to access the top of the two boilers. As the team prepared themselves on top, the video camera on the oscillating machine picked up a voice. It seemed to say, 'Always there' in an elevated content of speech, possibly masculine. It was at a different parallel to how Anthony and Shane talked through the upcoming vigil.

It was now quarter past midnight. Anthony had begun recording. The night vision camera had its infrared mode switched off: as the room was bright due to the inside motion sensor lighting. You had to watch your head with the scattered, large, overhead, hydraulic cylinders, the piping and the low ceiling. It was not easy underfoot either, due to the overlapping round tops of the boilers. We had to keep steady over an uneven base.

Shane was sitting down with a K2 meter in his hand. Sinead stood still, taking pictures of the area with the full spectrum camera. The female team member took up a comfortable spot by the far side of the boiler closest to the wall. Anthony and Shane started chatting about the raindrops that were coming in the room. Anthony and Shane's view from up above beaming was accurate. It was dour out there.

Back to the investigation, Anthony called out, "If there's anybody in the other room, can you throw a stone at us? Maybe a little pebble? Make footsteps around us? Sound of your voice?"

Anthony went on, relating his questions to tunnels and the little girl that was spoken of previously.

Sinead called out, "Is there someone by the name of Damien?"

All was silent.

Anthony asked, "Somebody by the name of Cecil?" Still, all was quiet.

Shane got back on his feet and walked over, resting his arms on a railing, staring intently at the K2 meter that he was holding. "I got something there," he declared.

He called out, "Was that you that was beside me? Come and say hi… like Anthony said, it's a grey box (K2 meter). It doesn't do you any harm. Come and say hi and see the lights?"

A dull echoing clamour could be heard. It was the sound of an aeroplane flying low over us.

"I felt something on my neck," said Anthony. He panned around to his right with the night vision camera. He called out, "Come out of the shadows?"

Everyone kept perfectly still, waiting for a reaction.

Anthony turned the night vision camera back to the left, aiming it at Shane, who was continuing to lean casually over a safety rail with the K2 meter. A bit of the glass doors could be seen in the background.

Anthony called out in Latin. After brief silence, Sinead decided to call out, "Are you down there? There? Near the door there?"

Anthony stood up and walked over to Shane. He knocked into something as he walked. It was an overhead spotlight. However, no damage was done, so he adjusted it back into position. He targeted the night vision camera at the room where the three triple extension engines were. He zoomed in and out. Not even the infrared camera could pick up anything specifically. Only a plasma TV with a fixed, static white screen offered any spectacle in this area.

Sinead continued to call out. "Could you make a noise on any of the metal around where you are, to let us know you are here?"

It remained quiet.

Anthony aimed the camera back to the left, at the back of the building. An off room was to the right, behind the two boilers. The room was highlighted with the brightness of a light source within it. Anthony raised his voice, hailing out a summoning-in prayer. He then slowly shouted out, "Come towards us now. Step forward."

The team heard what sounded like tapping.

Sinead stared out towards the off room. "If you're in the room there at the back, let us know; give us a few more taps there, if you can."

Anthony followed up by saying, "Throw a stone onto the piping?"

Anthony directed the night vision camera towards the entrance. Rainwater seemed to be seeping through under the glass doors. Suddenly, Shane grabbed everybody's notice. "Yeah, I got something here."

He walked over to a higher platform. Now he was overlooking a small narrow area near the back of the building. Anthony zoomed in with the night vision camera. While the K2 meter was flickering up to 10 milliGauss, we found out, shortly after, that this could be due to some power implement on the other side of the wall, in the room of the three triple-extension engines. The nearer the meter was to the wall, the higher the reading. Plus, it stayed constant, not erratic at all.

The female team member eagerly went down to the narrow passageway to the back of the building, where Shane had been overlooking. As she set foot on the ground, she was taken by surprise. "Wow! … that's weird," she said.

"Is it underneath there?" asked Anthony.

She replied, "We have got a tunnel."

Anthony echoed her words in excitement and disbelief, "We have got a tunnel. We have got a tunnel"

He aimed the camera down to where the female team member was. She was crouching down with her head torch on, its light beaming at a gap in the wall. She lay on the ground on her stomach. Going headfirst, she crawled halfway into the gap of the wall to get a better look inside the Tunnel.

Anthony turned away with the night vision camera towards the glass doors, glimpsing the entrance as if to say, 'do we dare advance further?'

The rain was bucketing down outside.

The female team member crawled back out from the Tunnel and addressed the team.

"I'm not sure whether it's safe in there."

Anthony and Shane took time out to survey an occurrence of the K2 meter going off.

A voice came over the night vision camera. It said, 'I like that' in a strong Irish accent, as if a Spirit was displaying a fondness towards the colourful flashing lights of the K2 meter. Two seconds later, there was a faraway noise. It sounded condensed and could easily be mistaken for a whooping cough. Was it coming from the Tunnel down below?

Anthony turned his attention to the female team member below in the passageway. He told her to stay down there while the rest of the team try to call out to get a reaction. No reply came back from her. He continued, "If you're down there," then let out a snigger.

A whispering voice could be heard saying, 'Yeah', as he turned the night vision camera back toward the glass doors.

Something was there, unknown to the team and it indicated some sort of recognition of our presence. We decided that it was time to explore, summon some courage, head down to the passageway and see exactly what was in that Tunnel.

The female team member was already inside the Tunnel, now holding the night vision camera, as Anthony crawled along the ground through the low gap in the wall. The opening only measured around one-and-a-half-feet square (1.5 x 1.5). Loose bricks on the floor inside of the Tunnel could indicate that it had been bricked up at some point in the past. The Tunnel seemed to lead back around to underneath the boilers, where we had previously been above.

Anthony scrambled to get inside. So tight was the Tunnel that once inside, there was little space to move. The maximum height of the round, arched Tunnel was about four-and-a-half feet, making it hard to even stand. The Tunnel was closed off about fifteen metres ahead. However, it may have progressed further than this, since another turn off to the far right extended another metre or so. The red-bricked flanking walls were full of decaying mortar.

Only a couple of metres in was a thin pale cement slab, which split the Tunnel in half. The slab lengthened for about a metre, obstructing the Tunnel slightly. The reason for this slab in the Tunnel was unknown. It may have been put there to stop the ceiling from collapsing or, it could have been used as a door. Either way, it was hard for Anthony to get past. The female team member handed the night vision camera back to Anthony before heading beyond the slab, further through the Tunnel.

Sinead and Shane declined the opportunity to enter the Tunnel. Given its increasingly limited size, this was likely a good decision. They were happy to stay on the other side of the opening, in the spacious passageway beside the boilers in the Steam Centre.

It was time to call out for anyone who could have been inside the Tunnel and listen in on who could be with us there. We would not be able to get away that easily.

The night vision camera was put back onto infrared mode. Anthony asked for the lights to be turned off, both inside and outside the Tunnel. He called out, "Okay, if there are any Spirits down here, we're underground now. You were talking to us earlier? Can you come and talk to us? Communicate? Can communicate through here? Can throw a stone? You can communicate… you can communicate through umm…?"

We could see orbs floating in the air and some individuals sensed that they had been touched. Anthony did a sweep with the night vision camera. First behind him towards the opening in the wall, then back again to the end of the Tunnel. A sense of feeling hot was becoming increasingly apparent. In such a constricted area, this was unsurprising.

Anthony directed his questions towards fire and Saint Kevin's Hospital. Shortly after, he thought he heard something. He called out to the rest of the team outside, "Did you lot make a growl? Groan then? Outside people, did you make a growl?"

Sinead responded, "Say again?"

Anthony again asked, "Did you make a growl?"

Sinead replied, "Growl? No."

Anthony then asked for a time check. It was now half past midnight.

He called out in Latin, "Whom? Name you are?"

We sensed the essence of smoke and a strong fire.

Anthony called out, "Did you die down here?"

A few seconds later, Anthony enquired if Sinead and Shane were getting anything where they were. Sinead responded, saying that the K2 meter was flickering.

The team members in the Tunnel then switched their head torches back on. On the far side of the Tunnel, puddles could be seen as light reflected onto the ground. It became clear that it was getting muddy beneath our feet.

The female team member heard a bang. She was standing at the far end of the Tunnel, ahead to the right, where the Tunnel extended slightly. Anthony shouted out, "Can you make that bang again?"

He went on to asking for all the lights to be turned off, "Lights off lads. All lights off. Turn it off."

There was a sound of a short, sluggish hum or moan. Anthony acknowledged that he heard a humming sound. He then questioned the team outside the Tunnel, to see if they were moving around. He called out again, "Can you make that moaning noise again?"

All was silent. Anthony called out, "Or a cough?"

About half a minute later, Anthony commented that he thought there was movement above.

The female team member turned her head torch back on and looked down to her left, to the wall at the end of the Tunnel. There was a gap in this wall as well.

"There is a blocked passage… actually, there is water seeping through," she declared.

Anthony replied, "Oh shit!"

"A lot," added the female team member.

The gap in this wall only seemed to be a foot in height and three feet in length, raised up from the ground to about knee level. It would be too constricting to go through. It was time to vacate the Tunnel and abort the mission. The female team member went to leave then, suddenly turned back, stating that she heard banging behind her.

Anthony turned away from her with the night vision camera. He got on the ground and started to crawl out. He passed the night vision camera to Sinead, through the low opening in the wall. The vigil had ended. All the team proceeded to gather back at the entrance by the glass doors.

It was quite fortunate that the investigation ended when it did: before any of our cases and bags of equipment were affected or destroyed by the puddle of rainwater that had crept into the Steam

Centre, underneath the glass doors. Our thoughts turned to how we would get back home tonight, with the deteriorating weather.

The video camera on the oscillating machine picked up what sounded like joyful humming. This was when the night vision camera was turned off and the rest of team were heading towards the Tunnel. It was separated into seven pieces: the first four were high toned, in quick succession; the last three, more separated, lower in tone with the last piece being the longest. It resembled a melody. Over two minutes later, a prolonged voice seemed to say, 'Hello' in an innocent, welcoming, childlike manner. Seconds before, the same type of voice was heard talking but it was hard to unscramble what was being said.

Because of the weather, we had to load up the car with equipment in a couple of stages. First, we went to the Visitor Centre, to shelter for a few minutes. This was close to our trek to the cars. The heavy rain showed no signs of letting up, so we made a quick dash and headed out into it. Going down the steps to the carpark, our jaws dropped but we had to keep on moving. There was no time to reflect or evaluate. The River Lee had burst its banks. We were met with two feet of rushing water, up to and above our knees in places. Thunder and lightning now became more pronounced.

We quickly got to the carpark beside the river and unloaded some of the equipment into our cars. We could not wait around or be hesitant. We put our foot on the gas and drove up to beside the Waterworks then stopped and got out of our cars in shallower water. We had to make a quick second trip up the stairs to the Visitor Centre, to collect the last of our belongings. Once back down again, we had to make a quick getaway. We did not want to end up submerged or stranded, as the water was already creeping in under the car doors.

The female team member and Sinead made the journey to the city centre. Sinead would be getting an early morning bus back to Dublin. Luckily for them, they would see the storm gradually unfold in the distance. Meanwhile, Anthony and Shane were to take the road back to Killarney, where the storm was headed. The air conditioning was on full blast. The windows on all sides of the car were fogged up; lots of moisture inside and out. All our clothes, socks and trainers were soaked through. It was miserable.

We were heading out of Cork City onto the Carrigrohane Road when we encountered, first-hand, the force of Mother Nature. About two miles ahead, along the straight road, we could make out a vehicle travelling in the opposite direction, back into the city. Suddenly, there was a big flash. A jagged bolt of lightning cut through the sky straight ahead and very close by. Instantly, the lines of streetlights ahead of us all cut out. It went extremely dark. The driver, in the vehicle in the distance, automatically switched on their full beam headlights. The opposing vehicle came closer: we noticed that it was a taxi. Once it passed us, the road was void of anyone else travelling in to or out of the city.

We took our time. We stopped off at a disused petrol station in Ballincollig, knowing that we could not keep going with the storm right above us. After about twenty minutes of waiting, Shane now being asleep, Anthony put the keys in the ignition and drove off. Steadily they made their way home.

Roads were flooded, with many rats scampering for territory from the hedgerows on approach. We put the hazard lights on in places. To avoid water and continue our route, we had to drive on the wrong side of the road. The journey took about three hours to complete, nearly three times longer than our initial journey to the investigation. We eventually reached our destination and Killarney. It was great to get out of our drenched attire, relax and get some sleep. We did not know then, to what extent the water would be a significant factor in the investigation that we had just completed.

After reviewing the audio on the digital sound recorder from the first separation, calling-out vigil, the word 'Speak' could be heard twice from the Frank's Box, within the first three minutes.

In between Shane's questioning, "Were you from Cork City?" the name, 'Limerick' can be heard twice, about fifteen seconds apart.

Names such as 'Marie', 'Bridget', 'Joseph' and 'Craig' were also picked up from the Frank's Box.

Shane had asked, "Does your boss care?", to which a feminine voice from the Frank's Box responded, 'Yes', followed by a deep masculine voice that stated, 'He doesn't'.

During Sinead's separation, calling-out vigil, the digital sound recorder picked out female voices and, early in the experiment, a child's voice. Like the video camera, 'Seven' was heard from the Frank's Box as Sinead asked how many Spirits were around. More names came up on the recording: 'Cecil', 'Thomas', 'William' and 'Bridget'.

Near the end of the vigil – when Anthony radioed in asking, *Do you want us to go into the engine room?* – a response came from the Frank's Box saying, 'No'.

We also experienced a similar decline of action in the Paper Office.

As Anthony asked on the walkie-talkie, *Do you like Sinead?*, a response, which sounded like it could be 'Cunt' or 'Couldn't', was heard from the Frank's Box. This was different to what Sinead perceived at the time. Nevertheless, the feedback was negative and identical to the action of the bell hitting into the body mood doll.

The weather about to take a turn for the worse as the River Lee rises

The outside of the building from where we parked

The magnificent chimney

Triple extension engines

A picture of some of the mechanics involved in the Cork City water supply

Things were not that easy before the Waterworks were built

This was where coal used to be weighed

Sinead prepares to go it alone in a separation vigil

Looking down from the boilers in the Steam Centre

What Sinead drew might be interesting!

Drowned-Out Voices Investigation footage can be viewed by

Watching the DVD that accompanies this book

Visiting our website

www.GhostÉire.net

Click on the button

Drowned-Out Voices Footage

and enter the password

YourNotAlone

Scanning the QR code

Enter the password

YourNotAlone

Location Background/Biography

The Waterworks is located on the banks of the River Lee in Cork City. It is widely acclaimed as one of the best-preserved industrial heritage sites.

Water has been supplied to the city of Cork since the 1760s. Architect and engineer, David Ducart (founder of The Pipe Water Company) designed the original Waterworks. Final construction was completed by Nicolas Fitton, in 1768. This Waterworks included a pumping house and open storage building at the same location as the present-day Waterworks.

Wooden pipes were used to pump untreated water from the River Lee to cisterns and public fountains in the city centre. Elm, Fir and Larch were used because of the resistance to rot. Gravity helped in transporting the water but, only locations below the level of the water basins at the Waterworks could receive it.

The water supply to the city was upgraded in the early part of the 19th century, due to population growth and the old wooden pipes being untreated. Thomas Wicksteed (a respected engineer of the East London Waterworks) was commissioned for his services in devising the recommended system. The Pipe Water Company was then taken over by the Cork Corporation. In 1857, new cast iron pipes were laid into the ground. These new pipes reached the military barracks on the Old Youghal Road by February 1859.

The Benson scheme, first introduced by John Benson, supplied water from the River Lee to two reservoirs, located on Prayer Hill. A metal waterwheel and two turbines were added to the reservoirs. In the summer months when the water was low, water was pumped up to the reservoirs by a 90-horsepower Cornish beam engine. The steam-powered engine required boilers to pump the water. Buildings were constructed to support the coal-fuelled boilers and chimney flue for emissions.

By the 1860s, three further beam engines were acquired, as the original Cornish beam engines was not providing sufficient power. New buildings had to be constructed to house these engines, along with a boiler house and coal store.

The Information Centre was built around the 1870s. It was used to accommodate the engineer and chief workmen.

In 1888, the turbine house (at the eastern end of the site, on the bank of the River Lee) was erected. The 'Streaky Bacon' effect given by the horizontal red brick, sandstone and grey limestone captured the attention of many.

The waterwheel was dismantled in 1889.

Between 1902 and 1907, Benson's scheme was altered as triple extension engines, made by Combe and Barbour of Belfast, replaced the Cornish beam engine. Two Lancashire boilers supplied the steam to power these great engines.

An engraving on the chimney from 1865 is dedicated to former mayor, Charles Cantillon. A stone plaque was erected in the north gable wall of the turbine house (visible from the road), which notes the names of the mayor, engineers and others who opened the building, in 1888.

Manifestation/Legend

There was no paranormal significance to this location prior to the investigation.

Conclusion

The automatic drawing/writing session had some thought-provoking detail to it.

Standing out was the picture drawn by Sinead, which resembled a woman in Victorian or Edwardian clothes. The wide brimmed hat was part of informal dress, in the Victorian era and was associated with the tea-party, in the Edwardian era. It is a piece of fashion item worn for a lady of importance and, with somewhat a trouble-free life. She drew what looked like smoke rising within an enclosed area and, what appeared to be ankle-high boots.

Excessive steam, causing mist and condensation, would have been customary in the Waterworks from supplying coal to boilers. Stokers or fireman would have worn boiler suits (overalls). Soot would have accumulated inside the engines, which would have to be cleaned out on occasion. Boiler suits would stop soot from entering the lower half of their clothing and, avoid it getting snagged on anything. Boots, ideally above the ankles, would be protective and lessen the chances of grainy fragments of coal escaping under the soles and heels of the feet.

When Shane was alone in the Steam Centre, he asked if there were any Spirits from Cork. A male and a female responded, 'Yes' from the Frank's Box. Later he asked, "Were you from the city?" a reply came back that said, 'Limerick'.

Another location came up on the box when Sinead was alone in the Steam Centre. After Anthony radioed in, asking about which city the Spirit lived in, a woman's voice clearly said, 'Tralee' (County Kerry) over the Frank's Box.

There was a correlation between the questions and the answers. We questioned where the Spirit was from and a received the name of a place in response.

There were more correspondences. When Shane asked if a Spirit worked at the Waterworks for possibly five years, there was a quick succession of numbers that came back from the box, counting from six up to eight. There was high pitched wailing coming up regularly during Shane's lone stint too. A distressed female voice said, 'Take me too' on the Frank's Box, shortly after the mention of Saint Kevin's Hospital over the walkie-talkie. Originally added onto Our Lady's Hospital, Saint Kevin's (Psychiatric) Hospital was opened in 1899 as an additional space to accommodate patients (men and women) with a capacity of up to 500.

We asked if any Spirit in the Steam Centre was twenty-three years old. Again, a number came through on the Frank's Box; not the same but, close enough with 'Thirty'.

A deep voice said, 'She looks pretty' at the start of Sinead's isolated period in the Steam Centre. This did not come from the Frank's Box! There seemed to be mixed emotion with Sinead's presence during this session. She received the number seven, from the number of people in the room. She also heard 'Damian' when she asked for a name.

There were a fair number of names coming forward throughout both solo segments in the Steam Centre. This probably bears fruit with the total of Spirits alleged to being around seven. At times, it seemed that beings from the Spirit world were willing to strike up a conversation with Shane and Sinead.

In the Paper Office, attention was drawn to a fire and the possibility of a little girl who died in the blaze, aged seven or eight. We wondered if this tied in with Jen's dream of a young girl, covered in soot, inside a tunnel? It appeared to. We found out, via the glass and the talking board, that the Spirit of a young girl was present.

In Jen's dream, she had a vision of red cobblestones. Paving with cobblestones is perfect for draining water, stopping the accumulation of mud or dust that occurs from dirt roads and giving better grip for horse-drawn carriages. The riverbeds around the River Lee would make it perfect for collecting smooth round stones for paving. Stones would have been laid in sand if mortar were unavailable or too costly.

The Spirit of the young girl confirmed that she died in a fire, somewhere close by or in the surrounding area. We had significant trust that this incident happened in the Tunnel. It was believed the house that she had lived in was not her natural home. She may have been an orphan. Saint Finbarr's Industrial School for Girls was situated in Sundays Well, not too far from the Waterworks. It first started up in 1870, where it would have taken in neglected, abandoned or orphaned girls. However, we could not find any record of a child dying in a fire at the Waterworks or, in any of the surrounding buildings.

We were to later discover a darkened Tunnel in the Steam Centre. The Tunnel may have functioned as an underground furnace in the past. When Anthony radioed into Sinead in the Steam Centre, to enquire if the Spirit had got caught in a Tunnel, the whimpering of a child could be heard.

As all the team prepared on the top of the boilers, a voice said, 'Always there'.

It was very clear and loud. It could well have been an indication that the Steam Centre was a hotbed of paranormal activity. Humming was caught on the video camera when Anthony and Shane were talking to each other, over the K2 meter fluctuations. Voices were detected on the night vision camera in this short space of time, when most of the team were up above on the boilers. Despite this fact, it cannot be ruled out that EVPs were created by the expressions of the team members.

Later, Anthony commented that he heard a humming noise when down in the Tunnel.

Old Cork Waterworks
Co Cork

WEBSITE: corkcity.ie
e-MAIL: lifetimelab@corkcity.ie
PHONE: 021 494 1500
FACEBOOK: corkcitycouncilofficial

Open every day from March to August. Open Monday
to Friday from September to February

Standing proud on a Cork hillside, the Lifetime Lab is an interactive exhibition for all ages. It provides scenic views of the River Lee. The venue holds a primary science education space, where children of all ages can conduct their own experiments.

The Waterworks is available to hire and comes with conference facilities.

A playground and garden are also located onsite.

Enochian Spells

Angelic script/language

Levitation = graupha + orh + you + graupha + t

(Whisper or chant, on your own or in a group and, in the presence of others)

See Spirits = ust + d + stall + o

(Whisper or chant, on your own or in a group and, in the presence of others)

Slow time = orh + i + y + r + gierh + machis + stall + yes

(Whisper or chant, on your own or in a group and, in the presence of others)

A gift = machis + nach + g + droux + you + graupha

(Only to be chanted by everyone within a group)

Spirit guide protection = ꓶꓴꓳꓶꓑꓶꓴ

(Not to be spoken, only written down on paper or marked on object)

Layout

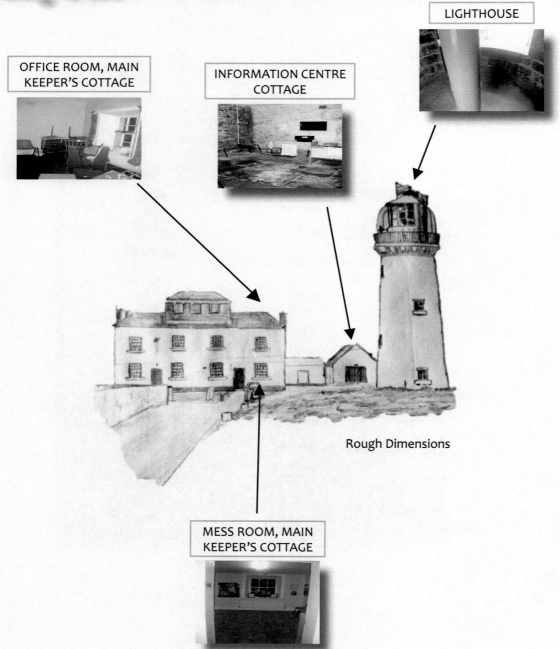

LIGHTHOUSE

OFFICE ROOM, MAIN KEEPER'S COTTAGE

INFORMATION CENTRE COTTAGE

Rough Dimensions

MESS ROOM, MAIN KEEPER'S COTTAGE

Chapter 18
Loop Head Lighthouse

Anthony's Journey

It was the start of another year. I was looking for places within County Clare for us to explore. Looking through the internet, I came across Loop Head Lighthouse and Keepers Cottages. My first thoughts were, *Yeah, it would be great to do another lighthouse again*.

With little hesitance, I sent an e-mail asking for permission for us to spend the night there, exploring the buildings for any possibility of paranormal behaviour. It was the year of 'The Gathering' – remembering all of those who have departed these shores.

The Lighthouse was newly opened, on a trial basis in June 2011, offering public tours of the site along with an exhibition on the working lighthouse's past. Loop Head welcomed former Taoiseach, Enda Kenny (*See Glossary*) in May 2012. Records state that his grandfather, James McGinley, had worked as a lighthouse keeper at Loop Head between 1922 and 1935.

It was not long before I got an e-mail back. We received news from Clare County Council and Irish Lights, granting us permission to be on the premises overnight. In fact, it would go out to the regional and national media that we would be carrying out a paranormal investigation at Loop Head. We were put in the spotlight. As Enda Kenny's grandfather had worked there, it had gone around the news circuit that we were on the hunt for Enda's grandfather! Anyway, we welcomed the challenge.

I decided to drop by at the Lighthouse a handful of weeks before we would do the investigation. I took my daughter along with two friends to see it. We took the ferry from Tarbert, County Kerry across the Shannon Estuary to Killimer, County Clare. This was quicker for us, cutting the journey and avoiding the longer drive through County Limerick.

Loop Head peninsula does not have many trees around. You could see pretty much into the distance but, there were quite a few ruined cottages, presumably suffering the effects of the penal laws and the famine.

Martin, one of the guides at the Lighthouse, showed us inside the Main Keepers Cottage. Afterwards, we were given a pleasant informative tour of the Lighthouse. We even managed to have a peek from the top, looking out to land and sea.

The wind was quite plentiful. The hood on my coat was useful to use on this occasion. Refreshed, impressed and satisfied, we made our way home. A date was pinned down for the investigation. It was set for the 9 April 2013. I could not imagine the excitement that was flowing through me. In the back of my mind, my thoughts were on what the outlook of the press would be on what we were doing, worrying that it could be inaccurate to the reader. We had to erase these worries from our minds and concentrate solely on what we would be doing that night. Experiments around a light theme were decided to be the best way to attract attention.

On the morning of the investigation, I received a phone call from an RTÉ news reporter. She was interested in popping down to us for an interview the next day, after the investigation. *Cool*, I thought. I hoped to make myself presentable although, we all knew that tiredness could be a key issue.

I got another phone call later that evening. We would be joined on the investigation, for a few hours, by a presenter from the local Gaeilge radio station, Raidió Corca Baiscinn.

Jen, Rhiannon and two team guests were already on the way to Loop Head when I managed to come off the phone. They had gotten the earlier ferry crossing over to Killimer. They cruised at a pleasurable pace, stopping off at various points, allowing myself, Sinead and a female team member to follow on. I had to get organised. No time to waste.

Later, we arrived at Tarbert and got in line to board the vessel. The ticket inspector directed the steady procession of vehicles as to where to park up. This was a good time to take a break, to get out on deck and to breathe in the fresh air. Looking over the side as we sailed, we noticed some dolphins swimming, surfacing on the waters at times and attempting to keep up with the speed of the ferry.

Back in the car and off the ferry, we met with the rest of the team and the guests at a restaurant in Carrigaholt. We all grabbed a bite to eat; it would be our last big hot meal for the day. The local cuisine of fish was highly recommended.

We did a protection prayer outside of the restaurant. It was gradually getting less bright in the sky, so as soon as we were ready, we departed for our final leg and to the Lighthouse. The darkness became ever more prominent but, we could see from afar the flashing beam of light from the Lighthouse. When we arrived, Martin, who would be handing over the keys, told us to drive through the gates so that we could park inside the walled perimeter. We stopped our cars beside the Lighthouse and started to unpack the car.

The cottages were split into three sections. The southern wing, to our left, was open to holiday makers. A family was staying there for a few days, so this cottage would be a no-go area for us. Another cottage, the original keeper's dwelling, was on the right. This has been made into an Information Centre Cottage. The Main Keeper's Cottage, straight on, was where we would be staying for the night.

We went inside the Main Keeper's Cottage, then made our way up some tight stairways. We unloaded our gear in the north and west view bedrooms, on the first floor. The bedrooms were very petite but habitable. We were right above the Mess Room, situated on the ground floor.

Jen went to the Lighthouse and took some photos from up top, looking down at the cottages below. Some were out of focus. This was mainly due to the digital camera trying to cope with the beamed rays circulating from the Lighthouse. She did manage to catch the few lit up windows from the cottages and the dense black of the night.

I did some baseline tests around the Main Keeper's Cottage, the Information Centre Cottage and the Lighthouse. I was not sure what the rest of the team or guests were doing. I was concentrating on what I had to do.

Jen met with me at the Information Centre Cottage to prepare a trigger object experiment. A chess board, with the majority of game pieces in starting formation, were placed on a three-and-a-half-feet thick, wooden partition. This partition blocked the lower half of what resembled an old doorway. On the other side of this, preventing us from entering, was an unfamiliar room. It was dark and void of any existence that we could see – or was it?

A direction board with a rotating pointer was placed on the ground, in front of the doorway partition. We hoped that at some point, a Spirit might be able to manipulate the pointer.

Jen readied the full spectrum camera, getting it in line with the doorway, chess set and direction board, so that it could record successfully.

Anthony then turned on the laser beam machine. A display of many shapes, patterns and configurations of red, yellow and green lighting projected on to the opposing trigger objects and behind it, into the dark room. Pictures were taken of the experiment. They came out really well.

I pressed the record button on the full spectrum camera and then, we left the Information Centre Cottage. The team and guests gathered outside of the Main Keeper's Cottage. I gazed at the Lighthouse. We then went inside to the Main Keeper's Cottage and into the Mess Room, on the ground floor. This would be where we would start our first experiment, using the laser board (*See Glossary*).

The Investigation

NUMBER OF TEAM 5

NUMBER OF GUESTS 3

It felt like we were in an altered dimension on the Loop Head peninsula. The terrain was something to behold. Nature ruled with harshness over humans, making it virtually impossible to coexist. The vegetation and trees that surround the area were either bare, leaning to one side or, in some cases, both, due to wind coming from the Atlantic. Stunning views can be seen of the surrounding cliffs, especially those of waves thumping against the rock face.

It was cold, with a reading of 6.4°C outside. A couple of layers were essential when we would be inactive. It was just a bit more comfortable inside the Main Keeper's Cottage, measuring a temperature of 8.9°C, compared to the Lighthouse at 7.8°C. It was fairly quiet within the compound of buildings.

Inside the Main Keeper's Cottage, the C low decibel level was at 45.6, making us feel encircled in calmness. It did feel tranquil.

The category of manifestation was thought to be intelligent and residual. It was observed as being pleasant so far. The humidity was appropriate for the given temperatures and cloudy sky: the Lighthouse recorded 85.4%, with the Main Keeper's Cottage lower at 71.4%. The towering height of the Lighthouse would be the reason for the difference in atmospheric moisture.

The celestial significance for the evening predicted that the waxing crescent Aries moon would turn up the heat but, there would be a struggle for independence. This might mean there were many Spirits assembled around us.

We all gathered into the Mess Room in the Main Keeper's Cottage for the first session of the night. Here, only the overhead spotlights produced any EMF alteration. On the walls were display boards, showcasing pictures of the Lighthouse, the scenery around Loop Head and information in regard to a keeper's daily life and duties. In addition, hung alongside, were framed black-and-white photographs of men and women from a bygone age, with the Lighthouse in the background. The people appeared happy and maybe that would rub off on the investigation too.

Glass cabinets of maritime memorabilia were put on show and a model of a tall wooden ship sat, in primary position, on a window ledge. Perched on top of a wooden table, in the centre of the Mess Room, was the laser board. This board was similar to the talking board but, a dial was used instead, to connect on at the middle of the semi-circle board.

A red laser light was set at the rim of the dial (pointing towards the edge of the board). The horizontal red beam from the laser light could target pieces of wood, positioned at the edge of the board, when it rotated. The pieces of wood had letters from the alphabet and the words 'yes', 'no' and 'change' marked on them. In short, a Spirit might attach to our energies, making the dial spin and the laser beam point on a letter or word.

The Mess Room was small but we had some good space to work in. The two team guests, who joined us for the trip, sat down on chairs at the fringe of the room, away from the action but in first-class seats, gaining a good view.

Jason, from Raidió Corca Baiscinn, was standing to the side of the board with his headphones on, attached to a sophisticated, state-of-the-art boom mic.

It was ten o' clock when we got under way. Anthony, Sinead and the female team member were the first ones to go on the laser board. After the customary greetings, Sinead started the flow of instructions.

"If you want to give us a name, an initial?"

The dial began to rotate slightly clockwise. It stopped with the laser not pointing to anything conclusive.

"Again," said Anthony in Irish.

The dial showed more pomp, leading those in contact to shuffle around the board, simulating the same course of movement.

Anthony put a point across to the Spirit world, requesting the intervention on the chess pieces and direction board in the Information Centre Cottage.

The dial stayed still.

"I can feel a little build up, a build-up, a rocky build up…" said Sinead, gesturing to her head.

Anthony asked, "Do you have a question?"

The dial rotated clockwise to 'Yes'. The Spirit did not muster up a question in the following minutes; the invitation quickly forgotten.

"Please Spirit, would you tell us your name? Please?" asked the female team member.

After some invigorated movement from the dial, a red dot from the laser light shone on 'W'. The dial twirled around one clockwise motion, continuing onto 'G'. The Spirit clarified that its initials were 'W' and 'G' by pointing the laser to 'Yes'.

The laser light moved to 'Change' on a further two occasions (possibly indicating a change of Spirit).

The female team member described sensing a quite a lot of energy around. When trying to come through, one over the other, they seemed to zap each other.

Whispering was alleged to have come over the night vision camera: a masculine voice said, 'I see May… see her'.

It does not seem likely that it came from Anthony, as he spoke at a higher pitch soon after. It is also unlikely to have come from the male guest or Jason. The only other likely explanation is that Anthony was trying to interpret what letters had come up on the board previous (I, C, C, R), as he thought out aloud.

Sinead came off the board and took responsibility of holding the night vision camera. Rhiannon had taken her place, connecting onto the dial. Shortly after, Jen replaced the female team member. A couple of minutes after the changeovers, it was noticed that the board was shaking.

Anthony asked, "Does your name appear in any of the writing on any of the exhibitions around here?"

A light, conspicuous knock could be heard.

"It's like a knock on the table," described Anthony.

The dial remained still, yet the activity was building all around.

Anthony asked, "Using the letters on the board, can you tell us how many Spirits in the room? A for one, B for two. If you can do that? Build that energy up…?"

The dial spun around to 'X'.

Anthony gasped, "Jesus! Twenty-four… is that correct? Twenty-four Spirits around us this present moment?"

The dial rotated counter-clockwise to 'Yes'.

Anthony recommenced by saying, "How many are men? Come on continue?"

The dial rotated to 'N', indicating fourteen male Spirits in close attendance.

"Are there ten women?" added Anthony.

It was all made certain, as the laser light pointed to 'Yes', confirming the total congregation of Spirits within earshot.

Anthony asked, "What year is it? Like, using A for one?"

The dial rotated clockwise to 'P'.

"Is it 1916?"

The dial casually rotated clockwise to 'Yes'. We were to discover that all these Spirit beings were from the same era.

"What month is it?" asked Anthony.

The dial did a couple of rotations, finally ending up at 'C'. We assumed that the Spirit on the board was using the letter to refer to March, the third month of the year.

"Go to C if the month is March now, please?" said Rhiannon.

The dial rotated clockwise but, as it just about finished moving, three brisk knocks could be heard. The dial ended up on 'M'.

"What! What that a…?" said a surprised Anthony looking over towards the female team member in the corner of the room.

"That was a knock," she replied, in a clear, concerned manner to everyone's shock.

A couple of the team members claimed that they heard three knocks. Many were taken aback by the importance of the number of knocks, linking it to the month of March.

Rhiannon remarked on hearing footsteps by the doorway, that split the Mess Room. Nobody else could hear them at that precise moment… but that would change.

A soft female voice said, 'I hear them' in a calm manner, followed by a whisper that possibly said, 'Turn it'.

It is not known if this came from anyone from the team or guests.

A few seconds later…

"I heard footsteps," said Anthony.

This time, the footsteps were heard by other members of the team, with some remarking that they saw a shadow passing by the interconnecting doorway. Sinead looked away from the laser board to the doorway. The adjoining area could be seen clearly on the night vision camera but was less illuminated. There was no intention of knowing what might lurk around all corners, beyond that doorway.

Anthony called out, "Is there? Is there people moving around… around us now, dear Spirit…?"

The laser light went to 'Yes'.

An icy exhale of breath could be seen coming from Rhiannon, who was connected on the dial. Sinead pointed out that she thought she saw a shadow through the door. Reviewing the footage afterwards, the expelled air was mistaken to be a shadow or an abnormality because of the distortion caused by the night vision camera screen.

"It's freezing now…" said Rhiannon.

Our attention was now directed towards the door.

It was discovered that there was a keeper, named Simon, who worked at the Lighthouse and he had something to do with a lovers' tiff. It was soon apparent, from the board, that this information was correct. Was there a keeper at the Lighthouse called Simon? Who started the quarrel? How did it end?

"Would you like us to move into the Lighthouse?" asked the female team member.

The dial did one clockwise rotation, stopping back on 'Yes'.

We went back to the suggestion that a death occurred as a result of an argument.

The female team member, who was in the corner of the room, asked a question in relation to a mistress' lover.

"… Can you tell me what you did? Can you tell me how you killed him?"

The dial went to 'K', 'O'.

Anthony asked, "Did you knock them out?"

The dial rotated clockwise, gradually stopping with the laser pointing at 'Yes'.

However, the word knockout could have meant an attractive or impressive person. It was thought there was more to it, however.

"Was there a shooting here?" asked Anthony.

The dial did one clockwise rotation, ending back on 'Yes'. There appeared to be more of a sinful side to this than first thought.

Leaving the Mess Room, there was time to check in on the laser beam machine in the Information Centre Cottage, before heading over to the Lighthouse. Voices could be heard coming in on the full spectrum camera footage; however, this could be attributed to people talking, as they made their way across the yard to the Lighthouse. The rest of the footage from the full spectrum camera played out with nothing baffling to report.

There was a continuous droned noise, credited as coming from the mechanisms at the top the Lighthouse from the lantern room. The noise inside the Lighthouse did contribute to about 80.8 decibels in C low level, making it fairly loud.

The power that supplied electricity to the lamp in the lantern room above could be found in the walled cabling. It measured up to

4 milliGauss in magnetic flux density, which was not an excessive amount.

The team and guests were divided into two groups to make use of the four floors in the twenty-three-meter building. Limiting the number of people per level was essential. The Lighthouse may have been tall but it was narrow and small in diameter. Anthony, Sinead, Jason and one of the team guests would occupy the third floor. Jen, Rhiannon, the female team member and another team guest took up their post on the first floor. Both groups would take it in turns calling out.

On the third floor, Anthony radioed in with a walkie-talkie to the crew and team guest on the first floor. "We are ready to go. Please press the Mel meter (*See Equipment*) on record and turn on the recorder (digital sound recorder) and we leave you to ask questions there for three minutes or so, five minutes. Over."

Anthony stood at a centre of the floor, peering towards the window. Although it was pitch-black outside, beams of light could be seen passing out the window onto the roofs of the neighbouring keeper's cottages. These rays came from the working part of the Lighthouse: the lantern room.

With no reply back from the walkie-talkie, Anthony went to the top of the staircase to shout down to the group below. Before he did so, he turned to everyone within the area and said, "Did you hear that?"

He took a step forward to the top of the stairs but quickly turned around. "Did you hear that?" he said again, in an inquisitive way, trying to get a response from someone.

He thought that he had heard humming but the team guest suggested it was the machinery up at the top that had created this sound. Quickly dismissed, Anthony yelled to the group below to turn their walkie-talkie on. Once done, instructions were sent over the portable radio.

Anthony returned to standing at the centre of the third floor, staring towards the window in thoughtful consideration. The aim was to keep quiet for now and hope the group below would ask the Spirit world to make themselves known to Anthony, Sinead, Jason and the team guest.

A minute or so in, on the third floor, the K2 meter situated on top of a tricolour flag on the windowsill began to flicker. Sinead zoomed in on the device with the night vision camera. The meter seemed to be fluctuating up to 10 milliGauss, rather more than recorded in the baseline tests.

In the following three to four minutes, the lights on the K2 meter lit up to 20 milliGauss. Anthony blamed the meter's lights flickering to mobile phones although Jason, listening through his recording apparatus, had a different perspective.

"I don't hear any interference on this… no, nothing," he replied.

A few moments later, Anthony radioed down to the group below. "Okay there, folks, we're going to ask a question there. You stay there. We're going to ask a question on the walkie-talkie for few minutes and then, you can do the same to us up here, without us replying. Us being silent. Over."

Anthony asked the rest of the group if they wanted to ask a question. "Anybody want to ask anything?" he said.

Sinead responded, "Umm… do you know of any bodies that were washed up here near the Lighthouse?"

Anthony spoke through the walkie-talkie, relaying Sinead's question down to the first floor. Roughly less than two minutes later, the group on the first floor repeated the process and put forward their questions, via the walkie-talkie, to a hushed and observant third floor. Before both groups contacted each other, Sinead explained that she could hear taps and Anthony thought that he heard moaning earlier, perhaps from the lower level, rather than from the noise coming from the lantern room above.

The two groups switched around. Jen, Rhiannon, the female team member and the team guest composed themselves on the third floor. The body mood doll was placed halfway up the staircase, leading to the lantern room. The night vision camera was in Jen's care. Everyone else remained silent. As Jen scanned the space, a voice was heard over the recording, 'I wanna be a ninja'.

The words were spoken by a child, as the voice was softer than the voices of the team and guest and, it was a type of talk that a youngster would use.

Jen pointed the camera to the window, where the familiar rays of light could be seen. A loud exhale was caught on the night vision camera. It was suggested, by the female team member, that a child or a cat might have produced the sound that was audible. It had been made even more likely that we had an adolescent personality amid us.

Anthony radioed in, concerned that he could hear someone breathe heavily up above. All on the third floor denied that the heavy breathing had come from them yet, they could only speak for themselves.

The Lighthouse was hopping by now.

"What is that?" said the female team member, looking towards the night vision camera in dismay. She radioed Anthony with the walkie-talkie that she was holding. "Is any of you knocking downstairs. Over?"

Anthony responded back on the walkie-talkie. *Yes, we are but whispering there, okay? Just stay silent, okay? We're hearing something up here like a sound moving amongst yourselves.*

The female team member's jaw dropped. She shook her head in disbelief and replied back to Anthony, "No, it's not the knocking. It's coming from above. Over."

Everyone was still on the third floor. Jen directed the night vision camera towards the bottom of the winding stairs, slowly inserting the upward steps into shot and then, she finally focused the camera above her head, close to where the lantern room was located. Over a minute later, Jen concentrated the night vision camera on the window looking out to the keepers' cottages below. The unmistakable beams of light from the Lighthouse could be seen penetrating the dark coastal skyline, leaving a persistent glimmer on the surrounding cottages.

Anthony radioed in. *Okay lads, you can ask questions away. We heard a few footsteps there. Would, would you keep your feet still?*

The female team member was quick to respond back on the walkie-talkie. "We are really still there. Over."

Before we left the building, Anthony verified the results from the Mel meter, which was left on the ground floor of the Lighthouse. Very little change had occurred in the temperature and in the electromagnetic field over the duration of time that they had spent in there. The Information Centre Cottage was our next call, to see if the trigger objects had been moved but everything was in the same place as we left it.

A break to take in refreshments, especially quiche and chocolate cake (made by Jen), was needed. It would be in the Office Room in the Main Keeper's Cottage where we would get underway again. Jason and the two team guests left the location, bidding their farewells and heading into the cold night. The GhostÉire team were left to their own devices.

The Office Room was small enough, about 16 by 7 feet in area. It was over the Mess Room that we had been in earlier and next to the north and west view bedrooms. A filing cabinet and a side table, full of necessities such as a kettle and fan heater, occupied the left side of the room. A clothes cupboard and wooden drawer were located in the right-hand side of the room. The EMF reading in the room was less than 1 milliGauss.

A pack of rune stones (See Glossary) was brought into the investigation. Each team member picked out one stone from a small bag. It offered a little enlightenment ahead of the next experiment.

We moved onto the laser board, positioned on top of a wooden table at the centre of the room. The dial was removed with the intention of using it as a talking board.

The earlier part of the session was dedicated to trying to find out the identity of a tattooed man, whose headless body was found washed up close to the Lighthouse in November 1940. There was a refusal to give any information at first but, why? It was sensed that a bullying or controlling force was behind the planchette in which, Jen, Sinead, Rhiannon and the female team member were connected on.

Sinead asked, "Do you feel like that? That they done you wrong?"

The planchette moved a fast, half, clockwise circle around the centre of the board.

"Would you like to get your revenge...?"

The planchette moved at speed, manoeuvring a couple of clockwise, half circles before knocking into the piece of wood that represented 'F'.

At one stage, it was noticed that the Spirit showed detest for the heater that was on in the corner of the room.

"How does that heater affect you... What does it do to you?" asked the female team member.

The planchette went to 'B', 'A', 'D'.

"Do you feel tired around that, that device there? Do you feel tired?"

The planchette proceeded to 'Yes'

This could shed a light on why often derelict, ravaged buildings possess haunting behaviour (possibly due to coldness and the fact that they are left in an idle state).

The Spirit went by the nickname of 'Faz'. Anthony asked, "Okay Faz, umm, what you, what is the tattoo you got...?"

The planchette moved a straight line, ten inches or so towards the centre of the board then continued to move a large, half, clockwise circle then a small, half, clockwise circle before briefly stopping.

'Artist', said by a feminine voice, could be heard breaking in on the recording.

The wooden, heart-shaped planchette gradually started to recommence its motion, moving five-and-a-quarter small, clockwise circles.

"Where were you born?"

The motion of the planchette took it straight to 'A' but its failure to add a second letter, with the number of clockwise circles, led us to believe the Spirit in contact was not going to comply.

'I'm a spy' was muttered in a male, Cornish (West Country) English accent.

"Ahh, they are a spy. Do you not want to answer any of our questions?" said the female team member

'Maybe' was the reply, in a similar low, masculine tone.

The planchette was totalling up to nearly thirty clockwise rotations as Anthony looked away with the night vision camera, examining the rest of the room.

Sinead asked, "Are you angry?"

Finally, the planchette became still.

Anthony commented that he could hear banging coming from down below. He focused the night vision camera in on the closed door, the only way in and out of the room.

"Wait there, there is another knock," said Anthony to the rest of the team, requiring them to stay quiet. He felt that something loomed the other side of the door.

Returning to the board, the letters 'F', 'E', 'D', 'E', 'R', 'A', 'L' were spelt out.

"Federal agent?" said the female team member.

The planchette moved a small, half, clockwise circle to 'Yes'.

"Feds, are you with the Feds?"

The planchette moved one counter-clockwise circle back to 'Yes'.

"Are you a sailor?"

The planchette did one small, clockwise circle to 'Yes'.

About three minutes later, Sinead put forward a question which revealed a gripping answer.

"Is there something that we shouldn't know about that happened here?"

The planchette moved at a fast speed to 'Yes'.

The female team member asked, "Is it something to do with the headless corpse?"

The planchette moved to 'N', 'A, 'M', 'E' and 'Yes'.

It seemed likely that we were never ever going to get the name to the person. Even in death there was secrecy. It was now half past two in the morning.

Anthony crossed the yard over to the Lighthouse and placed a digital sound recorder, attached to a small tripod, on top of an equipment case. It would document any unusual activity in the period of time that the GhostÉire team were in the Information Centre Cottage.

The EMF measurement in the Information Centre Cottage was high. The fuse box and emergency exit lighting peaked at over 10 milliGauss

In an open area of the cottage, an astrology board (*See Glossary*) was placed on top of a foldable wooden square table. The board featured a wooden, two-way, symmetrical pointer. The red, green and yellow coloured array could be seen flashing from the laser beam machine, onto one side of the table and board.

The floor was paved in flagstones and was slightly uneven in places. The gable-end wall was covered in sandstone bricks, coated with lime mortar. The far-end wall consisted of ragged, chipped pieces of stone. The room was plain except for a few red durable-plastic, metal-legged chairs and a desk draped in a red-and-white-chequered PVC sheet.

A seismometer (*See Equipment*) was placed on top of the desk. Anthony opened up by calling out incantations. The team rubbed their hands together and mildly clapped. Sinead held the night vision camera and Jen stood back from the table, taking photographs with her digital camera.

Anthony, Rhiannon and the female team member would be involved in the table-tilting experiment. They all bent down and lightly placed their fingertips onto the edge of the astrology board.

"Try and move the dial. Try and move the dial. Come towards us now. Step forward. Move the dial, the dial," asked Anthony.

The streams of light looked striking from the laser beam machine, posing as some sort of electrical charge running along the arms and hands onto those around the table.

"The constellations, the navigational, you're maybe towards a ship, come towards us."

He mentioned that the table was starting to shake.

"You can use your voice to sound out. Can maybe knock on the table. Bang. Make footsteps. Make a smell. Come towards us now. Step forward. Maybe show yourself?"

The table could be seen visibly shaking at this point. It gradually developed into a gentle, steady rock before the movement suddenly ceased. Anthony, Rhiannon and the female team member took a couple of steps back from the board and table to straighten their backs. Encouragement was given to the other side to independently move the pointer. So far, it was not forthcoming.

Anthony, Rhiannon and the female team member connected on the table. They chanted and hummed. The table instantly began to shake heavily.

Anthony called out, "… north, south, east and west; north, south, east and west…"

The table rocked on opposite legs. The astrology board slid slightly, to and fro. Surprisingly, the pointer did not spin with the unstable tossing of the table.

About a minute or so later, those who were connected on the table decided to step back again. The next thing to do was bring another person in on the experiment. Sinead would join them, with Jen taking over the night vision camera work.

As the team connected the table reconvened into its motion. The legs tapped off the surface of the floor. The astrology board had to be put aside, due to the strong essence of power. The team commenced their touch on the table and with greater impact it rocked heavily on its legs, back and forth. A minute or so later, the table became motionless.

Sinead stated, "I'm feeling real strange right now. I feel really like I'm been spun around the room a few times."

She felt disorientated.

Shadows were assumed to have been seen towards the dark area of the split room. Smugglers, pirates and fishermen were coaxed to make their existence known.

"Sounded like a big bang there. Did you hear that? Did you hear that big bang there?" said Anthony, looking over to where the shadows were apparently seen.

"Yeah," said Sinead in agreement.

Anthony turned the laser beam machine off.

The team reconnected back on the table.

It was only a matter of seconds before the table excessively rocked on its legs.

Anthony shouted out, demanding a reaction, "We believe. We believe. Believe. We believe. Levitate. Lift the table… into the sky… into the air… into the sky… into the air… into the light… into the atmosphere…"

As the table seesawed, Anthony pointed out that he could hear voices and ordered everyone on the table to close their eyes.

Anthony yelled, "Imagine a white light now. Imagine a white light now. Bring this energy in. Imagine a white light now. Levitate this table. Levitate it. Lift it; lift it…"

Instantaneously, Sinead abruptly walked away from the table.

"Oh my god. Oh yeah, yeah. Left there, I heard a big bang!" she said, looking over towards the direction of the dark side of the room, where the shadows had been seen.

The rest of the team relinquished their link on the table. The team were adamant that something was moving in that particular spot. We had only needed to make a few footsteps to see if we could find out.

Jen had a full shot of the team assembled around the wooden table in front of the partition. She also got a glimpse of the foreboding upper darkness from the other room, behind their backs. Even though a break was thoroughly wanted at this point, we pushed for one last bit of involvement on our part. Sinead, Rhiannon and the female team member connected on the table. Anthony clapped at a fast pace. Sinead called out, "Do you like parties, parties… dancing… dancing… dancing?"

The table rocked on its legs and began to twist counter-clockwise. It responded to Sinead calling out in Irish. "Craic and music," she said.

Anthony joined in on the table. He also spoke out in Irish, "Again, again, again, again, again, again, again… again, again, again."

Faint humming could be heard on the night vision camera footage. The table's legs were ponding on the ground, eventually stopping when it struck a member of the team on their knee. The table was placed back to its former position.

There was a reaction when speaking in Irish. It could also have responded to mentions of a pleasant, long-ago age. Mentioning music (a familiar comfort to everyone's hearts) made the table act with uttermost vigour. A tinge of sadness was felt as the table halted. The team had talked about drinking a Guinness and playing an instrument – a reminiscing of indulgences. The team quickly lifted the burden.

Anthony thought that he heard rustling behind him. He glanced slightly to his right-hand side, trying to get a peep of beyond.

"Don't have to be upset," said Sinead in a caring tone of voice.

In the following moments, to bring back the happiness, various members of the team sang songs.

"Could you hum a little please?" asked Sinead.

A cold draught was experienced by almost everyone. Sinead commented that she was freezing.

The table could be seen slightly shifting on its legs, one side to the other. Anthony said, "Would you be able to slant this table? Lift it?"

Sinead asked, "Yeah, just give it against the wall, maybe…"

The table slanted, swaying with a particular simplicity, so much so that Anthony and Rhiannon felt comfortable in disconnecting.

The shifting of the table continued; with each team member pressing only their index fingers on top. As they shouted encouragement, a dull hum developed, gradually becoming louder. The humming appeared on a couple more occasions and it was not going unnoticed by some people.

The team broke into melody to the song, *Danny Boy*. More humming popped up, giving off the impression that the Spirit was trying to join in. Something else was enjoying our musical performance!

The team took a brief break to stretch their backs and chatted about what had just gone on. The conversation turned to the humming, which was projecting in the background and the cold draughts.

The team got back on the table.

"There is nine minutes on this," said Jen, referring to the amount of battery time left on the night vision camera.

There was just enough time for one last press.

"Thank you, dear Spirit, dear comrade. Thank you for giving this; this is great. I know your singing…" said Anthony.

The table moved backwards and forwards. A groan (decreasing in sound to a hum) could be heard in the backdrop.

"It's there again," said Rhiannon.

"Did you hear that noise? Did you hear that noise?" said Anthony enthusiastically.

The team returned to putting their index fingers on top of the table, in the hope that the movement would persist or, better still, get more active with less pressure. Our animation was plentiful, so hopefully it would have helped. As the tune *Molly Malone* was belt out, a loud sustained humming sound, lasting for at least fifteen seconds, was caught on the video. There were a couple of slight pauses in between the humming, suggesting intakes of air. It may have come from one of the GhostÉire crew yet, the humming was similar in resonance to previous audio.

Anthony, Sinead, Rhiannon and the female team member swiftly removed their index fingers; the table had come to rest. They each placed one hand on the table. Instantly, there came a familiar motion by the table, tipping from side to side. Moments afterward, the table turned drastically clockwise, heading in the direction of a wall. Anthony had to disconnect, although it did not deter him from clapping his hands again.

We were now in the early hours, approaching four o' clock in the morning. The break of day was not far off. The team continued to sing and, apart from the rocking, the table undertook one last act. It flopped over and slid on the ground. The support of the legs had given way, causing it to fall on its side. That was it. At this stage, we had to finish. Everyone headed to the Main Keeper's Cottage, to get a few hours' sleep.

Only tapping and clicking noises were picked up by the digital sound recorder in the Lighthouse. In every respect, it was ordinary.

Anthony awoke the team from their slumber around eight o' clock. The sun was unforgiving to the eyes, high in the sky and reflecting from the whitewash of the cottages.

Wait and wait they did for the RTÉ news reporter but, disappointingly, there was no reply back on the phone. Missing a free breakfast, they had decided to head back to catch the ferry home. Instead, the dolphins in the Shannon estuary would be on the RTÉ *Six One News* that night. Well, you could say they took the limelight but, we got the Lighthouse.

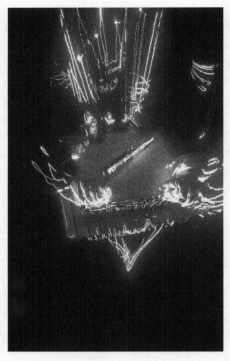

Some amazing pictures were taken with the laser beam machine

We were in the Information Centre Cottage, using an astrology board

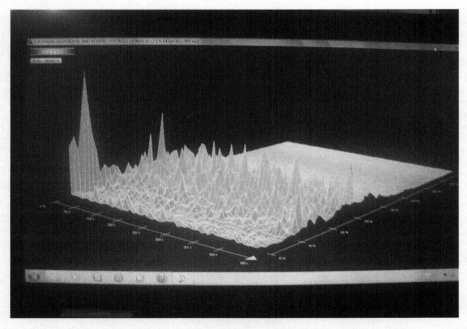

A graph indicates a high amount of background noise in the Lighthouse, with this rippled, wavy effect

It is easy to know why you need a Lighthouse here

A photo in the night looking down on the cottages

We have to go down to get out

Narrow stairs in the Main Keepers Cottage

What was in the dark room beyond? Maybe the laser beam will tell us

This was where coal used to be weighed

***Drowned-Out Voices* Investigation footage can be viewed by**

Watching the DVD that accompanies this book

Scanning the QR code

Visiting our website
www.GhostÉire.net

Click on the button
Drowned-Out Voices Footage

and enter the password
YourNotAlone

Enter the password
YourNotAlone

Location Background/Biography

Loop Head Lighthouse stands on the furthest point west on the County Clare coastline. The limestone-walled, white tower with a red balcony peaks at a height of 23 metres. There are a total of seventy-six steps from the ground floor to the top of the Lighthouse. Loop Head overlooks the northern shore of the River Shannon, high above the Atlantic-bombarded, cliff coastline.

The original Lighthouse beacon was built circa 1670, consisting of a cottage (Information Centre Cottage) with a large brazier on the roof, in which the Keeper and his family lived. It remains today, beside the Lighthouse, which was constructed in 1854.

For fifteen years, the light was a 'fixed' one until 1869, when the present 'intermittent' light, designed by George Halpin, was brought into operation. A screen rotated around a lamp to give the twenty seconds of light followed by four seconds of darkness vision. This was oil drawn until 1971, when it was powered by electric. The Lighthouse was automated in 1991, with a DGPS transmitting service being added in June 1998. A World War II (1939-1945) lookout point still remains around the perimeter walls of the Lighthouse.

Close to the Lighthouse, a British ship, *Water Lily*, sank off Loop Head on the 23 October 1836. The ship was set ablaze by a fire that originated with its cargo, with only one man from a crew of nine surviving.

Former Taoiseach, Enda Kenny visited the Lighthouse in 2012 with his family: his grandfather was a Keeper at Loop Head in the 1930s.

Manifestation/Legend

There was no paranormal significance to this location prior to the Investigation.

Conclusion

In the Mess Room, Sinead felt a build-up of some sort, possibly energy. The female team member also identified a lot of Spirits present, trying to scramble for command on the board. So, there was little surprise when it was revealed that there were twenty-four Spirits around us: fourteen men and ten women. All of these beings were from 1916 – the same era. It is hard to tell if all of them knew of our existence. The fact is that they all probably did and for a reason.

Furthermore, we got the month of March to the year of 1916. What rendered this time period important? Historical records state that on Good Friday, 21 April 1916, three days before the Easter Rising (*See Glossary*), an Eamonn Fennel of the 8th Battalion, Clare Brigade received information, in strict confidence from his brother, John Fennel, a lighthouse keeper at Loop Head Lighthouse, in which a British warship was spotted off the Kerry coast. The merchant steam ship, *Libau*, was easily visible off the coast of Loop Head Lighthouse on Thursday, 20 April 1916. This ship carried arms from Germany to Ireland, in preparation for the Easter Rising. An increase of anxiety and anticipation could have been felt within the walls. Everyone was on high alert in the weeks leading up to the Easter Rising.

On two different occasions, knocking could be plainly heard. The first time that this happened was when asking if a name appeared on any of the exhibition walls. Three knocks were noticed when discussion turned to the month of the year (March). It was not hard to discern that the Spirit was linking the number of knocks to the third month of the year. In between many team members reporting hearing footsteps. A female voice said, 'I hear them' on the night vision camera.

This could have come from a team member or guest but, at the same time, it was spoken softly, sounded unique and an unobtainable whisper soon followed. This whisper, which was perceived as 'Turn it' could have been an order from one Spirit to another on the dial, to distract the team from observing the space around them.

There was confirmation from the laser board that the Spirits were moving around us. At the beginning of the laser board experiment, the letters 'W' and 'G' were given for the initials of a Spirit. A William Gordon was believed to have worked at the Loop Head Lighthouse during the 1830s and, in addition, a William Gardner circa 1860s.

Would women have lived at the Lighthouse? On shore, lighthouses were able to accommodate the keepers' families. Women would have been able to live at dwellings near the site close to the husbands' work. Some women would have taken the profession of being a lighthouse keeper, especially if they had grown up there as children.

We could not find any trace of a shooting or any murder that took place on the site, mainly involving a keeper named Simon and a petty quarrel between lovers.

As Anthony, Sinead, Jason and the team guest remained silent in the Lighthouse, the K2 meter could be seen flickering up to 10 milliGauss. A possible explanation for this could be due to the night vision camera detecting interference from the mobile phone device that the guest had in his possession. For a brief period, the K2 meter's lights reached a reading of up to 20 milliGauss, this time without any cell phone interference caught by either the night vision camera or, Jason's microphone. We were in a Lighthouse and the differential GPS system (used by mariners for navigation and positioning) may have had something to do with the EMF fluctuations.

What was believed to be a child's voice said, 'I wanna be a ninja' to Jen, Rhiannon, female team member and guest on the third floor of the Lighthouse. A brief few seconds later, a loud breath was captured on the night vision camera, quickly followed by comments from the team of a high-pitch whoop sound, possibly coming from a child. The expelled air beforehand may have originated from a team member or guest. Anthony did hear heavy breathing coming from the room up above him, which Jen, Rhiannon, the female team member and guest member were in. Apart from that, it was fascinating that the group was at least able to detect the voice of a child on the camera and hear this voice for themselves in person. Again, children would have lived close to the area and may have accompanied the keepers, at times, to the Lighthouse.

In the 1960s, Japanese culture became fashionable as the prejudice that the western world held towards Japan, on account of its involvement in World War II, decreased. Was the child from this time period?

Anthony remarked on hearing footsteps above him. There were the odd few shuffles of feet from team members on the third floor and, perhaps, this was what he had heard.

Moving onto the Office Room, the team tried to collect information on the identity of the headless body that was found, washed up by the Lighthouse in 1940. What they received was the nickname, Faz — a federal agent who was a member of crew for a commercial or naval ship or boat. He did not want to disclose his real name. Faz may have worked for the United States during World War II. Where was he born? Only the letter 'A' came up on the board yet, a voice on the recording said, 'I'm a spy' in a West Country, English accent. Alternatively, these words may have been muttered by the female team member on initial reaction.

The headless corpse was found to have missing hands and legs when discovered, washed onto the rocks two hundred feet below, on the evening of 8 November 1940. The body was badly decomposed. Two £1 Bank of England notes were uncovered in a belt around the body's waist. There were no identifying papers on the body but there were a large number of tattoos: the head of a girl named Mary Barbara on the left wrist; a figure of Christ on the cross on the left bicep; a serpent and a ship on the right forearm and on the right shoulder, a tattoo of a girl with the words, 'Forget me not' over the head. The unknown man was believed to be a British merchant seaman and the county coroner concluded that the cause of death was from drowning.

In relation to body-markings, a woman's voice possibly said, 'Artist' after the team enquired about tattoos. Could one of the women (or possibly both) tattooed onto the skin be the tattooist?

The heater in the Office Room was reported to be bad for the Spirit. Hot air rises because it is less dense than cold air. The less thermal energy produced, the better. Possibly, Spirit manifestations enhance in colder environments because molecules are closer and do not expand as much (closer to a solid). It could all be to do with water in the air and how hydrogen bonds with it.

Banging and knocking were perceived to have happened in the Office Room, although nothing was captured on the night vision camera at that time.

In the Information Centre Cottage, Sinead felt that her head was spinning. At this stage, the laser beam machine was on. The irregular pattern coming from the lights of the apparatus could have been triggering this illusion, especially if it were in her eye line. This may have had something to do with the shadows that were seen by the spilt area on the other side of the room. Still, bangs were reported by Anthony and Sinead, believed to be originating from that particular section. When the team reassembled to that section of the room, the table's motion became more potent. Unintentionally, it may have been the team's desire and enthusiasm that drove the table's force.

The humming did leave us baffled. By simply singing, we achieved the foremost reaction. All of the team on the table declared hearing several humming noises. This would count out those in close presence of each other from creating this noise. Furthermore, it did not come from Jen behind the night vision camera. It was likely that a Spirit was trying to join in on our singing.

At one point on the night vision camera, the humming turned into a certain long groan when the group were not singing at all. Members of the team were either speaking or completely silent at that precise moment.

Loop Head Lighthouse
Co Clare

WEBSITE: loopheadlighthouse.ie
e-MAIL: tourism@clarecoco.ie
PHONE: 087 223 4263
FACEBOOK: clarecountycouncil

Tours are available daily from April to September. Check website for details.

The Lighthouse and Cottages are open for tours on an annual basis in conjunction with the Commissioners of Irish Lights and Clare County Council.

The tour involves looking at the lifestyle of a Lighthouse keeper, history of the buildings, the evolution of the Lighthouse through the years and much more.

The Light keepers House makes an ideal getaway, accommodating up to five people.

Nearby caves and rock faces are home to many animals. The cliffs offer a great viewpoint to spot seabirds, seals, whales and dolphins.

BALLINAMUCK 1798 VISITOR CENTRE

Layout

GREAT MEMORIAL HALL

COMMON ROOM

Rough Dimensions

Chapter 19
Ballinamuck 1798 Visitor Centre

Sinead's Journey

What can I say? Ballinamuck is a hidden, quaint, miniscule village in the depths of Longford. What on earth could be discovered there? Well, to be precise, bloody battles including the Battle of Ballinamuck.

In 1798, the British troops charged at the United Irishmen (accompanied by the French army) across the surrounding landscape as bugles blew, horses galloped and a total of 28,350 men fought – many of them to their death. It was Wolfe Tone (*See Glossary*) country and Irish rebels were out in force, in an uprising against British rule. Unmerciful killings and hangings were the factors at play for this investigation. Anger, sadness, revenge, pride and lost dreams were, more than likely, the emotions.

I decided that I would like to carry out a past enactment at this investigation, to try and enhance some Spirit engagement. Pulling out all the tricks and gathering a mixture of sounds together, I edited a four-minute audio piece, recreating the battle cries, bugles, galloping horses and clashing swords. To add to the effects, I wrote out a speech on a large scroll, with the intention of reading it out before the battle sounds commenced. An entire ten-minute act, it would be GhostÉire's rendition of the Battle of Ballinamuck (a new play in the making – or so it would seem).

Leaving work early that day and changing out of my formal, business-like attire to pursue other-worldly hobbies, I jumped on the Dublin to Athlone bus route. Smiling to myself about the contrasts of the two situations (the 'real world's' day-to-day normalities of life alongside the pursuit of fun, exciting and quirky interests), I texted Anthony and Jen to let them know that I was on my way. They were both travelling from Killarney, in County Kerry and would pick me up in Athlone, in County Westmeath, three hours later.

Dozing off on the bus due to the summer sun beaming through the windows, I nearly missed my stop. Lingering around the Athlone bus and railway station, waiting to be picked up by the others, I was surprised how deserted the place was. This place was more than likely bustling with activity in times gone by. Or else, I must have been there at the wrong time of day. It was probably the latter.

Train times were announced, over a loud intercom, to a near empty station as I wandered around, inspecting the old black and white photos on the wall. Since being on the team, I have been to every train station in Ireland; you would swear I was a railway enthusiast!

After about forty minutes, I called Jen to find out where they were. They told me to make my way to Athlone town. Looking around, I could not see any town in sight. Was I even at the correct place? I know that I was tired getting off the bus and was still a bit groggy but, I could have sworn I was in Athlone. Heavy rain pelting down, I hailed a taxi and leapt into the front seat. "Athlone town, please."

Zooming up the road, I jumped out of the taxi after five minutes and spotted Jen and Anthony's car in the town centre. I paid my fare, jumped into their car and flung my bag on the back seat with a sense of urgency. Then, away we fled. It was a relay race of transport in a way.

Darkness was beginning to sweep in. Time was running out (we had an hour left until our expected arrival), so we picked up the pace. With a lack of sufficient signposts, no satnav on board, nor any sign of civilisation nearby, the glorified road map was our only navigation tool. Fields galore on each side, positive uplifting music pulsating through the car, I was beginning to get pumped up for the evening. A happy mind-set leads to a free-flowing and successful investigation.

Darkness was catching up and we drove around never-ending windy bends, hoping to reach Ballinamuck by the designated time. After a wrong turn, we frantically scanned the map, looking for the correct road. We were lost in Longford, literally. What must it have been like for those who travelled the barren, lonely roads years ago, with no immediate transport or light available? We surely have it easy nowadays.

Down to serious business, we switched off the music and concentrated on the journey ahead. Within the car, silence prevailed and swerving around bends continued. Anthony upped the speed, realising that we were behind time. Formula One racing here we come!

Popping up out of nowhere, a tiny village appeared – this must be it! We had finally arrived at Ballinamuck 1798 Visitor Centre. Trying to comprehend the scene of the battle that took place over 200 years ago, I scanned the vicinity of the area, noticing the outlined historical information printed on large boards. Generally, I refrain from looking through any noticeable information about the investigations beforehand, as I thoroughly enjoy discovering the answers on the talking board as they present themselves. I guess you could say that I love surprises. However, in this case, due to the enormity of the battle and the number of soldiers that perished, I digested as much knowledge as I could.

Left palm up, right palm down, we joined in a circle outside the building and carried out a protection prayer. It was if we were also preparing to go into battle: armouring ourselves with bright white light, imaging that it would keep us safe from any unwanted entities, just in case. It can help your brain to calm down and your pulse rate to drop. Maybe we should open a meditation class as well, at this rate!

Also, possessing a clear mind-set is of ultimate importance. It can boost concentration levels and enable you to pick up subtleties in the environment a lot quicker. No need for any mental chitter-chatter when on investigations. Being totally in the zone is the key!

After Anthony wrapped up the protection circle, we grabbed the equipment and stepped forth towards the building. What type of Spirits would make themselves known? Could we match up the answers on the board with documented history? Would they make themselves known if they hear the recorded battle cries? Would we hear the battle cries instead? Feeling like a proud Irish rebel, it was time to enter the building and seek out some soldiers of the past…

The Investigation

NUMBER OF TEAM

3

2

NUMBER OF GUESTS

Sometimes when you travel, you easily pass a building, a village or town not giving a second thought to its composition. Today, society may not look beyond what it sees or does. We live in a fast culture. The majority of the time, there is no need to take lengthy journeys to far destinations. So, we might miss out on the stories that these places have to offer.

Our destination, this time, was Ballinamuck: a small rural village in County Longford with a particular building that, if it could talk, would have a surprising yarn to tell.

Anthony, Jen and Sinead arrived in Ballinamuck that summer evening at around half past six. Patiently waiting to see them were Paddy, Tess and Rachel. Paddy escorted the team to a particular area of the building, a corridor that led out to the Great Memorial Hall. Prior to the development, this museum had cells that housed prisoners when it was a former barracks. The team got down to business at a brisk pace. This would be a short investigation.

Stepping on a blue carpet with a white floral design and, taking a few steps up a flight of stairs, we paused, not for wanting to take off our footwear, on account of the comfortable underlay but because, amidst looking up over the white rail banisters, we came across a circular window with the Star of David symbol on it. This window faced the front of the building but from the outside, it had a different aspect to it: a clock face.

At the top of the landing, we made our way through a door towards our left, to the Common Room. There were two interior window reveals (large square gaps in the wall) that extended inwards to a smaller, framed window. These small, framed windows were of stained glass with yellow and maroon colour panes on the outside and a clear glass pane at the centre. Spying out through the clear pane of glass, we could see an overhead view of the Great Memorial Hall down below.

On the wall above the windows was a painting of an artist's impression of a particular feat: An act of courage in a scene from the Battle of Ballinamuck. It showed two United Irishman soldiers holding a cannon aloft on their shoulders. The muzzle or tip was raised in the air, pointing towards the direction of an advancing British cavalry. Lying on the ground are slain Irish and French soldiers. Their surviving compatriots were in an apparent state of disarray. Prominent and high in the fierce blazed sky was the Irish green, harp flag – a source of inspiration amongst a ruthless massacre.

After Paddy had shown us around, he said his farewell. Anthony gratefully thanked him and told him he would be in touch. Back in the Common Room, several items were placed on a rectangular table. For the first experiment, we would be using the singing bowl (*See Equipment*), a digital sound recorder that was mounted on a mini tripod and, a voltmeter (*See Equipment*) for a séance. Two glass tumblers and the colour mood frame were at the other end of the table; they would be used later on.

Sinead set up a microphone stand beside the table. A dynamic microphone was clipped into place via the flexible lead on top of the microphone stand. Sinead plugged the dynamic microphone into an old amplifier box. The box was positioned inside the colour mood frame, on the table a few feet away from the stand. The microphone had been set hanging down over the table. Any abnormal sound could be amplified for us at that present moment and, for the recording devices (on later review).

The temperature was warm inside at 19.2°c. The C low on the decibel level read 34.0 and the A low read 33.9. The building gave up very little noise.

According to the astrological significance leading up to the investigation, we would uncover tension in the air, with struggle over power and control, with the Sun opposing Pluto. It was time for a vital change. Could this justify the conflict between adversaries?

After Jen took several pictures, she helped Sinead organise the full spectrum camera and video camera into position. Both cameras were placed either side of the room, opposite each other, focused in on the table.

The time was now half past seven. Jen and Anthony took up their seats at the section of the table that was earlier assigned for the purpose of a séance. The digital sound recorder had been switched on. Sinead pressed the play button on the full spectrum camera and walked over to the table, pulling up a chair between Anthony and Jen. Tess and Rachel sat at one corner of the Common Room.

No doubt they were curious to find out what they might witness. As Sinead sat down, Anthony gave a clear description on the process of opening the séance and what was about to happen.

Quickly settled, one by one, everybody called out their names. Anthony began speaking, going into detail about the equipment we would be using to contact the Spirits.

"We're not here to cause you any harm. We're not here to be intrusive and thank you for communicating with us tonight."

He took the wooden paddled mallet in his right hand (a tool used for playing the singing bowl) and heavily beat the top lip of the instrument. He circled the top of the bowl counter-clockwise with the head of the mallet. In doing so, a tolling sound reverberated, not just in the Common Room but within the open spaces of the building. The humming chime lasted for about twenty seconds. As soon as Anthony placed the mallet aside, an EVP was picked up. What only could be described as a man's voice said 'What was that' in a surprised tone, potentially a distance away from the Common Room. We do not think that it was due to another human popping in that evening. Maybe it was a Spirit. We do not know for sure. Later however, we would receive vocal feedback to another harmonious implement being played.

Each team member had their palms flat down on the table. Jen and Sinead had their eyes closed, as though in a state of concentration, whilst being receptive and aware. If Tess and Rachel were not bewildered by now, then they never would be!

We carried on with the normal abnormalities. Days before the investigation, the team had jotted down a few questions that they wanted to ask, in preparation for the séance. Reading from his note pad, Anthony got started first.

"What sort of artillery did you use?"

There was a silence for a few seconds and then he asked another question.

"Did you pray before battle?"

He carried on calling out questions for the next two-and-a-half minutes. All was very quiet.

It was Sinead's turn next. She also made a tune with the singing bowl before reading from her note pad. She asked such questions like, "What regrets do you have?" and "What was this building used for?"

Yet again, there was silence.

Jen took over the next sequence of questioning. She opened using the singing bowl.

"Can you hear our voices?" she said.

Moments later, she added, "Let me hear your voice."

Questions flowed from Jen for another couple of minutes until everything had been asked and it was time for a bit of a change in the séance. The voltmeter was introduced.

Before that, Jen went over to the video camera at the other side of the room and turned it on. This would keep close sight of the pointer on the voltmeter, should the voltage increase or decrease. A black (common probe) and a red (circuit test) lead connected into the voltmeter. Anthony held the metal tip of the red lead in his right hand; Jen held the metal tip of the black lead in her left hand. The next bit of the séance link was fulfilled, with Sinead lightly clasping both Anthony's and Jen's spare hands.

The voltmeter was aligned to the current DC readings (most commonly used in battery powered electrics or the stability of dead circuits). We would be checking for minor spikes in the séance circle. Again, starting with Anthony, each team member called out when it was their turn. The pointer rose from 0 volts to 1.5 volts before Jen began to deliver her questions. The reason for this, at that time, was that each person had tightened their grip on the person next to them. The experiment ended with no sign of a flutter so far.

It was when the team got up from their seats and walked around that an uncharacteristic breath – an exhale – was picked up. Unfortunately, the digital sound recorder had been turned off beforehand; however, the full spectrum camera and the video camera managed to record it. It was like the sound made by fogging up a window or mirror with your breath, to sketch or write in the condensation.

Both Jen and Sinead turned their attention to the cameras that they had attended to earlier.

It was unlikely that they – or Anthony, who was in view of the two cameras at the time – made this EVP. Also, Tess and Rachel were talking to each other as it happened.

We carried on with our schedule. Hopefully, we would examine the strategic positions of both sides of the conflict, in the Battle of Ballinamuck, by using grid reference mapping. Jen had earlier cellotaped three laminated nationality cards on one side of the colour mood frame. Represented were the Irish green harp (Nationalist), as well as the French (Tricolour) and the British (Union Jack) flags.

An A4 sheet of paper, with a map of Ballinamuck and the surrounding area, was placed on the end of the table that we had previously

used for the séance. The map was grid referenced one to five on the
vertical axis and A to D on the horizontal axis. We had twenty
spaces to cover in total. In front of the map on the table, a chair
was left standing, allowing any Spirit of a military background
to sit down and give us their interpretation of how the battle
evolved and ended. On the side of the frame opposite to the
nationality cards (design test section) was a sheet of A4 paper.
Marked on it was the word 'Neutral'. If the glass should move in
this direction, it would mean an unallied portion of land.

The old amplifier box was placed down on a seat beside the table.
Sinead pressed the switch button down on the digital sound recorder.
Also, beside her was the body mood doll. We would need it to
diagnose any Spirit's final fate if they succumbed to an injury
during the battle.

Jen and Sinead took up their seats beside the colour mood frame.
Jen discarded one of the glass tumblers. The other one that we
would be using was put at the centre of the frame by Sinead.
Anthony walked over to the table.

"So, dear Spirits. I know you might be still around there. What
we're going to be doing is a bit of glass divination… only for about
twenty minutes or so. Umm, here is different colours representing
a mood. So, you might represent a mood that you're in… what I
got here… is a see-through map, gridded with Ballinamuck. Now,
I'm going to ask probably… three different armies representing… so
was three wasn't there? Umm, where your strategic positions were
before and maybe after…"

When Anthony finished talking, he went over to a vacant table at
one side of the room, pulled up a chair and sat down on it. Jen and
Sinead placed their index fingers on the upturned glass tumbler.
Who or what would make their first move? Anthony got things going.

"Dear Spirits, err, is there Spirits there from three armies
around? There is yes or no on the other side of the frame. Can you
move the glass towards that area?"

The glass went a steady pace, in a straight line, to 'Amber', to
specify 'Daring and Stimulating'. The glass was put back to centre
of the frame.

"Okay… can you tell me which army you represent?"

There seemed to be a purpose in the glass's movement. It moved
in a straight line, stopping alongside a nationality flag card.
The tip of the glass made a cutting noise off the surface. Jen and
Sinead declared where it had gone too. "France," they both said.
The glass was put back on the centre of the frame.

Anthony wanted to correctly understand if the French soldier in our company had survived the battle. Marked down on the other side of the frame (area designated as being neutral) were the words 'Yes' and 'No'.

"Can you tell us; did you survive the battle?"

The glass made a straight line for 'Yes'. The glass tumbler was picked up and put back to centre.

We had to establish if the Spirit knew how the grid reference mapping worked. Anthony asked a question relating to this. The glass went to 'Yes', confirming that we were good to go.

"Can you tell me… who occupied with the flags towards…?"

Before Anthony could finish off the question, the glass had moved a fast, straight line to 'Black', meaning 'Stressed, Tense and Nervous'. The glass was removed from the side of the frame and placed back to centre. It was our opinion that the Spirit felt this emotion. It was not understood if that emotion was sensed by the Spirit exactly before the battle or presently, with us.

Anthony continued, "Can you tell me who occupied…?"

Again, the glass indicated a state of urgency, moving in a direct line and smashing up against the side of the frame before Anthony could finish off what he wanted to say.

Jen called out where it had gone too. "Amber," she said. This meant 'Daring and Stimulating' and was dedicated to the first occupied region of A1. Jen put the glass back to centre.

We advanced towards the grid reference mapping. Anthony asked, "Can you tell me who occupied A1…?"

It took a few seconds this time. It moved a straight line at a slower pace. It slightly adjusted its grip on the tabletop surface, eventually stopping on the 'Irish' (Nationalist) nationality card. A further two more square regions were completed outright.

Anthony continued on, "Can you… A4?"

It took about seven seconds before the glass started to track a path across the table from the centre. It moved slow, knocking into the side of the frame to 'Red', describing 'Adventurous, Excited and Alert' as an emotion. Also, Jen indicated that it was close to the 'French' (Tricolour) card.

Everything was going fine with the experiment. The Spirit present was being very co-operative. We had come to a section on the map where the village of Ballinamuck was positioned. This area was described as being influenced by the British.

Anthony called out, "B4?"

The glass travelled from centre of the frame to 'Brown', meaning 'Restless'. It then moved a straight line, hammering into the side of the frame where the 'British' (Union Jack) nationality card was. The motion did not cease. The glass tumbler reverted back to 'Brown', then curtailed its force as it moved to the 'British' (Union Jack) card again.

Sinead said to Anthony, "Err, British."

Jen quickly commented, "Brown…"

The glass made a beeline across the inside of the frame, again to 'Brown'.

Anthony asked Sinead and Jen, "Brown, is it?"

Jen replied, "Brown…"

Sinead confirmed, "Brown… restless."

To signify the importance of this particular area of the map, the glass being touched by Jen and Sinead's right index fingers moved in a straight line again. It smashed into the side of the frame next to the 'British' (Union Jack) card. It ultimately sent the glass onto its side. Sinead picked the glass up and placed it back at the centre of the frame. A short time later, the activity of the glass tumbler changed.

"… C1?"

It slowly made four-and-a-half medium-sized, counter-clockwise circles before gradually stopping. It then moved in a straight line for a few inches, knocking heavily into the side of the frame, resulting in the glass slightly leaning over on its rim in front of Jen and Sinead. It had moved to 'Amber', noting 'Daring and Stimulating' as a potential sentiment.

Jen put the glass to centre. Sinead and Jen resumed contact on the glass. The glass made a line for the 'French' (Tricolour) card. Jen picked up the glass and positioned it back to centre of the frame. No sooner than Sinead and Jen had put their finger back on the glass, it showed no hesitation in slamming back into the 'French' (Tricolour) card. Maybe the Spirit was just making sure!

The remaining sections of the map were filled in a short time later. To clarify that all the information was accurate, Anthony called out "… was that before the battle?"

In quick reply, the glass moved across the table in a straight line, banging into the side of the frame marked 'Yes'. The glass was put back to centre.

Anthony continued speaking. "Would you be able to tell me the strategic positions after (battle)…?"

As he was talking, the glass had already started to move, circulating seven-and-a-half small-to-medium, clockwise circles and moving ten inches or so, in a straight line, to 'Yes'.

Sinead placed the glass to centre. Immediately, as Jen and Sinead both connected on the glass tumbler, it advanced six inches or so in a straight line to 'Black', referring to 'Stressed, Tense and Nervous'.

This was probably the current state that the Spirit was feeling, as this colour was singled out previously.

Anthony progressed onto the second part, attempting to discover where the soldiers were situated after the battle. He soon made a mistake by calling out the wrong co-ordinate. The glass moved quite slowly at this point. The Spirit must have been confused! He amended what he had mistakenly done.

"Did I say B2? Sorry, sorry dear Spirit. A2?"

There was no need to worry. The glass went from its indecisive pace, slowly circulating three small, counter-clockwise circles to a three-quarter, medium-sized, clockwise circle to the 'Irish' (Nationalist) card. It skimmed the inside of the frame a few inches to include the 'French' (Tricolour) card on its journey.

Anthony needed confirmation that two parties had occupied that space. The glass was put at centre.

"Was that Ireland and France?"

The glass moved from centre of the frame, stopping at 'Yes'. Subsequently, we would find out that a second area of the map was taken up by more than one army.

"B3?"

The glass did one small, clockwise circle, briefly stopping before returning to the centre of the frame. It began to move again, gradually picking up pace. It did a one-and-a-half medium-sized clockwise circle, knocking into the side of the frame, to where the nationality cards were, sliding up against the timber. It hit all three cards as it bypassed them back to the centre of the frame. The Spirit indicated that the British, the French and the Irish had all been within this spot.

There was an interesting motion by the glass when enquiring about (D,1). The glass made seven medium-to-small, clockwise, circular loops as it targeted the 'French' (Tricolour) nationality card. It made the same number of circles, with the same style of performance, in regard to (D,2). Why would the glass take this type of action? All was done within this part of the grid reference mapping. To make sure, Anthony asked, "… was that the battle after… the positions after the Battle of Ballinamuck?"

It took about four seconds for the glass to respond. It went straight to 'Yes'.

We thought that it would be fascinating if we could get an opposing opinion about what happened.

"Is there any… British soldier around?"

The glass moved a straight line from centre to 'Yes'.

The glass was put back to its original position by Jen.

"Did you die in battle?" said Anthony.

Quickly responding, the glass moved to 'Yes'.

The glass was put at centre.

"Using the colours around the frame, can you tell me…?"

The roar of the glass interrupted Anthony as it moved to 'Amber', meaning 'Daring and Stimulating'.

Anthony was unsure what this meant, so he asked, "Is that your feeling now?"

The glass tumbler went directly to 'Yes'.

Jen placed the glass back to the centre of the frame.

Anthony assumed that there might be only one set of questions (before the battle) with the grid reference mapping for the British soldier because of its untimely death.

"Can you tell me what…?"

Again, before Anthony could get his words out, the glass made its way to 'Amber'.

The glass was moved to the centre of the frame.

Anthony succeeded in his third attempt.

"Can you tell me where? Using the doll… on the… beside the frame, corresponding with the colours on the frame. Can you tell me which area did you get affected during the Battle of Ballinamuck? Which part of the body with the doll?"

Slowly, the glass moved as Anthony finished off the question. It went to 'Orange', which meant 'Unsettled and Mixed Emotions' but linked with the 'Neck' area with the body mood doll.

Jen placed the glass back at the centre of the frame. She said that she was not certain that this was correct. Anthony called out to the Spirit, "Is it, is it the neck? Is that correct?"

This time, the glass moved an unfamiliar path, moving a half, medium, clockwise circle and stopping at 'No'.

The glass was moved back to the centre by Jen.

Anthony whispered, "Is it the legs?" He called out louder to get an answer, "Is it the legs?"

In a straight line, the glass shot to 'Yes'.

The glass was picked up and put back to centre.

"Did you? Is that how you felt? That's what caused your death? Is it an injury towards your legs?"

The answer was 'Yes'. The earlier movement to 'Orange' may have been the result of the Spirit of the British soldier's regret about the injury that caused its death.

Anthony asked, "Can you tell me the positions of the British before the Battle of Ballinamuck?"

The glass moved very slowly this time, moving a one-and-a-half medium-to-small, clockwise circle to 'Yes'.

The glass was placed at the centre of the frame. As Anthony began to roll the co-ordinates, Jen suspected that all was not accurate.

"It's the Frenchman," she said.

There was a reaction to this. The glass moved to 'Yes'. We had not entirely asked the French soldier to step back and let forth the British soldier. When we asked for the British soldier to come forward, the answers we got before might have not been that precise. However, the French soldier could have been acting as a go-between. After a short while, we received indication that the British soldier was in control of the divination vessel.

Anthony called out, "Can you tell me what A1 is…?"

The glass moved three small, clockwise circles, converting into a straight line, finally ending up at the 'Irish' (Nationalist) card. Normal service had resumed.

Later, a whispering voice seemingly said 'Should be' in a soft tone. It was picked up over the recordings, possibly in reaction to the glass moving to the 'Irish' (Nationalist) card when Anthony called out, "B4?". Either Tess or Rachel (off camera) may have spoken these words unwittingly to us. It is likely that we struck an accord. We continued on…

"C5?" said Anthony.

It took about eleven seconds for the glass to respond to this question. It moved slowly up alongside 'Orange', meaning 'Unsettled and Mixed Emotions'.

The glass was picked up and put back to centre.

There was not any hurry to pick out a nationality card for this co-ordinate. This Spirit must have had reservations regarding this particular part of land, one which caused its passing.

Light rain had been forecast for the day. The lux reading was at 035, not that bright. Still, in the last few minutes, the room within grew darker. The final bits of the experiment were completed and the map was filled in. To finish things off, Anthony asked, "And dear Spirit. Was it you that… got hurt with the legs?"

We witnessed the glass move in a straight line, with no hesitation, to 'Yes'.

The glass was put back to centre by Jen.

"Was that before the battle?" said Anthony.

The glass moved a few inches in a straight line, completing two counter-clockwise circles before pulling up bedside 'No' on the frame. Looking back, it was likely that the details given by the British soldier concerned the battle in progress.

For the next part of the investigation, we took aim at what the Great Memorial Hall could deliver. The digital sound recorder was placed down on the creaky timber flooring. The hall was very spacious. Ahead of us was the stage, raised up about three feet from the ground. The back wall of the stage had a striking poster, which commemorated the bi-centenary year (1998) of the battle. The flash of the camera was acting as a counterbalance, as the words on the poster gleamed on the photographs Jen had taken.

On either side of the stage were toilets: the gents to the right and the ladies to the left. Chairs, which you would commonly associate with finding in a late twentieth century school, were stacked up in a perfect line at opposite flanks of the hall. Above these chairs, on both walls, were colourful paintings, symbolising peace and local interests.

Anthony was preparing the full spectrum camera to record. The legs of the tripod, to which it was attached, were fully extended, giving a perfect view of Sinead up on the stage, as she did a past enactment experiment. The digital sound recorder and the full spectrum camera were switched on. Jen quietly strolled around, randomly taking photos. Sinead was given the go ahead to start.

The sound of a bugle horn, orchestrating a rally to fight, came from Sinead's recording device. Once that was finished, she rolled out a piece of paper scroll. She had a speech prepared. Loudly she spoke, "Attention, attention. On this day on eighth of September, seventeen ninety-eight, in Ballinamuck, the French proudly joined forces with the United Irishmen to prepare for battle against twenty-six thousand British. British soldiers assembled by their viceroy Lord Cornwallis…"

She continued, detailing the repercussion of the event.

"For those of you who wish to seek your revenge or voice your opinion, now's your chance to step forward and let us know what happened on that day. I'm now going to play the French national anthem, so if there's any French Spirits here that like to come forward, please do. Say what, say what you want. If you want to seek revenge, please step forward."

She switched the recording device on.

An arousing performance of the French anthem, *La Marseillaise*, was playing. In the meantime, Anthony was analysing the change in temperature on Sinead and the area around her on the stage with the thermal imaging camera.

The anthem radiated in the background as Sinead took her time asking specific questions. Soon, the anthem rounded off. Following that came more bugles, calvary, shouting, roaring and sword-swiping noises. Amongst all this, a whisper was found on the recordings. It was believed to be that of an adolescent speaking but, it was difficult to know what was spoken.

Anthony picked up the tripod with the full spectrum camera attached and walked up closer to the stage. Sinead continued calling out.

Three minutes or so later, Sinead played a piece of audio on her recording device: a written text by Wolfe Tonne from 1798, when he was captured and sentenced to death. Four and a half minutes had passed when Sinead switched the recording device off and called out in French and Irish, seeking a response.

Anthony directed the full spectrum camera to the right of the stage, towards the gents' toilets and Jen, who was a metre from him. He then focused the camera at the front entrance to the hall. A voice was picked up. 'I'm tired', it possibly said. It echoed in the vast space.

Surely, only the living could make such a distinct vocalisation and this was different. Better still, thirty seconds later, after Sinead had finished off her questions, Jen made it apparent that she had heard a voice, possibly originating from the gents' toilets. Also, Anthony professed to hearing something, around the same time, in the background, a few moments beforehand.

We had done all we wanted to do. All that was left was to say a few words, with an honest thank you to all. Getting back to the car, we gathered the readings from the pedometers, which Jen and Anthony had put on after arriving at the location. In the space of over two hours, Jen had recorded a distance of 0.5km, whilst Anthony recorded 0.3km. There had not been much walking about in this investigation.

It had been exciting to co-operate with differing sides of the warring parties. We felt that an understanding had been accomplished. It seemed that the Spirit energies were still reflecting on what had happened in the past at Ballinamuck. Some are still clinging onto it; others, we hope, have moved on. A moment lasts in memory.

BATTLE OF BALLINAMUCK 1798

Fig 1: A FRENCH SOLDIER (SURVIVED) PERSPECTIVE 'BEFORE' THE BATTLE OF BALLINAMUCK 1798.

IRISH (NATIONALIST)   FRANCE (TRICOLOUR)   BRITISH (UNION JACK)

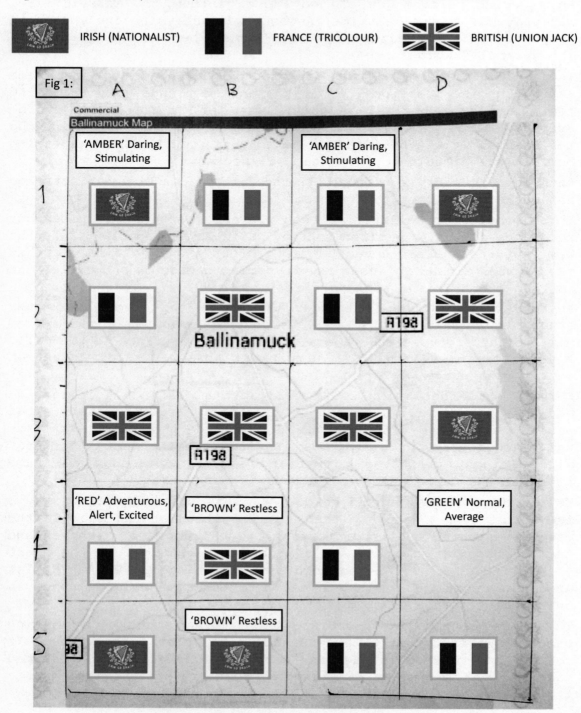

BATTLE OF BALLINAMUCK 1798

Fig 2: A FRENCH SOLDIER (SURVIVED) PERSPECTIVE 'AFTER' THE BATTLE OF BALLINAMUCK 1798.

IRISH (NATIONALIST)   FRANCE (TRICOLOUR)   BRITISH (UNION JACK)

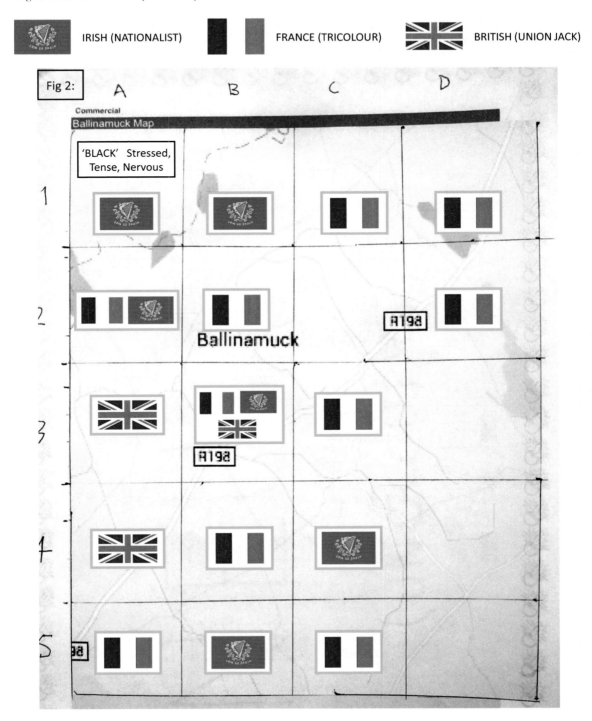

BATTLE OF BALLINAMUCK 1798

Fig 3: A BRITISH SOLDIER (DIED) PERSPECTIVE 'DURING' THE BATTLE OF BALLINAMUCK 1798.

IRISH (NATIONALIST)   FRANCE (TRICOLOUR)   BRITISH (UNION JACK)

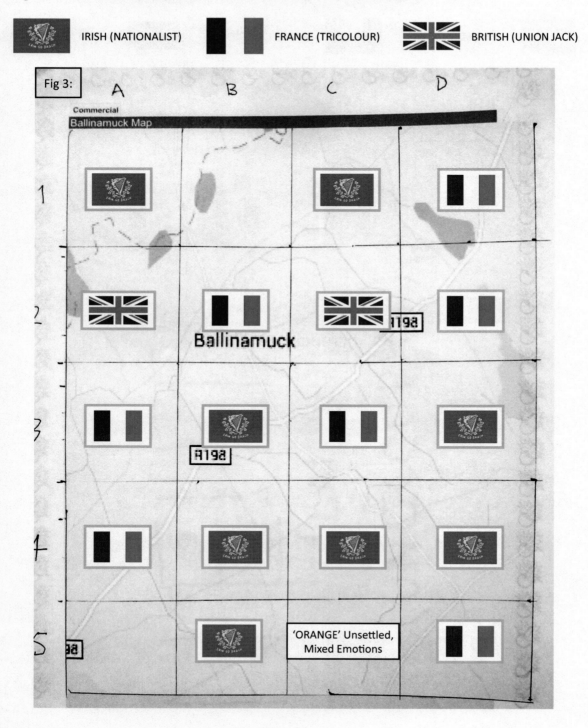

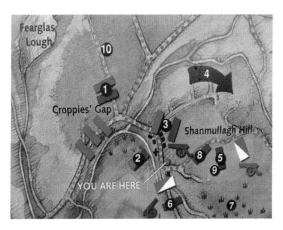

The strategic positions in the Battle of Ballinamuck are shown on this map

A corridor that had previously led to the cells in the barracks

The Star of David. The Visitor Centre was probably a masonic lodge at some point.

We just came up that way...

The Battle of Ballinamuck was gruesome

A thermal imaging camera pointed at the table in the Common Room

Let's see who's about using the nationality cards

Sinead read from a scroll on top of the stage

A wide view of the Great Memorial Hall

***Drowned-Out Voices* Investigation footage can be viewed by**

Watching the DVD that accompanies this book

Visiting our website

www.GhostÉire.net

Click on the button

Drowned-Out Voices Footage

and enter the password

YourNotAlone

Scanning the QR code

Enter the password

YourNotAlone

Location Background/Biography

The Visitor Centre was formerly an RIC (Royal Irish Constabulary) barracks, built around 1830, reputedly by the King/Harman family. The three-bay, two-storey building has been modernised and extended into a Visitor Centre, displaying the events before and after the Irish Rebellion of 1798 (*See Glossary*) associated at the Battle of Ballinamuck, from both sides of the opposing armies.

The walls of the Visitor Centre are made from sandstone. The clock face (previously a Star-of-David patterned window) is twinned with a Gaelic inscription centred above a timber door entrance. This could be why it was thought to have been a Masonic lodge at some stage. A Cannon sits on a sandstone plinth, which was also used in the Battle of Ballinamuck.

The barracks was attacked by General Seán McEoin (Blacksmith of Ballinalee, formerly St Johnstown) during the Irish War of Independence, 1919-1921. Originally, the building had two turrets/towers attached at either side of the barracks. They have not been seen since the attack, by General McEoin (IRA), in June of 1920. The building was restored in 1948 and was converted to a museum in July 1999 (opened by the President of Ireland, Mary McAleese).

The Battle of Ballinamuck is remembered every 8th September. The conflict details how a 2,350 strong, combined army of United Irishman and the French First Republic, with General Jean Humbert at the helm, struggled against a 26,000 British army, led by

Viceroy Lord Charles Cornwall and General Gerard Lake. A short artillery duel was followed by a dragoon (mounted infantry) charge on the exposed Irish rebels. As a result, the French surrendered. However, 1,000 or so Irish allies, under Colonel Bartholomew Teeling (an Irish officer in the French army), held onto their arms.

A further attack by the British scattered the Irish, who were pursued and slaughtered. Approximately 500 Irish lay dead on the field and 200 prisoners were taken in gathering-up operations. Almost all were later hanged, including Matthew Tone, brother of Wolfe Tone.

In the aftermath, the total of French prisoners captured amounted to 96 officers and 748 men.

Only a dozen of the British soldiers was reputed to have been killed in combat (although the figure was probably higher) in a battle that lasted little more than half an hour.

A detailed oral account by historian, Richard Hayes and the Irish Folklore Commission, gathered in the 1930s, gives a collected description of the events that occurred during the cataclysm of Ballinamuck.

Manifestation/Legend

There was no paranormal significance to this location prior to the Investigation.

Conclusion

There were a handful of EVPs of worth after reasonable, careful thought.

A voice was picked up possibly saying, 'What was that?'

We do not know precisely, if the vocalisation occurred in the Common Room, where we were or, if it emanated from another room. If it did, presumably it would have been on the ground floor below. We believe that no one else had access to the building, who could have been unaware of our presence and turned up out of the blue. They must have left quickly, assumingly alarmed by the ringing sound of the singing bowl. Another option is that it may have originated from the Spirit world, also acting in surprise to the reverberating sound.

A loud exhale was caught on the full spectrum camera and video camera, as the team were moving around between sessions. Not everyone was in view of the cameras, including the guests, so it may not have come from a Spirit at all. These breaths are quite common on investigations. It could be a process of manifestation — a type of awakening. Another explanation is that as we were moving around, our energy and the Spirit's energy had bound together in a particular space in the room.

As the grid reference mapping was coming to an end, a soft feminine voice said something similar to, 'Should be'.

Again, not everyone was in sight of the full spectrum camera and video camera. Sinead and Jen were but the two female guests were not.

Moving on to the Great Memorial Hall and the past enactment, a child's whisper had seemed to have come up on the full spectrum camera recording yet, it was difficult to make out what was spoken. Later, when calling out, a Spirit may have said, 'I'm tired'.

It was not as clear on the digital sound recorder as it was on the full spectrum camera. Although similar to the EVP before, the second one seemed even more like it was created by a child or adolescent. Like any other war, children bear the brunt of conflict. Some may have wanted to fight or were forced into it. Others were innocent and too young to understand.

What were the similarities between the grid reference mapping results to the Battle of Ballinamuck?

The French soldier (who survived the battle) gave the impression of top priority when coming forward. He felt stressed and maybe nervous in trying to interpret the details.

The daring last stand made by General Jean Humbert (French soldier) of Irish and French forces can be pinpointed to (*Fig 1*) the grid references of (A,1), (B,1) and (C,1). French forces held Ballinamuck (C,2). His left was protected by bog, his right by another bog and lake. Chances of escape were very low, due to the numerical advantage the British had. General Gerard Lake (Commander of British forces) was behind him, in the north, with 14,000 men and Lord Cornwallis (British Army General) was to the right, with 15,000 men.

Also, this might be the scene of the double-quick order that Humbert gave his grenadiers (armed with grenades) to rush British mounted infantry under the Earl of Roden and Colonel Crawford. The British officers rode out with their cavalry, under the false assumption that Humbert had surrendered.

Humbert moved up Shanmullagh Hill with 400 men (C,1). General George Blake (Irish Commander) led a battalion of pike men along with Captain Jobit (French Commander) towards a position along a road. Jobit ordered his grenadiers (A,2) to attack the British (B,2) across a bog but they sank and were forced to surrender. General Lake arrived in the valley (B,2) and attacked the left flank of Shanmullagh Hill. Irish pike men fought bravely and repelled Lake's advances.

Humbert withdrew his army from the hill (C,2) to another piece of high ground. Lake sent a detachment of cavalry and infantry around the hill, to attack Humbert from behind. This might coincide with grid references (D,4). Humbert, surprised by cannon fire and cavalry, surrendered in minutes.

Lake's cavalry (B,2) and (B,3) were pushed back by General Blake's pike men and James 'Gunner' Magee's (Irish soldier) cannon. Blake led his men towards Shanmullagh Hill. When he arrived, Humbert had already conceded. Realising that they would be shown no mercy, they fought with courage and desperation. Many of the Irish fled to the bog, where the cavalry would not pursue them but they were surrounded (C,3) by muskets and slaughtered. The French were treated with all the courtesies of formal surrender while the Irish were butchered.

Twice the glass made a spiralled pattern when asking for grid references (D,1) and (D,2). Both times, the glass halted at the French nationality card (*Fig 2*). It waltzed casually around the top of the table. This could have been where the French soldier ended up afterwards, situated east to where the battle had taken place and close to a lake, a natural resource.

The French prisoners were later taken, by barges, through the Grand Canal to Dublin and traded for British prisoners-of war. There is a doubt to the truth of this as there was no British contingent detaining the French outlined in (D,1) or (D,2).

The amount of effort that the Irish put into the battle either did not seem to be registered by the French soldier or, he was either too concerned for his own fate to recognise this. He was probably close to Humbert's side when they surrendered. This backed up the reason why he survived. There was an account from a British soldier, describing how they remained afterwards, burying the dead for days.

The repercussions of the battle (*Fig 2*) saw (B,3) marked with British, French and Irish soldiers. This area could have seen mass burials or, could have been a camping and holding site before moving on.

Less British soldiers (*Fig 2*) occupied the land although, there could have been many of them in a small space.

Many of the captured (Irish) were hung the following day, including General Blake and Magee (from the arms of a cart). The (B.1) grid reference proves accurate.

There were a number of French and Irish squares occupying the southern section, a few kilometres from the battlegrounds. Some soldiers (possibly wounded) may have gone into hiding or kept a watchful eye.

A British soldier came forward. It was assumed that he died as the battle was in progress. It was unclear where on his body the soldier may have been afflicted. The Sprit targeted the neck of the body mood doll yet, Jen sensed it was a leg (below the knee) issue that resulted in the soldier's death.

There was a lack of British influence (*Fig 3*). Maybe the British soldier felt enclosed and was caught off guard. This possibly happened in the very early stages of the battle (perhaps he rode out with the Earl of Roden and Colonel Crawford). The only emotion felt was for grid reference (C,5). This was far from battle and was likely where he lost his life. He possibly died alone and fell victim to his injuries at that spot.

Ballinamuck 1798 Visitor Centre

Co Longford

WEBSITE: visitlongford.ie
e-MAIL: ballinamuck1798@gmail.com
PHONE: 087 961 3312
FACEBOOK: 1798-Visitor-Centre-Ballinamuck

The 1798 Visitor Centre is open by request

This exhibition explains, in detail, the fateful events of the Battle of Ballinamuck, 8 September 1798.

Eyewitness accounts from local people and officers from opposing armies are presented at the Visitor Centre.

There are various walking trails in the area, that take you to notable historical sites associated with the battle.

The Garden of Remembrance, in the centre of Ballinamuck, commemorates those who lost their lives in the conflict.

BLENNERVILLE WINDMILL

Layout

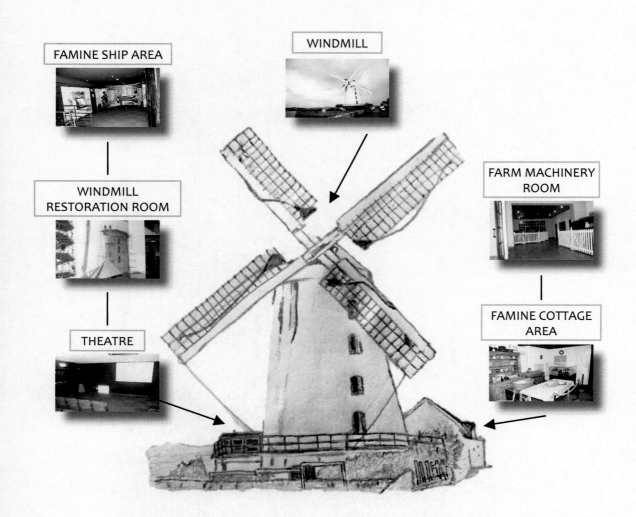

FAMINE SHIP AREA

WINDMILL

WINDMILL RESTORATION ROOM

FARM MACHINERY ROOM

THEATRE

FAMINE COTTAGE AREA

Chapter 20

Blennerville Windmill

Anthony's Journey

It was our first year as a paranormal team, the year being 2009. We had planned to hold a fundraiser on Saturday, 31 October (Halloween) to help us buy some much needed equipment. Our attentions were drawn considerably towards this. We had to raise some cash for a band to play that night and for some prizes. Our ideas turned to having some themed games for the party and a raffle. Decorating the location would also come at a cost.

A great effort was made in borrowing a mannequin from a local shop. My sister, Una, helped to dress it up as a mummy. We had also built a black coffin. This would help as an additional spooky prop for the fundraiser. The coffin would be used for an investigation at the Granary Bar and Restaurant, Killarney, County Kerry.

On that same day, we would travel to Blennerville Windmill in Tralee, also in County Kerry, for our second investigation. The date was the 21 October. As the Granary was a bar, we had to wait until punters left, around midnight, until we could prepare, set up and conduct the investigation.

After about three hours, we finished and our minds quickly turned to that afternoon/evening, when we would be travelling down the Tralee coastline to Blennerville Windmill. It was not the first time we had been in this particular neck of the woods. We had done the Kerry County Museum previously, in July.

I had met with Mike Curran at Blennerville Windmill a month prior to the investigation. Mike is a very knowledgeable gentleman, who knew everything that there is to know about the local history and the exhibits that fittingly occupied the museum. Considerable work had gone on in reconstructing the Windmill by the Tralee Urban Council, National Manpower and AnCO (later became FÁS and Kerry ETB). Blennerville has the honour of having Ireland's tallest windmill.

Farming machinery, a model of the nineteenth century emigration ship, the *Jeanie Johnston* and documents stating the names of passengers who left the coast of Tralee, to seek safer pastures, were just some of the exhibits that caught my eye. Pictures in the museum illustrated the painstaking work of building the Windmill. There was a short video presentation in the Theatre. The film contained information about the background of the area, as well as the Windmill itself. Inside the Windmill, you could get a glimpse of the mechanisms used and the way of life that the milling industry entailed, along with a spectacular view of the bay.

Via e-mail, I was given the contact details of a journalist, who was quite happy to do an article on us for Halloween. He worked for the *Irish Examiner*. He and his friend agreed that they would come down to Killarney, to join us for an investigation at the Windmill.

It was around four o'clock in the afternoon, on the day of the investigation, that we all met up outside the Granary in Killarney. A female team member and Derek went in one car whilst I took up the passenger seat, with another male team member, in another car. The *Irish Examiner* journalist and his guest followed us in their car.

I already felt quite drained from the earlier investigation that day. My exhaustion faded as we arrived at Blennerville, half an hour later, in the midst of darkness. I did some baseline testing whilst the male team member set up the night vision camera in the Farm Machinery Room.

Trigger objects were put in the Theatre. It consisted of a black snooker ball, placed on a round, wooden board. A groove, which circled the outer rim of the board, would help keep the ball steady and aid any movement, should a Spirit want to move it around the edge. The board had a pentagram symbol drawn on it.

Feathered wind chimes were placed on the stairs leading up to the Famine Ship Area on the first floor. Hopefully, this would make a noise if disturbed. The female team member and Derek got to grips with the surroundings of the museum.

Once this was all done, we waited for the photographer for the *Irish Examiner* to arrive. We went up the stairs to the Famine Ship Area and sat around a light, round table. A message came that the photographer was running a bit late. In the meantime, the female team member and Derek joined me in a spot of glass divination, using an upturned glass placed on a table.

Minutes went by, so to pass the time, we included the colour mood frame and another glass divination session before going into an instrumental trans-communication (ITC) experiment (*See Glossary*) involving a cassette radio.

Eventually, we received news that the photographer was nearing the museum, so we went down to the Windmill Restoration Area on the ground floor. Whilst we waited, we did glass divination for a third time. On this occasion, there was a wanting to be acknowledged. It did not take long for the glass to make a commanding motion.

A short time later, the photographer had arrived and was shown through the front door of the museum by Mike. He made himself welcome to the journalist, guest friend and the team. You could tell that they were astonished by what they saw in front of them with the glass.

Blennerville Windmill will always go down as one of my top places that I have visited: mostly because it challenged my belief about what a scary location should look like. Who would have thought a Windmill would be haunted? However, considering the history belonging to it and the glass vessel countlessly circulating the table, this place seemed like it was definitely haunted.

Who was to know?

The Investigation

NUMBER OF TEAM

4

4

NUMBER OF GUESTS

The time was about six o'clock in the evening. The team and guests had arrived at Blennerville Windmill.

Would we be naive as a group, as some of us have only recently been introduced to one another? How would we cope if we were too hasty or intimidating to some? We also had to show no fear. We had a safety strategy if something went wrong: trust and, of course, protection. We had all that covered and that brought about the added factor of enjoyment. You could not be more inspired. After all, we were nearing Halloween.

The forecast was for rain. An added bit of wind was expected to accompany it. With the wind, the external temperature was 8.3°C. In the museum, the temperature was at 15.3°C. So, conditions inside the building were easy and pleasant to work with.

The EMF read the usual fluctuations around exhibits and overhead spotlights. We would not see too much lighting during the investigation, as the rooms/areas that we would cover were deliberately put into darkness with a flick of a switch.

The Farming Machinery Room remained lit up. A night vision camera was set-up in the room, in full view of two enclosures of white fencing, which held exhibits. The room measured approximately 28x14 feet and could be accessed by a couple of steps. It had red-tiled flooring. One pen, at the far-left end of the room, held old agricultural machines and tools consisting of rakes and scales. There were toilets opposite, at the far right of the room. Another pen, on the near right-hand side, featured a green van.

Whilst waiting for the photographer to arrive, we quickly arranged an experiment in the Famine Ship Area on the first floor. We made a start with a glass divination session. Blue carpet and a matching blue ceiling gave a relaxed feeling. A tapestry hung from the ceiling above the place where the experiment would be concentrated. Created by local school children, it highlighted iconic landmarks around the area. Navigational tools, including a brass telescope and compass, were in a display cabinet to one side of a table that we would be using. Adjacent, a few metres away, was the model of the *Jeannie Johnston*. The audio production effects were still ongoing, with gentle, Irish-ballad themed, pan-pipe music playing in the background. The Famine Ship Area overlooked the ground floor reception, where Mike awaited the photographer by the front door.

The round table had four chairs circled around it. Anthony, Derek and the female team member sat down at the table and connected on the upturned glass. The journalist took up the other chair. The guest friend of the journalist generously offered to record the session with a second night vision camera. The male team member paced around, taking photographs, stalling at times to ponder. He looked onto the video screen of his camera to check if anything unusual or imprecise was pictured.

Each individual present called out their names. Anthony asked, "Try and move the glass to the edge, if you can?" He went on to say, "Thank you" in Irish.

The glass at the centre of the table moved very delicately, about two to three inches in a straight line.

Anthony directed the journalist to the EMF gauss-master meter, which he was holding. The journalist pressed a side button on the meter. The device signified that it was on by alerting us with two high-pitched buzzing sounds.

"It's getting more stronger."

The glass seemed to make a slow, small, three-quarter, counter-clockwise circle. As it was moving, Anthony encouraged more movement, to use the energies that were around and not to be put off by the heat, which was funnelling out onto us by a convector unit. He added, "We be around for the next few hours. If you can ask us any questions… if you're willing for us to ask you questions. Move this glass if a sign you be willing?"

What sounded like a murmur was heard on the night vision camera. It was either made in hesitation or agreement. The night vision camera was failing to pick up any distinct picture. The focus remained blurry.

The journalist lightly placed his index finger on the base of the glass.

"If you be able to make, make this glass go in a full circle around the table fast. If you can do so, use all our energies. Use the Spirits that, use… use our bodies. Use anything you can in our environmental surroundings to… show us that you are here with us tonight?"

The glass moved a slow, straight line to a position in between where Anthony and Derek were sitting and then, it moved a small, half-clockwise circle to where Anthony was sitting at the end of the table. It seemed as if the Spirit that was with us was accepting our existence.

Derek felt a presence behind him.

"Sorry, dear Spirit person for interrupting you. Can you please, ah, bring the glass to the middle of this circle please, if you can?" asked Anthony.

After a few seconds of inactivity, the glass was picked up and placed back at the centre of the table.

Next, we positioned a circular, cardboard disc on the table. The glass was placed at the centre of it. This was the template of the colour mood frame. Twelve colours and twelve matching descriptions of emotion were represented on it. Anthony, Derek, the female team member and the journalist reconnected back on the upturned base of the glass, situated within the cardboard disc.

"Okay, dear Spirit, we are going to ask you what mood you are in tonight and how you are feeling this present moment towards us?" said Anthony.

The glass moved to 'Pink', meaning 'Fear and Uncertain'.

We needed more light on the table. A debate happened over which torch to leave on.

Anthony felt heat on his hands. The beam of light shining down on the middle of the table could have being creating this sensation.

Anthony nudged the glass sideways back to centre of the cardboard disc. He asked, "And what way should us, that, that are around the table, what mood should we be in tonight around you, dear Spirit?"

The glass moved to 'Grey', meaning 'Very Nervous and Anxious'.

"Is there anything else? What other mood should we be in tonight around you?"

As the glass was moving, Anthony went on to explain to the journalist that the soul present might be warning us of an unpleasant or tricky Spirit around us. The glass finished up at 'Red', meaning 'Adventurous, Excited and Energy'.

As the glass slowly glided back to the centre of the disc, Derek stated, "It's right by me anyway."

Anthony took the cardboard disc off the table and placed it on the floor beside him. He connected back on the upturned glass. Similarly, Derek, the female team member and the journalist all did the same.

"Would you be able to move this glass in a full circle? Use our energies just to show everybody that's around us here there. Try and make a full circle. Use our energies. Come towards us…?"

The glass obliged, moving two large-to-small, clockwise circles and stopping at the centre of the table.

We tried another experiment, Instrumental Trans-Communication (*See Glossary*), using a cassette radio that was tuned into a long-wave frequency and placed on top of the table. The upturned glass was placed right next to it. We were hoping for some sort of a charge to occur and deliver some exuberance to the glass.

Anthony asked for any Spirits to come through the radio by calling out their names. Anthony, Derek, the female team member and the journalist all linked hands around the table to form a circle. After a minute, the tone of the radio's atmospherics changed.

Anthony placed the glass back to the centre of the table. All four participants placed an index finger on top of the upturned glass.

"We're going to turn the black box off there (cassette radio). We're going to be doing automatic drawing in a minute. You can write a message to us. You can do so, you happy with that?" enquired Anthony.

The glass moved, at a moderate pace, a quicker straight line to the edge of the table, to in between where Anthony and Derek were sitting. Anthony hovered with his left hand above the glass, making sure that it did not fall off the table. The glass was put back to the centre of the table.

Anthony asked one more question, "Thank you, dear Spirit. Just to let us know, where are you now around this table?"

The glass moved one medium, counter-clockwise circle, bypassing the cassette radio, which was still bringing in static feedback. The glass finished its motion by replicating another straight line, to in between where Anthony and Derek were sitting.

News had come that the photographer was on his way. The team and guests headed down below, to the Windmill Restoration Area on the ground floor. Pictures on the wall showed the scaffolding, cogs, cranes and hard labour put into the reconstruction of the Windmill. It can be seen how the Windmill progressed to its present glory. A miniature replica of the local landscape surrounding the Windmill – including buildings, bridge and coastline – were shown in a display cabinet. The photographer wandered in only to see the glass relentlessly moving in circles. Although we had primary control over the matter, it seemed that whatever Spirit was there was enjoying the limelight.

More pictures were to be taken inside the Windmill. Mike, with keys in hand, opened up the Windmill to us. We walked, a few yards, out to the back of the museum with the table in tow. We stayed on the ground floor, due to the complexity of moving the table up the steep stairs to the upper floors.

Anthony, Derek, the female team member and the journalist lightly connected on the table with their fingertips, whilst the photographer prepared them for the photoshoot. A quick table-tilting experiment had formed.

The earlier movement of the glass, to in between Anthony and Derek, in the Famine Ship Area might also have signified the direction that the Spirit wanted us to go in – the direction of the Windmill.

Immediately the table was rocking from side to side. It got suddenly active. It seemed promising. Anthony called out, "Move the table if you are able to walk amongst us? Maybe…?"

The table stopped rocking.

He added, "Move the table if you be able to make a noise inside here? Maybe whistle?"

The table rocked briefly, probably in a state of agreement, before it became stationary again.

"You be able to copy me?" asked Anthony. He whistled.

All was still and quiet for the time being. Anthony asked Mike about the rope behind him.

"Is that a pulley there, Mike? Yeah?"

Mike confirmed, "Yes, that's the pulley…"

Anthony commented that he may have rattled it.

Anthony told the male team member, who was holding the night vision camera, to keep an eye on the rope and chain, which were both dangling from a hole above them, through the ceiling of the ground floor. The male team member focused in on the chain beside the rope. The outside floodlights, used to illuminate the Windmill, were the only lighting offering guidance to walk around.

Anthony called out, "Dear Spirit. If your around us at the moment, can you move the table if you be able to make that chain beside me, to the left of me, maybe make it rock?"

The table slowly rocked, side to side, four times in a rhythmic pattern. Anthony, in astonishment, let out an excited cry, claiming that the rope or chain had moved. It was difficult to suggest this had happened. The night vision camera was not kept still by the handler, nor was it in view of the chain and rope. The table was repositioned.

Anthony called out, "Thank you, dear Spirit. That was brilliant. That's amazing what you done there now. Move the table and vibrate it if you be able to move the rope. Try and make the rope move. Use our energy…?"

Derek called out, "Come on dear Spirit. You know you can do it?"

The table started to rock heavily, to and fro, as the male team member kept the focus of the night vision camera on the chain and rope.

Thirty seconds later, Anthony asked, "Move this table if you be able to move that rope?"

The table abruptly ceased moving.

"Dear Spirit, if you can, move this table again?"

The table resumed its rocking motion.

"Would you be able to make the chain move back to us?"

The table stopped moving. By now, everyone was observing the chain. Derek claimed that he saw the chain move a small bit. Anthony concurred: he saw this too. Suddenly, more comments hyped up, suggesting that the chain was moving. The female team member stated that she was getting a freezing sensation.

The night vision camera focused in on the chain, as the participants re-gathered their connection on the table. The table rocked for about forty seconds. In the stoppage of time, when the table was still, the photographer started taking some more photos. The team and guests relaxed for a moment. In this pause, a deep sigh or breath could be heard. The female team member and a couple members of the team admitted to hearing a moan.

As they reconnected on the table, it began to rock slowly and steadily. Anthony called out, "Would you be able to moan again?"

The table slowed to a halt.

Anthony carried on, saying, "Would you be able to use your vocal cords to try and talk to us? Maybe anyway, even if it's slow."

Anthony demonstrated this by clearing out his throat. "Try and do it?" he asked.

Straight away, a whistle could be heard, something that Anthony had asked for earlier. The table steadily rocked again for a few seconds, then stopped after Anthony asked, "Do you want to whistle? Sing?"

All was silent. About eleven seconds later, another whistle occurred. It was a replica of the previous one in sound.

The table started to rock as Anthony asked the Spirit to try and twist the table around the room.

"Try and make the table move around. Try and spin this table if you can. Maybe, you can go clockwise; move this table clockwise if you can?"

The table took up a vigorous rocking movement. It rotated counter-clockwise, making the individuals connected on to follow suit and reposition their stances. Seconds later, it finished rocking.

Using the movement of the table, Anthony wanted to ask what century the Spirit present was from.

"Okay, dear Spirit, we're going to ask you some questions about what century you are from and you can answer by moving the table. Is that okay?"

As soon as Anthony finished the question, another whistle could be heard yet, it was fainter than before. Anthony informed everyone that he heard taps on the table. This was also confirmed to have been heard by the female team member.

Anthony called out, "Would you be able to tap on the table? Thank you… everyone quiet?"

The male team member, who was told to stand still, carried on taking steps. As Anthony was in the process of asking for taps on the table, the male team member began to take gradual strides up the wooden steps that led to the first floor of the Windmill. He got to the height of just a few inches above the first-floor level, sneaking a peak with the night vision camera.

"Shit," whispered the male team member.

As he slowly wandered up the steps to access the first floor, Anthony was calling out for movement on the table to confirm the century that the Spirit(s) were from.

"Eighteen hundreds?"

Four seconds later, a faint whistle could be heard on the night vision camera.

"Nineteen hundreds?"

About three seconds later, a toned whistle, similar to the majority of those that came before, could be heard on the night vision camera.

The male team member, who was now on the floor above, let out a deep breath. He called out for Derek's assistance.

The chains and robe extended up through the ground floor, to the first floor. The room was fairly bare; echoes could be heard from every step on the wooden floor.

The female team member trekked up the steep steps to join the male team member on the first floor. As they debated, they elected to creep up to the second floor. A blowing sound or lighter whistle was caught on the night vision camera. This was fainter than the whistling sounds that we had gotten earlier.

Anthony signalled for the male team member to come back down. The team posed for pictures alongside the table on the ground floor. As the team picked a stance, the journalist and the Derek lightly touched the table.

Another whistle could be heard. This time, it seemed to chime a melody. It ranged from high to low pitch twice, then finished at a high pitch. This was not heard by the team or any other individual. The only thing that they recognised was the table lightly rocking and making six rapping noises. This prompted some members of the team to giggle and to politely persuade the Spirit or Spirits, doing this action on the table, to chill out whilst the photographer was doing his job.

We moved back to the museum and into the Famine Cottage Room. We did a séance as the photographer took the final few photos. Miniature cottages could be seen within a display cabinet. We were sectioned off behind stanchions (standing poles) and a roped enclosure, in company with a wooden chest, a kitchen dresser (filled with crockery and baskets), cooking range and wooden table with imitations of several loaves of bread. The confined space probably matched what life was like in a small cottage centuries ago.

We did the séance but nothing remarkable came of it. Probably due to the heavy mass of the table, too much lighting, little time and lack of focus. The photographer said his goodbye and we carried onto the next session. We went back up the stairs of the museum to the Famine Ship Area. We situated ourselves in the same spot that we had been in before.

Two lined A4 white sheets of paper were placed alongside each other at the centre of the table. A blue biro was centred within a pentagon-shaped, wooden holder that rested on three caster wheels. It was a type of planchette drawing/writing experiment. Anthony, Derek, the female team member, the journalist and his friend lightly placed the tips of their index fingers on the wooden holder. The word 'Finish' was marked on the bottom centre of one of the sheets of paper. This might ensure that the drawing/writing would be the right way up on the paper. Also, a notification of when the session would be stopped, with the wooden holder moving towards it.

"We're sorry to ask again but, can you draw a picture for us?" said Anthony.

The wooden holder immediately started to move, twisting and moving in straight lines. What seemed to be drawn was a triangle, with two lines spreading ahead from the top point of the shape. The wooden holder/planchette was placed back to the centre of the paper, with the same individuals resuming contact.

Anthony talked about the circular board, with the pentagram symbol on it, in the Theatre on the ground floor.

"Okay, dear Spirit. We are asking you… there is a room down below. Would you be able to draw what's down below? What symbol you can see down below?"

The wooden holder moved a direct line, off the sheets of paper to the edge of the table. One of the caster wheels exceeded the edge, leaving Anthony having to grasp at it before it fell off the table. The wooden holder was placed back to the centre, on a fresh piece of paper.

"Dear Spirit. Would you be able to draw your name? Write your name… or your initials?"

The wooden instrument moved, in a direct line, off the sheet of paper. A swap-over occurred with the male team member, who was holding the night vision camera and Derek. The wooden holder was slower and moved less of a distance, presumably making a mark in detail. After about four minutes, the session stopped. What seemed to be drawn was another triangle and, alongside it, a tight, small, jagged mark. You could make up your own mind or come to many assumptions about what was drawn.

We stayed in the Famine Ship Area and did another glass divination test. Anthony, Derek, the female team member, the journalist and his guest friend participated. The glass was very vibrant during this session.

The night vision camera was put, stationary, on a nearby table overlooking the experiment, whilst fiddle music was being played off an iPhone.

There were numerous counter-clockwise circles being made by the glass. Anthony asked for the Spirit to manifest and reveal who they were.

"Dance, clap, even clap, stomp your feet."

Derek departed the table. He pushed his seat back, stood up and walked over, in the opposite direction, to the area where the model of the *Jeannie Johnston* was. He raised both arms up, lateral from his sides with both palms facing up. He was in a stance of offering or opening up.

After a brief pause, the iPhone was placed at centre of the round table. Anthony asked, "Okay, dear Spirit. Would you be able to move this glass around this electrical instrument there, which is playing the music… black, little box… to the music? Would you be able to do it to the music?"

The upturned glass started circling the device counter-clockwise. Anthony began to feel heat on his hand. The glass circled, at a reasonable pace, for about a minute. It slowed down when Anthony posed an impression, "Beautiful place called Tralee?"

This was possibly in disagreement to what Anthony had just said. It resumed circling the iPhone at a reasonable pace.

Anthony felt yet more 'pure heat' as the glass continued rotating. The female team member turned her head torch off. This torch being on might have interfered, causing the heat sensations.

The session ended. There was one last experiment to do. This involved using tarot cards (*See Glossary*). We used them to identify numbers from zero to nine. The ace represented one, with the other playing cards representing two to nine. One card was designated as zero (card facing down with deck motif facing up). The ten cards were positioned, in a circular formation, around the outer region of the table. Anthony described where all the numbers were, pointing to each one. Our main aim was to get a precise date as to when the Spirit was from.

Anthony, Derek, the female team member, the journalist and his guest connected on the glass. First up, Anthony asked for the Spirit to move the glass to the numbers he would call out. He called out three numbers; the Spirit managed to get the first two but stumbled on the third. It made amends by correcting its mistake, with the glass moving to the third number that Anthony had called out.

Anthony asked, "Dear Spirit, would you be able to tell me what year you were born?"

The glass moved, screeching as it moved across the surface of the table to '1' (Ace), '5', '9' and '4', before stopping at centre.

Anthony needed confirmation, "Okay, just to clarify again, dear Spirit, which year were you born?"

This time the glass moved to '1' (Ace), '8', '4' and '8' before heading towards the centre of the table.

Anthony shouted out to Mike, who was down below in the reception by the main entrance. Anthony asked if the year 1848 had any significance. Mike agreed that there would have been ships coming in and out of the Tralee Bay during that time.

As soon as Anthony reconnected on the glass, it moved to the numbers '1' (Ace), '5', '9', '4' and '9'. The first four numbers corresponded with the year we got before. The glass carried on moving back and forth on the table.

Anthony pleaded, "Okay dear Spirit, we're going to ask you another question. Would you be able move it to centre? Please. Please. Would you like to move the glass to centre?"

Eventually he grasped the glass. He talked about the subject of ships. Something was in the air and it felt delicate.

"Were you associated with the ships around here?"

The glass moved to '1' (Ace).

Anthony placed the glass back to the centre of the table, then immediately picked it back up. He tried to make it easier for the Spirit to communicate for the next series of questions. He pointed, with the glass in his hand, to '1' (Ace) for 'Yes' and '5' for 'No'.

"Are you associated with the ships around here?"

The glass moved to '1' (Ace), to signify 'Yes' and was then placed back at centre.

"Are you male?"

The glass moved in the opposite direction of the table to '5', to mean 'No'.

The glass was placed at middle of the table.

"What age are you now?"

The glass moved to '1' (Ace) and '6', then reverted back to centre.

Anthony pondered, "Sixteen. Ah!"

The female team member asked, "Did you sail in one of the ships around here?"

A few seconds passed.

"Were you captured on one of the ships here?" asked Derek.

The glass moved a straight line to '1' (Ace), to suggest 'Yes', then moved back to centre in a straight line.

Anthony asked, "Did you sail on one of the ships around here?"

The glass moved to '5', to mean 'No'.

Soon after, the Spirit said that she was kidnapped.

No movement occurred when Anthony asked, "Did you like being in this country?"

He went on to ask, "Did you sail to America?"

The glass moved from the centre of the table to '5', to indicate 'No'. It returned in a straight line to midpoint.

"Were you born in this country?" asked the female team member.

The glass went to '1' (Ace), to imply 'Yes' then went back to centre.

"Were you taken away from this country?"

The glass moved to '5', to mean 'No' and returned to the middle of the table.

At this point, the story that the Spirit was unveiling to us seemed harrowing.

Anthony asked, "Are you associated with this Windmill?"

The glass moved directly to '1' (Ace), to mean 'Yes', then continued back to the centre of the table.

"Did you live near this Windmill?"

The glass moved to '1' (Ace), to suggest 'Yes' and headed in a straight line to the centre.

Presumably, she was taken away from her home but, what we would discover next would be even more disturbing.

"Merchant's daughter?" enquired the female team member.

The glass moved to '1' (Ace) to mean 'Yes', then reverted to centre.

Anthony asked, "Is your father around you at the moment?"

The glass moved to '5', to signify 'No', then went back to the centre of the table.

"Do you like your father?" asked the female team member.

The glass went directly to '5', to mean 'No', then continued back to centre of the table.

"Did he trade with people from different countries?"

The glass moved to '1' (Ace) for 'Yes', then reverted to the centre of the table.

Anthony asked, "Did he trade you?"

The glass clarified by moving to '1' (Ace) to suggest 'Yes', then returned to centre.

We contemplated the situation.

The female team member asked, "Was there slavery here in this port?"

The glass moved to '1' (Ace), to mean 'Yes', then followed up by moving back to centre of the table.

The young woman or girl seemed displeased with her father and, rightly so. Used as a bargaining tool and exploited, she had lost her dignity and innocence.

Another date came through: the year '1' (Ace), '9', '4' and '8' – the date another Spirit was born. It seemed that our space was stricken and more Spirits were accumulating. Still, Derek sensed the Spirit of the young, sixteen-year-old behind him.

Anthony took his finger off the glass. He asked if anybody else would like to put forward a question. The female team member did so.

"So, when's the trading around here then?"

The glass moved, in a straight line, from the centre to the tarot cards '1' (Ace), '4', '8' and '5', before heading back to centre.

With no more questions being offered, Anthony resumed his connection on the glass. He said, "Okay, we're going to say goodbye."

The glass evidently moved to '5', to mean 'No', then moved back to the centre of the table. We asked some more questions. These further questions revealed that the Spirit had an interest in music, especially with the bodhrán (a shallow, one-sided drum) and dance. We requested a response, waiting to hear a beat off a drum yet, this failed to happen. After the silence and no sound phenomena, all five individuals connected back on the upturned glass. Anthony continued saying his goodbye.

"Okay, dear Spirit. We're going to say goodbye now. I know you don't want us to say it but, we'll probably come back to this place again. This place is a beautiful place. I hope you agree with us there. We're going to say goodbye."

The glass began to move. It built up its pace, circling clockwise six times before gradually stopping at the dead centre of the table.

"May you rest in peace."

The glass moved a few inches towards the '5' tarot card, which meant 'No' but declined from further movement until, in a moment of recognition, it reverted a few inches back to centre of the table.

It was now eleven o'clock in the evening and the end to a very long day. All the equipment was taken back to the car. We said our goodbyes.

The night vision camera that was set up in the Farming Machinery Room, revealed a similar whistle to that which was caught around the team in the Windmill. This happened about fifty minutes into the recording, when the team had returned to the museum, after being at the Windmill. Possible whispering was heard around one hour into the recording but, it is hard to identify what was being said.

Neither the black snooker ball in the Theatre, nor the wind chimes above the stairs leading to the Famine Ship Area, moved.

Over a week later, the Halloween two-page article in the *Irish Examiner* was published. The journalist wrote of his experience at Blennerville. He described that on leaving the location around midnight with the guest friend, a dim blue light materialised behind them in the car. It drew closer. They realised, to their dismay, that it was a garda (police officer) patrol car. After pulling them over, the garda officer enquired if they had been drinking. The journalist explained, in his own words "Garda, we've spent the evening in a Windmill, communing with the Spirits…"

The article specified in exact detail how the investigation went.

That Halloween night, we had the fundraiser. The weather was wet but that did not stop the excitement. We did not gain any money. Nonetheless, we did not lose any either. We managed to break even. We would have to wait longer to get the equipment we needed. What was fantastic though, was how much people enjoyed the entertainment and games. Watching people dance around a black coffin in middle of the dance floor, whilst listening to some upbeat tunes, was something that would never be forgotten. Smiling faces leaving the building early that morning, brought it home to us. Halloween was still popular in our culture and long may it be part of our festivities.

Tralee Bay, an emigration port of the past

Endless movement of the glass

Maritime exhibits

The Famine Cottage Room awaits us

The Famine Ship Area with a model of the Jeanne Johnston

Another view of the Famine Cottage Room

A model layout of Blennerville, with the windmill being a
notable landmark

A night vision camera was left recording
in the Farm Machinery Room

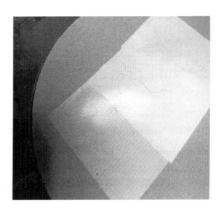

A drawing done during
planchette divination

Location Background/Biography

The Windmill was built in Blennerville, County Kerry around 1800. Sir Rowland Blennerhassett (1741-1821), a local landlord, oversaw the construction of the mill. It is likely that a millwright would have supervised the original building work.

Blennerville thrived as a major port and trading centre. Grain was milled on the site, available for local purchase and loaded onto sailing ships for export. The port also served as the gateway, from Kerry to North America, for emigrants throughout the nineteenth century.

Work stopped at the mill in the late 1800s. With the opening of the Ship Canal in Tralee, in 1846 and steam-powered mills being built in the nearby area, the mill began to deteriorate.

The property was under the ownership of Arthur B. Chute in 1856. By then, the property was described as being the "ruins of a windmill."

The mill was modernised by R. McCowen and Sons Ltd in 1880, with a steam engine installed. The Windmill was up for sale again in 1882.

The sails to the windmill were lost in the heavy gales of 1890. The cap (roof) also gave in with the 'Great Wind' of 1910.

In 1982, the mill was bought by the Tralee Urban District Council. A year later, the Blennerville Windmill Restoration Committee was established. The mill was finally opened in 1990, by Taoiseach,

Charles Haughey and by March 1992, corn was ground at the mill again, powered by the wind.

The mill has five floors and rises to a height of 18.3 metres (tip of roof). The span of the wooden breast rod sails is 22.5 metres.

Manifestation/Legend

The Windmill is reputed to be haunted by one ghost, Millicent Agnes Yielding (1742-1801), wife of Sir Rowland Blennerhassett. She was killed by a blow from a sail shortly after the mill had been opened. She may have been looking out from an upper door.

It was said that, before the Windmill became derelict, her name and perhaps, the date that she died, were inscribed in the woodwork of the door frame where the incident occurred.

Conclusion

During the first visit to the Famine Ship Area, there was believed to be a murmur or hum picked up on the night vision camera. It came after Anthony asked the Spirits if they wanted to put forward questions and suggested they should reply to the ones that they had raised. It was hard to know if the Spirit was giving their approval to do this. It may have been a form of dissent (not willing to comply) or, it may have simply been the only form of interaction that it had the capacity to enter into. It may have not come from a Spirit at all but instead, a team member or guest.

Shortly after, the Spirit used the cardboard disc (colour mood frame) to indicate that it felt dubious around us. The Spirit warned us that we could be in some stress for the rest of the night, with the glass moving to 'Grey', to imply 'Very Nervous and Anxious'. The glass moving to 'Red' on the colour mood frame was also a sign for us to be daring for the night ahead. On the whole, the 'good stress' would be relevant, with pulses quickening and hormones surging.

In the Windmill, the table-tilting experiment revealed that the Spirit at hand was not able to walk amongst us. It did not have the capacity to do this. This could simply indicate the Spirit's inability to do this action (to take human form) or else, its refusal to so.

The Spirit did affirm that it could move the chain and rope. Members of the team stated that they had seen the chain move yet, this was not captured on the night vision camera. Uneven flooring or, the abnormal stances that members of the team were positioned in could have created the illusion that the chain was swinging and therefore, produce false assumptions. It might have been the people that were moving, not the chain. A scientific device or test would be essential to measure any small movement (micro scale). The other possible explanation is that a sudden draught might have caused the chain to minimally move to the naked eye. This could also explain the freezing sensation that the female team member expressed shortly afterwards.

As for the table, it cannot be ruled out that the people caused the vigorous motion whilst they were touching it. The camera lens failed to pick this up most of the time. Instead, a reasonable amount of sound phenomena was found in this building. We noticed a breath and several whistling sounds. The whistling occasionally came on command and identical short breaths could be discerned. They could be heard as Anthony was pushing the Spirit to use its vocal cords, to whistle or to sing.

The surrounding area is known for its birdwatching therefore, birds cannot be ruled out as the cause of the whistling. The building may have created the sounds or, even, the photographer's camera too yet, it is likely that the source was from either a human or, to a degree, we believe, a Spirit.

There were comparable, faint, blowing whistles when asking if the period that the Spirit was from was between the 1800s and 1900s.

Millicent Agnes Yielding (wife of Rowland Blennerhassett) lost her life in 1801, in unfortunate circumstances (some share that it may have been a premeditated). We do know that she died from a blow to the head from the sails. The sails might have been rotating at a speed of up to 40.5km/h when it struck Millicent. We do not know if she died instantly or fell victim to the fatal injury at a later stage. Could it have been Millicent making the whistling noises?

There might be a slight impression that the coastal features (a map) of Blennerville were drawn out in the planchette drawing/ writing experiment. This might collate with the Spirit of a young girl, whom we would later make contact with.

There was an interest in the music being played over the iPhone but, that faded when Anthony mentioned Tralee being beautiful.

The Spirit of the sixteen-year-old girl was believed to have been captured or kidnapped. She was associated with the Windmill and one specific ship. Her father was a merchant, most possibly a sailor who, we discovered, had traded her. This was probably the reason why she displayed disappointment with the area (being left behind) and distaste towards her dad.

Twice, the glass moved to the tarot cards '1'(Ace), '5', '9' and '4'. This could have been when the girl was born, making the year that she died presumably around 1610. Around that span of time, the Gaelic chiefs had given up their land and fled to mainland Europe in the Flight of the Earls of 1607, as a result of the Nine Years War (1594-1603). The official Plantation of Ulster of 1609 soon followed. This saw Scottish and English Protestants settle in Ireland.

Blennerville functioned as the port of Tralee in the 17th century, importing coal, timber and iron and exporting emigrants. We believe that trading had started in the area in the year 1485. The Desmond Geraldines would have held power in the area up until this time period. Under the newly established monarch, King Henry VII (1457-1509), trade possibly flourished in Tralee.

Regarding when a Spirit had been born, we received an additional date – the year 1848. Ireland was in the grips of the Great Famine at that time. The approved valuation *Mill Book* of 1848 noted that the Windmill machinery had been removed. The building was up for rent or sale at that stage.

The *Jeanie Johnston*, a sailing vessel (a barque with three masts), was built in Quebec in 1847. It brought emigrants from Ireland to North America and brought back timber to Europe. She made her maiden voyage from Blennerville in 1848, with 193 passengers on board, soon to be added to when a baby boy was born aboard the ship. He was named Nicolas (after the co-owner of the ship) and Johnston (after the vessel). Nicolas Johnston Reilly was added to the passenger list.

Emigrants would have been loaded into smaller vessels that took them the *Jeanie Johnston*, where they would have clambered aboard. This task would have proved difficult for the heavily pregnant, Margaret Reilly. Barely on board, she went into labour and the day before the ship was about to sail, she gave birth. Nicolas was born in the harbour of Blennerville. He died in 1904.

The voyage would have taken forty-seven days to complete. Margaret and her husband, Daniel would have known, in advance, that the baby would be born on board. Maybe this was a code for us to work with that year in mind. Was a member of the Reilly family briefly making contact? The mental stress of reaching new pastures must have been overwhelming.

Another Spirit came forward, giving their birth year as 1948. We could not find any records connecting an individual to that date.

Blennerville Windmill
Co Kerry

WEBSITE: blennerville-windmill.ie
e-MAIL: blennervillewindmill@gmail.com
PHONE: 066 712 1064
FACEBOOK: blennervillemill

Opened from April to October from 09:00am
until 05:00pm

A short video presentation can be seen, in the Theatre, on the history of the Windmill and surroundings.

On display are emigration and maritime exhibits and, in particular, information on the ship, the *Jeanie Johnston*.

Guided tours are provided for the five-storey Windmill.

The Kerry Model Railway is of great interest to children and those young at heart!

The location is fantastic for birdwatchers. Many migrating species can be spotted within the area.

The Story of Sarah Reynolds

Killarney, a town in County Kerry, is renowned worldwide for its picturesque hotspots and one in particular – Muckross House, situated on the N71 on the Ring of Kerry.

About two kilometres from the Muckross estate, on the same road, is a concealed entrance that opens up to a grassy slope and further on, Killegy Cemetery (Church of Ireland). The majority of the graves are perfectly maintained yet, there is an essence that the land feels untouched. Steps lead down to various hidden tombs and a huge, twenty-eight-feet Celtic cross overlooks the National Park.

The pauper's area lies in a secluded part of the graveyard. Within it is a single standing headstone that reads:

In memory of Sarah Reynolds, aged 24
who died 7th of December 1862.
This stone was placed here by
Blanche Elanor Herbert

In 2012, the GhostÉire team conducted a paranormal study at the graveyard. Apart from gasps of air and whimpers caught on the digital sound recorders, there was a tendency by a Spirit present to only respond to questions put forward by female members of the group.

In other experiments, the glass moved predominately to the 'Whistler' occupation card, which signifies cloth bleacher.

The card displayed a picture of a skull and crossbones and a triangle. Later on, they used a tarot deck, where there seemed to be considerable liking to the 'Ace of

Pentacles'. This card resembled wealth, child or drink of poison.

The only relative question from a male that got an answer was when asking the Spirit present if they had a child. The K2 meter responded by hitting a high of 25 milliGauss from a baseline of zero.

On further questioning, they believed that they were in contact with a twenty-six-year-old woman who worked at the (Herbert) Muckross estate. She was inconclusive about her thoughts towards the Herbert family. She did not react to questions put in the past tense; instead, she expressed the view that she was still living. She also dithered when the subject of children was put across.

How did Sarah Reynolds die? Why was a headstone erected in the pauper's area of the graveyard? More importantly, who is Sarah Reynolds?

The publication, *In Search of Sarah Reynolds. A tale of Muckross House* (2016), produced by Janet Murphy and Eileen Chamberlain, states that a visit from a Mr and Lady Louisa Tenison to the Herbert Muckross estate, took place in the winter of December 1862. There was no account of Sarah Reynolds or her death at that time although, a newspaper article described how Lady Elizabeth Cuffe (Countess of Desart) and her daughter, Lady Alice had to cut short their stay at the Muckross estate in early December of that year.

Blanche (1845–1920) was the youngest daughter, out of four children, from the union of Henry Arthur Herbert and his wife, Mary[*]. Blanche must have had a strong bond with Sarah,

[*] Mary Balfour Herbert (1817-1893), wife of Henry Arthur Herbert, her niece was Eleanor Mildred Sidgwick (née Balfour; 1845-1936), a leading figure in the Society for Psychical Research (SPR). Eleanor's husband, Henry Sidgwick was the first president of the SPR – an organisation dedicated to examining events and abilities normally described as psychic or paranormal in its behaviour. This would make Eleanor Mildred Sidgwick and Blanche Elanor Herbert first cousins.

with roughly only seven years' difference in age between them. There is a compelling case that Sarah was a servant – a governess who tutored Blanche at the family estate. Blanche may have erected the headstone in her memory, as a mark of love and respect towards Sarah yet, was it done as a sign of compassion too?

Another paranormal study was organised at Killegy a few years later. Contact with the Spirit of Sarah Reynolds had been reputedly made during a talking board session. She gave her age as twenty-six – the same age as the female Spirit that the GhostÉire team had spoken to on the previous occasion. If this is correct, then the age marked on the headstone is wrong, meaning that Sarah was born in 1836.

Again, Sarah gave the impression that she was still living. She had earlier been walking the grounds of the graveyard and was in the kitchen and 'around the house' of the Muckross property. She was tentative regarding who her friends had been at the estate. It did not seem to be the servants although, she did refer to Blanche as a friend and, when asked if she had any friends or family on the grounds, the answer was six.

This information concludes that Sarah was a governess (a woman employed to teach and train children) at Muckross House. During the Victorian period, servants were not allowed to be in the presence of those they tended to. They were kept virtually invisible or separate, away from the upper-class. For Sarah, this was different – governesses had an awkward role, often secluded and socially detached from the upper and lower classes. They came from a middle-class background and were educated. Henry Herbert, his wife, Mary and their four children would make up the closest ties that she had at the house – totalling six. She also described being close to Henry Herbert.

So, when did Sarah arrive at Muckross? Sarah revealed that she was born in Belfast (in the north of Ireland) and had begun work at Muckross House at the age of fourteen (circa 1850). We do not know how Sarah came to know the Herberts prior to that date.

Mary and her four children returned to Muckross from London, England in late 1849. Blanche would have been five-years old at the time – the right age to learn and be tutored.

Sarah's services as a teacher and 'paid companion' to Blanche were coming to an end as Blanche hit her late teens and, especially after the costs of Queen Victoria's visit to the house (August 1861) had come to hit home.

What were Sarah's circumstances before her death? Sarah felt emotional pain towards Henry. She bore a child, a girl, who she saw only once before being taken away to England, under the care of a 'Sir Bart'. It does not come as a surprise as to who the father was!

She was twenty-three years old when she gave birth to the baby girl, whom she referred to as Deidre. The date would have been 1859 and a cover up would have been necessary, due to the lengthy number of years the Herberts took in preparing for Queen Victoria's visit. Any revelations would surely jeopardise their chances.

A Bart (Baronet) is a British hereditary dignity, ranking below a Baron but above a Knight. They are addressed as 'Sir'. Unfortunately, the surname was not passed on to Sarah, making it hugely difficult to find out where Deidre was taken to and, all the more so if her name had been changed.

What were Sarah's thoughts on her last moments before she left our plane? She explained that the last thing she remembered was being in the kitchen at Muckross House, before falling ill in the dining room. She clarified that she had no symptoms to show, before her death, that could indicate if she were suffering from a disease. She also made it clear that the cause of her demise was through taste (suggesting that she might have ingested a substance) and that she was suspicious in regard to her untimely death.

Most of the results gathered seem to compare with the paranormal study conducted in 2012. Wealth, children and poison – probably even bleach could have a link to Sarah. It was not until the Pharmacy Act of 1902 that it became illegal for bottles of dangerous chemicals to be identical in shape to ordinary liquids. We still cannot be sure if Sarah's death had something sinister behind it or, was an accident due to an unfortunate error.

Is there any evidence of Sarah left today? Sarah mentioned that the only couple of facts of her existence were from her grave and a blue coat she had worn, now in the attic of Muckross House. Governesses' wages around the mid-nineteenth century were extremely low. They would have worn simple clothing, ranging in functional colours, such as grey, black, dark blues and greens, only keeping a 'best dress' for special occasions. A coat would have been quite a distinctive item of clothing for Sarah, assuming the proportions of one of her prized possessions; hence, it was worth mentioning.

One of Sarah's final messages was to find her baby.

The last letters to come up on the talking board were:

'I',

'M', 'U', 'S', 'T',

'G', 'O',

'F', 'O' 'R'

'M', 'Y'

'W', 'A', 'L', 'K',

'T', 'O',

'T', 'H', 'I', 'N', 'K'.

She finished off by spelling out:

'T', 'H', 'A', 'N', 'K',

'Y', 'O', 'U',

'A', 'L', 'L'.

Layout

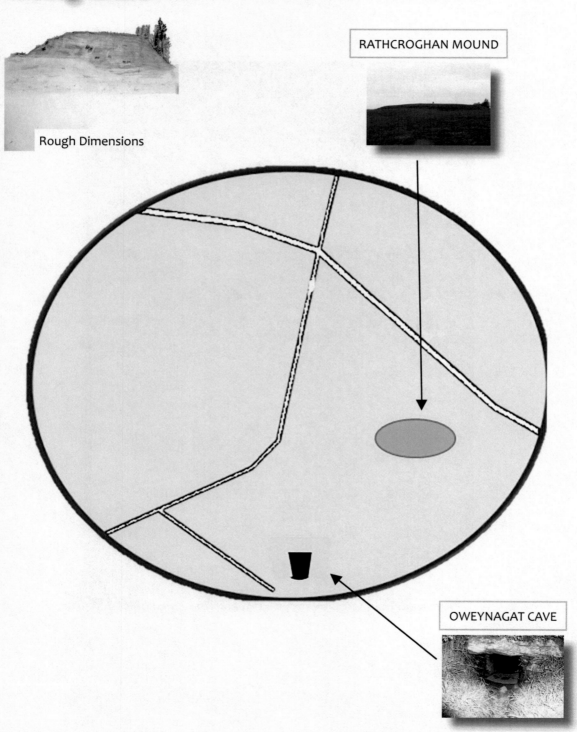

Rough Dimensions

RATHCROGHAN MOUND

OWEYNAGAT CAVE

Chapter 21

Rathcroghan/Oweynagat Cave

Anthony's Journey

We were to go on the search for the Morrigan yet again but, this time we would be much closer to her home. Rathcroghan (meaning 'Fort of Cruachan'), a vast ancient site set around the quiet village of Tulsk is where we would target. First, we would go to Rathcroghan Mound, the seat to the High Kings of Connacht. Then, we would travel a couple of kilometres to Oweynagat Cave, also named 'The Cave of the Cats' or, to religious scaremongers (to change people's minds, by spreading fear and getting them to follow their way of thinking, like sheep) as 'The Gateway to Hell'.

We did not buy into this! We were going to try and find out if there was a softer side to the Morrigan, which had a life story, rather than the several other stories that belittle her - for instance, praying over dead corpses. Have we lost or killed that part of our Irish ancestry - a type of genocide?

We had gone to Rathcroghan Visitor Centre in Tulsk on two previous occasions. We had gone the first time to seek permission to do an investigation on the Cruachan site and the other was around November of 2014, when the 'Goddess festival' - a day of several lectures on numerous topics, such as childbirth, Queen Medb and the Morrigan - had taken place.

Later that evening, we had gathered with a group of people at the mouth of Oweynagat Cave. Some of the group had decided to go the deepest bowels of the Cave by candlelight and torch. When reaching the bottom, they had quenched their light sources before making their way out of the cavern, with only the beating of drums from the outside of the Cave to guide them. It had resembled a type of initiation test, which would have happened in the past, proclaiming one's advent into adulthood.

The following year - mid-summer solstice of 2015 - we had done an investigation at Tulsk priory (over the road from Rathcroghan Visitor Centre) and then afterwards at Oweynagat Cave. The investigation had not gone to plan. The experiments had not been delivered properly. I am, in some ways, a keen perfectionist. One experiment - the direction board - had not aimed at the correct compass points. It did not accomplish anything to my satisfaction and to what we wanted to achieve. Although, one experiment had proved quite surprising.

Jen and I had been wearing the pedometers and we would both accumulate a distance of 2km. In our own reality, we should have only covered a couple of hundred metres, if that, with the strolling and scrambling we did in a short space of time yet, there could be no other explanation for that large amount of distance.

We turned on the pedometers when sitting in the car at a layby outside the priory. We would only walked a short distance around the priory before heading back to the car and driving to Oweynagat, where we would crawl in and climb out of the Cave. We would have to come back again and use the pedometers to see if there would be any comparison.

So, was there another dimension that we unknowingly went to? Another realm that we got lost in?

It was March 2016 when we revisited Cruachan. This time, we went with a more defined idea of what to look for. A few days before the investigation, Jen and I were familiarising ourselves with the ins and outs of electric fencing (*See Glossary*). We practiced in the garden of our home, trying to assemble the fencing in the shortest possible time. We would use this procedure up on top of Rathcroghan Mound. Our objective was not to keep things out but to withhold, enhance and withstand any energy within its perimeter. As ancient sites have an impression of being highly energised, we thought we would make it that much greater.

Another reason for rehearsing was, of course, down to the weather. Being on top of a hill in harsh conditions is not my type of pleasure, so we had to work quickly to get the electric fencing up and running. It was a good job that we had prepared because, it was raining non-stop on the day we drove up from Killarney to Roscommon.

There would be only three of us participating in this investigation. Cameron, Jen and I made sure we had the proper clothing and footwear for the harsh conditions. We definitely needed to use various methods to keep warm and dry. Heat pads, hot flasks of water and spare clothing came in handy.

We stopped at a restaurant in Roscommon town to get some warm feed. Getting back into the car, we drove another half hour, stopping at the carpark next to Rathcroghan Mound and with little daylight remaining, we steadied ourselves for the night's proceedings.

Cameron and I attached a pedometer to our clothing. All three of us carried some sort of equipment across the field and up the high gradient to the top of Rathcroghan Mound. The rain weakened but the big umbrellas we had brought with us were still essential in keeping us wet – rather than soaked!

I did the baseline testing; thankfully, not much had to be done.

Meanwhile, the electric fencing was being readied. Four posts were fixed upright into the ground and positioned to make a large square shape. Jen weaved white wiring in and out of the four posts. A battery pack was clipped onto the wiring, which in turn was earthed by a grounding rod. We hopped over the wiring. We were now all within the electric fencing enclosure. You could see a great view to afar from up the top of the Mound.

The wind, which made things even colder for a moment, had stopped. However, only a handful of minutes later, we had to switch on our head torches. It was time to turn the battery pack on, charge the area and return the power back into Rathcroghan.

The Investigation

NUMBER OF TEAM

3

0

NUMBER OF GUESTS

The rain pelted off the window as the team sat comfortably in the restaurant, waiting for the order of food to arrive. Looking out from the window, there were light grey clouds above in the sky and a slight feeling of optimism for the night ahead – but that soon dwindled.

We saw people dashing in and out of their vehicles in the carpark. We had an objective, however and the weather was not going to stop us. We set off on our final part of the journey – driving to Rathcroghan Mound.

Visibility was low, especially when stuck behind other motor vehicles, the backward spray hampering our view. The windows inside the car were misty with condensation; they had to be opened. The splashing sound of driving over waterlogged asphalt magnified. We were, indeed, in for a wet one; the forecast for the investigation would be rainy.

The team would have to act swiftly after they arrived at the carpark beside Rathcroghan Mound. Anthony, Jen and Cameron each secured a pedometer to their clothing inside the car, before heading out across the saturated long grass, up the high gradient towards the top of the Mound. It was still quite bright, with the lux at 432 but it was half past five in the evening and the light would soon fade.

At the top of the Mound, Anthony did a quick EMF test. Surprisingly, in particular of the Mound, there was a constant measurement of 0.5 milliGauss. It has been reported that there is a metal pole extending underneath the earth, which may have caused the reading. There were electrical cables from pylons over surrounding fields yet, the EMF gauss master meter gave a weaker read-out when held high and around the edge of the Mound's summit.

Understandably, the false anomaly risk was rated as being very high due to our circumstances. The humidity was 100%, due to moisture and the temperature at 5.5°C, meaning that conditions were harsh and unpleasant. It would be hard to concentrate.

Jen and Cameron had sufficiently laid out the electric fencing. Practicing the set-up had made a difference. The umbrellas the team had gave brief shelter from the teeming rain. Jen put the video camera into action. She panned around the Mound. It was a gloomy sight.

She passed the video camera to Cameron. He focused on the red heart-shaped planchette at the centre of a tetradecagon (fourteen-sided) shaped board. This oddly shaped creation is known as the manifestation board (*See Glossary*). It can be used in identifying the most common types of Spiritual beings, according to human knowledge.

Thirteen types of beings were represented by miniature figurines, relating to how they are envisaged, forming a mental picture of how they might look. The thirteen figurines were slotted into their allotted spaces. One space was left free – the unknown section, an entity undetermined by man.

With urgency, Anthony began introducing the experiment as he and Jen connected on the planchette.

"Okay dear Spirits, thanks for contacting, we're asking you for clear positive answers now because we're in the soaking rain. You might be able to clear the rain. Can you move the planchette in a circle? Thank you. Use the energies. Come towards us now very strongly. Come towards now. Move this planchette in a circle. Come towards us there…"

Anthony continued talking briefly but there was no motion from the planchette. Maybe the drops of rain were hampering it. Shortly afterwards, it was repositioned by Jen.

As Anthony disconnected, he looked at his right index finger which had been touching the planchette. He got startled. "Shit, I got blood!"

Jen immediately laughed.

Cameron quickly pointed out it was the paint from the planchette. On account of the rain, the red dye had started to run. The minor hiccup was solved.

Anthony reattached his right index finger, joining Jen back on the planchette. Unlike previously, Anthony offered better instruction for what he wanted the Spirit world to do.

"Can you move the planchette… to what Spirit are you?"

The planchette moved a small, narrow, half, counter-clockwise circle.

Anthony repositioned his right index finger. In doing so, the stickiness and release of pressure on the planchette made it swivel partly clockwise. There were a few more minor movements temporarily before Jen and Anthony adjusted their placement on the planchette and initiated a summoning-in prayer.

The planchette moved more directly to the 'Poltergeist' section on the board.

The planchette was placed back to the centre of the board.

"What kind of Spirit do you think we are? Use the planchette. Move it there?"

The planchette moved a straight line about twelve inches or so to the 'Demonic' segment of the board.

One would be rather nervous at this point but, this did not overwhelm the team – especially Anthony, who was more concerned with the slippery exterior of the planchette.

"Okay, what categories of Spirits are around?" asked Anthony, eagerly this time as the wind blew a gale and the rain continued to pour.

There seemed to be a rapid act of sympathy – the planchette drove in a straight line to the 'Angel/Spirit Guides' section.

Straight away, Jen placed the planchette back to the centre of the board.

"If there's no more, can you move it in a circle?"

The planchette moved a small, half, counter-clockwise circle, stopping momentarily before heading in a straight line to the 'Magic' section of the board.

The planchette was picked up and placed back to the middle of the board.

Anthony wanted further clarification on the questions that had been asked. As a result, the planchette went to the same sections of the board as before.

The team moved promptly to the next experiment. It would involve a séance but, without the sitting. There would be a succession of questions from each person. Two members of the team would stand with their hands face down on the table, one with both palms down on top of the other person, each clasping an energy probe (*See Equipment*) with both thumbs. The two probes were unbalanced at the base and so had to be supported and held to stop them from falling.

The third team member would call out. They would sit on a makeshift throne, which consisted of long, thick, scarlet fabric draped over a camping chair. A claymore sword had been set up nearby, piercing the ground to symbolise ceremonial rites of power.

Cameron and Jen were first up on the table, as Anthony sat down on the chair, holding the video camera. Each member of the group introduced themselves, calling out their names and then, Anthony read out the questions he had already prepared.

"Was there, was this an inauguration site?"

Amid the swirling wind Anthony mentioned that he felt something weird. He looked at the sword. Through the viewfinder of the camera, it was swaying slightly.

"The sword's moving anyway, huh, that could be the wind," said Anthony.

He swung the video camera towards his right. Only a dot of light could be seen in the far distance.

Anthony asked another four questions in a space of over a minute but, nothing prevailed.

It was Jen's turn to sit on the throne, call out the questions and hold the video camera. Cameron and Anthony connected on the table.

Jen called out loud, "Are you buried standing up?"

About ten seconds later, she moved onto the next question.

"Who was your one true love?"

The sound of the wind could be heard battering the Mound.

Jen asked another three questions over a period of about a minute and a half. The rain had subsided but, with our clothes saturated, a feeling of dampness and coldness seeped into our skin. Our hopes of getting anything here were diminishing.

Cameron was last up. Jen and Anthony were on the table.

Cameron introduced himself, calling out in Irish, "My name is Cameron Murphy... what is your name?"

Less than ten seconds later, Cameron went onto the next question, calling out in English, "Do you live here?"

Anthony peered to his right, looking into the distance.

Cameron finished his final (sixth) question just over a minute after he started. As he did, a prolonged gust of wind made its approach.

Never mind if a Spirit had responded in the meantime; it was difficult enough to even interpret what Anthony was saying. We hurriedly forfeited the experiment.

The energy probes were placed onto the ground. Immediately, Jen and Anthony reconvened their contact on the table, placing all of their digits lightly on top. They were about to do a spot of table tilting. There was a wide enough space for it to be done and it might just click with the mystical side, plain and simple and easier to establish a relationship.

Cameron carried on filming.

"Now's your chance… two minutes…" said Anthony.

The table instantly started to rock back and forth. Anthony continued coaxing, "Come towards us now. Step forward. Try and lift this table up. Maybe lift it into the sword… come towards us now step forward… we mean you no harm… Queen Medb if you're around come towards us now… goddess of the earth…"

Anthony removed his left hand from the table. It continued to rock but sloped to a higher degree. Another lengthy strong gust of wind made Anthony pause the flow of the prayer he was using to summon the Spirits. He placed his left hand back on the table. The motion of the table weakened as Anthony expressed thanks.

This is a typical reaction from the table-tilting experiment (movement becoming less) when there is an inclination from a person before a break or, when thoughts are turning to ending the session. Very rarely would a table get more energetic with individuals' intent on concluding or finishing a session. Anthony pointed out that the table was nimble in the short space of time and that a livelier experience may have occurred, given a longer period.

It was seven o'clock. Anthony, Cameron and Jen carried their possessions down the Mound and filled the boot of the car. It would be a short drive, just over a kilometre away, to Oweynagat Cave, where they would continue the investigation.

Anthony drove the car down a boreen road. The narrow lane would lead them to a dead end (next to the Cave) yet, there was enough room at the rear of the road to do a three-point turn and to pull up, facing the opposite direction.

Once parked up at the side, the keys were turned, switching off in the ignition. The team picked up the bare essentials from the car. They passed through a gate on the side of the road that led into a field and walked a few metres to the entrance of the Cave.

The temperature outside was getting lower. It was at 4.5°C – a degree colder than a couple of hours earlier.

They would have to squeeze in through the mouth of the Cave one by one, either by crawling or hunching down low. Any lighting would become vital once inside, as darkness would envelop them and there would be limited room to manoeuvre. Turning one's body around was difficult, making claustrophobia a potentially significant factor for some.

After a few metres in, there was a turning to the left. The team would have to watch their footing; the uneven rocks protruding from the ground made it virtually impossible to progress whilst squatting but, shuffling on one's backside was an option. For a person heavy on their legs, entering the Cave might prove difficult. Thankfully, the cavern opened up soon after and eventually, leg room was available. The team had to negotiate a few more rock boulders downwards before they could walk into the main chamber.

Anthony did some more baseline tests within the Cave.

It was quieter than up at the Mound. The C low level had halved. We were far away from any noise. This would make doing a calling-out vigil (an EVP session) a good way of gathering proof but, consideration had to be taken on account of our surroundings. Dripping sounds were frequent and the magnitude of any noise funnelling in from outside would increase immensely inside. The Cave acted like some sort of ear trumpet.

It was still damp and moist inside. The humidity was at 100% but the temperature had risen to 9.2°C, on account of the tight space that we were in. There was a reading of up to 1 milliGauss at its highest peak. The rock in the Cave may have had something to do with this. The lux was at 002, meaning that we were in complete darkness.

Cameron and Jen peppered the area with small, lit candles. A large candle attached on a cane was embedded into the ground. It gave off a good deal of light, so much so that we could turn off head torches and ultraviolet torches (*See Equipment*). Jen snapped a few coloured glowsticks, placing them into crevices around the walls of the Cave. We were about to get underway with a calling-out vigil.

A digital sound recorder was placed on the ground ready to pick up on any strange audible phenomena.

Anthony held the full spectrum camera, pressed record and proceeded to ask questions.

"Do you reside in this cave?"

Cameron stood a few metres away at the Cave's border, with mud-splattered ground between him and Anthony. It was important to stand still, to avoid making squelching sounds.

"Does the Morrigan live down here?"

Now and then, Jen took a picture with her digital camera (*See Equipment*); a flash would spread within the confines, separating the contrasting walls.

Nearly three minutes later, Anthony asked Cameron if he wanted to ask a question. He accepted.

"Are you stuck here?" Cameron asked.

There was no response as of yet.

"Is there anyone buried here?"

A few seconds later, Anthony described that he thought he heard a groan, although Cameron said he heard cackling. Anthony was convinced the sound came from behind him (towards the front of the Cave). Jen, the only person standing behind Anthony at the time, quickly renounced that the sound had come from her.

Jen raised the question, "Are there bones down here?"

Moments passed, then Anthony mentioned he heard another noise, resembling a wail.

"Did you?" asked Cameron, looking for an explanation from Anthony.

"Outside, it could be, sounds like sometimes that it's coming from outside the Cave," replied Anthony.

Later, Jen asked, "Have you seen anything strange down here?"

Silence ensued, until Cameron commented that he heard a rattle. He went to saying that it came from the entrance of the Cave.

Anthony giggled, then explained that he thought the same noise had come from the opposite end of the Cave, to the rear, where Cameron was situated.

Anthony pointed the full spectrum camera towards Jen. She was facing in the direction of the entrance, with her back turned to Anthony. A thick mist could be seen as she breathed out.

"Have you seen any strange faces?" she asked.

About thirty seconds had gone when Anthony described that he heard another wail. Anthony asked Cameron, "Did you hear that?"

Cameron shook his head.

"Suppose it's the sound vibrating everywhere really; isn't there?" contemplated Anthony.

The calling-out vigil came to a close about ninety seconds later.

The digital sound recorder was turned off.

The manifestation board was put up again.

Cameron and Anthony connected on the heart-shaped planchette, whilst Jen videoed with the full spectrum camera.

The thirteen miniature figures were left in the box, in the boot of the car. We thought it best not to bring them, just in case they got destroyed or lost inside of the Cave.

A K2 meter was placed high up on a flat piece of stone at the back of the Cave, right behind where Cameron had been standing. The board was positioned in the centre of the main chamber.

Anthony squatted down beside the board. It took a while for him to get comfortable. In the meantime, Cameron looked relaxed, sitting down on the mucky floor next to Anthony. It took some time before we finally had a reaction from the planchette.

"… What category of Spirit are you? Come towards us now. Step forward. Use the energy. Build the energies. Come towards us now, step forward," asked Anthony.

The planchette was slow-going. Presumably, the Spirit controlling it was weak. It ended up split between the 'Elemental' and 'Poltergeist' segments of the board.

The planchette was placed back at centre.

"Can you make that clearer, thank you…?" Anthony requested.

Again, the answer was indecisive – the planchette stopped between 'Elemental' and 'Poltergeist'.

Cameron placed the planchette back to centre and asked, "Can you move it too, once more please?"

Anthony affirmed by saying, "Once more, more direct."

The planchette moved in a straight line, ten inches or so to the 'Elemental' section of the board.

The planchette was placed back at the middle.

Cameron asked, "Are there any other Spirits present with us that you recognise on the board?"

The planchette went straight to the 'Elemental' part of the board.

Anthony placed the planchette back at centre.

The Elemental Spirit proclaimed that, we the team, were identified as being supernatural or mysterious individuals. The planchette had moved to 'Magic' in relation to what it sensed we are.

The manifestation board was overturned. We could ask some questions in planchette divination.

Anthony managed to get himself rested by sitting down on the dirt. Anthony offered the Spirit either to move the planchette to himself, for 'no' or to Cameron, for 'yes'.

Cameron asked, "Are you a male?"

A heavy exhale could be heard on the full spectrum camera, a second before the planchette moved from centre of the board towards Cameron's direction, to indicate 'Yes'.

The planchette was placed back to centre.

Anthony said, "Are you representing the elements?"

The planchette moved a straight line, eight inches or so, stopping towards Cameron's direction for 'Yes'.

The planchette was placed back to middle.

A soft feminine voice seemed to be detected in the recording. Three syllables may have been spoken but it is unclear what was said.

"Did you have human form?"

The planchette only moved a few inches this time, towards Cameron, briefly stopping before moving another inch or so in the same direction.

Four knocks were heard. The first three knocks were in quick succession, with the fourth, slightly separate from them. The knocks seemed distant from the board, though it was the only wooden material that we had brought down with us into the Cave, that we assumed could have caused the response.

The planchette was not as clear but moved towards Cameron's direction, suggesting 'Yes'.

"Do you reside in this cave?" asked Cameron.

The planchette showed more force, again moving in a straight line, ten inches or so towards Cameron's direction for 'Yes'.

In fact, the planchette kept going towards Cameron's direction for several answers afterwards and seemed incapable of going towards Anthony's direction, for 'No'.

The Spirit confirmed all our beliefs. There was a pathway to another dimension that we did not know about, on the other side of the boundary, which we could travel to in our own lifetime. It was cut off by Christianity.

The Elemental Spirit specified that it was a woman, contradicting what it had said earlier. Maybe this being had no gender distinction or, had a combined masculinity and femininity. It was something we could associate with being a person, linked to human nature.

Was the reason why we were getting the affirmative responses down to us hitting the nail on the head repeatedly?

Anthony prompted the Spirit into action.

"Come on. Move it in a circle… a circle."

The planchette did show signs of moving in a circle. It was what Anthony said next that made the movement more vigorous.

"Change in the seasons."

The planchette circled the board, at a rapid pace, believably showing excitement.

The conversation turned to the Morrigan.

The planchette turned in approximately forty-seven-and-a-half clockwise circles, starting small and then increasing in size, before returning to its small, curved plane.

It slowed down when Cameron asked, "Is this a nice place?"

The Elemental Spirit admitted that it was, finishing up by heading towards Cameron to indicate 'Yes'.

The planchette was picked up and placed at centre.

Anthony asked, "Was it meant believe that it was a bad place?"

The planchette moved a straight line, eight inches or so towards Cameron for 'Yes'.

Cameron placed the planchette back to centre.

"Was their bodies found down here?"

The planchette at first did a small, half-clockwise circle before heading in a straight line, five inches or so in Anthony's direction, to signify 'No'.

The planchette was put back to centre.

"Was, was this a sacred place?"

The planchette moved positively in a straight line towards Cameron's direction, for 'Yes'.

Cameron pointed out that he would love to know when this vital force was from.

In further questioning, it was found that the Elemental Spirit was present when bodies were buried at Rathcroghan Mound. Astonishingly, the Elemental Spirit specified that it was Christian. We got the date 400AD for the time period that the Elemental Spirit was from.

Next, we would be using the reversion and altered speech device, with a digital sound recorder to attract and discern any strange audio disturbance. To make sure, we asked the Spirit if it could make a sound with its voice for the experiment. It confirmed that it would – the planchette moving to Cameron, implying 'Yes'.

There was a short recess where the team readied the equipment. We were going to use the Nintendo DS for the reversion and altered speech test. We would have a ten second timeframe to talk into the Nintendo DS. It recorded what was intended to be said (mainly a question), then changed the pitch of our voices or, even reversed them. Compact battery speakers were plugged into the Nintendo DS to give it extra amplification.

Jen focused her attention on the Nintendo DS. She directed Anthony and Cameron on when to call out. We decided that we would each take turns speaking through the device.

Cameron took hold of the full spectrum camera. Anthony pressed record on the digital sound recorder. We were prepared and rather enthusiastic about the minutes ahead.

Anthony was up first. He told Jen when he was about to start talking. As he gave the all-clear, Jen pressed a button on the touchscreen of the Nintendo DS. It would duplicate what Anthony was about to say.

"Are you Christian… let us know… please?"

The device stopped recording.

Jen replayed the question, first in slow motion at a low key. It recreated a resonant deep voice. After a few seconds of silence Jen replayed the question again. It sounded freaky – something that you would hear straight out of a horror movie. Jen adjusted the settings to a high pitch.

Cameron remarked, "He's probably going, *What are these guys doing?*"

Jen played the question once more, at a high pitch and at a fast speed. This time, the voice sounded like something out of a children's show. It proved to be quite interesting. It makes you wonder how tone of speech plays a big part in our lives.

Cameron was next to call out.

Jen pressed record on the Nintendo DS.

"We will be leaving soon but, are we welcome? Please give us a sign?"

As soon as the time lapsed, Jen tapped the touchscreen. Twice she replayed Cameron's voice in a slow deep pitch.

Anthony looked around, peering first out towards the entrance then behind him, to the rear of the Cave.

Jen adjusted the speed of the voice recording, making it quicker, thus shorter in length.

In the passing time of quietness, an unusual noise was picked up on the full spectrum camera. It is difficult to describe, with possibly similar qualities to a low grating voice, like a snarl. It comprised of two syllables, in close succession. The second syllable seemed to have an echo. In the circumstances, it is reasonable to suggest that there could be something else that had created this unfamiliar sound, like a droplet of water or an animal.

Jen reproduced Cameron's question, keeping with the low tonality at quite a slow speed. She changed the settings on the Nintendo DS, tapping the screen. She managed to reverse what Cameron had spoken, this time at a normal pitch. It had a taste of a mysterious, archaic language to it. It sent a quiver in Anthony and Jen's voices, enough to cause shivers down their spines.

Shortly after, Anthony explained that he thought he heard a voice (possibly from the audible earlier) when Cameron was asking the question, coming over the recording of the Nintendo DS device.

Cameron turned the full spectrum camera to Jen. It was her turn to ask a question.

"Are you searching for something?"

Anthony intervened before the time had elapsed on the recording. "Was magic performed in this location?"

As Jen tapped on the screen of the device, looking to replay the questions, Cameron expressed surprise.

"Did you hear something there?" he asked, directing his question towards Anthony.

"Yeah," replied Anthony, in a pondering way.

"Like a rumble," Cameron explained.

Jen found the recording, slowed it down and lowered the tone significantly. She then went onto reversing the words.

Cameron disclosed, "I just had a really, really full body, shivering sensation there."

Jen replayed the reversed version of the voice recording again.

Anthony agreed with what Cameron had said – he got the same. He mentioned that it was getting a bit nervy with the ultraviolet torches turned off.

"As long, big draught coming in there, like," said Anthony.

Cameron told Anthony that the full spectrum camera had unexpectedly turned itself off. It would be the start of further technical issues.

On the digital sound recorder, as Anthony was talking to Cameron, a female voice appeared in the background.

"Who's there?" it whispered.

Anthony was trying to find an explanation for the full spectrum camera cutting off. As he was thinking, the Nintendo DS played a short snippet of a recording made a few seconds previously. It had also picked up on the female voice, clearer and louder. At the same time, Jen was baffled as to how it had managed to unintentionally record.

Anthony took over from Cameron in holding the full spectrum camera. We were going to put a bit more oomph into the experiment.

Cameron resumed his position at the back of the Cave. He stood tall, legs slightly apart, adopting a stable stance with his arms down by his sides. He looked down towards the muddy surface.

Again, there seemed to be a hitch with the Nintendo DS. It got Jen flustered for a moment. She soon got it fixed and gave Anthony the all-clear to proceed.

Anthony shouted out, "Hear these words. Hear these cries, Spirit from the other side. Come to me. I summon thee. Cross now the great divide. Hear, hear, hear, hear us."

Anthony turned the full spectrum camera back around, scoping the front of the Cave.

Jen reshaped the invocation, lowering the pitch and reversing it. She replayed it about four times, gradually speeding it up and slowing it down.

Anthony swung the full spectrum camera back in on Cameron, who was staring straight ahead. He turned his attention away to the entrance of the Cave again.

"Uh, I got a chill on my right hand," said Anthony.

Anthony turned the full spectrum camera in the opposite direction, towards Cameron.

"I have a sensation that something's behind me," said Cameron.

Anthony concurred, believing that the darkness or light had something to do with it. Cameron described that the feeling was not bad.

Cameron called out next, showing a calm and relaxed demeanour, "Spirits, thank you for communicating with us… Do you have a message for any of us or for someone else?"

Jen programmed the device to play at a slow speed, with Cameron's voice at a base pitch.

Anthony zoomed in and out on Cameron.

Cameron stood still, looking straight ahead, back down the lens of the camera.

Jen replayed Cameron's voice backwards.

Cameron raised his right forearm, releasing the grip of his hand. He moved it slowly inwards, towards his waist as though he was feeling the air.

He then raised both arms up from his sides, palms wide open. He closed his eyes and slightly bowed his head. He was isolating himself, connecting with his mind. Seconds later, he tilted his head back, opening his physical body to what was around him.

Jen replayed Cameron's question three more times.

Cameron mentioned he heard a noise, presumably behind him.

Thoughts had turned to other dimensions and other realms prior to Anthony putting forward his query.

"Does doing reversion speech, talking backwards, bring us into another realm, where you can communicate?"

Simultaneously, Cameron was blowing air out from the cheeks of his mouth, creating a mist that could be seen in front of his face.

Jen prodded the touchscreen.

Anthony's voice could be heard in a slow, full-toned style.

"I heard something there; like a scream or something…" said Anthony.

"Behind me?" asked Cameron.

Anthony replied, "Yeah."

Anthony asked Jen if she heard it; she confirmed that she did.

Nevertheless, there was no scream in the recording but there was what seemed to be a yelp, similar to that which a dog would make.

There was one last activity we intended to pursue – the use of shadow play figures (*See Glossary*) in a past enactment.

Jen had crafted three animal images, cut out of card with each one attached to a stick. She held up one at a time, holding a torch in the other hand, casting a silhouette on the Cave wall.

Anthony aimed the full spectrum camera at the first shadow figure – the head of a goat.

Cameron welcomed the prospect of calling out.

He asked, "Can you copy my whistle please?"

Cameron proceeded to let out a loud whistle. There was a brief period of silence before Cameron called out again.

"Can you make a tapping noise… on the stone…?" He tapped four times on the wall. "… like that?" he added.

The second shadow shape used was a wolf, presented in a threatening alert state.

Anthony spoke out, "If you are aware, this is a wolf. Was the Morrigan anything to do with the wolf? Can you give us three knocks?"

There was no apparent response in the ample time provided.

"Is this the Cave of the Cats? Can you make a sound with your voice?" asked Anthony.

In the period of silence that ensued, there was a distant noise.

"Did you hear that?" said Anthony.

Cameron imitated a moan similar to what he thought he had heard.

"Very clear that was," Anthony added.

Cameron expressed his point of view that the Elemental Spirit could affect the flame on the small candle he was holding.

Anthony asked, "If you're something associated with earth, or fire, or air, or water, can you use that element to show yourself in here?"

The last shadow figure was held aloft – a crow. Anthony called out, asking for a reaction.

"The crow – the Morrigan – the bringer of death to the battlefield… a deity who welcomed the Spirits… of those who died on the battle and scavenged upon them. Would you be able to make the whining sound again with your voice?"

Soon after, a clear plain whistle was caught on the full spectrum camera.

Anthony also reported it, "Did you hear that?"

A second or two later, there was another whistle, fainter than the previous.

"Like a whistle," Anthony said. He went on to ask, "Can you copy me?" followed by letting out a whistle of his own that echoed along the cavern.

About twenty seconds later, Anthony declared, "There was another voice there."

He described it as being a groan, yet nothing was caught on the recordings; nor did any of the rest of the team indicate hearing it either.

The shadow puppets had worked perfectly. Maybe they resembled cave drawings, casting a shadow of a story.

The investigation was complete. The team gathered up all the candles, glowsticks and equipment and scrambled up out of the Cave, back to the car where they were finally able to change into dry clothes. It was ten o'clock in the evening and the time had flown by.

We detached the pedometers but, what did they register?

Cameron on the throne, with sword in hand

It can get quite tight before you get to open space in Oweynagat Cave

Electric fencing on top of the Mound

Cameron and Anthony investigate in the dark Cave

Cameron stands still, sensing the atmosphere

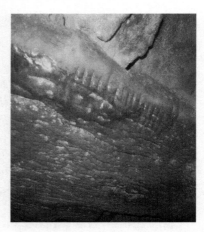

Ogham writing at the entrance

A shadow of a wolf

It can get claustrophobic but Jen crawled on through

Air to breathe can be quite limited

Drowned-Out Voices **Investigation footage can be viewed by**

Watching the DVD that accompanies this book

Scanning the QR code

Visiting our website
www.GhostÉire.net

Click on the button
Drowned-Out Voices Footage

and enter the password
YourNotAlone

Enter the password
YourNotAlone

Location Background/Biography

Cruachan is situated about two kilometres north-west of the village of Tulsk in County Roscommon. It is the celebrated seat of the High Kings of Connaught and, one of the four major ancient royal sites of Ireland. A total of over 240 archaeological sites covers over four-square miles, making it the oldest and largest royal complex in Europe.

Many Kings are said to be buried in the mounds in or around the surrounding area. Queen Medb is renowned as the local Earth Goddess and is associated with the land at Cruachan. To become King meant marrying and merging the two together.

'The cattle raid of Cooley', a battle between two bulls – one from Connaught and the other from Ulster – is said to have taken place close by.

Rathcroghan Mound stands at a height of 6 metres and a diameter of 88 metres. This circular mound is a prominent sight – a dedicated place of burial, gatherings and inaugurations. Access to the top of the Mound can be made from east and west by walking up a slight incline.

With the use of geophysical technology, it is believed that the surrounding entrance and trenches, close to the centre of the Mound, may have formed an area in which a wooden structure would have once stood.

Very little excavation has been done at Rathcroghan but radar and magnetic surveys have revealed similarities with Tara and Navan Fort.

Oweynagat Cave, which means 'The Cave of the Cats', is said to be the gateway to the other world. It lies just over a kilometre south-west of Rathcroghan Mound. A limestone lintel hangs over the entrance gap to the Cave. Ogham writing is inscribed on the lintel. In translation, it means *The stone of Fraech, son of Medb*.

The low entrance opens up to a boundary an overall total of 50 metres in length yet, this may have extended further.

Manifestation/Legend

The Morrigan (Goddess of War, battle and strive) is portrayed as a shape-shifting crow, werewolf and triple-headed creature. She is assumed to reside within the dark walls of Oweynagat Cave. The Cave acts as a portal to the otherworld and its power increases extensively close to Samhain (November 1st). In Christian texts, the Cave was otherwise known as the 'Gateway to Hell' or 'Hell mouth of Ireland'.

Conclusion

At Rathcroghan Mound, a Spirit identified itself as a poltergeist with the manifestation board.

This type of Spirit was capable of physical disturbances and loud noises. The loud noises did not happen yet, the table instantly rocked during the table-tilting experiment. This sits well with poltergeist behaviour. However, with the bleak weather, team members on the table might have been looking for a fast reaction and, therefore, unintentionally exerted pressure to produce a quick outcome. If they had not, then the Spirit may have understood the situation and acted rapidly.

Is a poltergeist a ghost? Alternatively, did Jen or Anthony (or even Cameron) either individually or, as a whole, produce the mental effort that affected the physical environment and caused the table's movement? This is known as psychokinesis or telekinesis.

If supernatural powers gave this entity its existence, then the mention of a magic essence around us is not surprising. There used to be gatherings at Rathcroghan during important times of the year, to mark the changing of the seasons.

It is also the location of twenty-eight burial mounds and where kings would have been crowned or inaugurated and married to Queen Medb of the Earth. Ceremonies were common.

In addition, there were Angels or Spirit guides around us. We do not know if they were associated with or separate from the team but, we do recognise that they were providing a service.

The poltergeist affirmed that the team were demons! One interesting fact was that we were holding up umbrellas at the time. They may have looked like shredded wings. Demons are prevalent in religion, described as malevolent fiends. They are fallen angels and unclean.

The Ancient Greeks had an entirely different view on demons. Their word for demon meant to divide or distribute and stood for a divine power. It was later interpreted negatively by Roman and Christian empires, which saw cult statues of demons from pagan beliefs as no longer beautiful or pleasing.

We could have been perceived as good-natured if the Spirit were from a pre-Christian era, when Rathcroghan Mound was first constructed. Possibly, the Spirit may have thought we were unworldly characters, demi-gods to its time – its realm. The word demonic also means indwelling spirit or genius.

In Oweynagat Cave, Anthony reported hearing groaning and wailing on a couple of occasions but, they were not captured on any of the recording devices. Anthony, most probably, perceived them incorrectly.

The continuous sound of water dripping in the cavern, along with having to adjust your feet in the unsteady, very soft ground, meant noises were predictable and keeping still was impossible. Noises may have come in from the outside environment of the Cave too.

There was a rattle picked up on the full spectrum camera, which Cameron commented on. It did come from within the Cave and after, Jen asked if there was anything strange seen down here. Anthony stated the rattle came from behind him, as Cameron said in front. So, the source of the sound may have occurred between Cameron and Anthony, just past the midpoint of the Cave.

There could be a similarity to the rattle – strange things been seen - and the female voice captured on the digital sound recorder and reversed/altered speech experiment that said, 'Who's there?'

The Spirit present expressed dismay at the same point that we had an issue with our equipment.

An Elemental (linked to the four elements of nature – earth, water, air and fire) Spirit had appeared to have made contact with us on the manifestation board. It is alleged that these types of energies may gain physical form and shape-shift.

The Elemental replied that it was male and female and may have taken a human form back in the 5th century (possibly the same date as the ogham stone lintel was placed in the Cave) and had Christian beliefs. It is assumed that the introduction of Christianity came to Ireland from Roman Britain, around that time. The first Irish monastery was founded by Saint Enda of Aran (born in County Meath), in Killeaney on Aran Mor around 484.

The Spirit may have lived as a Christian and in death, changed its faith towards something resembling an Elemental.

The planchette moved rapidly when mentioning the changing of the seasons and the Morrigan. From experience, this was a sign of positivity or shared opinion and interest.

There might have been more than one Elemental present with us. Did they change their beliefs too?

In a space of just over thirty seconds, an exhale, a female voice and knocking were caught on the full spectrum camera. There would be a tad of scepticism – that the sounds were due to team members and environmental factors – on top of how we interpret them although, they were extremely noticeable.

There have been no excavations at this site. According to the Elemental, there were no bodies found in the Cave and that appears to be true.

The cave is also a pathway to other dimensions. This would probably relate with the magic energy (also recognised as being the team) and, maybe with our pedometers, which gave an unusual reading in the previous investigation at the cavern.

There is a tale written, in the 18th century, of a woman who followed a runaway cow into the Cave, only to end up at Keshcorran Caves in County Sligo.

On this occasion, the pedometers Anthony and Cameron had on them only recorded a maximum distance of about 0.5km each. It also must be taken into consideration that Rathcroghan Mound is further from a carpark than Tulsk Priory was from the layby. It highlighted how bizarre the pedometer readings were the year before, on the mid-summer solstice evening.

Cameron and Anthony had experienced shivering and cold sensations. Cameron also felt a presence behind him. The sensations are most likely down to adrenaline (strong emotion) spiking just after questions were played back slowly in a deep (voice) tone and reversed, exposing a mix of excitement and terror. The point where Cameron had first felt a presence behind him was when speech had been replayed in a similar process. Cameron had been meditating (tuned in to his surroundings) and yet, he had stated that it was not bad.

If the device had been spreading fear, then Cameron's claim offered reassurance that we would be okay. Also, it came unexpected at that stage — making it reliable.

Later in the same experiment, Anthony had mentioned that he had heard a scream, after asking a question about reversion speech and other realms. A yelp or bark from outside the Cave (most probably from a dog at a neighbouring house) was the noise captured after reviewing the full spectrum camera footage.

When analysing the recording of the shadow play figures experiment, a distant deep groan or moan was picked up, though we did not judge it to be as far away as the earlier noise from the dog. It happened just after Anthony queried if this were the 'Cave of the Cats' and if a noise with the voice could be made.

Jen was holding up the wolf shadow figure at the time. This must have been one other form of communication but there would be another method of making contact.

Cameron had asked if a Spirit could copy his whistle. About four minutes later, what sounded like two sharp whistles were heard, as Jen was holding the crow shadow figure and Anthony was talking about the Morrigan.

It is important to note, Anthony had asked for a whine, not a whistle. The dripping water in the Cave may have caused the whistling sounds or, it may have unintentionally originated from a team member (who was unwilling to say they had done it), apart from Anthony, who had remarked on it. However, the groan/moan and whistling had occurred when prompting a reaction other than speaking.

Rathcroghan/Oweynagat

Co Roscommon

WEBSITE: rathcroghan.ie
e-MAIL: info@rathcroghan.ie
PHONE: 071 963 9268
INSTAGRAM: /rathcroghan/

The visitor centre is open Monday to Saturday,
9am–5pm and Sundays from May to August.

You can experience stories, archaeology, history and prehistory of the royal capital of Connacht at the educational visitor centre.

A total of thirty-five artefacts, discovered in the nearby landscape, are on display at the centre, along with audio-visual presentations that bring Ireland's past and legends to life.

The Táin Café is an ideal spot to relax and refresh with a coffee or tea. The café also provides hot food, sandwiches and desserts

Guided tours are available of the Rathcroghan archaeology complex.

FRANK McCOURT MUSEUM

Layout

Rough Dimensions

CLASSROOM, FIRST FLOOR

ROOMS/AREAS, SECOND FLOOR

ANGELA'S BEDROOM

CORRIDOR

ROOMS/AREAS, BASEMENT

DINING ROOM, BASEMENT

BILLIARD ROOM

POOL ROOM

Chapter 22

Frank McCourt Museum

Sinead's Journey

Have you ever read *Angela's Ashes*? It is a story depicting a family living in poverty in the 1930s, in a state ruled by the Catholic Church, where strict morals and unspoken dreams were plenty.

Welcome to our next investigation – The Frank McCourt Museum. Compared to our other locations off the beaten track, this one was quite central – Limerick City. It was the Georgian quarter of Limerick City to be precise. What was once known as Leamy's School – attended by Frank McCourt and his brothers - had now been turned in to a museum – one that re-created the memories of strict headmasters and oppressive class rules. I wondered what this investigation would bring up.

Departing work early that day, I made a swift exit towards the nearest train station, to venture forth towards the midlands. Fields of green, cattle and sheep galore! One thing that evoked my imagination was listening to my favourite music whilst lapping up the Irish landscape. Peace and tranquillity, here I come!

However, no more than about thirty minutes into my journey, any existing tranquillity disappeared in a flash. Without hesitation, a lady boarding the train decided to budge in beside me, plonking her screaming baby on the table with an assortment of rattles and other baby products. Was I supposed to entertain her child as well? Make googly eyes and cooing noises? No thank you – not today!

Giving an insincere smile, much to the parent's dismay, she proceeded to open two bags of crisps, handing one of them to her child. As the baby crawled across the table, smashing the crisps up with their hands, wailing and stretching their arms out towards me, the mother laughed on in amusement. Was I supposed to validate or congratulate? I honestly did not know but I decided to ignore the whole situation for the next two hours and focused on the evening ahead instead.

Stepping off the train, I meandered up the Limerick streets towards my overnight hotel. On entering, I felt like a spy on a mission. It was quite deserted, with a handful of people lingering around the reception area.

Was I here for business?

No.

Visiting relatives?

No.

Taking in tourist attractions?

No.

Did I come for leisure?

Well, maybe – if you could call it that.

Exploring other realms?

Probably, yes.

Running behind time, I dumped my bag in my room, grabbed my keys, then I legged it down the road at top speed and followed my phone's GPS, as my eyes scanned the vicinity for the Frank McCourt Museum. James Bond, eat your heart out!

I was fascinated by the silent, cobblestone streets. Unlike Dublin, they were slanted and crumbling away. If I tripped up here, I could have easily disappeared into the crevasses of the curb. Who knows? The streets looked quite unstable. It was like stepping back in time to the Victorian era.

Having travelled from Kerry, the rest of the team were already there, waiting for the owners to arrive with the keys. Once inside the building, I was quite mesmerised by the entire set up. There were rooms resembling old Victorian bedrooms, rocking chairs and old religious iconography. An old classroom stuck in time – desks lined with old ink wells. Photos of past school children lined the wall, dating back to the late 1930s. A mannequin of a boy was sat on one of the desks.

While Anthony carried out the base testing, the rest of the team helped set up the cameras for the first round of experiments in the classroom. If anything were to be heard here, it would echo through the entire building!

After exploring the building and setting up the equipment, we were ready to roll. We had a group consisting of guests and the owners of the building sitting in with us for the evening. Everyone was psyched up.

Before kicking off, we had one last thing to do – our protection prayer. We decided to carry out our protection prayer at the back of the building, down a delinquent, dodgy laneway. For a moment,

I thought that it would be a better idea to protect ourselves from being attacked by real people, rather than from any other entities.

If any member of the public sauntered by, they would have seen a group of strangers in a circle, eyes closed, speaking about 'blinding white lights' and 'invoking the violet flame'. It reminded me of cartoon I used to watch when younger called *Captain Planet* – fighting crime with a group of friends. Maybe we would start a new superhero craze in Limerick, sweeping the alleyways around the quiet quarters of the city. I could only imagine.

In a way, it was like our own secret society, miles away from regular day-to-day life. Sure, what else would you be doing on a sunny evening in spring?

The Investigation

NUMBER OF TEAM

4

5

NUMBER OF GUESTS

It is believed that the book, *Angela's Ashes* is one of the best things to come out of Limerick city. The author, Frank McCourt, gives a detailed account of what life was like in Brooklyn, New York and in Limerick. His struggles at home, work and school were easily recognised in the memoir but are juxtaposed with amusing content.

We visited Leamy School (as it was previously known) a few days before the investigation. This was where Frank McCourt was educated between the ages of five and thirteen.

We were interviewed by the *Limerick Leader* newspaper about our first impressions ahead of the upcoming investigation.

We met with the owner, Una. Shortly afterwards we were introduced to Rob, Tara, Michael and his wife. They are fine enthusiasts of his literature and had great knowledge of the premises, the surrounding area and of course, Frank himself.

A few areas caught our fancy. The largest room in the building, the Classroom, was half set up to resemble what a schoolroom would have looked like in the 1930s. The other half of the room displayed memorabilia dedicated to Frank McCourt and the former school.

Opposite the reception, up a small flight of stairs to the second floor, was a door leading to Angela's Kitchen and Angela's Bedroom. Both areas represented the appearance of the house in Roden Lane, where Frank and his family grew up.

The Basement, previously a billiard and pool centre, was partly decorated into a house of horrors, for entertainment purposes, for the festival of Halloween.

The date for the investigation was 19 March 2015. It would be our first of the year, with a gap of about eighteen months between this and the last one that we had done.

Anthony, Jen and a female team member had arrived at the Museum around four o'clock that afternoon. On the leaving the parked car,

Jen was given a pedometer to measure the distance she would cover over the entire evening ahead. Another pedometer would be given to Sinead on arrival.

There was a low amount of EMF emitted around the whole house. The majority of it was produced by the typical sensors, sockets, cabling and overhead lighting.

It was a cloudy day. The moon, which was a waning crescent, was 6% full. Its influence on the star sign Pisces would bring a scattered feeling. As Mercury was in conjunction with Neptune, there would be a tendency to drift off. The more we relaxed, the better it would be for Spirits on the other side.

There was a bit of noise in the air with the C Low level at 53.4, showing a disturbance by noise pollution, probably coming from outside of the building, mainly caused by traffic as O' Connell Street was nearby.

The Museum would be closing to the public at five o'clock.

As most of the baseline tests were done and equipment dropped in, it was a good time to get some food to fill our tummies for the evening.

There was a residual energy around the building. This would later be emphasised when the team and Una returned to the Museum after the break.

Anthony was setting up equipment in the Classroom. As he was attaching a video camera to a tripod, he swore that he heard a humming sound, similar to the noise a child would make in mid-thought.

Jen and the female team member arrived in the Classroom after their walkabout. Anthony told them what he had heard. To their astonishment, they immediately disclosed to Anthony that they had both individually heard a similar sort of hum before they entered the Classroom. It brought to the fore that we might be dealing with past pupils of the school - that we were not the only ones who might be learning that day!

Sinead appeared around seven o'clock. A pedometer was provided for her to wear.

The team made their way to a lane around the back of the Museum, gathering themselves in preparation for the hours ahead with a protection prayer, to preserve well-being and to prevent any harm or injury to us and to others who would be attending tonight's search at the Museum.

The team gathered back at the front of the building. Each member had their picture taken using a thermal imaging camera at the front door. Their entire bodies were photographed. The same would be done at the end of the investigation, to analyse anything exceptional.

Joining GhostÉire for the evening were Una, her partner John, Michael, Rob and Tara.

Everyone congregated in the Classroom, on the first floor, in an attempt to talk beyond in a séance. There would be a different layout, a new plan of dialogue. Five questions would be read out and translated into five languages: Irish, Spanish, French, old English and English.

A full spectrum camera had a good overhead view of the Classroom. It was put high above a doorway, which connected to the reception. Situated at the front of the Classroom was the school headmaster's table. Positioned around it were notable items, such as a globe, bell, cane, encyclopaedias, books, academic hat, briefcase and a gold-framed, black-and-white photograph of the past school headmaster (decked out in a gown and ceremonial sash). Those observing the séance sat a few metres away to the right-hand side of the table.

In front of the school master's table were wooden desks that would have belonged to past children who attended the school. The desks had the capacity to sit two people. A mannequin of a child was seated halfway down the arrangements of desks.

Large maps of Europe, North America and Ireland, a black board and an old-fashioned clock took up the majority of the wall's space on this side of the room.

The other half of the room had glass cabinets, featuring schoolbooks, Frank McCourt's personal copy of *Angela's Ashes* and the robes he wore when he received an honorary degree at the University of Limerick in 1997.

On this section of walls were black-and-white images of Frank McCourt's close family; framed, coloured illustrations of Leamy House and local landmarks painted by the owner and a local artist, Una Heaton.

Jen, the female team member, Anthony and Sinead took up their seats at the school master's table. Anthony and Sinead sat on one side, facing the front of the Classroom. Jen and the female team member settled on their chairs opposite them – the same side of the desk that the school master would have sat at.

A digital sound recorder was fixed onto a small tripod. It was placed on one of the school children's desks back behind Anthony and Sinead.

A video camera was positioned overlooking a talking board at the centre of the school master's table. The video camera was attached to overhead copper piping. Black industrial tape held it in place. The piping extended outwards for about five feet, curving downwards at a height of seven feet. To keep it stable, the piping was tightly fastened around a microphone stand beside the table with yet more black tape.

On the talking board were a school bell and a toy of a green double-decker bus.

Beside the school master's table was a single seater desk that showed signs of deterioration: the wood was slightly worn. It had the sole purpose of being up at the front of the class, under the teacher's nose, to serve as a place to punish for any misbehaviour.

On this desk were offerings of a cup of water, half a loaf of bread, two poems on paper (one of which was called, 'The brat'), a bowl of earth, another school bell, a thin stem of a plant and a mini-Saint George's flag together with an Irish tricolour.

We hoped to guide or lure the Spirits in with synchronised timing. The full spectrum camera, video camera and digital sound recorder were switched on to record all at the same time.

It was eight o'clock and it was time to begin. The team lightly linked hands, resting them upon the table. A silence took over. Irish would be the first language we would use. Each team member called out their name. The female team member called out the first question of the night.

"What is your name?"

Ten minutes passed with questions being asked in Spanish and French until it was time to use the old English dialect.

"Your name?"

A couple of seconds later, what could be understood as a distinct shout came through on the full spectrum camera. It is unclear what was said and, if it precisely had come from someone's tongue.

When the English questions were asked – the final of the five languages – we had come to the point where we needed to strike more of a balance and calmly speak out, negotiating to try and spark off something.

"If the lady who's being hiding in the corner… like to know who she is please do so… It's okay; your safe with us," said the female team member.

Two clear knocks came through on the full spectrum camera recording. They seemed to be identical in pressure. As well, the same knocks came through on the digital sound recorder.

The séance would take a whole new twist a couple of minutes later.

Anthony's concentration was fully on the green double-decker toy bus. He stared at it for a prolonged period.

The female team member said to Anthony, "It's not going to happen. Is it?"

She was suggesting that the toy was not going to move with just mind control.

Anthony remained fixated on the toy. He let out a loud groan. This startled the female team member. Her bowed head rose to attention. The groan showed up easily on the digital sound recorder and on the video camera above the school master's desk.

Anthony chuckled. He spoke yet, the sound of his voice sounded suppressed. "I'm small…" he said then his voice reset to how he would normally talk but the vocabulary was strange.

"No, I'm not saying anything."

Quickly, he followed up by saying, "That's just me talking, Anthony."

It would be fair to say that another Spirit had channelled into Anthony's soul and, partially, his body. The groan representing the Spirit had entered Anthony.

The Spirit established that they were young, slight in height.

When Anthony regained his voice, he commented that he had not been talking. It is likely that he had recovered full control of his speech at that point. Shortly afterwards, he remarked that he realised he had spoken by stating his name.

During the séance, Anthony could be seen swaying side to side after the question, "What's your occupation?" was asked in French. That was another sign that something was manifesting.

After the séance had ended, each team member and those who were in close attendance took a pen and paper and wrote down the personal experiences they had sensed or, any information they had perceived during the session.

When they had finished, the piece of paper that they had written their names on would be folded and placed through the slot of a small, square, cardboard box. The cardboard box would be opened at the end of the night.

It was during this time of contemplation, when everyone was writing or in thought, that some unaccountable incidents occurred.

A voice was caught on the video camera above the school master's desk and on the digital sound recorder. It was when Sinead was debating whether to discuss with the female team member what she had felt during the séance. She said, "Yeah, yeah, yeah but I can't… it has, it has to be into the box at the end."

A feminine voice said, 'It has to be up to you'.

For sure, the reply could have come from somebody present, yet everybody present knew for a fact that, for the experiment to work, nothing on the piece of paper could be disclosed for now. Set aside from that, it sounded dissimilar and was pronounced very slowly and clearly.

About three minutes later, a conspicuous breath was caught on the same video camera by the school master's desk and the digital sound recorder. Unfortunately, the full spectrum camera that had a great view of the room had shut down, the battery emptied, making it difficult to decide if the breath had come from a human being. People had been moving around at the time but it sounded like the perpetrator had been expelling out air deliberately.

Another EVP was picked up by the digital sound recorder. What could be best described as a muffled, male voice possibly said, 'Confidence to the rule' or, 'Come into the room'.

It was said in a controlling manner, probably by someone in authority.

There were similarities to what people had written down on the sheets of paper. There seemed to have been reactions to Spanish questions, a presence by the back of the Classroom, whispering, footsteps and food or the lack of it. Also, the names coming forward were mostly masculine.

A time for conversation and refreshments ensued, including tea, coffee, sandwiches and biscuits.

We would make our way to Angela's Kitchen and Angela's Bedroom on the second floor. Only one observer, Tara, joined the team for a host of calling-out vigils.

Anthony had prepared two doorway motion detectors on the floor, in the Corridor to Angela's Bedroom/Kitchen. Hopefully, there would be intent by a Spirit to disturb the infrared beam between both components.

One video camera was placed in Angela's Bedroom. It had a great visual of a typical 1930s wooden bed, with an old military tunic used as a blanket; it would keep a person warm yet, this tough garment would harbour lice at the seams.

The wallpaper was very plain. There was a white and blue speckled design on one side of the bedroom and a blue with white floral design on the other. The paper was peeling off the wall and a representation of dark mould on the walls gave meaning as to how people struggled in such living conditions.

Underneath the bed was a porcelain chamber pot. A simple wooden chair was to the right of the bed, next to a window, which was concealed by white, sheer-draped netting.

Above the chair and the head of the bed, hanging off the wall was a black-and-white photograph of a woman (perhaps that of a relative of Frank McCourt). On a small shelf in that corner of the room was a Jesus of Prague statue.

Splitting the room in half were three metal stanchions (standing poles) with two blue ropes loosely connected in between them, forming a line divider.

The digital sound recorder was put on a table in the room. Sinead pressed it to record. At the same time, Anthony pressed record on the video camera.

Anthony and Sinead met the rest of the team next door, in Angela's Kitchen. Anthony remained standing whilst Sinead took up a chair to sit alongside Jen, the female team member and Tara at a dining table, which was congested on top with items. Crockery, silverware, a shot glass, a jug and a jam jar occupied the top of the table, along with unfamiliar household objects seen today, such as a cast iron tea kettle, clothes iron, oil lamps and candles and, a Guinness Extra Stout bottle.

Other noticeable things included the blue and white printed wallpaper. Inside, on the right of the room, was an imitation fireplace and above that was a picture of the scared heart next to a small, square piece of cardboard, with a text of a prayer on it.

Also, around this tight corner of the room was an old ceramic sink, with various utensils stacked untidily next to it. Near the sink was a scrubbing board and a vintage pram. A Victorian window shutter stood idle, giving sight to white, floral-patterned window netting.

Another video camera was positioned on a tripod, overlooking the dining table.

This time Anthony, opened up by calling out to the Spirits.

"You can come towards us. You can make footsteps. Move within the room. You can make knocks… taps… make a sound with your voice. We have three boxes here but they don't mean you any harm. They're only for our benefit – just to record… Come in between those… Make yourself known."

At nearly six minutes into the calling-out vigil, Anthony described that he was getting a dead bell in his ear.

Shortly after, the female team member got three names in her head. Francie (undecided if male or female) came in very strong, then Breda and Katie. Tara declared that she was getting the name 'Anne' coming into her mind.

Continuing on, Anthony described that the dead bell was in his ear again. A minute or so later, Anthony called out for an intervention.

"Can you maybe… close one of the doors?"

Murmuring or humming, possibly made by a child, emerged on the recordings.

There was a sense of a woman and especially a nun being present on this specific floor. Also, hunger was suspected.

"Did you lose a child?" asked Sinead

Tara was suddenly overcome with a cold shiver. "Yeah, that's it," she replied.

Tara was not the only one who sensed this being a prominent aspect. So did Sinead.

After fifteen minutes, the team left Angela's Kitchen and headed into Angela's Bedroom. Before departing the area, a scent of carbolic soap could be smelt in the air.

In Angela's Bedroom, Anthony sat down on the bed that was in front of the video camera. The female team member sat on another bed opposite. Sinead and Tara had taken up their seats away from the video camera's range of vision, while Jen stood and took a few snapshots with her digital camera, before sitting down beside Anthony. We advanced quickly to the second calling-out vigil.

Anthony called out, "Okay, if there's an Anne, a Francie, Katie… Breda…"

The female team member felt a cold shiver; Anthony remarked that his bum had got freezing too.

Nearly five minutes had passed when the female team member felt a Spirit energy coming forward, associated with making clothing. They were stuck in the process of that activity. The female team member described what this Spirit had said. She shouted, "I make my own clothes."

She added that there was a strong presence of a woman who believed that surviving day after day; getting food on the table was the fundamental part of existence for her.

A couple of minutes later, factory work was sensed coming in strongly.

Anthony turned his head to his left and glanced at the female team member. "Shall we move on?" he said.

The motion sensor light by the doorway in the Corridor had turned on. Jen was on her feet at the time, taking some photographs, so she might have triggered it as, at that point, she was moving close to the Corridor. Yet, she denied her involvement, maintaining that she was the same distance away prior to the sensor being activated.

The team were curious and so they carried on calling-out in Angela's Bedroom. After around twenty-eight minutes or so, after both calling-out vigils were completed, it was time to vacate.

As everybody was leaving Angela's Bedroom, a clear female voice spoke, in the aftermath of Anthony asking a question to the team.

"Should we go straight down and do it?" he asked.

'Jesus!' was the reply.

The response was made in an irritable way, rather than in a self-soothing manner. It had a distinct tone, that of a mature lady speaking in a native Irish accent.

It should be pointed out that this retort happened when the team were being indecisive about leaving, especially too much dithering on Anthony's part – the only man present.

Jen, Sinead, Anthony and the female team member met with John outside the Museum. John opened the door to the connecting building that led down to the Basement. We were now below the Museum.

The lights were switched on. There was a definite chill in the air. John stayed by the reception area in the Basement. A motion detector was placed in the same area, directed away from John towards another area – the Dining Room.

The team went to the Pool Room. Chairs and snooker cues were scattered across the red carpet. Up against a white, lime-coated wall were folded trestle tables. The whitewashed wall was probably the outer shell of the school in its day. The Pool Room was a former playground.

We would be doing a past enactment experiment in this area. We would be using a recording of children at play from an iPhone.

The female team member was finding it hard to get the infrared motion nature camera (*See Equipment*) to work. It would not happen. It was not suitable for this type of purpose. Jen would have to use the digital camera to record footage. All of our visual recording equipment either needed charging or, was dispersed across other areas of the Museum. The digital sound recorder was placed on a small flight of stairs that led to an emergency exit door. Anthony was holding the thermal imaging camera. He would check if any changes would occur on the temperature scale.

Jen pressed the iPhone play button. The sound of children playing in a playground could be heard throughout the room. The team refrained from talking. After the experiment had finished, the female team member suggested that the energy had changed.

Jen was the first to go back into the Billiard Room. She pulled aside a ragged curtain. To her left were standing trestle tables, square classroom tables and modern school chairs. The room looked completely different compared to when the team had last visited. The three snooker tables and overhead hanging lamps were nowhere to be seen. The room was now being utilised for educational needs.

The team walked to the bottom of the room. The female team member stood in a particular open spot. She was getting goose pimples.

"It's full in your head," said Jen.

She described that it was similar to having a headache.

The female team member said, "This is where I got the choky and I'm feeling it now here."

She signified her feelings to the rest of the team by retching.

The team pressed on. Sinead went to retrieve the digital sound recorder from the Pool Room. On her return, Anthony led the team to the Dining Room. To get to there, they had to walk past the reception in darkness. They were directed, by John, to a light switch inside the Dining Room. Jen pressed the switch. The overhead fluorescent tube lighting briefly flickered, illuminating the room.

In the centre of room, straight ahead was a large trestle table swathed in white linen. On either side of the trestle table were two round tables, also draped with linen sheets. Two wooden chairs with red upholstery lay on the opposite end of the trestle table, facing each other. The presentation of crockery, silverware, napkins and candles on the tables was eye-catching. Who was inviting us to dinner?

It was not the only veiled object in the room: the resting, shrouded figure, representing a dead corpse, was stretched out on the long, wooden bench ahead. It was all for show - the theme for a Halloween haunted house of horrors. The room was sectioned off by wooden chipboard panelling. Doorway cavities in the panelling opened up a makeshift maze of terror on the other side.

We walked in on the red and green chequered carpet. Sinead put the digital sound recorder up on top of the dining trestle table. Sinead was excited, as she had never been in the room before.

"That's so strange," she said.

"Yeah, they have a haunted house here at Halloween," replied Jen.

In the wake of giggles, a voice was picked up on the digital camera that Jen was holding. It sounded like a soft, female voice. It might have said, 'Ah it so lovely', 'Ah, you smell lovely' or, 'Ah, you're so lovely'.

Sinead, who was in shot at this point, did not look as though she had moved her lips but, it should not be ruled out that it was her who was speaking. This expression could not have come from Jen and the female team member. One thing is for sure: somebody or something else had expressed gratitude to the matter.

Anthony noticed temperature differences with the thermal imaging camera around the spout, handle and base of a brass teapot. A reflection from another light source could have caused this.

Not long after, the team made their way out of the Basement. The three video cameras that were left playing in the upper floors of the building, failed to trace anything of further importance. The equipment and other items were picked up and carried out to the car outside, on Hartstonge Street.

The team came back into the Museum to say their goodbyes, thanking Una and John for their hospitality.

Outside of the front door, the final pictures were taken of each team member, using the thermal imaging camera. The outcome was a mixed bag. The heat had increased on the upper body but decreased on the lower half of the body by the end of the investigation.

Leaving the building, the team members would have encountered the cold air on the legs and under the feet whilst walking out to the car: conduction - when standing for pictures. Also, the temperature inside the Museum would have fallen throughout the night. The reason for the upper body (hands, arms and head) being warmer was probably down to exertion - carrying equipment to the car.

The time was now half past eleven, so the team went back to the car.

There was quite a contrast in the pedometer results. Jen clocked up 1.2km in seven and a half hours. Sinead walked a distance of 0.5km in three and a half hours. Jen had walked further but, in over double the amount of time. Jen had covered a considerable distance when setting up equipment and taking photographs (getting the best camera angle) in different areas of the building before Sinead had arrived. She may have achieved the 0.7km difference in the build-up to the investigation. There was only the steady process of concentration, calling out and working of various rooms (with Sinead, Jen and the rest of the group) after the investigation had begun.

Anthony, Jen and the female team member got into the car and were soon on their way home. Sinead departed, only a short walk away from the hotel. Their lessons for the day had ended. Still, some homework had to be done.

A painting on the wall of a young boy at the entrance of the museum

Formally Leamy School, the Classroom still holds one pupil

Fancy a game of Snooker?

A mannequin representing 'Angela' can be seen through a curtain on the second floor, Angela's Kitchen

The headmaster's desk - we wonder what we might learn today?

The school now houses a museum to *Angela's Ashes* and the book's author, Dr Frank McCourt

The Tudor-listed building with the bust of Frank McCourt, commissioned by Limerick artist, Una Heaton

Sinead stood still in Angela's Bedroom in a calling-out vigil

The Dining Room in the basement; fake dead bodies lie under the sheets, ready for a scare!

A view from an upper floor down on the Classroom

Drowned-Out Voices Investigation footage can be viewed by

Watching the DVD that accompanies this book

Visiting our website

www.GhostÉire.net

Click on the button
Drowned-Out Voices Footage

and enter the password
YourNotAlone

Scanning the QR code

Enter the password
YourNotAlone

Location Background/Biography

The Frank McCourt Museum, also known as Leamy House, is located on Hartstonge Street in Limerick city. The Tudor-style listed building was designed by William Atkins.

Atkins, who was from County Cork, would later design Eglinton Lunatic Asylum (1847) and St Mary's Priory (1850) in Cork City. The building was erected in 1843 by William Leamy, as a memorial to one of Limerick's indigenous benefactors, Lady Lucy Hartstonge and her husband, Sir Henry Hartstonge. Lady Lucy was the sister of Edmund Sexton Pery, who entered the House of Commons in 1751 and was Speaker of the chamber from 1771-1785.

Before William Leamy died, he generously left a large sum of money (£13,300) in a trust for the education of poor Protestant boys. With dwindling numbers in 1880, Leamy School, as it was known became the National School for Catholic boys up until 1953.

With the help of Jack Heaton, the Crescent Clothing Company took over the premises in 1956. They manufactured in men's clothing up until 1993.

In 2009, Limerick Artist Una Heaton opened up a gallery at Leamy House. She commissioned a bust of the late Dr Frank McCourt (author of *Angela's Ashes*) and undertook the transfiguration of this unique building to the Frank McCourt Museum.

The museum showcased old photos of what life was like in Limerick City, with schoolbooks, a classroom presentation of the 1930s and a replica of the McCourt home, which included an early 20th century-styled, themed Bedroom and Kitchen.

The contrasting exterior of Leamy House includes the limestone and sandstone gargoyles and ornamented chimneys along with turrets and clock tower. The three-storey over Basement, red-bricked building stands out from other Georgian terraced buildings on Hartstonge Street.

Manifestation/Legend

There was no paranormal significance to this location prior to the investigation.

Conclusion

Unfortunately, there is no proof of humming before the investigation started, only statements by team members. It is, indeed, unusual that individuals had heard these identical sounds, at the same time, in different areas. There might had been more than one child making the noise. The reason for a child to hum is to self-instruct their progress: a method of concentration.

Humming or murmuring had also occurred later, when the team were in Angela's Kitchen. The owners and the majority of guests who had not been participating at that point, were nearby. They may have contributed to this type of noise by talking – their voices reverberating around the building, causing a dissimilar audible noise on our recording devices.

A child had been assumed to have channelled through Anthony during the séance in the Classroom. He had started swaying earlier in that session, when questions were asked in French. He had stopped when the English language was applied. This may have grounded Anthony, bringing back familiar words that were common to him.

The female team member had mentioned Anthony was focusing hard on the green double-decker bus when he groaned. Nobody had mentioned the groan. People may not have heard or had been too stunned by the reaction to say anything about it. The toy bus that Anthony had tranced on and used to ask for a child to come forward, had been the subject of conversation for two minutes before the voice came through Anthony saying, 'I'm small'.

Anthony had quickly remarked that he had not spoken those words. At six-foot-three, Anthony is anything but small, which brings us to the conclusion that a child had been looking for our attention.

Leamy School had provided education to both Protestant and Catholic pupils (in separate rooms). In 1885, Catholic children were withdrawn from the school.

The distant shout that we thought we had caught after "Your name?" was asked in old English, might have originated from Una, who was seen opening her mouth as if to yawn.

There had been two knocks or raps detected when asking the lady, hiding in the corner, to let us know who she was. This might have been the same lady who had said, 'It has to be up to you', in reply to Sinead, twelve minutes later. The Spirit had been offering Sinead a bit of direction over her indecisiveness.

Soon after, an obvious breath had been picked up; most probably recognised as an expel of air from a female. This breath could have been from a Spirit regenerating in our atmosphere or, a reaction from people moving about (end of the session), invading its space. It could also, quite simply, have been a person trying to gather themself after a lengthy sit-down. However, there had been a purpose and intent to it.

According to parliamentary papers of 1890, there had been at least one mistress; a female teacher at the school – a Miss Mary Mercer.

A Mrs Young, a teacher who lived on Hartstonge Street (most likely the school), had died in June of 1859.

A male voice had been picked up, shortly afterwards, on the digital sound recorder. It may have said 'Come into the room'. It had been spoken with serious intent but had been muffled. It is reasonable to suggest someone displaying superiority would have spoken in a manner like this.

A William Mercer had been headmaster of the school during the late 1800s (at the same time as Miss Mary Mercer).

A commissioner's report from 1857 summarised that there had been no flogging at the school, though attendance was poor, mainly due to poverty. This report also described that the headmaster – a Mr Joseph Hosford - would not like himself to go to school with a hungry belly! We do not know if this statement had been made by the teacher regarding the children's predicament (starvation), stopping them from going to school or, if it had been a dig at the teacher's appearance (overweight) by the inspector.

Anthony had written down on paper that he had felt a yearning for oranges. This fruit does not spoil as easily as others. It had been rare and expensive to buy but a special treat to receive during the 19th century. It became popular as a gift for Christmas during this period. The oranges could have been an affordable delicacy for a teacher.

The female team member had sensed hunger, which linked with how the children must have felt.

Anthony and the female team member had both experienced a reaction when questions were asked in Spanish.

The commissioner's report from 1857 specified that this language had not been taught to pupils at the school. It is likely that it was part of the curriculum further down the line.

Members of the team had shared a feeling of a presence by the back of the Classroom, along with footsteps and whispering, likely assigned to the lady in the corner.

A wide variety of masculine names had been written down but none with a surname. This makes it hard to identify a person.

On the floor above, in Angela's Kitchen, female names had been prevalent. Likewise, without any surnames, there was no genuine guarantee of establishing a connection with a person and the building.

For the team and guests, their feelings towards getting names might have been influenced by the rooms that they were in. In the Classroom, the mannequin of a boy, exhibits dedicated to Frank McCourt and the cane, briefcase and photograph of a former headmaster had been all aligned with masculinity.

Angela's Kitchen and Bedroom were the opposite - women. A mannequin of Frank's mother, Angela and the surrounding décor reminded us of what a woman's role was in a family in bygone days. These ladies' stories told us a life of hardship.

The scent of carbolic soap was smelt. This red soap, that has mild antiseptic qualities to help fight infection on the skin, became mass-produced in 1894. Carbolic soap was the first of its kind to kill germs and maintain hygiene, making it a necessity for a school to have.

The fact there was a sink and a scrubbing board in Angela's Kitchen might have caused the scent to be smelt. Can inoperable objects release such smells? There had been no sign of this soap lying around.

A nun was believed to be close.

With further research, we cannot find any records of nuns being on the property. Because girls also attended Leamy School up to end of the nineteenth century, there is a possibility that nuns or sisters may have had an active part in the education of children at the site, even when it became a Catholic, all-boys school.

In Angela's Bedroom, the female team member had sensed a Spirit (possibly female) who was in the process of tailoring. The building used to be called the Crescent Clothing factory. The firm was founded by Mr Jack Heaton and employed a total of 150 (women and men) to make suits and jackets. Unfortunately, we were unable to get a name for this Spirit, who seemed hard-pressed in its work, even to this day.

The light sensor in the Corridor had been activated when Anthony requested, "Shall we move on?"

Just a few seconds beforehand, the female team member had confirmed that a factory worker was very dominant in the area. As we did not have a complete view of the Corridor, we cannot deny if a person caused the sensor to trigger, especially Jen, who had been close to that spot taking photographs at that time. After it happened, she stated that she had not moved whilst looking down at her feet. Nonetheless, other parts of the body cannot be ruled out from causing this incident to happen. In spite of that, had we been shown the way to leave?

As the team departed Angela's Bedroom to go to another part of the building, a female voice, in a strong Irish accent, had said 'Jesus'. It sounded as though that we had been a hindrance and that we had needed to be gone quickly. It may have come from the factory worker Spirit, quite possibly occupied, who was working towards a deadline.

Again, the team members or Tara (guest) cannot be excluded from having created the vocalisation, as their faces had not been in the frame of the static video cameras at that precise moment.

The headache and choking sensation in the Billiard Room might have been a consequence of the overhead florescent lighting. The florescent lighting gave a read-out of 2 milliGauss. Low levels of EMF are believed to cause headaches and nausea but according to the WHO (World Health Organisation), there is no scientific evidence to support this.

Other environmental factors have to be taken into consideration, such as infrasound and ultrasound (*See Glossary*) and the circumstances leading up to the person's acknowledgement of a symptom (for instance, health and diet).

It is hard to really unearth what a female voice had said in the Dining Room of the Basement. We do know that the words were either said with gratitude (knowledge of what was in front of them) or, with a nicely surprised attitude. If it had been to do with a pleasant scent, it could have been in relation to how the room (or an object) had smelt in a previous era.

The female Spirit might have been following us around and entered the room at the same time as we had. If so, the Spirit might have perceived an alternative smell to what the team found with the room. If the words had not mentioned the sense of smelling and just gratitude and surprise – such as 'Ah, it so lovely' – then we had potentially just been perceiving what the room had looked like to the female Spirit in front of them. It is unlikely that the words had been uttered by a female member of the crew.

The Dining Room used to be an open yard to the school toilets.

Frank McCourt Museum
Co Limerick

The building is now under private ownership.
We thank Una, John and all the guests for their
time in helping in our studies.

Layout

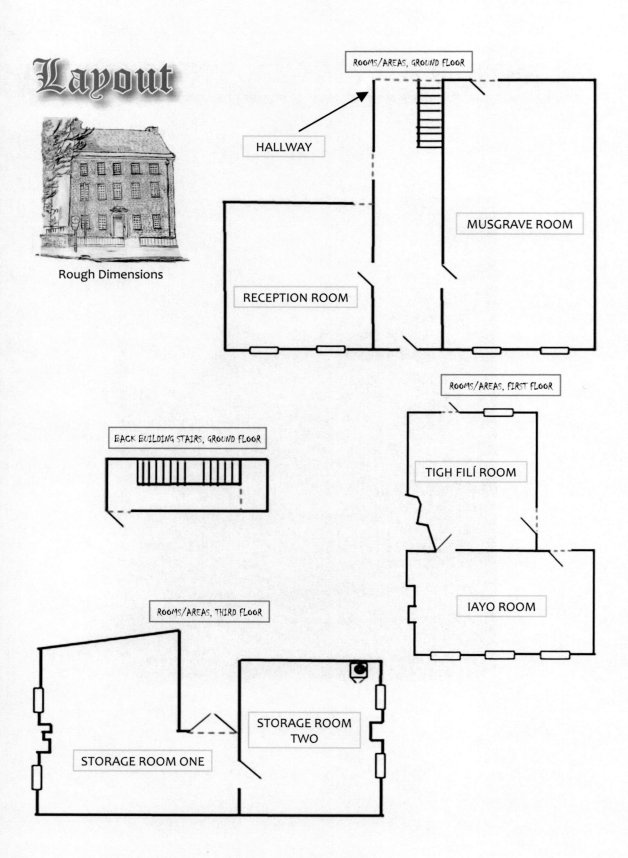

Rough Dimensions

ROOMS/AREAS, GROUND FLOOR

HALLWAY

MUSGRAVE ROOM

RECEPTION ROOM

ROOMS/AREAS, FIRST FLOOR

TIGH FILÍ ROOM

IAYO ROOM

BACK BUILDING STAIRS, GROUND FLOOR

ROOMS/AREAS, THIRD FLOOR

STORAGE ROOM TWO

STORAGE ROOM ONE

Chapter 23

Arts @ Civic Trust House

Jenifer's Journey

On our last visit, we were introduced to many of the staff who worked at the Arts @ Civic Trust House. The four-storey building had offices dedicated to running many of Cork's arts festivals.

One of the staff that day, who showed an interest in the paranormal, would join us on a future date, when we would explore what lurked during the quieter hours at this busiest of places.

The investigation was conducted on the 26 April 2013. We had arrived outside of the Civic Trust House, on Popes Quay, at about half past eight on the night of the investigation. We stood across the road from it. What an iconic building – standing out from modern suburban society.

In my own thought, it resembled a red-bricked doll's house, with white square-framed windows. You wanted to open it up from the side to expose its interior. In a different way, we would be doing that tonight.

The staff member, Aoife, arrived by bicycle. She held the key to open the house. Anthony, Rhiannon, a female team member and I were ready to enter the building but, something was missing or, somebody. Poor Sinead! She got a bit muddled. A phone call later, a search party went out for her. Eventually, she was found.

In between this time, I decided to go, as usual, on my own to take pictures of the now-vacant rooms. It was quieter than the last time we were here. The wide, imbalanced front stairs gave a quirky image to the past, hidden behind modern familiarity. I felt even more distant from the team with each floor that I went up.

Unexpectedly, it felt much tighter on the top, third floor although, there were smaller rooms in the building. You could say that trekking up so many flights of steps, you would become breathless but, I took my time. I was drawn to this particular part of the building. I looked out of a window from Storage Room 2 and saw the glare of the city lights reflected on the River Lee. Briefly, time stood still.

Eventually, I made my way down and met with Anthony in the Reception Room. I helped him set up the trigger objects, which included medical instruments and a toy. A key was turned to switch on the laser-beam machine. An erratic display of red, green and yellow colours targeted an empty armchair. As this was the Reception Room, maybe someone would be waiting for their appointment. Would we be the ones to see them?

Anthony wanted to conduct another experiment using a prism (*See Glossary*) on a video camera. To ensure this, we cordoned off an area - the Back Building Stairs. More modern to the eye, this was a perfect choice.

The video camera was set up, looking down some steps to another floor level. It was watching over what you would not expect!

Replica human skeletal bones were placed on the ground.

Once everything was checked over and the okay to go was given, we all gathered outside the front door of the building. The blood pressure (*See Glossary*) was taken of each team member. As I waited for my turn, I took a picture, peering through the glass window into the Musgrave Room. The normally empty room, with just chairs and a large dining table, looked barren but, it would not be for long. It would soon fill up. I knew, as I was taking the picture, that it was expected.

The Investigation

NUMBER OF TEAM **5**   **1** NUMBER OF GUESTS

Being the oldest house in Cork City, an abundance of tales is marked in its framework. The office-style interior could have impeded this but that was not the case. There was something significant about this place. Team members were expressing the unusual before the investigation even got started.

A photograph that Jen took outside of the building seemed to reveal, on later inspection, a menacing face of a person looking out from the second-floor landing window. This was before the team went back into the premises to get things underway. Now, reflections from walled material (posters, signs or pictures) on the inner walls on that landing might have triggered the illusion of a face.

Workers at the Arts Civic Trust House have had spoken of stomach-turning sensations in Storage 1 and 2 on the top floor. The team picked up on this similar experience. It made the hours to come mouth-watering as to why it had happened.

There were considerable high spikes on the EMF gauss master meter. The reading in Storage Room 2 was over 10 milliGauss, mainly due to the emergency exit lighting. This might give a clue to the abdominal impression that everyone had described.

To the eye, the rooms resembled your typical office-like space, with desks and adjustable nylon chairs, computers, printers, bright florescent-tubed lighting and other technical assortments, all contributing to this hard-working principal in a friendly and comfortable manner.

A doorway motion detector was positioned in the Hallway outside of the Reception Room, alongside the old front stairway. This motion detector fed an infrared beam onto a receiver, spread out less than a metre apart, facing opposite each other. Should anyone or anything step past its beam, it would activate by sounding an alarm or chime.

The petite Reception Room consisted of a couch, armchair, desk, cabinets and a wide variety of stationary. Another motion detector was set-up. Instead, this observed a wider angle, focusing on the trigger objects, which were placed on the floor. They included a green toy lorry, a mouth mask, two plastic tubes and a syringe.

A temperature gauge (*See Equipment*) was also placed within the room. It worked off the old-fashioned style format, mercury, to give a measurement in Celsius and Fahrenheit. This instrument had three dials on it: a blue dial, which indicated the minimum temperature; a red dial, which showed the maximum temperature; and a black dial which measured the current temperature.

The laser-beam machine was also activated; its point of interest was the couch.

Smell buckets (*See Glossary*) were put in many of the rooms. Each white tub gave out a different aroma, hopefully letting off a stimulating scent or odour. In this case, antiseptic fluid was used in the Reception Room. The bucket was placed on a wooden chair.

We would wait to see, until after the investigation, if there was to be any substantial alterations with the experiments in this room.

Next up was the Back Building Stairs. An area identified as being one of the most active areas/room alongside the Storage Room 1 and Storage Room 2.

Two sets of replica human bones belonging to the arms – the humorous, radius, ulna, carpels, metacarpals, phalanges (hands) – and the legs – the femur, tibia, fibula, tarsals, metatarsals and phalanges (feet) – surrounded a cranium skull on an intermediate landing.

Spying on these objects was a video camera, which had a small triangular refraction prism attached in front of the lens. The prism allowed a split screen view, looking down the stairs onto the trigger objects.

The astrological significance revealed that the night would run smoothly, with Mars/Neptune sextiling. There would be a comfortable aroma with a willingness to help one and other.

The forecast was clear and the moon was at a waning gibbous phase, at 99% full.

The temperature outside was 6.2°C yet, it was much warmer inside, at 18.0°C. The humidity was at 51.2%.

The lux was at 002, on account of the lights in the house being switched off but, influence from outside illuminations would brighten some sections of each room that we went into.

With the noise from outside, the false anomaly risk was very high. The C low level read 52.1.

It was now coming up to ten o'clock at night.

The Musgrave Room was to be where we would start our first meeting. Numerous boards were disposed on a large dining table. Frankincense was put in a second smell bucket. It was placed on the ground in front of a large fireplace, which occupied a somewhat plain room. It would not be void for long, however – it was about to fill up with character.

Some of us would be disguised. The female team member wore a mask, which resembled an alien. Aoife was wearing a black mask; Rhiannon had a similar shaped mask which was white. The masks they were wearing covered their faces. Sinead wore a black, themed plague mask, with the familiar bird-like beak nose that covered the upper half of her face.

The four of them connected on the heart-shaped planchette, which was situated at the centre of the colour mood frame. Anthony was recording with the night vision camera whilst Jen strolled around taking photographs.

There was clear instruction, on our behalf, as to what we would like to happen. The Spirits were invited to participate. We would guide them through the various boards/experiments chosen.

The planchette slowly circled within the colour mood frame. Then, it hugged the inside of the frame, rubbing tightly against it as it travelled in straight lines to all four corners. The planchette slid on the table surface slickly, occasionally making a whining sound.

It was quite a stretch to reach over the table to connect. It was advisable to take the finger off should it move too far away and, to reconnect once the planchette was more approachable.

"What kind of mood are you in dear Spirit? … What kind of mood are you in?" asked the female team member.

The planchette moved to 'Orange', which meant 'Unsettled and Mixed Emotions'.

"Is that because we're here?"

The planchette moved a straight line to 'Yes', the base of the instrument acting as a pointer.

"Do you want us to leave?"

The planchette moved along the inside of the frame, stopping at 'No' and then progressed back to the centre of the frame.

"Would you like to tell us, what kind of mood we should be in… or what mood do you think we should be in?"

There was no straightaway, decisive answer as the planchette moved to in between 'Yes' and 'Finish'. Eventually, it did a half, counter-clockwise circle to 'Yellow', indicating 'Imaginative' and to 'Pink', to mean 'Fear and Uncertain'.

Seconds later, the planchette moved to 'Change', possibly to mean a different type of mood, which we should adopt or, simply correcting the previous response. It followed up by moving a large, half clockwise circle to 'Amber', meaning 'Daring and Stimulating', then a straight line to 'Finish'.

To confirm, the planchette again moved a straight line to 'Amber' and then to 'Yes'. We were told to show bravery and be courageous. Would we be up for the challenge?

The noise that the planchette was making on the table was becoming more prevalent. We discovered that there was a dominant female energy present.

"Are you a woman of God?"

The planchette moved towards the centre of the frame, as the female team member continued her questioning.

"Do you believe in God?"

Whilst still in motion, the planchette altered its direction, turning around and moving directly to 'No'.

"Are you a nurse?"

As this was asked, the planchette did a half, medium clockwise circle and made its way to in between 'Brown', which meant 'Restless' and 'Yes'. The planchette seemed to be more fixed towards 'Brown'. We found this to be accurate shortly afterwards.

"You're a restless Spirit?"

The planchette went to 'Yes', then moved in a straight line, about five inches or so, towards the centre of the frame before reverting its way back to 'Yes'.

"There are a lot of restless Spirits in here tonight."

Twice the planchette moved away from 'Yes' then back onto it. It was a similar reaction to the question previously posed. There was no doubt about it. There must have been some unease that tarnished the walls.

"Are you usually here?"

The planchette moved to 'No'.

Soon after, the Spirit declined the prospect of us proceeding to another board.

On countless occasions, the planchette bounced off the side of the frame to 'Yes', to indicate its preference for us to take off our masks. The Spirit also agreed that they had been able to show their face on the reflective surface of the shiny dining room table.

"Okay, so if we took our masks off, you show your face?"

The planchette, which was at the centre of the frame, moved straight to 'White', meaning 'Bored and Frustrated', then to 'Yellow', which meant 'Imaginative'.

Obviously, the Spirit was unenthusiastic about the masks. It preferred that we concentrate on gazing in on the surface of the table, similar to the act of scrying.

We carried this forward. Sinead, Rhiannon, the female team member and Aoife took off their masks to reveal their faces and stared down onto the dining room table, whilst calling forth the energies.

Anthony turned the night vision camera towards his left, to a door that led out to the front of the Hallway.

A simple battery-powered, cone-shaped lamp at the centre of the table emitted enough light for reflections to be seen.

Draughts were felt around the table yet, we spent little time making a full hearty go of seeing anything unexpected. The reason being that it was too strenuous to lean over the table, on account of the boards situated around the edge, which got in the way of a closer view.

The emphasis was to get onto the next board session - but which one would the Spirit/Spirits pick?

We had two talking boards, an ogham board (*See Glossary*), a days-of-the-week board (*See Glossary*), a direction board, an astrology board and two planetary boards, all of which were situated around the edges of the table. The planchette was placed at the middle of the table.

A school bell was rung, cleansing and alerting all around.

Anthony did a quick scan around the room with the night vision camera, including right behind him to the two large Georgian windows. He walked down to the opposite end of the table to get the opposing view of his previous position.

Sinead, Rhiannon, the female team member and Aoife connected onto the planchette.

"Step forward. Please dear Spirit. Use the energies of the building," asked the female team member.

The planchette moved a straight line on the table beside the days-of-the-week board. The board was picked up and placed at the centre of the table. Subsequently, the planchette was picked up and positioned at the boards centre. They connected on the planchette again.

"Can you tell us what day of the week it is now?"

The planchette rotated on its spot three quarters of a counter-clockwise circle as it moved a straight line to 'Tuesday', then did another half clockwise circle twist on its spot.

"Can you tell us what day of the week you have as a rest day?"

The planchette moved to the opposite side of the board, stopping right near the edge, finishing up in between 'Friday' and 'Saturday'. The planchette then reverted to 'Tuesday' and it continued moving in a medium, narrow, three-quarter clockwise circle, stopping at 'Monday'.

This left us a bit curious but not baffled.

"Can you tell us, dear Spirit, what day do you go to church?"

The planchette moved directly to 'Sunday'.

"What day do you go to confession?"

The planchette moved a short distance to 'Monday'.

"What day do you go to work?"

The planchette moved to 'Wednesday', 'Monday', 'Friday', 'Sunday' and then stopped at 'Wednesday'.

Fascinating stuff, we thought. The Monday to Tuesday and the Friday to Saturday were days of relaxation.

"Can you tell us, what day of the week it is today, please?"

The planchette half-circled the board counter-clockwise, stopping at 'Friday'.

The Spirit earlier identified Tuesday as the present day of the week. So, there must have been a mix up!

There might have been a fracas of opinion by a number of Spirits on the other side who were trying to come through, though that did not seem likely. Later, Anthony referred back to the same topic for reassurance.

"Okay, so we're gathered… so it's Tuesday today, dear Spirit?"

The planchette answered by moving a straight line to 'Friday'.

It was Friday today in our world too. So, the Spirit, intelligent as it was, had an inkling as to our situation. Or perhaps, it was just coincident that it was Friday in their reality too. At least it had been confirmed twice.

There was no mistake with the next question we put forward.

"Can you tell us what day of the week that you died on?"

The planchette moved to 'Sunday'. We asked this question again during the experiment. We received the same reply.

Anthony called out, "What day of the week is the most activity in this building?"

The planchette moved a three-quarter, medium clockwise circle, to 'Friday'.

We asked another question but, before we could get an answer, Anthony butted in. He thought he had seen something.

"Is that flashing going on there?"

The planchette made a full, counter-clockwise circle on its travels, covering each of the day sections on the board and then, gradually, stopped on 'Friday'.

"All week," remarked Rhiannon.

We mentioned aloud that we would be taking on another board soon. The Spirit took advantage of the situation. The planchette hopped over, off the side of the days-of-the-week board and up onto a small, squared, framed mirror. Then it spun off onto the table before stopping beside a planetary board.

The Spirit indicated what it wanted us to use next. Instead, we opted for the other planetary board. This board gave easier direction because the planetary board the Spirit selected had a horizontal, lined formation. Marked on the board that we would be using were twelve symbols of heavenly bodies. The symbols encircled the planchette that we had placed at centre.

"Now, dear Spirit, you recognise this? Can you tell us, which symbol, which planet, obviously you know the planets you're most familiar with please?" asked the female team member.

There was a cold breeze right above the board by Rhiannon and Sinead.

The same four individuals as before connected on the planchette. We were twenty minutes into the investigation. The planchette moved slowly towards the 'Neptune' planetary symbol and carried on, circling counter-clockwise over the symbols.

Four loud, dull thuds could be heard on the night vision camera just before the planchette stopped on the 'Mars' planetary symbol. Then, the planchette carried on in a straight line, pointing to the 'Neptune' planetary symbol. Interesting, as tonight, both Mars and Neptune were sextiling. This was our window of opportunity.

Could the four dull thuds represent the fourth planet from our sun?

"Are you an astrologer? That's really coinciding with tonight?"

The planchette went off the board, onto the table and halted beside the talking board. The energy sagged as we tried to reach out with divination tool. The connection proved strained for some.

The talking board was put into the prime position at the centre of the dining room table. Sinead, Rhiannon, the female team member and Aoife engaged on the planchette. Sinead called out this time.

"Would you let us know what your name is? The first initial, if you can?"

The planchette moved from the centre of the board, back and forth, between 'Yes' and 'No'. Its flow interrupted as a question was asked.

"English?" asked the female team member.

The planchette returned to 'Yes'.

"Do you speak Gaeilge?" She asked in Irish.

The planchette remained still.

"Do you like Irish?"

This time, the planchette made a more decisive action and picked up pace, moving straight to 'No'. Not only was this resolute but a whispered voice came up on the night vision camera stating, "No", just as the planchette ceased its motion.

In the following minutes, we discovered that there was a police officer in close attendance – that there were eight Spirits around us but not all of them were supposedly friendly.

We called upon the Spirit, who was in charge at the premises, to step forward. We suspected this entity had come forward; we asked for its name. We did not get the answer that we had been hoping for on the board.

"Do you want to try another board?"

The planchette moved to 'Yes'.

Anthony spoke out to his colleagues, "Maybe ask direction. What direction they're in? Which direction we should be?"

The planchette went off the left-hand side of the talking board onto the table. It carried on its journey, making its way on and off the planetary board to the edge of the table with ease. Its purpose and focus were directed towards Jen, who was now sitting down at the dining table. Jen put her right index finger on the planchette. The small wooden board now retraced its path back to the centre of the table, to the talking board.

Jen stood up and took position at one side of the table from where the female team member had discontinued and vacated. Immediately, the planchette began to head in all directions around the board, twisting uncontrollably.

Sinead asked, "First of all, maybe, what year is it?"

This question was ignored; there was no doubt that more energy had come upon the planchette after Jen made contact. The Spirit was more interested in this flow of movement than in answering us.

The planchette did twenty-one medium-sized, clockwise circles.

"Use the energies that are in the building," said the female team member.

The planchette briefly slowed but it carried on circling.

Anthony pointed the night vision camera away from the board, targeting it on at the walls and the fireplace to his right. He panned the night vision camera the opposite way to the door, which led out to the front of the building and the Georgian windows to his left. Gentle humming was caught on the recording.

Anthony went back to observing the talking board. The planchette had been rotating around the board for the past fifty seconds. It did another two medium, clockwise circles, eventually stopping at 'O'.

The planchette's movement became erratic. It was trying to spell out something but, it was not recognisable.

The female team member placed her finger back on the planchette. As she touched the top of it, the planchette moved a straight line to the bottom centre of the board, half overlapping the edge, then resorted into making a three-quarter, clockwise circle, extending over the edge again.

The planchette continued to move, overlapping the four sides of the board. The female team member withdrew her finger. It continued on its path along the edge, from right to left until it fell onto the table.

Only Jen's and Rhiannon's finger remained connected as the planchette on the dining room table went into a three-quarter, small, counter-clockwise circle, before heading in a straight line for about four feet and stopping at the direction board.

The school bell was rung very loudly.

The direction board had now come into play.

Jen and Rhiannon placed their index fingers back on top of the planchette. Immediately, it swerved off from centre to the 'North – East' section off the board, onto the dining table. It drastically encircled the talking board and direction board, moving three times counter-clockwise around them.

It changed direction, slowly moving this time a small distance onto the small, squared, framed mirror.

The night vision camera caught a loud, peculiar screeching sound.

Briefly, Jen glanced to her left. She did not say anything.

Several fast, small, clockwise rotations occurred in the mirror; the Spirit fascinated by what was in front of them on the table. As this was happening, Anthony suggested a question to the team.

"Okay, ask them what direction of the building…"

Sinead cut in with a question.

"You want us in a specific room?"

Anthony finished off what he was trying to say. "Ask them where they are now on the direction thing."

The planchette came off the face of the mirror, making its way over to the side of the table, just in front of Anthony.

"Can you point to where you are in the room right now?" asked the female team member.

We were looking for direction and we got it.

The planchette made its way, with ease, back onto the direction board, stopping at 'North'. The area that it pointed to was the door that led to the Back Building Stairs.

Anthony wanted clarification from one of the team members. "North. Is that north? Is it?"

At the same time, Sinead called out, "Are you here over my left? Could you really make a noise within the room itself?"

The planchette went off the 'South' side of the direction board, travelling a few feet and stopping up alongside the talking board at the centre of the table. The pointer underlined the word 'Yes'.

The direction board was checked to see if it precisely indicated the actual compass points. All was correct when analysed with a compass.

A succession of muted tapping could be heard on the recording, approximately six or seven in total, accompanied by a short whistle and a sorrowful whine. Something was trying to get our attention!

The planchette carried on moving around the table. Anthony discussed what to do next with the team.

"Can we get a sort of, a birthday? What month of the year they were born, with the star sign, yeah?"

Another whistle came through on the night vision camera, this time a bit weaker.

The talking board, at the centre of the table, was put to one side and replaced with the astrology board. Symbols dedicated to the signs of the zodiac would help us find answers regarding the months of the year.

Providing the energy for the planchette next were Jen, Sinead, Rhiannon and Aoife. The planchette went straight to one corner of the board and then, it made twelve small, counter-clockwise circles as Anthony asked, "What month is it now?"

The heart shaped device stopped in between 'Pisces' (19th February – 20th March) and 'Aries' (21st March – 19th April). We might be on the borderline of the two, around 20th/21st March, according to the Spirit.

"Which star… which star sign's your birthday?" asked Anthony.

The planchette had moved only an inch or so, homing in on 'Aries' (21st March – 19th April).

Which world was this soul born into though? This could mark a death. The question should have been less obscure, as it could have had another meaning.

"Is there any particular month you're most active?"

The planchette went in a straight line towards the centre of the board. It then came back in a straight line, stopping over the 'Aries' (21st March – 19th April) star sign symbol.

We could assume that the Spirit's death, in our realm, was the act of coming into existence in another state. Less than a minute later, we would get the hint of an accurate answer.

"What month did you die? If you could move the planchette, if you can ask me, if can?"

From centre of the board, the planchette moved a straight line over the 'Aries' (21st March – 19th April) star sign symbol. It retracted a couple of inches to point more directly towards the symbol. We came off the astrology board two minutes later.

For the first time during an investigation, we would use two talking boards at the same time. Sinead, Rhiannon and Aoife connected on an old-fashioned glass on the talking board that we had been using (Talking Board A), positioned at one side of the table whilst on the other side of the table opposite, Jen and the female team member connected on the planchette (Talking Board B).

The number '9' showed up as being significant, early on, for both boards. We figured that this meant the date of a particular month.

As soon as one divination tool completed its movement, the other would become mobile.

On Talking Board A, the glass moved to '9', 'J', 'E', 'N'.

The female team member on Talking Board B called out, "Jen's on the board."

The glass moved to 'Yes' on Talking Board A.

Rhiannon responded by saying, "They want her on this board (Talking Board A)."

The glass moved about four to five inches away, in a straight line only to reverse back onto 'Yes' again.

"Yeah, well, move over to this board," said the female team member on Talking Board B.

Immediately, the planchette moved on Talking Board B, which Jen was on. It proved too quick for Anthony to keep track of with the night vision camera.

The planchette stopped exactly on 'Yes'. Laughter broke out, presumably in excitement as to what had just happened. The Spirit present was hopping back and forth from each talking board in reply.

"Give us your second name?" requested Anthony.

The planchette moved several circles - clockwise and counter-clockwise, large and small - twisting in all directions as it travelled off the bottom-right corner of the board onto the ogham board, which was right beside it. It continued moving, passing over a few of the hallmark symbols used in the old ogham alphabet script.

The letters on the ogham script the planchette had moved to were 'F', 'O', 'E'.

We knew what 'foe' meant but our and, maybe the Spirit's understanding of the language of the script went missing as the planchette soon after went to 'H', 'P', 'Q'.

The planchette came off the ogham board and onto the dining table. It was put back to the middle of Talking Board B.

The female team member on Talking Board B spoke out, asking aloud for the Spirit to give its name on the Talking Board A. The planchette, as she was speaking, made a narrow, clockwise circle before moving one counter-clockwise circle and stopping at centre. As she concluded her question, she flipped the planchette upside down to prevent any other movement occurring.

The glass instantly moved on Talking Board A. It went to 'I', 'M', '9'.

Sinead asked, "Is that how old you are?"

The glass moved a straight line to centre, then changed direction to 'Yes'.

Shortly after, the glass moved to the letters, to make up the words 'Adam' and 'God'.

We were not entirely sure that this Spirit energy was being genuine.

The glass was turned over, back to drinking side up, so that our attention was diverted back to Talking Board B. There was a refusal to give a name. The planchette was on 'No'.

"Okay, are you Catholic?" asked the female team member.

The planchette moved a small, three-quarter, counter-clockwise circle. The female team member's index finger briefly moved off the planchette. She quickly reconnected and the sharpness with which the divination tool was moving was surprising. It finished up at 'No'.

"Are you a Quaker?"

The planchette moved a narrow, three-quarter, counter-clockwise circle to 'Yes'.

"Did you come off a boat?"

Back at centre of the table, the planchette moved to 'Yes'.

"Can you tell us what year it is, please? Thank you, Sir?"

The planchette moved a straight line to 'S', 'H', 'O', 'P'.

Now it felt clearer that the Spirit was using the tip of the planchette as an indicator. It carried on towards 'G', 'R', 'A', 'N', 'G', 'E', 'R'.

"Shop granger?"

At a distinct fast pace, the planchette went to 'Yes'.

"Is that the name of a shop near here?"

A large, narrow, clockwise circle was made by the planchette as it reconnected back on 'Yes'.

"Were you the owner of the shop?"

There was a similar motion as before. The planchette finished back at 'Yes'.

"Did you use to make anything to do with bars… beer?"

The planchette made a half, medium, clockwise circle and a small, three-quarter, clockwise circle before changing into a half, medium, counter-clockwise circle, resulting in it stopping back on 'Yes. It continued to move a half, medium, clockwise circle to 'No'. It moved back and forth between 'Yes' and 'No' a further three times.

"Butter?"

Involuntary, the planchette twisted twice, clockwise and then counter-clockwise. The female team member's finger came off the planchette. Still, it moved, as if to shun any connection she had on it.

Jen's finger remained in contact but, for that split second, it seemed that the planchette was being moved by an unseen force, as the female team member tried to connect. A handful of seconds later, the planchette was placed back to the centre of the board.

Anthony felt it was time to move on and try something a bit different. We made one last go of it.

"Can you tell us what year it is?"

The planchette directed us to '1', '8', '2', '6'.

Straight away, Anthony asked, "And what's the number of the building here? Thank you. What's the number of the building here?"

The planchette moved to '6', '0' (zero).

The Spirit was not too sure. The planchette ended up finishing at 'No'. Maybe the wooden planchette was pointing inaccurately or, we misinterpreted what it was targeting. It might have been intended to indicate '5', '0' (zero).

Next up was a séance.

A digital sound recorder was put into play. It sat on a tripod, raised about four feet off the ground.

All the boards were taken off the dining room table. The cone-shaped lamp remained within the middle section of the table. We also introduced onto the table a school bell, the grey alien mask, a sound monitor and the body mood doll.

Sinead took up the job of holding the night vision camera. Anthony, Jen, Rhiannon, Aoife and the female team member sat at the table. They placed their hands flat on top of the table in front of them, forming a circle as their little fingers touched the other person's on either side of them.

We felt that the name Barry was coming in strong at the beginning.

The conversation was relaxed and the tempo was slow.

The table was already showing signs of shaking. It would take something immense to move this hefty piece of furniture.

Anthony requested that Sinead look into the equipment bag and dig out the seismometer, then spent a couple of minutes trying to insert a battery into the meter. Once successful, Anthony placed it at the centre of the table.

The Spirits were asked to make their presence known.

Rhiannon sensed a breeze to her right, between her and Jen. Moments later, she described the table as rocking stronger on that side than the other.

Anthony sped up in pursuit by speaking quickly.

"If you once lived in this building - maybe you used to frequent this building - if you used to live around this building, come towards us now. Step forward. If you were a patient in this building, if you used to live here, come towards us now?"

He quickly responded to the rest of the team in regard to what word, previously said, that made the table shake with a bit more force. "Stronger, thought with patient. Was it?"

"Yeah," replied the female team member.

"Okay," said Anthony.

Nearly three minutes later, Anthony confirmed that he may have heard a sound towards his left, just above between where he and Aoife were sat. He put it down to his feet underneath the table making the noise but he then decided that the sound, which was tapping, had come from the alien mask beside them.

Sinead declared that she could see the body mood doll wobbling.

Rhiannon commented, "There's like a breath behind – between me and Jenny."

Excitement began to brew with the alleged Spirit activity. All of a sudden, the team were asking for replica responses to whistles that they had made and, for the Spirits to move an arm on the body mood doll. One thing at a time would have been better!

The body mood doll seemed to be shaking yet, the seismometer lights had not flickered but, it was not long before they did. Two to three of the seismometer green bulbs lit up.

Sinead stepped to one side at this moment. Her movement on the stiff, wooden flooring may have triggered the meter to illuminate.

The séance was about to spring more into life.

Anthony chanted, at a fast pace, "Light as a feather, stiff as a board…", repeating the words several times.

The seismometer faintly lit one bulb for a few seconds (there are ten bulbs in total).

Anthony urgently asked for more involvement from the Spirit realm. "Make a sound with your voice. Show yourself. Touch one of us."

Sinead intervened by calling out, "Make a noise upstairs… on… even on the stairs."

The body mood doll was still holding its stance on the table yet, unbeknownst to the team, it wavered for a few seconds. There was not a clear indication by the seismometer that the table underneath had caused this movement from the doll.

Our attention was drawn to what we believed were noises coming from in and from outside of the room. Anthony decided it was time to switch on the sound monitor. It played the regular noise of a heartbeat.

Anthony placed the device back at the centre of the table and called out, "Okay, there's a heartbeat now. Try and use that heartbeat. Come forward. Be physical again. Step forward. Use the energies that are around?"

There was silence. The body mood doll had given the impression that it was doddering as Anthony called out again, "Come towards us now, dear Spirit, dear comrade. Step forward and use the energies that are around. Move around the room…"

The female team member interrupted, "Cold draught on my right hand."

Anthony was concentrating with his eyes closed and his head bowed. Quickly, he praised the Spirit for making contact, "Okay, thank you, thank you, thank you…"

A couple of the team claimed that the large table underneath the palms of their hands was shaking continuously, keeping up with what seemed to be the beat of the sound monitor.

Anthony let out a loud whistle. A cold draught became apparent.

Anthony called out, this time with haste, "If you want to make your presences known more, you have to do a bit more stronger. Make it move stronger."

The female team member called out at the same time as Anthony, "Come on, use the energies."

The seismometer bulbs flickered three times, lighting up to two to three units. The disturbance in balance would change further as certain team members chanted, "Light as a feather, stiff as a board…"

The team engaged in different vocalisations, including various chants, humming and whistling. The seismometer flickered more frequently, up to about twenty times, reaching a peak of approximately four units. At the same time, the body mood doll was seen clearly shaking through the night vision camera, backing up the opinion that the table was becoming less firm. Was this down to desire from the Spirits or, just us?

We asked for more but all we got was the seismometer lighting up, the dull shaking, cold draughts and an assumption of a shadow being seen. There was nothing too out of the ordinary.

Jen took the night vision camera from Sinead.

Sinead, Rhiannon and Aoife came away from the large dining table to a foldable, small, wooden, square table a couple of metres away. They crouched down and lightly touched the edges with their fingertips on top of the table. Their contact was limited due to the direction board (that now had a wooden, two-way symmetrical pointer affixed to its midpoint) taking the majority of inner space on top.

Anthony remained with the female team member at the dining room table. Both stretched their arms out across the table, to make contact with the other person opposite them.

The team came up with more questions and chanting. Anthony's head was bowed yet, he was involuntary nodding. This action may have been due to the shaking of the table.

The dialect went at a fast speed and voices became even more raised. The team hummed, howled and even started singing.

The seismometer was now flashing constantly, with the body mood doll looking like it was dancing a jig.

A short time later, Anthony and the female team member swapped places with Sinead, Rhiannon and Aoife on the versatile, foldable, square, wooden table. They both connected with only one hand on the table and chanted. The table swayed at times but this was not enough; we needed something remarkable. On a final attempt, Anthony hummed out loudly, gradually breaking into a fast chant "… in the world that I walk, in this circle, this flies…"

The female team member across from Anthony loudly hummed a constant note. Both invited the table to be lifted up from the ground, to levitate above their own eyes. Each time the table refused this notion, becoming still. Later, as the table declined for the last time, a deep groan was caught on the night vision camera. This was captured by the digital sound recorder at the same time. A fainter groan followed up shortly after.

Jen had put her thought into aiming the night vision camera at the front windows, away from the individuals at this particular point in time; so, it is hard to consider this EVP extraordinary or peculiar, as it could have been caused by someone but it would come as a surprise if they had intentionally made that noise.

We split into two groups and headed upstairs to the first floor. Sinead, the female team member and Aoife entered the Tigh Fílí Room whilst, Anthony, Jen and Rhiannon were in the IAYO Room.

A Frank's Box session would take part in the Tigh Fílí Room, which was smaller in size than the IAYO Room, the space being limited due to the customary office material.

The IAYO Room, which had much of the same appliances and furnishings, would be where the planchette drawing/writing experiment would take place.

An A2 paper pad was placed on the floor, opened up to a blank white sheet. Anthony, Jen and Rhiannon sat on the floor. A black marker pen pierced through the centre of a pentagon-shaped planchette. It was supported by a square frame mounted above four caster wheels, separated at each corner.

Jen and Rhiannon connected onto the outer square frame of the instrument. When they did, the planchette manoeuvred around the sheet of paper just as Anthony started to record with the night vision camera. The nib of the pen lightly touched the paper. It looked like nothing had been drawn. Anthony turned on the light in the room to get a better look. Numerous squiggly lines had unfolded on the paper in front of their eyes.

Anthony asked, "Okay, dear Spirit, can you move the planchette towards me if you are making a picture?"

The drawing instrument quickly moved towards Anthony's direction, as if to say that the irregular movement that had occurred earlier had served a purpose.

"Okay, continue. Thank you," responded Anthony.

What had been sketched did not show any accurate detail.

"I wonder if they're a child," pondered Anthony.

The planchette stopped moving immediately.

"Go on, continue. Thank you, dear Spirit."

The drawing mechanism circled clockwise at a quick pace three-and-a-half times. The pad was turned over to reveal a clean, blank sheet of paper. The black marker pen was taken out from the centre of the planchette.

Anthony wanted to know what exactly the Spirit wanted to draw. He placed his index finger, along with Jen's and Rhiannon's, on the outer square frame of the device.

He called out, "Err, towards myself for Yes, dear Spirit. Do you understand?"

The planchette moved towards Anthony's direction.

"Okay and towards Jen… for no."

The planchette went the opposite side of the sheet, towards Jen. We had an understanding.

Anthony continued to call out, "Okay, do you like to draw again?"

The planchette moved away from Jen's side of the sheet, stopping at the corner between Anthony and Rhiannon. As it stopped, a hushed whisper could be heard on the night vision camera. It resembled another being saying 'Yeah' but, before that, something much more defined – a clear vocalisation which, we believed, belonged to a young child, had come forward.

'My name is Cedric,' said the Spirit.

Further on, the Spirit rejected the idea of drawing a symbol or an emotion; instead, it chose to do a portrait. This was our chance to get some sort of facial recognition from the drawing. A red marker pen was fixed into the centre of the planchette. Again, straight away, the planchette went about its business.

On the second sheet, it looked like a crescent moon had been drawn. This was disproved by the Spirit; the planchette moved a straight line in Jen's direction. What was drawn was not distinguishable enough to compare it with a portrait. We needed much more precise detail to identify any features of the face.

Moving on from that, we had a bit more time to spare, so Anthony decided to call out and for the Spirits to respond. It was important that we immersed ourselves in other conditions to open up: either us to them or vice versa but, hopefully both.

Anthony scanned the area of the room, from side to side, several times. Somehow, we concluded that the Spirit of a child was close by – not that we had heard the earlier EVP of a child talking to us but, that we were possibly interacting with the Spirit world.

The time was half past twelve; Sinead had to leave to catch the bus to Dublin. She said her goodbyes and left.

We got some hits by using the Frank's Box.

Sinead had asked, "How many of you are with us?"

A masculine voice with a brawny Irish accent said, 'Eight' from the Frank's Box.

Afterwards, Sinead very clearly called out, "Could you give us a number please?"

A child-like, high-pitched voice said 'Five' from the box.

To the question, "What place of worship do you go too?", a very clear masculine voice replied, 'Here' from the Frank's Box.

"Were you killed?"

Straight away, a second or two later, a clear 'Here' could be heard in an Irish accent from the box.

The predictable 'Leave' word, heard on many occasions from the Frank's Box in investigations, was plainly heard. This reply came when a question was asked about the subject of diseases.

We did a quick check at the Back Building Stairs. Anthony and Jen made their way up the stairs. They paused in front of the trigger objects and video camera that was set up. Following them was Rhiannon, holding the night vision camera. As Jen took a picture, a deep husky sound resembling the words 'Scared away' was picked up on the recording. It would not be the last time this style of tone would be heard.

Anthony took the decision to glance at the video camera. The prism had fallen off and was lying on the step of the stairs. Anthony explained that it was obviously the weight of the prism, along with the adhesive tape not giving enough support, which had contributed to it falling a few inches to the ground. We would have to wait and see the footage afterwards to determine what had happened.

Next up was the Reception Room. Jen opened the door; Anthony disarmed the motion detector and picked up the temperature gauge that was on the floor. He gave out the readings. The lowest temperature was at 13°C; the current temperature was not that far off at 14°C. The highest temperature recorded was 18°C. There was a difference of five degrees.

It did not seem that the trigger objects had been disturbed in the room.

We picked up the equipment and headed up the front staircase to the third-floor storage rooms.

The digital sound recorder and the tripod would be used in Storage Room 1. The smell used in the bucket for this room was bleach. The smell bucket in Storage Room 2 would contain the colourless pungent gas, ammonia.

The team split into two, to do some automatic drawing/writing.

Jen, Anthony and Aoife would be in Storage Room 2 for the first ten-minute vigil, whilst Rhiannon and the female team member would be in Storage Room 1.

They would put down on paper any names, places, sensations and pictures plus, any questions that needed to be asked. We would use these questions for a final calling-out vigil near the end of the investigation.

Rhiannon and the female team member picked up on a girl in rags, between the age of five and seven, who was shy and hiding. There was a feeling of restlessness, tiredness, deep thought and trying to remember something. They also collected the names 'Mike' and 'Sarah' and the recognition of a coal man.

In Storage Room 2, Anthony, Jen and Aoife picked up the sense of frustration, mercy and panic. Jen drew a picture of a man grasping a woman. The woman was shouting, 'No'. The scene was set in a wooded landscape. She also drew what looked like a map. The name 'Joseph', loitering around and a mangle (a mechanical laundry aid) were sensed.

Both groups swapped over again, spending ten minutes in the alternative room.

A seismometer was placed on a desk behind both Rhiannon and the female team member in Storage Room 2. It was in view of the stationary night vision camera, placed on the desk opposite. The seismometer failed to light up but Rhiannon got a vision of a middle-aged woman, scared, her hair in a bun and wearing white clothes. Other feelings detected were hunger, vomit and belly ache.

In Storage Room 1, Jen drew a picture of a person kneeling beside a bed saying, 'When will I go home?'

She also drew another picture of flowers in full bloom.

The names 'Geraldine', 'Margaret' and 'John' were thought to be closely linked to the building.

Anthony drew a picture of what seemed to be a pregnant woman with, at the bottom of the bed, a lot of scribbling, so the intent seemed obscure.

There could be comparisons of what both groups obtained in the one room. We would have to hope that what information we picked up – whatever it resembled to us – could be useful in getting a hint when asking questions later. We all had something to ask and it would not go unnoticed.

It was in Storage Room 1 where we would set up our operation. Everyone took up their preferred seats at the desks, got comfortable and relaxed. The connecting door between Storage Room 1 and 2 was left half ajar.

Anthony stood up. He tried to figure out which switch would turn off the main lights to the front staircase. It proved unsuccessful. He sat back down and carried on recording with the night vision camera.

Each person would take a turn calling out the questions they had written down previously or, remark on a certain matter that they felt the Spirit might relate to.

Anthony sharpened his attention with the camera on the female team member who was about to speak. 'Is it dark where you are?' she asked.

There was a pause and silence for about five seconds. She continued to ask another question.

'Who are you hiding from?'

It only took two seconds for a response to come back, though everyone was unaware of what had just been said. Identical to the voice captured on the Back Building Stairs was another vocalisation. Clear as day, it said 'Hiding from you' in a similar whispered or somewhat husky, deep, sinister tone of voice.

The room was ignited by flashes from Jen's digital camera.

"Does the water frighten you?"

Anthony focused the night vision camera back on the half open door into Storage Room 2.

Within the next minute, the female team member's subject of interest revolved around the Magdalene sisters, who they were or, if they were involved with them.

There was a cold breeze felt within the room.

Anthony called out, "Can you move something?"

Just as he finished the sentence, a whistle was heard. Anthony, on hearing this, asked everyone else, "Is that you?", directing his response to the team and Aoife. The whistle was rapidly nullified by everyone. It seemed to have come from outside of the building, from the city streets.

Moments later, another voice on the film occurred. It sounded similar to a human saying, 'We'll think about it'.

The voice did have a Scottish/Irish twinge to it. If this EVP was correct, then 'we' meant many. 'Thinking about it' could have been in relation to making something move and having a conscious mind.

"Can you make a smell?" asked Anthony.

Very slowly, Anthony shifted the night vision camera towards his left, towards the rest of the team, then back to the right towards Storage Room 2. He turned the camera back behind his left shoulder. "What are you getting, Jen?" he asked.

Jen looked at the piece of paper she was holding. She raised it to a height that she could successfully see it with. Thanks to the small amount of light being emitted from the front stairs, she was able to put forward a question.

"Where are you now?" she asked.

Anthony switched his attention back to the door and repeated what Jen had just said. There was no response.

"Why were you taken away?" said Jen.

Shortly afterwards, Rhiannon mentioned she had heard a noise from the other room (Storage Room 2) and Anthony recalled that he had heard shuffling.

The activity throughout rest of the vigil decreased to a gentle conclusion.

For the final part, everybody assembled into Storage Room 2.

The connecting door was now wide open. Anthony had a great vantage point of most of Storage Room 1 from where he was sitting on the floor, with the night vision camera. He could see a red speckle of light, which was coming from the digital sound recorder situated waist-high on the tripod in Storage Room 1.

The seismometer looked minute in size. It was positioned on the floor of Storage Room 1. It was closer to the team than the digital sound recorder but it looked a far distance away. Not too far however, to be accurately seen if any lights should activate, should anything or anyone want to walk in there.

Back in Storage Room 2, there was a disused dumb waiter rooted into one of the walls, which also took Anthony's eye. He spent some time trying to take in the surroundings with the night vision camera. There not much else to see, so he directed the night vision camera to the extended darkened room next door. With the number of components in the office, there was a possibility for some altering circumstances.

We began to call out.

"Are you trying to escape?" asked Anthony.

The female team member stressed that she had a banging headache.

"Are you panicking?"

Rhiannon explained that she was feeling the impression that there were two people colliding. One of them was scared, stopping the other one who wanted to tell someone something. As soon as she stopped talking, a woman's voice popped up on the night vision camera. It sounded like, 'Out you come'.

Amazingly, the female team member described what she got earlier on in Storage Room 1. A skinny, young girl, about five or seven years of age, in rags and filthy, was hiding because she had been taken away. Was the voice we picked up seconds earlier that of a woman, trying to coax a young child out from its hideaway?

Anthony engaged, appealing for the Spirit world to draw near, to indicate that they were there.

"Somethings changed," said Anthony in a hesitant approach.

A foreboding feeling of sadness, dizziness and stomach pain was felt. Shadows were reported to have been seen.

Anthony beckoned for one last reasonable sign of importance. "Try and move something. Try and walk. Try and come down the steps. Try and close the door if you want."

We started to discuss the explanation for why belly or stomach pain was so influential. Some reasons, we thought, might be to do with labour pains or birth. Anthony raised his voice. "Did you have a baby here?" he asked, channelling his question towards the vacant Storage Room 1.

A suspicion of panic arrived after a draught of cold air hit Rhiannon.

"Make just one sound with your voice. We're going now – any minute now."

An utterance was heard, caught by the night vision camera, as Anthony talked. It was hard to describe what had been actually said because of its quiet-spoken temperament.

To some degree, we got the idea that there was a mortuary associated with the house. We failed to elaborate on this theory, proving it inconclusive and so, we decided to call it a day.

When all was done and the Civic Trust House was locked up, we took a timeout and settled into the final process of taking everyone's blood pressure. Only Anthony's pulse rated higher at the end than at the start of the investigation. Jen, Rhiannon and the female team members were lower at the end.

Could the women in the Art Civic Trust House be influenced more than the men? Or was it the simple matter of Anthony trying to prepare himself for the sole purpose of driving all the team back home in the early hours of the morning?

Going back to the video camera incident in the Back Building Stairs, the recording had failed to back up the EVP captured by the night vision camera when the team re-entered the area. The battery had already died. It did pick up on the prism sliding off the front of the lens, due to the weak support from the tape.

There was an influence of all life (work, rest and play) but there was a sombre edge to the house, indicative of much harder times. You could sense it on every brick, making Cork City's oldest building an important arcane idol.

The stairs, leading up to the front of the building

At the Back Building Stairs, replica copies of a human skeleton are prepared

The laser beam machine targets a couch

A motion detector positioned in the Hallway

Storage Room One

Several experiments were done in the Musgrave Room

Anthony looks on. Who's on the other side of the door?

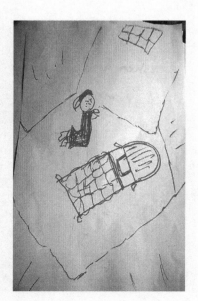

A drawing by Jen but, what did it reveal?

***Drowned-Out Voices* Investigation footage can be viewed by**

Watching the DVD that accompanies this book

Scanning the QR code

Visiting our website

www.GhostÉire.net

Click on the button
Drowned-Out Voices Footage

and enter the password
YourNotAlone

Enter the password
YourNotAlone

Location Background/Biography

The Arts @ Civic Trust House is located on 50 Popes Quay, Cork City. This noticeable, red-bricked building built during Queen Anne's reign, between 1700-1730, is regarded as the oldest house in Cork City.

It is alleged that it was erected to facilitate the 4th Earl of Cork - Richard Boyle - who had the nickname 'Apollo of the Arts' but, it is doubtful that he ever lived there.

Henry Maultby took over ownership of the property in the mid-1800s; it became the hub for the cooper and butter merchant. An adjoining building to the house was used to expand the business, where barrels for the city's ale and casks (firkins), for his world-famous butter were made. Later, Maultby moved to Australia with his family.

The building was opened as a hospital, on the 31st of October 1876, for brief period and was known as 'The County and City of Cork Hospital for the Diseases of Women and children'. The patients of the hospital were successfully transferred, on 16th September 1885, to the Victoria Hospital in Cork City.

It was noted, in the 1901 census, that the household had five occupants residing at the house. A Maria J. Geaney was head of a household, which included her sister and two lodgers - one of them a priest from France named Louis Bertent - and their servant, Bridget Desmond.

A Sergeant Patrick Ryan in the RIC (Royal Irish Constabulary) was the next owner of the house. The 1911 census recorded ten other family members registered as living along with Mr Ryan at the building. Ryan would also take up the role as the School Attendance Officer in the city.

The daughters of Patrick Ryan then took over ownership of the house, letting it out to lodgers; an acceptance for schoolteachers was preferred. An annual treat for locals was to visit Mrs Ryan's home at Christmas time, to sneak-peek at the beautiful, decorated interior and her fine clothes.

The house fell into disrepair and was saved from dereliction in the 1980s by Cork City Council. It was used, for a short period of time, for the Graffiti Theatre Company. Since 2006, with the support of the Cork City Council, it has been home to eight professional arts organisations.

The building has four floors and is neighboured by the Dominican Friary. It overlooks the River Lee and Cork City Opera House.

Manifestation/Legend

There was no paranormal significance to this location prior to the investigation.

Conclusion

The picture of a face in the window might clearly be pareidolia – an incorrect perception of an object, pattern or meaning to an observer.

Seeing shapes in clouds and rock-faces (Man in the Moon) and hearing voices in audio recordings are just a few of examples of pareidolia. People tend to make faces out of patterns of light and shadows. There is a tendency to be interested in shapes, patterns and familiar faces as a baby after three months of age. Babies are fascinated by their parents' and their own faces, in particular, recognising their personal identity for the first time. Our early ancestors would have used mythological figures to identify constellations (group of stars) to tell stories. So, seeing a face in a window would be quite common.

As there was a total of eight Spirits believed to be in the Musgrave Room, it is no wonder we had varied attitudes towards us and emotions.

A female nurse was first up. She was restless and only visited the room/house on occasion. The house, established by a Protestant charity specialising in medical treatment for the sick, did operate as a hospital in the late nineteenth century, although, nurses also visited homes for other issues, such as inspecting and advocating hard work and moral living.

Tuesday was the day of the week that the Spirit thought it was *now* but on two occasions, acknowledged Friday as today's day. 'Now' and 'today' might be two completely different stories or, to be precise, domains. It might have been Tuesday in the Spirit's world but, as it was intelligent and was in and out of our domain, it accepted that it was Friday – the actual day for the investigation.

We were lucky, as this was the most active day as well, which supports why the Spirit was present – she may only be active at this particular time – when the office was quiet. With the rest days and working days figured out, the female Spirit may have worked long afternoon/evening shifts at the house on Friday and Sunday to Monday, with an easier shift on a Wednesday. Friday to Saturday and Monday to Tuesday were periods of getting valuable relaxation. Thursday – which was not chosen - may have been a day for pleasure.

The Spirit selected Sunday as the day to go to church. This would have been the traditional day that Christians would gather for worship. Monday was the day the Spirit went to confession. If it was the Spirit of a nurse, she had earlier pointed out that she did not believe in God. It may have just been an observation on her part that she never attended religious services or repented sin. The Spirit also chose Sunday, twice, for the day that it had died on.

A cold draught was felt by Rhiannon and Sinead above the dining table when the planetary board was introduced. Having two people back up that there had been a breeze was convincing. The team members had been well away from any windows but a fireplace was close by and it could have also been a breath from other participants, leaning over and preparing to touch the planchette (the female team member and Aoife).

The planets Mars and Neptune were favoured. Maybe the Spirit had known of the significance of these planets for the evening or, had knowledge of the movement of celestial bodies above the Earth – that we would have a smooth night.

Four knocks had been heard on the night vision camera when the planchette moved to Mars on the planetary board. Other knocking sounds had been heard at the same time – not as prominent, which could discredit the value of this piece of evidence being exceptional. The knocking seemed to have come from up above the room. It had been deemed worthless, as we had discovered there were two members of staff in the building working late. They had left a short time later.

The Spirit had claimed to be English and, when asked if the Spirit liked the Irish, the planchette, without hesitation, went straight to 'No' on the talking board. A voice whispering 'No' had been picked up at the same time. This had likely been done by a team member or Aoife, in response to where the planchette had moved to.

Who was this Spirit who had claimed to be English? There are a number of possibilities as to who it could have been.

A police officer was alleged to have been on the board at that point. A Sergeant Patrick Ryan lived at the house in the early 1900s. He served in the RIC (Royal Irish Constabulary), the police force of Ireland, which had been under British administration. He may have served in the RIC until it was disbanded, in 1922. Mr Ryan had been born in County Tipperary in 1862. He is down in the 1911 census records as being Roman Catholic. He married his wife, Elizabeth in 1890. In his years of work in the RIC, he would have probably faced criticism and threats from his fellow countrymen. There may have been a fair amount of resentment felt by Mr Ryan towards this.

Vibrations on the planchette came to the core, along with strange sound phenomena when Jen joined in on the experiment. Even her name was spelt out on the talking board.

The humming came when the female team member was offering positive instruction, when everyone present was concentrating. The hum was expressed as a way of looking for awareness.

A screeching sound was heard, similar to a mocking snigger. It may have been noticed by Jen, as she had glanced away momentarily from the planchette that would soon move onto the small, squared, framed mirror. The sound may have come from the outside street but it had been very loud and within proximity and unlikely to have come from any the team or Aoife.

In a space of five seconds, light tapping, muted whistle and whine had been captured on the night vision camera. This had been an unusual amount of unexplainable behaviour in a short time frame, with little logic behind them. To add to this, the Spirit had previously moved onto the direction board, pointing the planchette at 'North', to where they were.

It means the Spirit had been explaining where they were positioned: not in the Back Stairs Building but within the Musgrave Room, around the dining table to Sinead's left. It just could have been a coincidence that Sinead asked for a noise and we received the tapping, whistle and whine a short time later. It is a common enough practice to ask for noises on paranormal investigations. However, the planchette had also moved up beside the talking board, to 'Yes', to clarify it could respond.

It is likely that at least one child was in attendance at this juncture of time.

'I', 'M', '9' were gathered from Talking Board A. The name 'Adam' had appeared on the same board, along with the word 'God'. We did not find an 'Adam' on any available records for the house.

There had been a different Spirit on Talking Board B. It came across as being a member of the Religious Society of Friends (a Quaker) who had been a farmer (granger) and owned a shop nearby. This Spirit had been indecisive when it came to the topic about manufacturing beer.

In the Aldwell's *General Post Office Directory* of 1845, a Henry Maultby was listed as a Master Cooper, residing at number 43 – the Civic Trust House. He was also registered in the Pigot and Co.'s *Directory of Cork City*, in 1824, as a Cooper but living at Sand Quay (350 metres away).

A Cooper is an occupational name for a maker or repairer of wooden vessels, such as barrels, tubs and casks. We know that Maultby was involved in the industrial production of barrels and casks for ale and butter.

There were several coopers living by him as well, according to the 1845 Directory: James Noonan at house number 39 and a John Farmer at number 44. They could have worked under Mr Maultby.

It is not forbidden for Quakers to drink alcohol but it is considered wise, by them, to only consume moderate amounts. Many became brewers. They could be trusted to deliver a decent, well-measured beer.

Henry Maultby could have been an ancestor of Samuel Maultby, who had served in Oliver Cromwell's parliamentarian (New Model) army in 1649. Quakers and Puritans had several similarities; one of them was to purify the Church of England (mid-1600s). There was a difference in that Puritans were intolerant of other religions, while Quakers believe that everybody could be saved – the light within. So, we are unsure if Henry Maultby was a Quaker.

The Maultby surname literally means 'farmstead or village of a man called Malti' or, 'where the malt is made'. The Spirit stated that it was a farmer. We know that Henry Maultby was renowned for his butter. He possibly owned land in which cattle could graze. The milk from a cow goes through a churning process in developing butter. The movement of the planchette became odd when butter was mentioned.

In the *Slater's Directory* of 1846, Henry Maultby was entered as a cask inspector at the Butter Weigh House on Mannix Street.

The year 1826 was specific. What is the significant of 1826 to Henry Maultby? His wife, Mrs Anne Maultby died "leaving a large and youthful family", in the first week in May of 1826. Henry Maultby may have been living at the Civic Trust House around this period. He was suspected of moving to Australia later in life. In the investigation, the question was asked if the Spirit came off a boat. The answer was 'Yes' on the board. We do not know if this was in reference to after Henry Maultby's birth (if born outside of Ireland), death (travelling to Australia) or dealings he had throughout his life, possibly with ships.

It was assumed the planchette had moved to '6', '0' (zero) for the house number but, this was incorrect according to the Spirit (presumably Henry). The planchette was probably pointing to the number five, instead of six. During Henry Maultby's time, the number of the house was forty-three. Notwithstanding, if it was Henry or another intelligent Spirit that was present, then it would have knowledge of the current number of the building being fifty. Did Henry evoke a memory to come back to the Civic Trust House?

Masks were worn at the start of the investigation. The Spirit present at that time felt annoyed with the inability to see the faces of the team and Aoife. There was also a sense that if we wanted to see the Spirit's face, we would have to envisage it in our minds.

The planchette went to in between Pisces and Aries on the astrology board, in relation to the month it was now. This could have been around the date of 20th/21st March. This was different to the date of the investigation yet, not too far off.

The Spirit identified Aries (20th March – 21st April) as the month in which they were born and had died. There might be a parallel between the two. Rebirth might occur after a biological death in a form of a mind, consciousness, soul and, in another body for reincarnation. This might be the reason why the location was at its most active, according to the Spirit and that it roughly coincided with the date of the investigation (26th April).

Anniversaries may prove essential in heightening activity at a location. Taking into account the current date that the Spirit was in (20th/21st March), then we assume that we had only been at the beginning of a more intense stage. So, hauntings could depend on the actual time that it is for the Spirit in their realm.

Rhiannon had experienced the table shaking, a breeze and a breath between her and Jen in the séance. They were close to the end of the table, where the Spirit had earlier directed where it was with the direction board.

Cold draughts had been felt throughout the séance. At one point, after Anthony whistled, the female team member felt a sensation of a cold draught on her right hand. She was almost directly across from Anthony; the forced breath from him most likely caused her reaction. When keeping still, especially in a séance, the body loses heat. A protective warm layer forms around a person. Cold draughts become apparent when motionless.

There was an unusual hollow clunk heard by the team when Sinead and Anthony asked for movement elsewhere, especially on the stairs. Everybody looked still in front of the night vision camera. However, those involved in the séance may have hit the table with their legs unintentionally. Going by people's interpretations, it seemed to have originated from another area. It would have been better if it were from inside the room, as yet again, interference from outside the building or piping/guttering could have caused the clunking or gurgling noise.

The small, square, wooden table rocked strongly but was not able to create a spontaneous movement and, when asked to levitate, abruptly stopped. Levitation (counter-gravity force) might only exist when intended and, if not, only in our own minds. Trickery, illusion, hallucination and natural causes (such as magnets and wind) could cause what one would believe is an object being held aloft, without support, in a stable position. The Spirit was probably looking for us to take a more sensible approach instead.

The groaning sound may have been from Anthony, on his part displaying displeasure that the table did not hover or, relief (on his back) in being able to stand upright again.

A child was alleged to have been in the IAYO Room. Anthony may have come to the assumption that there was a child around because of the squiggly lines drawn on the A2 paper with the planchette drawing/writing instrument. The erratic motion from the device failed to show any features and there was little attempt to mark in finer detail. The instrument briefly stopped moving after Anthony remarked on a child, indicating that something significant had been said.

What had been thought to be a portrait could only be made out as a crescent moon, drawn on the second sheet of paper although, there had been more purpose behind it. There is a possibility that the crescent moon resembled a hammock. This type of canvased bed would be ideal as a cheap cot for babies/infants/young children to fall asleep faster. Hammocks take up less room than beds and are easier to change, compared to soaked mattresses from patients suffering with fever and infectious diseases. However, they are more often suited for children.

There was also a voice of child that said something like, 'My name is Cedric' followed by a whisper that said 'Yeah' after Anthony asked if the Spirit wanted to draw. There was likely more than one Spirit present at that precise moment. Were we picking up on children when the Civic Trust House was a hospital?

The name Cedric became popular after the children's book *Little Lord Fauntleroy* was published in 1885. Therefore, we should consider that this Spirit of a child was from the period of the house's history, in between 1885-1901. Though the child's voice might not have come across clearly, it did have a serious hesitancy or shyness about it.

The Frank's Box experiment in the Tigh Filí Room revealed that there were eight Spirits present - the same sum that had been in the Musgrave Room. Furthermore, one of them might have been a child.

Following Sinead asking, "Could you give us a number please?", a child's voice plainly replied 'Five', presumably from the Frank's Box. Was this the age of the child - possibly Cedric?

When asked "What place of worship do you go too?", a distinct clear masculine voice said, 'Here'.

There are three religious sites in the vicinity of the Civic Trust House. Saint Mary's Priory (Roman Catholic) is next door. Saint Mary's Holy Roman Catholic Priory is around the corner and just a short walk away is Saint Anne's Church/Shandon Bells and Tower (Anglican).

This male soul may have meant the Civic Trust House. There might have been a chapel in the building at some stage or, the Spirit could have been referring to a different matter, in awe of the place.

After the question, "Were you killed?" was asked, a masculine voice, in an Irish accent said, 'Here'. The reply was quick. Was this an act of urgency? Did something need to be known? Did this person get maliciously murdered or, did his death happen accidentally? Could it have been stopped?

Doctor Henry McNaughton-Jones was a medical officer (1874-1880) and consulting surgeon (1880-1883) for 'The County and City of Cork Hospital for the Diseases of Women and Children'. McNaughton-Jones was a professor in midwifery, a gynaecologist (women's reproductive system), an otologist (inner ear) and ophthalmologist (eye and vision) specialist.

In 1880, McNaughton-Jones was accused of administrating a drug too soon to a patient but because of failed medical expertise elsewhere, was actually too late. The male patient was suffering from scarlatina (scarlet fever – bright red rash, sore throat and fever). A nurse did not want to torture a blister the patient had on his skin and McNaughton-Jones' assistant thought rolling in blankets would suffice. By the time the patient was seen by McNaughton-Jones, to administer the drug, it was too late. McNaughton-Jones moved to London in 1883. He had five children. He died on Friday 26th April 1918 – ninety-five years to the day of the investigation.

Some of the sensations felt on the third floor could be linked to when the house was a hospital. In Storage Room 1, there were drawings of a person beside a bed, wanting to go home; a pregnant woman; flowers and a feeling of restlessness, tiredness and deep thought. The same types of energy were picked up during the calling-out vigil later, in Storage Room 2, such as labour pains and a cold draught when inquiring if babies were born in the building.

In the same session, when Anthony asked, "Are you trying to escape?", the female team member felt a headache. Soon after he asked, "Are you panicking?"

Rhiannon sensed two people clashing over something. One was scared, trying to stop the other person from opening up. Maybe the words that Anthony had used triggered something, making team members open up to what was around them or unbeknown to them and causing them to be led up the garden path – slightly deceived into believing that what he had spoken had some sort of significance. If what we presumed was correct, then we could have unearthed a secret. There may have been an attempt to escape but panic had set in.

Previously in the same room, for an automatic drawing/writing experiment, a middle-aged woman was noticed by Rhiannon. She wore a white dress with her hair tied up in a bun. She was scared. This was probably the person whom Rhiannon had sensed trying to be tight-lipped. An EVP was caught of a woman speaking, a couple of seconds after Rhiannon disclosed what she had felt. It said, 'Out you come'. Maybe this was the secret.

Seconds later, the female team member sensed a small/skinny girl, between five and seven years of age, all in rags and filthy, hiding from being taken. She had written about this child earlier in Storage Room 1. Did the row between the two people have a connection with the girl?

The middle-aged woman might have been related to the young girl in some type of way. Although she wanted to, she could not escape the house with the girl because of a predicament – the best thing was to leave the girl in alternative care (maybe within the hospital), instead of her being taken out the building to fend for herself.

Hunger, vomiting, bellyaches and frustration were also recorded in Storage Room 2. 'Mercy' was also written down. It is not known if this was in relation to offering compassion or, looking for it.

Anthony wrote down the words, loitering around. There were a number of possibilities for why people would have been hanging around the house. For example, partners or parents may have been concerned about their loved ones' well-being at the hospital.

Jen drew a man grasping a woman by the arm in a wooded area. The woman (presumably a mother) said, 'No' on the picture whilst a small figure (possibly her child) had its arms stretched out, up high. One would assume that the child was looking to be picked up. The landscape looked like it was set in the countryside. Many diseases, such as cholera and smallpox, were widespread in Ireland in the late nineteenth century. The rural community would have suffered the most. There is a strong possibility that the story behind the picture was that of a child being left abandoned in the woods.

There were believed to be a few EVPs captured on the night vision camera on the third floor. In Storage Room 1, when the question, "Who are you hiding from?" was asked, a husky voice said what was possibly, 'Hiding from you'.

The reply could have been an amalgamation of noises (for example, group members breathing) but there were defined syllables in the sentence. If we accept that the response was real, then we had a Spirit who wanted to go unnoticed. Unfortunately, we do not know the identity of this being and why it wanted to be elusive.

There was a voice which possibly said, 'We'll think about it'. It came across slightly muffled and could easily be interpreted as something else. Just a few seconds earlier, Rhiannon was explaining what a previous sound from outside the building was (a whistle) and she may have continued to put forward an explanation for this by mumbling.

The last EVP captured on the third floor was when Anthony called out, clarifying that the investigation would be finishing up. The words 'big belly' could be made out. The team members were talking about labour pains, birth and babies just beforehand, so it is quite reasonable to suggest that the voice had come from someone in the group, especially as it sounded similar to the female team member's voice.

Noises and shuffling were reported after Jen had asked, "Where are you now?" and, "Why were you taken away?"

Although these sounds never came over the recordings, the questions asked may have had importance to the young girl who was hiding.

John was the only name the team picked up that had any known relevance to the history of the house. The eldest son of Sergeant Patrick Ryan and Elizabeth Ryan was John Dommick Ryan. He was born in 1894. A surname would have been preferred, to attain a perfect connection.

The temperature change in the Reception Room was not abnormal. The highest reading was at 18^0C – exactly the same temperature as at the start of the investigation. When the team entered the area to set up experiments, the door was left open. The hot air would have escaped through the upper half of the doorway. The temperature would have decreased shortly afterwards, only faintly rising once the door had been kept closed, as a result of heat flowing from a high concentration to a low concentration within the room.

A hoarse voice was captured on the Back Building Stairs when the team went to check on the trigger objects. It very clearly said, 'Scared away'. At the time, Rhiannon was holding the night vision camera in front of her, up close behind Anthony (right shoulder) and Jen (left shoulder). They all stood facing the video camera (with prism) and replica bones ahead of them. Once again, it cannot be ruled out that a team member had created the vocal: probably from a male; most likely Anthony. That being said, Anthony spoke at a different pitch just as the vocalisation stopped, ruling him out from creating the audible.

The team were discussing the banging noises from up above moments before but credited them to the draughts coming in and out, which were causing the doors to shut. If it was a Spirit, we do not know for sure who was scared or what made them be afraid! Was it to do with the replica bones? On the other hand, a Spirit may have been curious to stay in the area and quickly left when the team had returned.

Also, who was the Spirit giving the information? They were either determined or possibly dropping a hint that someone had fled the scene at some point.

Arts @ Civic Trust House
Co Cork

WEBSITE: civictrusthouse.ie
e-MAIL: info@civictrusthouse.ie
PHONE: 021 421 5101
FACEBOOK: civictrusthouse

The house is open to visitors by appointment.

The boardroom (Musgrave Room) is available to hire. The dining room table seats 10-12 people and can be adjusted to accommodate between 23-30 people in the room.

Broadband is available in the boardroom, along with access to a projector. A kitchen amenity provides tea/coffee.

Office spaces are convenient to art firms and freelance individuals at an affordable rate.

Cork Film Centre, Corcadorca Theatre Company, Cork Jazz Festival and Cork Midsummer Festival are just few of the resident companies situated at the Civic Trust House.

CLONONY CASTLE

Layout

RECEPTION ROOM

BANQUETING ROOM

Chapter 24

Clonony Castle

Jenifer's Journey

The Kings and Queens of England have such inviting tales to tell and some untold. Who could not be captured by sagas of power, love, betrayal and death, to list a few? Ireland's link to this empire was one of discontent on many factors. Though, some Irish landowners had many privileges, none so more than the Butlers of Kilkenny.

Who would have thought a woman of Irish ancestry would become Queen of England? One of the privileges given by King Henry VIII to Anne Boleyn's father, Thomas, for Anne's hand in marriage was the estate of Clonony Castle, County Offaly. It is said to have been lived in by descendants of Thomas Boleyn's bloodline, during and after his death.

We did a paranormal investigation at Clonony back in June 2010. Things did not run as smoothly as we had hoped, mainly due to national tabloid antics, photoshoots and pain in the arse ex-team members and their guests. Things got a bit rushed, undermining and strenuous. We have learned from that now. A pre-visit should have been recommended as little was done that night to our satisfaction.

The welcome that we received, however, from Rebecca, the owner of the castle, was helpful in catering for all our needs. This meant we needed to come back again, to give it our fullest attention. We knew, in our own minds, that we would come back again when the time was right.

Four years later, I was lucky enough to be taking a trip to London for a family celebration. As I was there, I paid a visit to the historic, Tower of London. It was around Remembrance Day, early November. Poppies filled the outskirts of the Tower. I walked into the chapel renowned to be the final resting place of Queen Anne Boleyn. A basket of red roses on the ground marked where she was meant to be buried. Wandering around the grounds of the tower, I was drawn to particular areas that were strictly forbidden to go into. I wondered, what could be behind closed doors?

Fast forward to 2016 and we were ready to do Clonony Castle again. Rebecca was more than delighted to have us. Months of preparation had been done ahead of the investigation. We arranged to meet Rebecca beforehand, to catch up on the past few years and arrange a date for an investigation.

Before we arrived, Anthony and I stopped at a petrol station in Cloghan, to get biscuits for the tea that we would be having. It was nice to see that nothing on the outside had changed once we were allowed inside the gates of the castle. The hawthorn tree still stood beside a stone slab on the grass. The same slab indicated that all is not right in the history books.

Rebecca, in company of Oscar, the dog and Emmy, the cat led us up the spiral stairs to the Reception Room on the first floor. Anthony and I relaxed on the sofa whilst Rebecca brewed the tea. A lot of hard work has gone into the restoration of this fine structure. Since our last visit, plumbing to facilitate a toilet in the garderobe had been added, among other, numerous fixtures. The castle had come a long way compared to how it looked when Rebecca first set her eyes on it.

After some catching up, I took some photos whilst Anthony did some baseline testing.

A fine tapestry hung off the wall, portraying a gathering of women in luxury dresses, with bonnets on their heads.

We headed down to the Banqueting Room on the ground floor. On the wall to the far left of the room are three portraits, two of which are the Boleyn sisters, Elizabeth and Mary (said to be great-granddaughters of George Boleyn), who lived within the confines of the castle. Below these, is a portrait of Queen Elizabeth I.

On the way out of the castle, before we said our goodbyes, a group of tourists had arrived. Rebecca greeted them whilst Anthony and I wondered around the grounds. I took some pictures of the outside of the castle, at many different angles. How nice it was to be back at this magnificent place. We then said our goodbyes but, not for long – we would be back in two weeks.

Anthony booked a holiday cottage for two nights for the team beside Lough Derg, in County Tipperary. This would be a stop off point to shorten the journey for the investigation.

The day came, Anthony, Sinead, Cameron and I departed Killarney. I had just finished work. It was around one o'clock in the afternoon. That day, we relaxed and got our bearings. Some fun and laughs were to be gained. Basketball, soccer, board games and charades were played. Two team guests arrived later that night.

The next day we took a spin up the road to Portumna, to do some sightseeing. Sinead stayed in bed. After a few hours, we returned to the holiday cottage, to get some sleep before the night's investigation. The alarm was set for five o'clock. We managed to get a good rest, awakening one by one.

We gradually started to pack the car with equipment, food and refreshments. I felt excited and the rest of the team were in that category too. Forty minutes by car and we would be there.

We left the holiday cottage around six o'clock that evening. Anthony, Cameron, Sinead and I went up in one car whilst the two team guests followed us on. We stopped off at a restaurant in Birr on the way, to get a warm, hearty meal. This was needed, to keep the energy flowing for the next few hours.

As only I and Anthony knew the location of the castle, the car behind had to keep in close attendance. This made it funny when we deliberately circled a roundabout three times. When we got to our destination, Anthony rang Rebecca to notify that we were there. She opened the gates for us.

We got everything we needed out from the car and gathered it all in the Reception Room. Anthony did the remainder of the baseline testing whilst I went about setting up the CCTV surveillance night vision cameras. The rest of the team and guests had a look around.

Surprise, surprise, I had left the continental adaptors for the CCTV surveillance night vision cameras back at the holiday cottage. Typical!

Meanwhile, Sinead got changed into a medieval dress. This style of clothing would help liven things up in a later experiment.

After Anthony had finished the baseline testing, he helped Cameron place some cards and slips of paper on top of a table. I took a few snaps, with the digital camera, of how they were laid out.

Once everything was set up, we went outside and sat on the steps leading up towards the castle. Sinead blended into the background, behind us, posing like a person from a different era. One of the team guests, at this point, took several photos of us, all in front of the castle.

After this, we decided that a good place to do a protection circle was by the hawthorn tree. We asked for clear answers for the investigation through our Spirit guides.

This would be the last investigation we be doing this year. I was already three months pregnant.

Anthony and Sinead would be busy preparing our first book for its release and Cameron would soon be leaving, for UN duty abroad.

We were ready to go all out. What Boleyn secrets would be revealed through the night? Well, it did not take long for us to know…

- To Be Continued -

GLOSSARY

Here are descriptions, explanations, experiments, historical factors and iconic persons you might encounter in the chapters and need more information on.

Acoustic Camera 64 Array (See Bonus Footage)

This flawless piece of kit arranges sound into vision. It is essential in recognising noise and vibration inconsistencies within a particular space, area or room. The data collected through the device is easily simplified using the wide range of software analysis, such as near and far-field imaging, time lapse, spectrogram and spectrum features. The handheld assembly has sixty-four miniature microphones and a HD camera, streaming measurements of below 1 kHz and up to 20 kHz, which can be connected into a laptop or tablet. It also comes with a tripod. It has a simple purpose of distinguishing between Spirit sound occurrences and the usual domestic noise pollution that we find in our daily lives.

All-Seeing-Eye Pyramid Scrying

Images of eyes can help avert evil. The use of charms and decorations, called 'Nazars', are used in west Asian and Mediterranean cultures whilst the 'Eye of Horus' was used by Ancient Egyptians, to bring protection and for rebirth into the Underworld. The 'Eye of Providence', an eye inside a triangle is used in Freemasonry. The all-seeing-eye pyramid scrying board is decorated in gold paint. Sticking out at the base of the board is a piece of wood, providing the platform for a small mirror and a candle/torch to be placed. Before working with the scrying board, we can find, with the colour mood frame, which reflective colour mirror any Spirits would prefer to come forth in.

Astrology Board

The zodiac is a belt of the sky about 8° of the ecliptic (path of the sun, moon and planets) and divided into twelve divisions, known to us as star signs. This square board features these twelve signs of the zodiac (Aries, Taurus, Gemini, Cancer, Leo, Virgo, Libra, Scorpio, Sagittarius, Capricorn, Aquarius and Pisces), which are represented with symbols, in a circular formation, at the centre of the board.

Athlone Siege Figurehead Cards

These cards display pictures (from sculptures featured in the museum exhibition) of the main military commanders and leaders at the Siege of Athlone of 1691. Names of persons involved are shown on the back of the card.

Aura

The aura is an assumed emanation (flow) around a human being, animal or living organisms that radiates a colour in varying sizes. In alternative medicine, the human aura is believed to affect the health and mood of a patient. There is no scientific evidence to suggest auras exist yet, psychics and holistic practitioners maintain otherwise.

A simple way to see your own aura is to stand in front of a mirror (in front of a white background) and stare a couple of inches away from a particular part of your body, until your vision becomes slightly out of focus. You might see a different colour.

Automatic and Planchette Drawing/Writing

Automatic drawing/writing is a method of receiving information from the Spirit world through an individual's clear mind. With the hand, lightly gripping on a pen, pencil or chalk and lightly touching the surface of a piece of paper or slate, a possible message might be displayed, drawn or written out a short time later.

The planchette was regarded to have been invented by French spiritualist, Mr Planchette in 1853. This is a heart-shaped piece of wood, with wheels or coasters that are commonly used with a talking board. Planchettes that have wheels can be utilised for a drawing/writing experiment. A downward pen or pencil (at centre) is used to support the other wheels. Individuals connect on this divination tool and with its versatility, the instrument can move around in all directions. This is ideal for a Spirit to draw a picture or write a message.

Body Mood Doll

The doll is configured with similar colours to the colour mood frame. The aim is to find out, using a divination tool on the frame, what injury, illness or area of the body brought about the prognosis of death. The colour on the frame will link to the area of the doll of interest to which the Spirit can relate to.

Another use for the doll is when a Spirit can affect a certain area of the body of a team member. It can help pinpoint where a Spirit might touch or affect a person (without them knowing) in a separate session elsewhere at the location.

Calling-Out Vigil

Sometimes, being at the forefront, calling out questions or just relaxing into the atmospheric surroundings in the vigil could influence a presence to manifest. You could do this during a separation vigil or as a group. Asking relevant questions to the location, connecting in with your personal thoughts, feelings and exchanging them with present team members might get credible results. Other team members might have similar experiences or, they could clash and be different to yours. You might get a reaction back on your visual and audio equipment, as well as other altering factors to your senses, as you take time to concentrate on what is around you and, in the background, compared to other experiments in the foreground.

Channelling and Mediumship

Channelling or Mediumship is the perceived transmitting or exchanging of information (sharing), from a Medium between humans and Spirits. It is not to be confused with possession: the control of an evil Spirit or Demon over a person.

In Spiritualism, a Spirit guide is often used by a Medium to open and close communication and offer protection. The technique of channelling can come through many ways: through seeing (clairvoyance), hearing (clairaudience), smelling (clairalience), feeling (clairsentience) and so on.

Cleansing

To cleanse is to make pure and clean and get rid of unpleasant occurrences and negativity. All four natural elements have a purpose in cleansing.

Water cleansing may involve swimming in the ocean or river, standing in the rain and drinking plenty of water. Earth cleansing would entail walking in a wood, hugging a tree and following a healthy, green diet. Fire cleansing can be achieved by meditating in candlelit area/space or letting sunlight into a room. Lastly, air cleansing can be accomplished by focusing on breathing and being outside, in the open, on a windy day.

Coat of Arms Shield

Sometimes you need something to distinguish yourself to what you represent at a location. The GhostÉire coat of arms shield was created by team member, Jenifer Kerrigan. The harp represents the symbol of Ireland, while the snake relates to pre-Christian times with paganism. Using this shield as a trigger object is possible too. It lets the 'Spirits' know who we are and where we come from. A place such as a castle or a location of a siege or battle is an ideal place to display our colours.

Colour Mood Frame (Spirit Mood Frame)

The main aim of the mood frame is to establish communication with an individual Spirit, to see what emotion it is in or how we should feel around it. Team members connect on a divination tool (glass or planchette) and ask questions. It takes out the 'Are you bad?' and 'Do you mean us any harm?' scenario. A more established picture of how the Spirit is feeling is accomplished.

Certain colours are used in our daily lives to help us in our routines. For example, red on the board means 'Alert, adventurous and excited'. This colour is used at traffic lights, as a warning to stop and with road signs with eventual dangers when driving. Light Blue on the board means 'Calm, relaxed and lovable'. This colour is used by many of the hospital fraternity, to ease certain pain and to relax a patient's prognosis.

The mood frame has a 'Yes', 'No', 'Change' and 'Finish' lettering on it. There is a section for pre-planchette drawing divination experiment on one side of the frame. These descriptions help determine what a Spirit will draw.

Compass Table

This white bar table can be used in a séance or table-tilting session. The aim is to substantiate which direction the table is moving too and to what degree. Inscribed on the top circular surface of the table are four arrows. These arise from centre (90^0 apart), expanding out to the edge in four directions – North, East, South and West. These four principal compass points are marked with the letters N, E, S, W. Prior to the session starting, a compass is placed at the centre of the table, to verify the correct bearings and can remain in the same spot for the duration of the session, to measure any impetus.

Consumption (Tuberculosis)

An infectious disease caused by mycobacterium tuberculosis bacteria, spread by coughing and sneezing tiny droplets into the air and can affect many parts of the body but, largely the lungs.

Some parapsychologists believe that when fraud is not involved, suggestion and a multiple personality disorder can be explained for the Medium's actions.

Custom House, Dublin

Construction of the building was eventually completed in 1791. The architect, John Gandon (1743-1823) was asked to draw up the plans for Custom House, to be built from an idea conceived by John Beresford (Chief Revenue Commissioner). First used as the main office of the Commissioners of Custom and Excise, it would later serve, from 1872 onwards, as the headquarters for the Local Government Board for Ireland.

On the 25 May 1921, Custom House was burned out, resulting in most of the Board's records been destroyed. The Irish Republican Army (IRA) was responsible for the attack, sparking the end to the Irish War of Independence (1919-1921). Restoration was done at the house and completed by 1928.

Days-of-the-Week Board

A board dedicated to the days of the week. It has many qualities that can help gather more information on a Spirit's 'way of life': for example, finding out what types of daily activities were done or are still going on.

The square board features an outline of a circle, with the seven days of the week – Monday, Tuesday, Wednesday, Thursday, Friday, Saturday and Sunday – sectioned within it. A divination tool is used to obtain an answer.

Direction Board

A square board composed with the four cardinal and four intercardinal direction points, labelled on the outside of a marked circle. The four cardinal points – North, East, South and West – are represented with the letters N, E, S and W and the intercardinal direction points – Northeast, Southeast, Southwest, Northwest – with the letters NE, SE, SW and NW respectively. Extending from centre of the board are four arrows (90° apart), pointing towards the edge of the board in the direction of each cardinal point. Smaller arrows also emerge from centre (90° apart), showing the intercardinal directions. Before the session starts, the correct orientation needs to be confirmed, in order for the experiment to work.

Easter Rising (24th-29th April 1916)

The Easter Rising was an armed uprising organised by Irish republicans against British rule in Ireland. The planning of the Rising was done by the Irish Republican Brotherhood, under such leaders as Thomas Clarke, Sean Mac Diarmada, Patrick Pearse and James Connolly. The forces included 1,200 people from the Irish Volunteers (under Pearse), the Irish Citizen Army (led by Connolly) and the Cumann na mBan (an Irish republican women's organisation) that took control of several key buildings, including the GPO (General Post Office) and Boland's Mill, on the Easter Monday of 1916. The Proclamation of the Irish Republic (document proclaiming Ireland's independence) was read outside the GPO on that day.

The failure to seize Dublin Castle and Trinity College (for arms and ammunition) and the railway stations and docklands, meant that the British could respond with a large number of armed troops moving into the city. The rebels were under siege from heavy artillery, eventually abandoning the GPO on the Friday. Patrick Pearse surrendered the next day.

A total of 485 people died in the six days of fighting. The majority were civilians, of which, 260 had died. 66 were Irish rebels and 143 represented the combined forces of the British Army and Royal Irish Constabulary (RIC). Most of the leaders of the Rising were executed, fourteen of whom were shot dead by firing squad, at Kilmainham Gaol, in a ten-day period in May of 1916.

Electric Fencing

It is wise to do this experiment on a piece of land. The idea is to condense the energy inside a boundary, providing a positive active space.

Four standing posts are positioned into the ground, to form a shape of a square. Steel wire is wrapped between the four posts to make the outer perimeter. Afterwards, the wiring is connected to a fence energiser (providing the electrical pulses), which is attached to a ground rod (no less than two feet away) placed into the earth. An EMF meter is used to see if the electric fencing is working and a stepping board or stool is handy to get in and out of the enclosure, to prevent getting a shock.

Enda Kenny

Born on 24th April 1951 in County Mayo, Kenny served as Fine Gael (political party) leader from 2002 to 2017. In 2011, he became the thirteenth Taoiseach to be elected to office.

Enda Kenny officially opened up the Loop Head exhibition in 2012. His grandfather, James John McGinley was principal keeper at the Loop Head from January 1933 until October 1934.

EVPs (Electronic Voice Phenomena)

Sounds captured on electronic recordings believed to be of Spirit voices, unintentionally recorded or on purpose, when requested. Scientists believe these voices are misinterpreted, originating from random background sounds or, initially, living people and animals – a type of apophenia (a form of recognising patterns in random information).

Flying Columns

A small, military land unit mainly made up of volunteers. Ideal for ambush situations with a hit-and-run tactic, where independent individuals could escape been caught or killed. Flying Columns were effective for the Irish Republican Army (IRA) during the Irish War of Independence (1919-1921). They became essential in robbing trains of British supplies, plundering mail for who was secretly communicating with Dublin Castle and attacking military barracks to attain small firearms. Bicycles were the easiest form of transport for the flying columns to evade being tracked.

Frank's Box (Ghost Box, Spirit Box)

This was created in 2002, by Frank Sumption, as a type of communication, using a combination of AM radio frequency and white noise to relay voices.

The key to using it is to call out questions or, remain silent and wait to hear a response come back from the box. The device scans the airwaves, sweeping back and forth and picking out snippets of sound. Some sceptics believe the voices are coincidental but others refer to them as being accurate to the credibility of the location or situation that they are in.

In some cases, during the experiment, vocals or other sound occurrences could emerge from another source and not entirely from the box. In general, these devices can enhance but also disguise genuine phenomena.

Glass/Planchette Divination

An experiment that is less precise in achieving answers but assumed to be a safer method to using than the talking board.

This is another type of divination, seeking communication by channelling Spirit energy, through human energy, to an instrument.

For example, an upturned glass is commonly used, placed on a smooth surface of a table. Placing the index finger lightly on top of the glass, the Spirit allegedly determines what direction the glass moves in. The glass may minimally or vibrantly move, go in straight lines or circular motions, topple over or even fall off the side of a surface that it is connected on.

Other tools that can be used for divination are planchettes, coins and even toy cars.

Great Famine (Irish Potato Famine, 1845-1849)

Mass starvation and disease struck Ireland in the mid-19th century, due to consecutive years of failure with the potato crop. Potatoes were affected by blight, a disease that destroys the plant, resulting in about one million people dying and a further one million emigrating abroad. The country's population fell by almost a quarter.

Grid Reference Mapping

A piece of paper with a townland, building or map is employed, with several grids marked on it. A vertical (numbers) and horizontal (letters) axis is used to indicate a particular area of interest.

Hearing Aid

Ear trumpets or ear horns were the first implements used for hearing loss in the 17th century. With the advent of the telephone, the modern-day hearing aid progressed and was widely available by the end of the 20th century. Hearing aids today are classified as medical devices. They use an electroacoustic set-up that transfigures external sound to audible for the user. This device manages to pick up discernible sounds on a personal basis, to which normal hearing would not catch.

Infrasound and Ultrasound

Infrasound can be produced from natural and man-made sources, such as earthquakes, waterfalls, meteors, mountain airflow, wind turbines, supersonic aircraft, factories, nuclear/chemical explosions. Some animals use it to communicate. It is also known as a low-frequency sound, below the lower limit of human hearing (less than 20 Hz). Although the ear may not be able to sense the low sound it is believed to affect the body. Vertigo, disorientation, nausea and bowel spasms are just few of the symptoms connected with exposure to infrasound.

Ultrasound can be found in a wide range of areas of our daily lives, such as automatic door openers, motion sensors, flowmeters in piping, from wireless charging of phones and, in the future, cars. The hearing range of dogs and cats extends into ultrasound. Bats use it to detect prey and dolphins, for navigation. Ultrasounds are sound waves with frequencies higher than the human range of hearing (above 20,000 Hz). Symptoms like headaches, tinnitus, nausea and coronary heart disease are reported to be linked to exposure to ultrasound.

Instrumental Trans-Communication (ITC)

Instrumental Trans-Communication (ITC) is the practice of using electrical appliances for contact with the Spirit world, such as televisions, tape cassette recorders, radios, computers, tablets, walkie-talkies and the Frank's Box. It is suggested that Spirits either make their presence felt through appearance, sound or both. To make the experiment successful, video cameras or digital sound recorders are essential, in order to later review recordings.

It was German physicist, Ernst Senkowski who devised the phrase, Instrumental Trans-Communication, in the 1970s.

Irish Confederate Wars (1641-1653)

Also known as the Eleven Years War. It started with the Irish Rebellion of 1641 (*See Glossary*) and ended with the Cromwellian Conquest of Ireland (1649-1653).

The Confederate Catholic Association was formed at the Confederation of Kilkenny, at the end of 1642. Its aim was for self-government. Several battles and sieges took place between the Confederates and English/Scottish Protestants, with some victories for the Confederates: notably, the Siege of Limerick (1642) and Battle of Finnea (1644).

At the end of the summer of 1649, Oliver Cromwell and his New Model army arrived in Dublin to quell the Confederate revolt. The Parliamentarians, under Cromwell, took Drogheda in the northeast, together with Wexford and Waterford – crucial ports in the southeast. The last strongholds for the Confederates were besieged – Limerick and Galway. They were eventually taken by Cromwell's forces by 1652.

At the end of the summer of that year, Parliamentarians passed an act that confiscated Catholic-owned land and executed those responsible for the Irish Rebellion (*See Glossary*). The last battle took place in the spring of 1653, with Philip O'Reilly's Irish Catholic army surrendering at Cloughoughter, County Cavan.

Irish Free State (1922-1937)

The Irish Free State was set up after the Anglo-Irish Treaty of December 1921. It was comprised of twenty-six of the thirty-two counties on the island. Northern Ireland was formed from the six counties who disagreed on joining the new state.

The treaty concluded the Irish War of Independence (1919-1921), which was fought between Irish (Irish Republican Army – IRA) and British Crown forces. However, after the treaty there was a split in the IRA. As a result, the conflict of the Irish Civil War (1922-1923) saw former brothers in arms now fighting against each other. The National Army (pro-treaty) manage to overpower the IRA (anti-treaty) and, by May of 1923, the war had ended but, with a cost: an estimate of up to two thousand people had died.

A new law of the land, Bunreacht na hÉireann (Constitution of Ireland) was successfully passed, by plebiscite, in 1937, driven by Éamon de Valera (leader of the Fianna Fáil party) with the state being renamed "Éire or, in the English language, Ireland."

Irish Rebellion (1641)

Catholic fears spread with the imminent occupancy of Ireland from English and Scottish Protestants. Tensions grew more with Protestants holding the majority in Irish Parliament (easier to pass anti-Catholic legislation).

Phelim O'Neill, leader of the rebellion, managed to seize fortifications in Ulster. It sparked the rise of many Catholics to join the cause in Leinster and Munster. An estimated 4,000 Protestants were murdered by the end of 1641. Support for Charles I (1600-1649) had dwindled in England and Scotland, due to many reasons. These included the increase of taxes, with an indifference towards Parliament; his religious approach (having a Catholic wife) and a call back of English Parliament to pay for war against Scotland.

The Irish Rebellion caused the English Civil War (1642-1651) between the Royalists (under Charles I) and Parliamentarians (after a disagreement over who should command an army, over in Ireland, to crush the rebellion). This gave Catholic Ireland a chance to regroup for a united front, which would, eventually, form the Confederate Catholic Association of Ireland and lead onto the Irish Confederate Wars (Eleven Years War, 1641-1653 – *See Glossary*).

Irish Rebellion of 1798

The rebellion was an uprising by United Irishmen against Britain, in trying to establish an Irish Republic, built on the concept of the French Revolution.

A botched attempt to invade Ireland, by French veteran troops accompanied by Theobald Wolfe Tone, was made in December of 1796. Bad weather hit them off the coast of Bantry Bay (County Cork). The rebellion faulted, as it failed to launch a nationwide coordinated attack. The rebels could not secure Dublin but there were clashes in other counties of Leinster and Antrim and Down in the north.

The French (army of 1,500 men) landed in Killalla Bay, County Mayo. Accompanied by the United Irishmen, they defeated British forces at Castlebar, County Mayo and Collooney in County Sligo. However, the French surrendered at the Battle of Ballinamuck on 8 September 1798. Hundreds of Irish were executed. The rebellion was finally quelled on 12 October 1798, after Wolfe Tone, with a French force of 2,000 men, strived to land in County Donegal but were met by a sizable Royal Navy fleet. An estimate of between 10,000-70,000 people died in just three months of conflict.

Irish War of Independence (1919-1921)

A guerrilla war fought between the Irish Republican Army (IRA) and British forces. The war began with an ambush by IRA volunteers, Dan Breen and Seán Treacy at Soloheadbeg, County Tipperary on 21 January 1919, the same day that Dáil Éireann was formed (the lower house of parliament in the Irish Republic).

Slowly, IRA activity picked up pace with the freeing of prisoners and seizing of weapons. With further attacks on RIC (Royal Irish Constabulary) barracks and British Army patrols, the British government enlisted former World War I (1914-1918) soldiers, to be known as the Black and Tans, together with the Auxiliary Division, to help the RIC gain back control and repress the situation. Conflict escalated as the British forces carried out reprisals, looting, arson and extrajudicial executions.

21 November 1920, (also known as Bloody Sunday) saw some brutal killings. The IRA assassinated fourteen men, eight of whom were British Intelligence officers. In revenge, British forces shot dead fourteen civilians at a Gaelic football match at Croke Park in Dublin.

A truce was negotiated on 11 July 1921. About two thousand people had died in over two-and-a-half years of conflict.

Laser Beam Machine

The laser beam acts as a type of portal for the Spirit world. It can emit three colours – red, green and yellow – and can also be programmed for the same three colours to be used at the same time. Numerous sequences of shapes are shone in various directions, at several different speeds, onto a wall or surface. It is most effective when used in a darkened area, pointed at a certain object or area of interest, with a visual recording device (video camera) set up in view.

Laser Board

This is a semi-circled talking board with twenty-nine vertical pieces of wood positioned at the edge. Inscribed on the inside of each piece of wood is a letter from the Theban alphabet (ancient Greek, popular with occultists). The words 'Yes', 'No' and 'Change' are also featured. In the middle of the board is a circular dial, with a red laser pen located on the rim. The dial can rotate clockwise or counter-clockwise when individuals connect on it. When asking certain questions, the light from the laser may point to a certain letter or word around the board. It is effective when used in the dark.

Manifestation Board

The manifestation board focuses on the different types of energies that we believe, to our knowledge, exist inside and outside of our realm.

The various types of manifestations are represented by thirteen small iron figures on the board, each one spread out into sections. One section of the board lies vacant, to account for a type of being unknown to humans. By asking the right questions we are able to find out what is in contact with us, what other energies are around us and what type of entity they think we are.

Each section of the board has a (square hole) cut-off point, so the divination tool (such as a glass or planchette) can be disabled from knocking into the miniature figures, should a malevolent or energetic Spirit cross our path. So who knows what beings are out there - intelligent, faerie, vampires or elementals?

MilliGauss (mG)

A unit of magnetic flux density named after German mathematician and physicist, Carl Friedrich Gauss in 1936. 1000mG is equal to 1G (Gauss).

Mobile Robot

This device uses ultrasonic waves to detect obstacles in its path when moving. Should anything be in its way, it alters the general line into a clear space.

This instrument is handiest when left in a locked-off room to do its thing. Visual and sound equipment attached to it may pick up on a presence. What could prove useful are certain light objects placed on top of it. A digital sound recorder, replaying a certain sound (singing, music, etc) might attract a reaction. A small tub, test tube or container that releases a certain aroma could also be effective or, even an artefact (trigger object). It has two timer settings: One is for half an hour, the other, more generous, lasting an hour.

Mortician (Undertaker)

A profession otherwise known as a funeral director that offers its services to the deceased and their survivors. This usually involves the arrangements of the funeral ceremony and preparing the departed. The funeral director would undertake duties in embalmment, desairology (hair, skin and nail care), dressing of the clothing, casketing (placing the human body into a coffin), cossetting (treating the dead body with cosmetics) and finally, a burial or cremation.

Motion Pressure Board

Would it be interesting to measure the force or weight of a Spirit? How can footsteps or tapping be heard?

The experiment consists of two boards, measuring approximately 3ft by 1.5ft, that sandwich a motion pressure pad. Underneath the bottom board is a tractor tyre tube. The air pressure (kg/cm^2) is measured by an air pressure gauge before and after an investigation or vigil. Weight of the surface, gravity and force applied might offer a theory.

Tests have been done in the past. In 1907, Duncan MacDougall conducted experiments based around the measurement of the human soul.

Nationality Cards

Sometimes it is interesting to find out where the Spirit came from: if they came from abroad or, if they found an alliance or enemy with certain nations. This experiment with grid reference mapping can give an ideal point of view towards how a battle happened before, during and after. Using a divination tool, we can find out what nationality the Spirit is. Along with the body mood doll and colour mood frame, we can find out how the Spirit died or felt in battle.

Nine Years War (1594-1603)

A rebellion that took place involving the Irish alliance (Old English and Gaelic Chieftains), led by Hugh O' Neill (Lord of Tyrone) with the support of the Spanish, against the New English Reformists. After the Tudor Plantations, there was a call by the English for the end of Gaelic Law, especially for Ulster to be replaced by the Queen's law (Elizabeth I). As a result, O'Neill enabled an army but after some early battle victories against the English, they lost at the Siege of Kinsale (1601-1602) and decisively, the campaign.

Occupation Cards

This experiment involves, in great detail, the Spirits working life. They also can relate to the symbols. On the cards are the old names for old jobs that would have been used from Middle Ages onwards (for example 'Fletcher' was an arrow maker). Some of them are still common today. Using a divination tool the Spirit can pick out what card they find appealing, which could give inkling as to how they lived or are still living.

Offering of Fire (See Bonus Footage)

Fire has been used by humans for thousands of years as a source for heating food (thus reducing disease) also, helping to keep warm in cooler climates, for the light it produces, to warn off predators and to guide. Two fire gloves (left and right) are soaked in water, squeezed to semi-dry and then fitted on each hand. A second pair of gloves is worn over the first pair and a very small amount of lighter fuel is dripped onto the outside of the hand and fingertips. When lit, the combustion period lasts for about twenty seconds.

Ogham Board

Ogham writing dates from the 4th to the 10th century. The 'Celtic tree alphabet' was native to Ireland and is also linked to the Brythonic (such as Pictish and Welsh) languages. The board presents twenty letters of the ogham alphabet (Beith-Luis-Nin) and the six additional letters.

Oliver Cromwell (1599-1658)

English general, politician and leader of parliamentarian forces who ousted King Charles I and his royalist supporters in the English Civil War (1642-1651). He became Lord Protector of the British Isles from 1653 up until his death. He is widely despised in Ireland, due to the ruthless campaign he led with the Cromwellian Conquest of Ireland (1649-1653), replacing the Irish Catholic landowners with British colonists, although accounts of massacres of civilians are still disputed today.

Oubliette

An underground dungeon used in medieval times to hold prisoners. Access out of it would only be through a trapdoor in the ceiling. It originates from the French word meaning, 'forget'.

Past Enactment (Singapore Theory)

The origin of the name of this theory is unknown but, the method has been around for some time. It is a form of ritual or action that may evoke a Spirit entity to become active. If the Spirit wrote poems, read a poem. If the Spirit was a musician, play their favourite instrument or song. Sometimes, dressing up in period attire or using trigger objects from that era can attract a strong effect.

If a particular event in history happened at the location you are investigating, a dramatisation of what had or perhaps, should have occurred (changing the history for that time), may bring back the memory for that Spirit to manifest.

Pedometers

You can come across locations that are large and spacious; you will also come across places that are small and compact. Time spent on an investigation could prove crucial too. Transporting equipment can be arduous on occasions, so keeping an eye on how much distance is covered becomes handy, especially when dealing with fatigue.

Some pedometers have a reading for steps; ignore this, as people's strides are different. Instead, the mile/km reading gives a more accurate result. If you are lucky, you might come across a location where readings are too high or too low. This might be to do with something unexplainable (As an example: elapse of time in another dimension.), so make sure that a few team members have one on them and start and finish at the same time. Results may vary depending on how much work is done by an individual.

Planchette

The planchette is regarded to have been invented by French spiritualist, Mr. Planchette, in 1853. The planchette is usually heart-shaped yet, forms can be diverse. It is mainly made of wood, with wheels or coasters beneath it.

With its versatility, the planchette is commonly used on a talking board. Individuals who connect on it aim to receive an answer/message from the route or letters it lands on.

Planchettes that have wheels can be utilised for a drawing/writing experiment. A downward pen or pencil (at centre) is used to support the wheels. This is ideal for a Spirit to draw a picture or write a message.

Planetary Board

A board featuring planetary astronomical symbols frequently used in astrology, astronomy and alchemy (representing metals linked to the planets). Symbols such as the Sun, Moon, planets (Mercury, Venus, Mars, Jupiter, Saturn, Uranus and Neptune) and minor planets (Pluto, Chiron and Ceres) are presented on the board.

Prisms

A polished, transparent, flat-surfaced object used in optics, with at least two surfaces that have an angle so as to refract light. They can be triangular- and rectangular-shaped and can be used to reflect and split white light into a spectrum of colours.

Using prisms with an artificial light in a dark room, we can try to see if the colour bands can be disturbed or, the white light disoriented when shone against a piece of white card or paper.

Reversion/Altered Speech Device

Using a Nintendo DS that has a ten-second record time, a simple question, prayer or chant in any language can be replayed and reversed back. The backwards speech may put shivers down your spine; you may also notice some recognisable wording when you listen back over it.

This experiment can be used in séances. It is even more effective when done over a walkie-talkie in vigils, where a team member receiving is alone.

It adds another twist. With the Nintendo DS, you can make the reversed recording audible in a high and low pitch and also, control its speed. There are extra features as well that can distort the voice recorded.

Rune Stones

Dating back to the 2nd century, the runic alphabet was used to write various Germanic languages. There were also Scandinavian and Anglo-Saxon forms. These stones come in different materials, such as wood or glass, in a set of twenty-four, each bearing a symbol of the ancient alphabet. They are used to predict the future.

Scrying

This method of impression has been used for centuries in discovering past/future events upon reflection. Mirrors are commonly used; you can also use water (black base), a crystal ball or other reflective surfaces.

If you gaze for a long period of time, your face might start to disappear or, you might see images in the background. Often, experiences can include seeing different surroundings, a change of facial features or taking on a non-identical emotion. All in all, every one of your senses could be affected in doing this type of experiment.

It does not have to stop with reflection. Visions can be perceived by using fire, smoke, the sky or staring at the inside of your own eyelids and so on. It can be effective in candlelight or very dim lighting.

Sceptics advocate that low level sight of edges, outlines and lighting of the face causes hallucinations or illusions.

Séance

In French, this means 'sitting'. It is a way for a group of individuals to seek Spirit communication from the dead or, seek a physical manifestation. Preferably, a 'medium', if not a 'main sitter', should be the only person to ask questions to the otherworld.

Comfortable chairs are recommended and a suitable table. A quiet room is also needed, with no distractions. Other instruments, such as trumpets, bells, cabinets, slates and a rapping hand can be used during the session.

The first recorded séance is said to have taken place in 1659 but a wider, worldwide interest came about with the Fox sisters in 1800s, with the introduction of Spiritualism.

Separation

Often working with big groups, it is hard to give everyone a chance to communicate with the Spirit world. The Spirit may wish to communicate with smaller group numbers, to a gender (male or female), character or appearance of a particular person. More ground is covered if you are investigating a large location. However, it is always responsible to have some sort of contact with the rest of the team when on your own, in case of emergency.

When in solitude, the senses might intensify, depending on many factors: where you are, knowledge of the area, how far away you are from team members or, best still, simply from a Spirit making contact. However, being more aware might make you more perceptible to false speculation.

Sept/Clan Cards

A sept is a division of a family. It may derive from the Latin word, meaning 'fold' or 'enclosure' or, from the Irish language – 'seed' or 'progeny'.

Many regions in Ireland were ruled by dynasties at different periods of time. Each card has its very own coat of arms and clan name. Using a divination tool, we can find out what clan represents the Spirit in contact. We can find out what areas were their strongholds by using grid reference mapping. We can also find out who they fought and who they formed allegiance to.

Serotonin

A chemical which acts as a neurotransmitter (carries messages from the brain), sending signals through nerve cells that contribute to well-being, happiness and, among other important uses, it regulates the bodies internal clock, sleep-wake pattern. It is found that there is an increase in serotonin when people are dying or having a near-death experience.

Shadow Play Figures

Shadow play is a type of entertainment that involves storytelling. It is thought to have originated as far back as 1 AD in southeast Asia and first became popular in Europe in the 17th century.

A light source (such as a torch) is shone onto a piece of card (shaped to represent a particular character) creating a shadow onto a surface behind it.

This experiment works well as a type of past enactment, in a location with a diverse history, compared to other places and, with possible spectres of children.

Smell Buckets

This is a different technique in attracting Spirits, by using the sense of smell. It is known that some Spirits can create scents or odours, to remind us that they are present. If a Spirit is aware of its surroundings in our realm, then it will be attracted to certain smells that they can remember – love or loathe.

A small bucket is sealed up with a specific fragrance or stink. The lid is removed at the start of the investigation or vigil. Either way, you get a reaction, either from the Spirit world or colleagues.

Remember, each human being lets out a type of body –odour that can cause an allure. Spirits may do this too! Most males find floral scents appealing whilst females go for a 'woody' approach.

Sound Monitor

This device helps in relaying certain atmospheric sounds to a vigil. Apart from the heartbeat recording, other sounds, such as thunderstorms, white noise, streams and rainfall are included. They offer a pattern to what the energies are familiar with when they were alive in our realm.

To promote more activity, it can also add a rhythm that the Spirit world can interact with. It helps draw on the spirit vibrations and performs an enactment.

Spirit Guides (Angels)

This is an entity that provides protection to human beings and is believed to be of discarnate existence. They play many roles in our lives and can be most apparent in affecting times, even to unaware persons. Those that do acknowledge, sense a loving presence near them and are able to receive a name for their Spirit guide.

There is a likelihood that information and wisdom can come through when connecting with your Spirit guides with meditation.

Strobe Lighting

When working in the darkest of locations, strobe lighting can bring in some added exposure. Some strobe lighting appliances come with many special features: such as different colours to illumine the area/room; the speed in which the light flashes or sequences and other modes.

Using the light as bate could trigger a reaction in some shape or form. The lightning effect may make you see shadows. It might heighten that sense of fear that brings in that energy.

Table Tilting (Table Tipping)

Table Tilting originates in Victorian times, highly popularised by the Fox sisters in the mid-1800s.

Fingers are lightly placed on the table whilst individuals are standing up or sitting down. The table might shake, rock, rotate, slide and sometimes even hover when commanding a movement to happen. A light circular table is recommended.

The phenomenon has been opposed by many sceptics, claiming that the movement is caused by muscles moving unconsciously, by trickery or, quite simply, from expectation and demand.

Talking Board (Spirit Board, Ouija)

Believed to be of Ancient Egyptian and Chinese (Quanzhen school of Taoism) origin, the talking board is thought to have been around for centuries. The use of the board may have been kept underground, due to it being frowned upon by society, with the penalty of death. It is also known as the Spirit board (Ouija). It came to prominence in the 1800s, with the advent of the Spiritualist movement, the American Civil War and an open Victorian society in Britain.

Businessman, Elijah Bond patented the planchette (meaning 'little plank') – a device that users connect on (to acquire an answer) – which was sold with a board with the alphabet on it. There are many versions around the world. Christians and occultists have associated it with evil. Numbers 0-9, letters A-Z, Goodbye, Hello, Yes and No are normally printed on the board.

Tarot Cards

A type of divination, this is a card game that goes back to the fifteenth century in parts of Europe, laying claim to being associated with gambling.

A usual pack consists of seventy-eight cards. The Minor Arcana cards have four separate suits (wands, pentacles, swords and cups); numbered from one (ace) up to ten including four face cards (king, queen, knight and jack/knave). There are twenty-two Major Arcana or trump cards.

Tarot is used by mystics to foresee future events. Tarot can be used to see a location's past or future, to a type of haunting, a Spirits story or, just used as trigger objects and other particular experiments.

Trigger Objects

Sometimes, old artefacts or materials that are or were commonly linked to the building or, the persons that haunt the location, can trigger the Spirit to show themselves.

Leave an object placed on paper and draw around it or, surround it with powder in a corner of a particularly active room. You may get movement. Make sure to have witnesses with you when leaving and re-entering the room/area and, photograph before and after the object to see any changes.

Water Submersion Test (See Bonus Footage)

Not all hauntings happen on land. Water covers nearly three-quarters of the surface of our world. It is known for its purity, cleansing and vital necessity to all known forms of life on this planet. Honoured, it can also claim mortal beings due to unforeseen or tragic circumstances and transport carriers of the dead (*Charon* – the ferryman).

Some bodies might never be recovered and left at the bottom of the sea (Davy Jones' Locker). Mythological stories of sea, lake or river monsters may have been far-fetched but, there may have been logic behind them. The tales of sunken cities cannot be ruled out either.

This experiment involves being in shallow water, up to knee height, with just enough depth to lie down and rest the back of the head. The chin is slightly tilted upwards, to allow the flow of air to the lungs. Controlled breathing is aided by a snorkel, while a nose clip prevents any water coming through the nose. Goggles are also a welcome addition. When relaxed, it is possible to get into a meditative state.

The test can last up to about ten minutes, depending on the individual, temperature of water and other factors and can work well on its own or, with separate experiments happening nearby, at the same time, involving the rest of the group.

The Luftwaffe (German Air Force) carried out bombing raids at numerous places in Éire-Ireland during Second World War. These included counties Wexford (two raids, which included the first recorded bombing on Irish soil, with three deaths), Dublin (four raids – the last one causing twenty-eight deaths), Wicklow (two raids) and (one raid) Monaghan, Meath, Kildare, Louth and Carlow (three deaths).

Wolfe Tone (1763-1798)

Theobald Wolfe Tone was born in Dublin. His father was a coachbuilder and an Anglican whilst his mother was Catholic, before converting to her husband's faith.

Wolfe Tone studied law at Trinity College, Dublin prior to heading to Middle Temple in London, where he trained to be a barrister.

He became one of the founding members of the United Irishmen (a republican group that revolted against British rule in Ireland). Tone spent some time in America before heading to France, to gain support for a revolt. He became leader of the United Irishmen in the Irish Rebellion of 1798.

Tone was later captured and taken prisoner upon the destroyed ship called the *Hoche*, on 12 October 1798. He was taken to the Royal Barracks in Dublin, court martialed and found guilty. He pleaded for a soldier's death, in front of a firing squad but was denied. He was sentenced to be hanged two days later however, before it was carried out, he attempted suicide by slitting his throat with a penknife. He was found covered in blood the next day but still alive. Tone remained in agony for the following eight days until his death on 19 November 1798.

World War II (1939-1945)

The Second World War involved a great number of the world's countries and was a struggle fought mainly between the Allies (Soviet Union, Great Britain, United States and China) against the aggressors – the Axis (Germany, Italy and Japan) who fought for independent purposes. It stands today as the deadliest conflict in human history, with between seventy and eighty-five million fatalities.

The invasion of Poland in 1939, by Nazi Germany (led by Adolf Hitler, 1889-1945), prompted Great Britain and France to declare war on Germany. The war ended on 2 September 1945, when the Japanese surrendered.

ACKNOWLEDGEMENTS

We would like to extend our gratitude to the following people, who are included in helping with our chapters and publishing the book.

Thank you to Sir Charles of Blarney Castle and Gardens for having us.

To Patricia, Donal and staff of Tarbert Bridewell Gaol and to the contributors of *Brigid's Fire* magazine – David, Harmonia and Rick – a thank you for a wonderful evening.

We like to show our thankfulness to Nuala and Jack for your hospitality, fine food and fond memories at the Old Fever Market Hospital.

We are grateful to Mary (who now works at Belvedere House, Gardens and Park); her friend, Emmanuel; Carmel at Athlone Arts and Tourism and to Westmeath County Council, for letting us investigate Athlone Castle.

Thank you to Dermot of Applerock Studios for sharing your experiences, knowledge of the place and joining us on the night.

To Cork City Council, Mervyn and staff at the Old Cork Waterworks, we would like to offer our appreciation in allowing us to be at this impressive location.

Many thanks to Clare County Council and especially to Ger, for respecting us and Peter, for showing us around at Loop Head Lighthouse.

It was a pleasure to spend time at the Ballinamuck 1798 Visitor Centre and chat with Paddy, Rachel and Tess, who have amazing knowledge of this wonderful building and area.

To Mike, Anne and all the staff at Blennerville Windmill, we value your generosity and helping us with our research.

We would like to say thank you to Daniel of Rathcroghan Visitor Centre, for giving us a tour of the wonderful sites, including the mysterious Oweynagat Cave.

We had an amazing experience at the Frank McCourt Museum, thanks to Una, John, Michael, Rob and Tara, that will stay with us forever.

To Nicki, Aoife and all the staff at the Arts@ Civic Trust House, we cherish your acceptance in having our group at this adorable property.

Acknowledgements

Thank you to Rebecca, Oscar and Emmy of Clonony Castle. It was a privilege to visit this terrific tower and explore its fine history.

To Richard Kelly and family of Killarney Video Productions, we are grateful to you for editing our recorded footage.

We would like to share our upmost appreciation to Olive and colleagues at Creative Writing, for their time and work.

We would like to give a special mention to Oscar of The Manuscript Publisher, for showing faith in us and getting our experiences and studies out to print.

A thank you to everyone who we met and joined us on our travels, including those who did not want to be named and those who should not.

Finally, thank you to you for buying or reading this book but in all… to the Spirit world – those that have contacted us, to point us in the right direction and for protecting us. We adore you and hold you close.

Other Books in this Series by GhostÉire

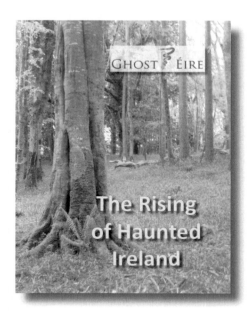

The Rising of Haunted Ireland

Anthony Kerrigan, Sinead Houlihan, Jenifer Kerrigan (GhostÉire)

First published in 2016 by The Manuscript Publisher
ISBN: 978-1-911442-05-9 (paperback) and 978-1-911442-06-6 (hardback)

Join GhostÉire paranormal research team as they travel around various regions in Ireland, investigating plausible hauntings. Experience what they have encountered and their reasons for unexplainable happenings. Step into the world of whispering lighthouses, misty islands, mind-bending gaols, vanished forts and spirits in public houses. Enjoy tales of sailors, smugglers, pirates, Irish rebels, Vikings and spies, at places you would not expect. Come to your own conclusion as to the world that is GhostÉire.

"A riveting read, best enjoyed with the bed covers pulled right up to your ears. Better have Ghost Eire's phone number on speed dial though. This is spine-chilling stuff." – **Alan Jacques (*Limerick Post*)**

Available to buy online (in print and e-book editions)

For further information, please visit:

www.GhostEire.net